THE FRENCH REVOLUTION

HIPPOLYTE TAINE

THE FRENCH REVOLUTION

HIPPOLYTE TAINE

Translated by

John Durand

Introduction by

Mona Ozouf

VOLUME I

LIBERTY FUND

Indianapolis

This book is published by Liberty Fund, Inc., a foundation established
to encourage study of the ideal of a society of free
and responsible individuals.

The cuneiform inscription that serves as our logo and as the design motif
for our endpapers is the earliest-known written appearance of the word "freedom"
(*amagi*), or "liberty." It is taken from a clay document written about 2300 B.C.
in the Sumerian city-state of Lagash.

Frontispiece from Corbis

The French Revolution is a translation of *La Révolution,* which is the second part of
Taine's *Origines de la France contemporaine.*

Printed in the United States of America

02 03 04 05 06 C 5 4 3 2 1
02 03 04 05 06 P 5 4 3 2 1

Library of Congress Cataloging-in-Publication Data

Taine, Hippolyte, 1828–1893.
[Origines de la France contemporaine. English. Selections]
The French Revolution / Hippolyte Taine; translated by John Durand.
p. cm.
"The French Revolution is a translation of La Révolution, which is
the second part of Taine's Origines de la France contemporaine"—T.p. verso.
Includes bibliographical references and index.
ISBN 0-86597-126-9 (alk. paper) ISBN 0-86597-127-7 (pbk. : alk. paper)
1. France—History—Revolution, 1789–1799. I. Title.

DC148.T35 2002

944.04—dc21 2002016023

ISBN 0-86597-126-9 (set: hc.) ISBN 0-86597-127-7 (set: pb.)
ISBN 0-86597-363-6 (v. 1: hc.) ISBN 0-86597-366-0 (v. 1: pb.)
ISBN 0-86597-364-4 (v. 2: hc.) ISBN 0-86597-367-9 (v. 2: pb.)
ISBN 0-86597-365-2 (v. 3: hc.) ISBN 0-86597-368-7 (v. 3: pb.)

Liberty Fund, Inc.
8335 Allison Pointe Trail, Suite 300
Indianapolis, Indiana 46250-1684

CONTENTS

INTRODUCTION

"MY BOOK," Taine wrote Ernest Havet in 1878, "if I have enough strength and health to complete it, will be a medical consultation."[1] Dr. Taine in effect sat himself down at the bedside of a country exhausted by the war and the Commune to write *Les origines,* the record of his examination of contemporary France. He never tired of comparing historical research to medical research, of demonstrating his scientific credentials, or of inventing metaphors for his profession: in his 1884 preface, introducing his study of the revolutionary government, he claims to have tracked the animal "when it lay in its lair, when it chewed, when it snatched, when it digested." He said he cared less about writing the history of the Revolution than about its "pathology." Contemporaries like Amiel thought they detected in the book the "odor of the laboratory."[2] He insisted, moreover, that the purpose of the enterprise was therapeutic: to make a diagnosis, write a prescription, find a "social form" that the French people might take on. Like Jaurès' history, which though quite different in its choices was also immense, purposeful, and militant, Taine's *Origines* was shaped by a representation of the future. The word "militant" might seem surprising: yet Taine wrote

1. Letter to Ernest Havet, March 24, 1878, in *H. Taine: sa vie et sa correspondance,* Paris, 1902–1907, vol. IV. He adds (thereby providing evidence for the hypothesis of a "German crisis" in Taine's thought): "two of the patient's fingers, Alsace and Lorraine, have already fallen."

2. This, moreover, is how Taine himself defined his life, as a "laboratory where one thought."

Albert Sorel in 1870 that free minds would henceforth be obliged to mobilize for "instructive and disagreeable"[3] lecture tours, so that by engaging in a vast, public self-critique the nation might avoid repeating its errors.

Because of its heavily didactic quality, Taine's uncompleted work, thought spectacularly successful at first, fell into discredit soon after. It was easy to argue that it had been conceived and written out of a combination of political passion, fear, and resentment.[4] For while Taine prided himself on approaching the history of the French Revolution in exactly the same spirit in which he would have treated the revolutions of Florence or Athens, his book was nevertheless intimately linked to two discoveries he had made a short while before: Germany, the fatherland of his intellect, now struck him (and also Renan and Fustel de Coulanges) as a brutal, despotic, and barbaric country;[5] and France, the fatherland of his heart, had just witnessed the reawakening of its old revolutionary malady. Taine's prognosis, shaped by these twin traumas, was one of disaster: the "gray" idea he had always had of France now turned decidedly blacker. This pessimism was precisely what made his book unacceptable; he wrote it in the years when the history of France was converging on a republican form, when Ferry gambled and won on rebuilding national unity around the principles of 1789. Squarely aimed at those principles, Taine's history thus went against the grain.

3. H. Taine, *Les origines de la France contemporaine,* Preface, Paris, 1886. Taine adds that this social form is not "a matter of caprice, but determined by the character and past of the people who claim to enter it."

4. Jacques Godechot interprets the *Origines* as the conventional product of the visceral fear of a landowner: "his social origins, the traditions of his family, his property, his kind of life, his milieu: all predisposed him to enter the ranks of the conservatives and to write a history violently hostile to the Revolution." J. Godechot, "Taine, Historian of the French Revolution," in *Romantisme.*

5. Letter of February 7, 1871, to Emile Planat, in *Correspondance,* op. cit., vol. IV: "The war," wrote Taine, "brought to light the bad and nasty side of their character covered by a veneer of civilization. The German animal is, at bottom, brutal, hard, despotic, barbarian; and the German animal is, moreover, frugal and wastrel. All this just showed itself and caused horror."

Nor was it fully assimilable by the Catholic and monarchist opposition. His portrayal of the Ancien Régime as responsible for the revolution, his arraignment of royalty on the charge of absolutism, and his anticlericalism (never far below the surface in this fervent Stendhalian) limited the extent to which his work could be taken up by the reactionaries.

Hard to classify politically (the image of Taine as an opponent of the Empire was still fresh in the minds of contemporaries), Taine's abundant output was also hard to classify philosophically—another reason for the public's incomprehension. It was apparently empiricist, because Taine revered facts and collected them with the zeal of the genre painter who fills his canvas with details. Yet he also insisted, and it was no small claim, that history obeyed fixed laws. His work was apparently idealist as well, since the causal principle of history was for him the spirit of the peoples and, for France, the classical spirit, but with the proviso that "this spirit is not distinct from the facts through which it expresses its character." And it was apparently positivist, because he believed that facts were related to one another; but positivists "relegated causes outside science," whereas Taine wanted science absolute and unbounded. His work was further influenced by materialism, which earned him the occasional sympathy of Mathiez;[6] the materialist aspect became increasingly pronounced as the years went by and Taine's pessimism increased, to the point where he asserted that "man's masters are physical temperament, bodily needs, animal instinct, [and] hereditary prejudice."[7] It is not hard to see why contemporaries hardly knew what to make of the massive meteorite that had somehow fallen among the flowerbeds of a history just beginning to hedge itself about with documents and preach the religion of neutrality.

The embarrassment caused by Taine's history soon turned into

6. See *Les Annales Révolutionnaires,* review essay of the work, April–June 1908.

7. H. Taine, *Les origines de la France contemporaine,* op. cit. "The Old Regime," Third Book, chap. IV: "Construction of the Future Society."

an indictment by the professionals. Official history charged him with having anointed himself historian without any knowledge of the historian's methods or techniques. It deplored the accumulation of anecdotes (catalogued by Aulard in an incredibly uninspired book[8]) with which Taine sought to "pressure the distracted and flighty reader, besiege him, overwhelm him with a surfeit of sensations and proofs."[9] It rejected the tyranny of the race-milieu-time theory already widely celebrated in literary history and transported without change to history proper. Above all, it cast a critical eye on a historian who, though dependent on circumstances himself, set little store by them in the history he wrote. Taine neglected the resistance of the refractory clergy, the flight of the king, the court's entente with Austria, the Prussian invasion, and, more generally, the foreign peril. Hence it was hardly surprising, Aulard and Seignobos agreed, that he depicted the Jacobins as madmen;[10] eliminating circumstances and doing away with partners and adversaries alike turned crucial actions into senseless gesticulations. At once prolix and superficial, anecdotal and didactic, vague and peremptory, Taine thus exhibited all the flaws of the bad historian: the great monument already lay half in ruins, to borrow Seignobos's lapidary description.[11]

Was Taine's work really a product of circumstances? If, as Taine himself maintained, the history of the Revolution depended on the

8. A. Aulard, *Taine, historien de la Révolution française,* Paris, 1907.

9. Letter from the end of January, 1861, to Edouard de Suckau, *Correspondance,* op. cit., vol. III.

10. For Aulard (op. cit.), Taine shows the fury of the revolutionaries without explaining why they were furious, and this fury—thus unexplained—has the air of a folly, the folly of "reason reasoning, the folly of the classical spirit, the folly of the revolutionary spirit." Seignobos echoes the thought: "The violent measures of the Directory are presented without taking into account the royalist conspiracies and the threat of foreign invasion that motivated them. It is the portrait of a duel in which one of the two adversaries has been effaced, and which gives the other the look of a madman." Ch. Seignobos, "L'Histoire in Petit de Julleville," in *Histoire de la langue et de la littérature française,* Paris, 1899, vol. VIII.

11. Seignobos, op. cit.

definition of the French spirit, he had defined that spirit much earlier through comparison with England. In his *Histoire de la littérature anglaise,* the monumental work that occupied him in the 1860s, by which time he was already obsessed with his discovery of a unique explanatory principle and anxious to characterize the English spirit, he believed that with the sense of liberty he had hit upon the way to do so. The great idea of the English "is the conviction that man, having conceived alone in his conscience and before God the rules of his conduct, is above all a free, moral person."[12] Taine traced English liberty to two fundamental sources: Protestantism, a moral religion purged of all sensuality,[13] and participation in public life. Civic activity was embodied first of all in "democratic aristocracy" that had had the intelligence not to cut itself off from the life of the county or parish and had thus retained not only its rank but also its purpose (Taine was a careful reader of Guizot and Macaulay).[14] But such activity also extended well beyond the circle of notables: newspapers and meetings gave "Parliament the nation for its audience," and public affairs were linked to the lives of individuals by a thousand local roots. From this web stemmed the "superabundance of political life"[15] that Taine discovered in England.

From his knowledge of English writers Taine very early drew the conclusion that this precious political liberty was the fruit of accep-

12. H. Taine, *Histoire de la littérature anglaise,* Paris, 1892, vol. IV, Conclusion: "The Past and the Present."

13. Thanks to Protestantism, and "by the suppression of legends and practices," man's thought had been concentrated on a single object, moral improvement. *Ibid.*

14. Taine admired Guizot's solidity (cf. *Essais de critique et d'histoire,* Paris, 1858). As for Macaulay, his admiration lasted through the years. Even in 1888, he wrote to the Viscount M. de Vogüé: "You are quite right to reread and to love Macaulay: he has the healthiest of heads and hearts; and as for his style, he has no equal in Europe." *Correspondance,* op. cit., letter of October 20, 1888.

15. "One can say that by the newspapers and meetings, a great universal parliament and many smaller ones disseminated throughout the country, and prepare, control and bring to completion the work of the two Houses." Cf. Taine, *Notes sur l'Angleterre,* Paris, 1876.

tance of inequality and toleration of disorder. The English Constitution was a complex, ancient, organic accumulation of privileges and "consecrated injustices." In this confusing mass of contracts each person could identify his rights and carve out his own protected domain, certain that no one—neither king nor lord nor community—could interfere with it. The state refrained from intervening in this ancient and often-patched edifice, whose older parts were gradually reshaped and fitted to new uses. Government offered guarantees and protections but delegated to others functions that it was incapable of carrying out—commerce, agriculture, industry—and that could be filled more effectively by free individuals, notables, or associations.

For Taine, this conservative tradition, an amalgam of civic spirit, moral virtue, and practical sense, clearly explained why revolution was unthinkable for the English. Yet they had made two revolutions: the *Times*'s reviewer reminded him how much difficulty England had had in recovering from one of them, the "little Cromwellian revolution," and Taine himself criticized Guizot for failing to convey its ferocity and energy. For him, however, the point was that these revolutions had not destroyed the monarchy. They had only forced it to adapt, thus revealing the English genius for improvisation. The English had reformed everything: "Bakewell their livestock, A. Young their industry, Adam Smith their economy, Bentham their penal code, Hutcheson, Ferguson, Joseph Butler, Reid, Stewart, and Price their psychology and their ethics."[16]

Can it be said that it was through this encounter with the English temperament, at once practical and moral, that Taine discovered—by contrast—the "French spirit" that would become his central explanation of the revolutionary phenomenon? Or did an implicit definition of the French spirit guide the selection he made among the facts of English history? The second hypothesis is more plausible, for it is striking to see how he attenuates or sharpens characteristic

16. Cf. *Histoire de la littérature anglaise,* op. cit., vol. III, Third Book: "The Revolution."

features of the two countries in order to heighten the desired antithesis. If he glosses over the discontinuities in English history, if he is silent about English Catholicism, if he overstates the uncouth and rustic character of the English, it is because he desires contrast and is quietly comparing two alternative courses for European history. In the 1860s, in other words, Taine was fascinated by the idea of two peoples hurtling without their knowledge toward an inevitable clash, each heightening its own characteristic features—the one feral, Christian, inegalitarian, and conservative, the other sociable, free-thinking, egalitarian, and revolutionary. The first had not destroyed its national community even with its "revolutions," while the second had demolished its national community well before the Revolution.[17]

In other words, the war and the Commune may have been responsible for the bitterness of *Les origines de la France contemporaine* but not for its philosophy. And Taine, much less difficult to classify and much less isolated than has been said, made use, not always with explicit acknowledgment, of the work of earlier historians, especially Burke and Tocqueville, who like him had recognized the exemplary value of English history.

From Burke, to whom he had devoted a laudatory passage in the *Histoire de la littérature anglaise,* Taine borrowed a portrait, a sentiment, and an idea, which he left unchanged in substance but amplified by rhetorical skill. The portrait was of the French revolutionaries: insane with abstraction, persuaded that the bedrock of human life was the elementary (and not the complexity in which Burke saw men immersed from the beginning), obsessed with the geometric spirit (to the point of performing surgery, as Burke put it, on their own soil), cynically reductionist (reducing man to "naked nature" by stripping him, as the revolutionaries had done to the queen Marie Antoinette over whom Burke had wept, of the gracious

17. The comparison between France and England is conducted throughout his work. On this point, see Taine's "M. de Troplong et M. de Montalembert," in *Essais de critique et d'histoire,* op. cit.

or decent drapery of ornament), and stupid in their pretension to create a new constitution ("rushing in where angels fear to tread"). The sentiment was one of the extreme fragility of civilized society, the slow product of compromise and adjustment, which was viable only if built on custom, enveloped in the reverence due everything that has endured, supported by church and state, and shored up by a hereditary class of notables. It is noteworthy that Taine, who rarely quoted other writers, did make an exception for Burke's statement that if a reformer laid hands on the defects of the state, he must do so as if touching "the wounds of a father, with pious veneration and a trembling hand." And finally, the idea, which Taine the scientist long hesitated to accept but which he made his own in *Les origines,* was that reason had played a limited role in the evolution of humanity. Burke had written that it was far wiser to perpetuate prejudice, with the reason it contains, than to cast aside the shroud and retain only naked reason, because prejudice makes reason effective. Taine responded: "Reason is wrong to become indignant when prejudice guides human affairs, for in order to guide them it too must become a prejudice."[18]

Taine's debt to Burke was therefore immense. But Burke also bequeathed to Taine his perplexity at the incongruous spectacle of the French: where they might have scoured the storehouse of their history for useful remnants of their constitution, instead they had inexplicably preferred the bewilderment of a new constitution. Taine was a born explainer, however, who could not leave such strangeness alone. For him, deformity had to have a form. So where an astonished Burke saw the French ignoring a rich tradition in favor of the nudity of a clean slate, Taine responded that it all made sense if in fact the clean slate was itself a French tradition.

Thus we come to the heart of Taine's history, the celebrated hypothesis of the classical spirit. In the beginning was a *racial* trait, a fixed form of intelligence given to rational and oratorical argument. This inclination found its ideal environment in the seventeenth-

18. Cf. *Les origines de la France contemporaine,* op. cit., "The Old Regime," Third Book: "The Spirit and the Doctrine."

century salon, and its *milieu,* the literary circle, in which an art of conversation was perfected based on ease and a stylized diction that invariably favored the general over the particular. The literary critic, familiar with English works that always informed the reader about their hero's profession, marital status, physical peculiarities, and fortune, could no longer abide a French literature filled with Damises and Cléantes (signifying employments, not individuals) and, later, with Iroquois and Persians as flat as playing cards and talking like books. Already well established in the seventeenth century, this abstract and simplifying vision was wedded in the following century, Taine argued, to the scientific spirit. This marriage might, for a scientist, have been a happy one. But French rationalism, because it was the offspring of an already mature classical spirit, had shunned the beneficial fertilization of experiment. Hence out of this wedlock came a monster: the idea of man in himself, liberated from all determinations, always and everywhere the same (physically, morally, and intellectually)—the source of all revolutionary aberrations.

Once this creature of reason entered the realm of history, the way was clear for all the philosophical offensives of the eighteenth century: that of Voltaire, directed against religion; that of the Encyclopedists and materialists, against custom; and the final efflorescence, that of Rousseau, against society. Here the philosophical nihilism of the eighteenth century found its true doctrine, and the Revolution, its true master; from then on, Taine maintained, it would do no more than fulfill the requisites of the Rousseauist vision, whose two sides were anarchy (since the form of government is subject at all times to the general will) and despotism (since individual rights are alienated in the community). This theory is the capstone of Taine's conceptual edifice: a racial trait, the classical spirit, which had long since found its milieu, in 1789 encountered its *moment.* In other words—and Taine never shrank from a striking formulation—Saint-Just and Robespierre were the direct heirs of Boileau.[19] And far from being a rent in the fabric of the nation, the Revolution was

19. This idea is expressed with incomparable clarity in a July 31, 1874, letter to Boutmy: it is a question of showing that "Boileau, Descartes, Lemaistre de

in fact the expression of the national genius. And thus Taine discovered Tocqueville.

That discovery seems to have come rather late for the needs of his enormous book. A letter to his wife shows how much Taine admired Tocqueville's predictive powers: "What a distressing thing, to see all our ills so thoroughly understood, and yet that understanding still so little disseminated!"[20] He studied Tocqueville to the point where he hoped to treat the very subject that Tocqueville had singled out in a letter to Kergorlay—how the Empire was able to establish itself in the midst of the society created by the Revolution—and answer its central questions: "Where did this new race come from? What produced it?"[21] He took from Tocqueville both his summary of the Revolution's effects and his arsenal of causes. Among the effects listed by Taine we find, as in Tocqueville, the establishment of equality (not simply abstract, theoretical equality but an equality almost achieved during the Empire, with all "great lives barred,"[22] a host of petty employments, and not a single position worthy of ambition except perhaps—a Stendhalian stroke—that of bishop) and the completion of state centralization, leaving a provincial wasteland eroded by ennui. Establishment, completion: the very terminology suggests a terminal process; it attests to the deep roots that link the Revolution to the Ancien Régime. In exposing those roots Taine showed little originality. He took from Tocqueville both the material causes ("abuses," seigneurial oppression without compensating ser-

---

Sacy, Corneille, Racine, and Fléchier are the ancestors of Saint-Just and Robespierre." *Correspondance,* op. cit., vol. III.

20. Letter of August 28, 1871, to Madame Henri Taine, *Correspondance,* op. cit., vol. III.

21. The idea of a "new race"—somnolent until then and coming to life with the advent of democracy—runs throughout Taine's work. Cf. *Histoire de la littérature anglaise,* op. cit., vol. IV: "The Modern Age."

22. *Les Carnets de voyage; notes sur la province 1863–1865,* published after Taine's death, (Paris, 1897), shows the aversion Taine felt towards provincial life under the Second Empire because of its parsimonious, skimpy, "rational" character.

vices, a useless nobility, an infuriatingly wealthy clergy, centralization and destruction by absolutism of natural groups, local life, and intermediary bodies, and fiscal irresponsibility) and the intellectual causes (the royalty of the humanities and the political radicalism of the philosophes). In the dark years while he was writing *Les origines* he was even prepared to add to this portrait the substitution of philosophy for religion, a change that deprived the popular classes of the firm mooring of faith.

These unoriginal materials were treated in a very original way, however. While Tocqueville sketched a whole host of causes and was content to lay special stress only on the *tabula rasa* created by the monarchy, a void that was quickly filled by public opinion, the true queen of kings, Taine tended to rest his entire architecture on a single pedestal, the intellectual cause. He had a far greater taste than Tocqueville for what he called the "productive element." For him, the essence of intellectual activity was to subordinate the effects of all particular causes to "the effect of a unique cause capable of accounting for the infinite complications of individuality."

This conception of causality, which dominates Taine's history, is worth exploring further. For him, the ideal type of science was deductive science. He never forgave Stuart Mill for limiting himself to inductive science by viewing causality as simply constancy of succession. He was equally hostile to Maine de Biran's concept of causality as an intimate force, a mysterious bond between cause and effect, as well as to Kant's synthetic a priori.[23] The only conceptual model of causality left was that of the relation between the whole

23. Taine's ideal is the establishment of a deductive chain without any discontinuities, constituting the essential thread of empirical reality, and the ultimate reduction of all facts and partial laws to a single law. The Kantian critique seemed empty to him: the human spirit knows reality in itself, and is capable of absolute knowledge without any limitation (see *De l'intelligence,* Paris, 1870, vol. II). As for Maine de Biran, Taine mocks the Birannian idea according to which the physicist, master of phenomena, does not grasp because all causes are immaterial (see *Les philosophes classiques au XIXe siècle en France,* Paris, 1857, reprint, Geneva 1979).

and its parts. In this model, cause and effect are not only inseparable but homogeneous. The world is made of one fabric. What we call cause and effect are two aspects of a single reality.[24] This explains Taine's fondness for a phrase he coined, "causal fact," which links the abstract and the concrete: the abstract is in fact an extract, taken out of the concrete. To find a causal relation is simply to bring to light a logical relation, to apply the principle of identity to history.

Whence the rigorous atmosphere, the invariable lighting, the emotional unity, and the monotonous tone of *Les origines,* despite the abundance of facts and the dynamic appearance due to the vigorous rhythms of Taine's prose. In this deterministic history of the Revolution it is absolutely impossible for a people to resist the inclination of its national character. At times Taine seems to regret the heavy shackles he himself has forged. Since his ideal is a country with local liberties (Holland or England) or a free Protestant country (Schleiermacher's Germany), he allows himself a moment's dream: France had simply taken a wrong turn, but what if it had taken another—would these destinies be "equally open" to it? But he quickly comes to his senses: "When I say 'equally open,' I am speaking *in abstracto.* Given the circumstances, the passions, and the ideas, scarcity, the peasant's misery, bourgeois and French envy, the laws of the Constituent Assembly and the final upheaval were inevitable."[25]

In such a static history it obviously becomes difficult to single out "moments." Unlike Tocqueville, Taine saw no bright episodes in the Revolution—not the revolution of liberty that preceded the revolution of equality nor what Louis Blanc called the revolution of Voltaire that preceded the revolution of Rousseau.[26] The Revolution

24. Cf. *Les philosophes au XIXe siècle en France,* op. cit.

25. Letter of October 31, 1876, to E. Boutmy, *Correspondance,* op. cit., vol. IV.

26. For Louis Blanc (*Histoire de la Révolution française,* Paris, 1847–1862, Book One, chap. II), the individualist principle and Voltaire's version of Enlightenment (Voltaire was the thinker of the bourgeoisie according to Blanc)

was all Rousseau's from the beginning. It was scarcely possible even to say that the Revolution became more radical. Like Bonald,[27] Taine believed that everything was decided the moment the Estates General became the National Assembly. The total destruction of the old order was already visible, as well as all the revolutionary *journées,* all of which were alike, moreover, in that they were emblematic events, mere developments of the insurgents' invariable principle: "I am the representative of right, of the general will." Thus the Revolution did not turn to the Terror. The Terror began on July 14, as Malouet, that "impartial man," had so keenly observed. October 5 and 6 were also days of Terror, as would have been evident to any reader of Burke. By the time the September massacres came, and later the governmental Terror, Taine had already exhausted his reserves of indignation. Nor does he discriminate between Assemblies: all were anarchic as well as despotic, and the worst of all, Taine confided to Francis Charmes in 1876, was the first, the Constituent Assembly. The others had done no more than apply the system they had taken from Rousseau: "To turn France into a dust of separate, equal individuals like so many grains of sand."[28] Taine had no regard for the Constituents' attempts to compromise, for their desperate efforts after Varennes to exonerate the king and strengthen his authority.[29] What ought to have appealed to the adversary of universal suffrage in him, the distinction between the active and passive citizens that marked the Constituent Assembly's retreat from the legiti-

---

are at the heart of 1789 and beyond, until the rise of the Girondins. But another principle, inspired this time by Rousseau, the philosopher of the people, is not the heart of Jacobinism seen as an annunciation.

27. See Bonald, *Démonstration philosophique du principe constitutif de la société,* Paris, 1830, vol. V.

28. Letter of August 28, 1876, *Correspondance,* op. cit., vol. IV.

29. Taine remained indifferent to the version of the constitution which, after the king's flight to Varennes, aimed to satisfy what Barnave called "the instinct for tranquility" and to bring about an acceptable compromise between the king, the Old Regime, and the Revolution.

macy of numbers, found no grace in his eyes. Even their final decision on the ineligibility seemed to him to hasten the disaster (though his reasoning on this point was not very consistent).

Thus no historian was more indifferent than Taine to the vagaries of politics or worked harder to ignore circumstances. Taine described July 14[30] without mentioning Necker's dismissal or the stationing of troops around Paris. He recounted the September massacres without breathing a word of the foreign menace. Was this silence because of political bias, as Aulard and Seignobos maintained?[31] It was more a matter of philosophical consistency. Taine was indifferent to the circumstantial causes. Only the efficient cause mattered. Hence there was nothing random in the history he wrote: "At the moment the Estates General began, the course of ideas and events was not only determined but visible."

As one might expect, this understanding also meant that it was illusory to distinguish between one set of rulers and another. The Girondins[32] until August 10 indulged in all the practices that would be used against them after August 10. In reality they shared the same political ideal as the Montagnards, namely (it will come as no surprise), "a state in accordance with Jean-Jacques's formula." Jacobins and Montagnards were two names for the same thing, and for Taine the Montagnard dictatorship was subsumed in that of the societies. When he dealt with individuals, he again perceived differences, the "little true facts" that he had learned to appreciate in Stendhal and the "particularization" that he admired in Sainte-Beuve; Marat's monotonous febrility, Danton's jovial cynicism, and Robespierre's lit-

30. When Taine turned to the Parisian insurrection and its causes he devoted only these elliptical lines to Necker: "a hue and cry rose in the Palais-Royal the 12th of July, at the news of the dismissal of Necker." He says not a word about the causes of dismissal.

31. Aulard (op. cit.) notes that in one hundred and ten pages devoted to 1793 there are only six lines on exterior dangers. The same is found in Seignobos, op. cit., note 10.

32. The Girondins, on whom Taine pronounces a less severe moral judgment than on the Montagnards, are no less than the latter presented as pure logicians who know only how to conceive of man in general.

erary decorum furnished the material for portraits[33] in which one recognizes the hand of the artist. Yet since each of his heroes also has to embody and epitomize the Revolution, Taine quickly squanders the benefits of his acute observation. Marat, though mad as a hatter, was nevertheless "clever enough to pick up the fashionable foolishness, the *Social Contract*." Danton understood "the inherent characteristic and normal procedure of the Revolution, popular brutality." Robespierre is of course even easier to reduce to the spirit of the times. In short, since Taine portrays all the revolutionaries as interpreters of the one and only revolutionary principle, he can distinguish them only by degree or moment (after three years the proper Robespierre rejoined Marat and "adopted the policy, goals, means, and works of the madman"). The diagnosis being inevitable, the patients' diversity vanishes in the uniformity of the disease, and the physician inevitably repeats the same old story. Yet his motivation, to reiterate, was not political malevolence. That sentiment did exist in Taine, quite obviously, but language and intelligibility took precedence. Taine laid out the theory in his acceptance speech to the Académie Française: since society consists of groups of people who are similar in condition, needs, and interests, "if you see one, you see them all." Science studies "each class of objects on the basis of selected samples."

Taine's favorite sample, and his primary contribution to the history of the Revolution, was the quintessential Jacobin, for if the Jacobin was defined, according to Taine, by a fixed idea, Taine also had a fixed idea of a Jacobin. Cochin[34] hailed Taine as the man who had spent twenty years circling round the mystery of Jacobinism, yet he also noted his indifference to Jacobin procedures in them-

33. There are nuances of difference between Marat, who, if the Revolution had not occurred, would have ended up in a mental hospital; Danton, who would have become a filibuster of law; and Robespierre, who in all likelihood would have remained a third-rate provincial lawyer. But all three were clothed with the same ferocity, united by the spirit and functions of the legal profession.

34. A. Cochin, *La crise de l'histoire révolutionnaire. Taine et M. Aulard*, Paris, 1909.

selves. This assessment is not entirely accurate, however, for it is not difficult to find in the pages of *Les origines* the same mechanisms that Cochin himself inventoried: the manipulation of electoral assemblies by a militant, active, and enterprising minority, well versed in the formulation of motions, the drafting of minutes, and the fabrication of unanimity; the tyranny exerted over the Assembly by the Jacobins and over the club itself by the galleries; the series of purges; the importance of the correspondence committee; and the vigilant presence of manipulators among the manipulated, for Taine even deals with what Cochin called the "inner circle," which he baptized "the band in the midst of the mob." Taken together, these mechanisms constituted a "machine"[35] whose purpose was to fabricate "an artificial, violent opinion that would have the appearance of a natural and spontaneous wish."

If Taine did not pull these scattered observations together, it was because he was again concerned not so much with describing the mechanisms of power as with reducing them to the "principle" of Jacobinism. For him, that principle was the suspension of reality, or voluntary blindness: the Jacobin did not want to see, and actually did not see, individual differences, personal qualities, and talents unequally distributed by nature and history, or age-old bonds among men.[36] If he did see them, he chose to renounce them for the sake of the community. As always in Taine, the diabolical pact, once made, determined everything. With the ground thus cleared and

35. One even can suggest that it was Taine who by his repeated use of the word "machine" (see, for example, *Histoire de la littérature anglaise,* op. cit., vol. III) inspired Cochin to use the term in order to signify the thousand wheels of Jacobin conduct.

36. "Of real men, no concern: he does not see them; he does not need to see them; his eyes closed he imposes his mold on the human material that he ruins. He never thinks to imagine beforehand the teeming, complex material of peasants, artisans, bourgeois, priests, and nobles at their plow and their workplace, in their sacristy and hotels, with their inveterate beliefs, habitual inclinations and actual desires." *Les origines de la France contemporaine,* op. cit., "The Revolution," II. "The Jacobin Conquest," chap. I: "Formation of a New Political Organ."

leveled, the state was free to exercise unlimited power over people and property. It imprisoned, confiscated, and punished, but above all it sought to educate, for Taine had understood that the teacher was the king of the Revolution, and the school the temple of the Jacobin people.[37] In other words, Jacobinism revived a backward conception of the state, eighteen centuries old, according to which a despotic power might reign legitimately over all aspects of personal life if in return the individual was allowed to share in political power. Clearly Taine incorporated his reading of Constant, in a schematic and rigid form, into his description of Jacobinism.[38] Constant had argued that modern society became less and less susceptible to despotism as private pleasure proliferated and developed, but Taine saw modern society in its Jacobin form marching straight toward despotism. For centuries public power had grown broader and more intrusive in France at the expense of private activities. "A nation changes little": Voltairian fixity remained Taine's credo.

Dr. Taine had promised remedies he could not deliver because his book remained unfinished. At a deeper level, however, one may ask whether his method would have allowed him to formulate any prescriptions. If history is truly logic in action, if it has the capacity only to realize and never to emancipate or innovate, then how can one avoid the conclusion that the future is already implicit in the present? Taine occasionally rejected this logic: he said that "reforms *might* have sufficed" in 1789, that the intendants *might* have provided the reform movement with leaders and organization, and that the

37. "If it is important to preach civic spirit to adults, it is even more important to teach it to children, because children are easier to shape than adults. Over these still malleable souls we (Jacobins) have complete control and by means of national education we gain control of the new generation." *Les origines de la France contemporaine,* op. cit., Second Book, chap. I: "The Jacobin Program."

38. B. Constant, *De la liberté chez les modernes,* Paris, 1880. Constant maintains that the "liberty of the ancients," which consists in active participation in the collective authority, is henceforth behind the French. For Taine, on the contrary, the Jacobins resurrect the model of the ancient city.

Assembly *might* not have capitulated to riot. But a Hegelian sense of the ineluctable led him to correct himself at once. The means were simply inoperative: "Nature and history made the choice for us in advance." Hence there was no "English way" for the French spirit. Taine had created a gulf between the two histories that he never could bridge.

Taine had said of Marcus Aurelius that he was a "pilot without hope." The description fits himself as well. The pessimistic determinism that is the essence of his thought prevented him from believing in remedies. Contrary to what is often said, it also quelled his reactionary passion: Taine knew that a nation can never turn back. And it also destroyed his ability to make short-term predictions. At the very moment when the Revolution's fecundity was exhausted, he thought that France was about to be caught once again, "in the fatal circle of revolutions and coups d'état."

Yet even if the immediate future proved him wrong, it did not discredit his insight. His stubborn intelligence uncovered two ideas that still have currency today. First, the democratic experiment is threatened by the isolation and anonymity that it imposes on individuals. The resulting feelings of uncertainty and insecurity give rise to a renewed need for the mystical unity of community, which gives despots their opening. Bonaparte fulfilled the promise of Louis XIV: "The only way out of anarchy is despotism, with the chance of encountering in one man first a savior, then a destroyer, and the certainty of being ruled thereafter by the unknown will that genius and common sense, or imagination and selfishness, will form in a soul inflamed and deranged by the temptations of absolute power."[39] For Taine the "bitter fruits of social dissolution" were abstraction, once again, and the common credo and secret alliance of democracy and despotism.

Taine's second idea was that the fabric of culture is extremely tenuous. Not only do bestiality and madness pose a constant threat

39. *Les origines de la France contemporaine*, op. cit., "The Modern Regime," Second Book, chap. I: "Formation and Character of the New State."

to mankind, but murderous folly lurks at civilization's gates. Though his prescience was dimmed for the 1880s, it has been astonishing for the twentieth century, in which he divined "the promise of massacre and bankruptcy," "the exacerbation of international rancor and distrust," "the perversion of productive discoveries, the perfection of destructive applications, the backward march toward the selfish and brutal instincts, the mores and morals of the ancient city and the barbarian tribe." His suspicion of progress, his anticipation of future disasters, his obsession with signs of the inhuman, all things that made him unreadable a century ago, are precisely the things that cause us to listen to him attentively once again. The "monument half in ruins" therefore remains in excellent shape.

Mona Ozouf

BIBLIOGRAPHY

Ayer, Alfred S. *Logical Positivism.* New York: Free Press, 1966.

Castex, Pierre Georges. *Critique d'art en France au XIXe siècle.* Paris: Centre de documentation universitaire, 1966.

Castiglioni, Guilio. *Taine.* Brescia: "La Scuola" editrice, 1945.

Charlton, D. G. *Positivist Thought in France during the Second Empire, 1852–1870.* Oxford: Clarendon Press, 1959; Westport, Conn.: Greenwood Press, 1976.

Chevrillon, André. *Taine; formation de sa pensée.* Paris: Plon, 1932.

Ciureanu, Petre. *Renan, Taine et Brunetière a quelques amis italiens: correspondance.* Florence: Institut français de Florence, 1956.

Codazzi, Antonella. *Hippolyte Taine e il progetto filosofico di una storiografia scientifica.* Firenza: La nuova Italia, 1985.

Engel, Otto. *Einfluss Hegels auf die Bildung der Gedankenwelt Hippolyte Taines.* Stuttgart: F. Frommann, 1920.

Eustis, Alvin. *Hippolyte Taine and the Classical Genius.* Berkeley: University of California Press, 1951.

Evans, Colin. *Taine: essai de biographie intérieure.* Paris: Nizet, 1975.

Gautier, Théophile. *Honoré de Balzac, sa vie et ses oeuvres: biographie par Théophile Gautier; analyse critique de la Comédie humaine, par H. Taine.* Bruxelles: Melina, Cans, 1858.

Gibaudan, René. *Idées sociales de Taine.* Paris: Éditions Argo, 1928.

Giraud, Victor. *Essai sur Taine, son oeuvre et son influence.* Paris: Hachette, 1902.

———. *Hippolyte Taine: études et documents.* Paris: J. Vrin, 1928.

Goetz, Thomas H. *Taine and the Fine Arts.* Madrid: Playor, 1973.

Gummere, Francis Barton. *Democracy and Poetry*. Boston: Houghton Mifflin, 1911.

Jeune, Simon. *Poésie et système, Taine interprète de La Fontaine*. Paris: A. Colin.

Kahn, Sholom J. *Science and Aesthetic Judgment: A Study in Taine's Critical Method*. New York: Columbia University Press, 1953.

Kuczynski, Jürgen. *Muse und der Historiker: Studien über Jacob Burckhardt, Hyppolite Taine, Henry Adams*. Berlin: Akademie Verlag, 1974.

Lacombe, Paul. *Psychologie des individus et des sociétés chez Taine, historien des littératures*. Paris: F. Alcan, 1906.

———. *Taine, historien et sociologue*. Paris: F. Alcan, 1909.

Léger, François. *Jeunesse d'Hippolyte Taine*. Paris: Albatros, 1980.

———. *Monsieur Taine*. Paris: Critérion, 1993.

Leroy, Maxime. *Taine*. Paris: Rieder, 1933.

Petitbon, Pierre Henri. *Taine, Renan, Barrès: étude d'influence*. Paris: Société d'edition "Les Belles lettres," 1934.

Pozzi, Regina. *Hippolyte Taine: scienze umane e politica nell'Ottocento*. Venezia: Marsilio, 1993.

Roe, Frederick Charles. *Taine et l'Angleterre*. Paris: É. Champion, 1923.

Rosca, Dumitru D. *Influence de Hegel sur Taine, théoricien de la connaissance et de l'art*. Paris: J. Gamber, 1928.

Saint-René-Taillandier, Georges. *Aupres de M. Taine: souvenirs et vues sur l'homme et l'oeuvre*. Paris: Hachette, 1928.

Schaepdryver, Karl de. *Hippolyte Taine: Essai sur l'unité de sa pensée*. Paris, 1938.

Schuin, Anik. *Pessimisme historique au XIXe siècle: Hippolyte Taine*. Genève: Institut universitaire de hautes études internationales, 1982.

Seys, Pascale. *Hippolyte Taine et l'avènement du naturalisme: un intellectuel sous le Second Empire*. Paris: L'Harmattan, 1999.

Siqueira, Esmeraldo. *Taine e Renan*. Rio de Janeiro: Pongetti, 1968.

Taine, Hippolyte. *Ancien regime*. Translated by J. Durand. New York: H. Holt, 1896.

———. *Arte en Grecia*. Madrid: La España moderna, 1893.

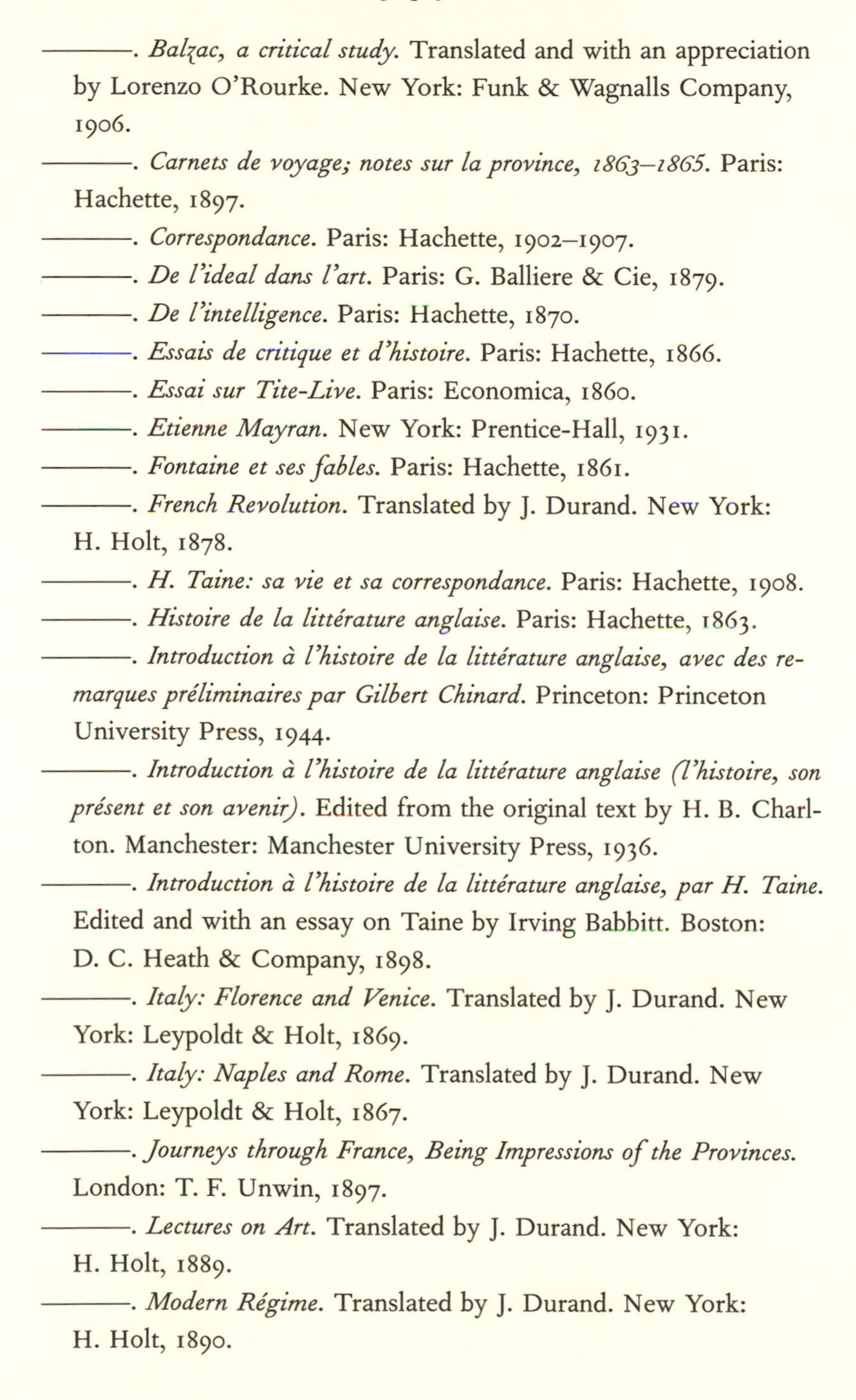

———. *Balzac, a critical study*. Translated and with an appreciation by Lorenzo O'Rourke. New York: Funk & Wagnalls Company, 1906.

———. *Carnets de voyage; notes sur la province, 1863–1865*. Paris: Hachette, 1897.

———. *Correspondance*. Paris: Hachette, 1902–1907.

———. *De l'ideal dans l'art*. Paris: G. Balliere & Cie, 1879.

———. *De l'intelligence*. Paris: Hachette, 1870.

———. *Essais de critique et d'histoire*. Paris: Hachette, 1866.

———. *Essai sur Tite-Live*. Paris: Economica, 1860.

———. *Etienne Mayran*. New York: Prentice-Hall, 1931.

———. *Fontaine et ses fables*. Paris: Hachette, 1861.

———. *French Revolution*. Translated by J. Durand. New York: H. Holt, 1878.

———. *H. Taine: sa vie et sa correspondance*. Paris: Hachette, 1908.

———. *Histoire de la littérature anglaise*. Paris: Hachette, 1863.

———. *Introduction à l'histoire de la littérature anglaise, avec des remarques préliminaires par Gilbert Chinard*. Princeton: Princeton University Press, 1944.

———. *Introduction à l'histoire de la littérature anglaise (l'histoire, son présent et son avenir)*. Edited from the original text by H. B. Charlton. Manchester: Manchester University Press, 1936.

———. *Introduction à l'histoire de la littérature anglaise, par H. Taine*. Edited and with an essay on Taine by Irving Babbitt. Boston: D. C. Heath & Company, 1898.

———. *Italy: Florence and Venice*. Translated by J. Durand. New York: Leypoldt & Holt, 1869.

———. *Italy: Naples and Rome*. Translated by J. Durand. New York: Leypoldt & Holt, 1867.

———. *Journeys through France, Being Impressions of the Provinces*. London: T. F. Unwin, 1897.

———. *Lectures on Art*. Translated by J. Durand. New York: H. Holt, 1889.

———. *Modern Régime*. Translated by J. Durand. New York: H. Holt, 1890.

———. *Notes on England.* Translated by J. Durand. New York: H. Holt, 1872.

———. *Notes on England.* Translated, with an introductory chapter by W. F. Rae. London: Strahan & Company, 1872.

———. *Notes on Paris.* Translated with notes by John Austin Stevens. New York: H. Holt, 1875.

———. *Notes sur Paris, vie et opinions de M. Frédéric-Thomas Graindorge. Recueillies et publiées par H. Taine, son exécuteur testamentaire.* Paris: Hachette, 1868.

———. *On Intelligence.* Translated by T. D. Haye. New York: Holt & Williams, 1872.

———. *Origines de la France contemporaine.* Paris: Hachette, 1899.

———. *Origins of Contemporary France.* Translated by J. Durand. New York: P. Smith, 1931.

———. *Philosophes français du XIXᵉ siècle.* Paris: Hachette, 1860.

———. *Philosophes français du XIXᵉ siècle, extraits.* Paris: J. J. Pauvert, 1966.

———. *Philosophie de l'art, par H. Taine; leçons professées à l'École des beaux-arts.* Paris: G. Baillière, 1865.

———. *Positivisme anglais: étude sur Stuart Mill.* Paris: G. Baillière, 1864.

———. *Taine's Notes on England.* Translated with an introduction by Edward Hyams. Freeport, N.Y.: Books for Libraries Press, 1971.

———. *Tour through the Pyrenees.* Translated by J. Safford Fiske, with illustrations by Gustave Doré. New York: H. Holt, 1874.

———. *Voyage aux Pyrénées.* Paris: Hachette, 1860.

———. *Voyage en Italie.* Paris: Hachette, 1866.

Weinstein, Leo. *Hippolyte Taine.* New York: Twayne, 1972.

Wiarda, Rein. *Taine et la Hollande.* Paris: E. Droz, 1938.

PREFACE

THIS second part of "Les Origines de la France Contemporaine" will consist of two volumes.—Popular insurrections and the laws of the Constituent Assembly end in destroying all government in France; this forms the subject of the present volume.—A party arises around an extreme doctrine, gets possession of the power, and exercises it in conformity with that doctrine; this will form the subject of the second volume.

A third volume would be required to criticize authorities. For this I have no room, and I merely state the rule that I have observed. The most trustworthy testimony is that of the eye-witness, especially when this witness is an honourable, attentive, and intelligent man, writing on the spot, at the moment, and under the dictation of the facts themselves—if it is manifest that his sole object is to preserve or furnish information, if his work is not a piece of polemics planned for the needs of a cause, or a passage of eloquence arranged for popular effect, but a legal deposition, a secret report, a confidential dispatch, a private letter, or a personal memento. The nearer a document approaches this type, the more it merits confidence, and supplies superior materials.—I have found many of this character in the national archives, principally in the manuscript correspondence of ministers, intendants, subdelegates, magistrates, and other functionaries; of military commanders, officers in the army, and gendarmerie; of royal commissioners, and of the Assembly; of administrators of departments, districts, and municipalities, besides persons in private life who address the King, the National Assembly, or the ministry.

Among these are men of every rank, profession, education, and party. They are distributed by hundreds and thousands over the whole surface of the territory. They write apart, without being able to consult each other, and without even knowing each other. No one is so well placed for collecting and transmitting accurate information. None of them seek literary effect, or even imagine that what they write will ever be published. They draw up their statements at once, under the direct impression of local events. Testimony of this character, of the highest order, and at first hand, provides the means by which all other testimony ought to be verified. The foot notes at the bottom of the pages indicate the condition, office, name, and dwelling-place of those decisive witnesses. For greater certainty I have transcribed as often as possible their own words. In this way the reader, confronting the texts, can interpret them for himself, and form his own opinions; he will have the same documents as myself for arriving at his conclusions, and, if he is pleased to do so, he will conclude otherwise. As for allusions, if he finds any, he himself will have introduced them, and if he applies them he is alone responsible for them. To my mind, the past has features of its own, and the portrait here presented resembles only the France of the past. I have drawn it without concerning myself with the discussions of the day; I have written as if my subject were the revolutions of Florence or Athens. This is history, and nothing more, and, if I may fully express myself, I esteem my vocation of historian too highly to make a cloak of it for the concealment of another.

December, 1877

BOOK FIRST

Spontaneous Anarchy

CHAPTER I

I. *The beginnings of anarchy—Dearth the first cause—Bad crops—The winter of 1788 and 1789—Dearness and poor quality of bread—In the provinces—At Paris—* II. *Hopefulness the second cause—Separation and laxity of the Administrative forces—Investigations of local Assemblies—The people become awake to their condition—Convocation of the States-General—Hope is born—The coincidence of early Assemblies with early difficulties—* III. *The provinces during the first six months of 1789—Effects of the famine—* IV. *Intervention of ruffians and vagabonds—* V. *The first jacquerie in Provence—Feebleness or ineffectiveness of repressive measures.*

DURING the night of July 14–15, 1789, the Duc de la Rochefoucauld-Liancourt caused Louis XVI. to be aroused to inform him of the taking of the Bastille. "It is a revolt, then?" exclaimed the King. "Sire!" replied the Duke, "it is a revolution!" The event was even more serious. Not only had power slipped from the hands of the King, but it had not fallen into those of the Assembly; it lay on the ground, ready to the hands of the unchained populace, the violent and overexcited crowd, the mobs which picked it up like some weapon that had been thrown away in the street. In fact, there was no longer any government; the artificial structure of human society was giving way entirely; things were returning to a state of nature. This was not a revolution, but a *dissolution.*

Two causes excite and maintain the universal upheaval. The first one is a dearth, which, being constant, lasting for ten years, and aggravated by the very disturbances which it excites, bids fair to inflame the popular passions to madness, and change the whole course of the Revolution into a series of spasmodic stumbles.

When a stream is brimful, a slight rise suffices to cause an overflow. So was it with the extreme distress of the eighteenth century. A poor man who finds it difficult to live when bread is cheap, sees death staring him in the face when it is dear. In this state of suffering the animal instinct revolts, and the universal obedience which constitutes public peace depends on a degree more or less of dryness or damp, heat or cold. In 1788, a year of severe drought, the crops had been poor; in addition to this, on the eve of the harvest,[1] a terrible hailstorm burst over the region around Paris, from Normandy to Champagne, devastating sixty leagues of the most fertile territory, and causing damage to the amount of one hundred millions of francs. Winter came on, the severest that had been seen since 1709: at the close of December the Seine was frozen over from Paris to Havre, while the thermometer stood at $18\frac{3}{4}°$ below zero. A third of the olive-trees died in Provence, and the rest suffered to such an extent that they were considered incapable of bearing fruit for two years to come. The same disaster befell Languedoc. In Vivarais, and in the Cevennes, whole forests of chestnuts had perished, along with all the grain and grass crops on the uplands; on the plain the Rhône remained in a state of overflow for two months. After the spring of 1789 the famine spread everywhere, and it increased from month to month like a rising flood. In vain did the Government order the farmers, proprietors, and corn-dealers to keep the markets supplied; in vain did it double the bounty on importations, resort to all sorts of expedients, involve itself in debt, and expend over forty millions of francs to furnish France with wheat. In vain do individuals, princes, noblemen, bishops, chapters, and communities multiply their charities, the Archbishop of Paris incurring a debt of 400,000 livres, one rich man distributing 40,000 francs the morning after the hailstorm, and a convent of Bernardins feeding twelve hundred poor

1. Marmontel, "Mémoires," ii. 221.—Albert Babeau, "Histoire de la Révolution Française," i. 91, 187. (Letter by Huez, Mayor of Troyes, July 30, 1788.)—"Archives Nationales," H. 1274. (Letter by M. de Caraman, April 22, 1789.) H. 942 (Cahier des demandes des Etats du Languedoc).—Buchez et Roux, "Histoire Parlementaire," i. 283.

persons for six weeks.[2] All was not sufficient. Neither public measures nor private charity could meet the overwhelming need. In Normandy, where the last commercial treaty had ruined the manufacture of linen and of lace trimmings, forty thousand workmen were out of work. In many parishes one-fourth of the population[3] are beggars. Here, "nearly all the inhabitants, not excepting the farmers and landowners, are eating barley bread and drinking water"; there, "many poor creatures have to eat oat bread, and others soaked bran, which has caused the death of several children."—"Above all," writes the Rouen Parliament, "let help be sent to a perishing people. . . . Sire, most of your subjects are unable to pay the price of bread, and what bread is given to those who do buy it!"—Arthur Young,[4] who was travelling through France at this time, heard of nothing but the dearness of bread and the distress of the people. At Troyes bread costs four sous a pound—that is to say, eight sous of the present day; and artisans unemployed flock to the relief works, where they can earn only twelve sous a day. In Lorraine, according to the testimony of all observers, "the people are half dead with hunger." In Paris the number of paupers has been trebled; there are thirty thousand in the Faubourg Saint-Antoine alone. Around Paris there is a short supply of grain, or it is spoilt.[5] In the beginning of July, at Montereau, the market is empty. "The bakers could not have baked" if the police officers had not fixed the price of bread at five sous per pound; the rye and barley which the intendant is able to send "are of the worst possible quality, rotten

2. See "The Ancient Régime," p. 34. Albert Babeau, i. 91. (The Bishop of Troyes gives 12,000 francs, and the chapter 6,000, for the relief workshops.)

3. "The Ancient Régime," 350, 387.—Floquet, "Histoire du Parlement de Normandie," vii. 505–518. (Reports of the Parliament of Normandy, May 3, 1788. Letter from the Parliament to the King, July 15, 1789.)

4. Arthur Young, "Voyages in France," June 29th, July 2nd and 18th.—"Journal de Paris," January 2, 1789. Letter of the curé of Sainte-Marguerite.

5. Roux and Buchez, iv. 79–82. (Letter from the intermediary bureau of Montereau, July 9, 1789; from the *maire* of Villeneuve-le-Roi, July 10th; from M. Baudry, July 10th; from M. Jamin, July 11th; from M. Prioreau, July 11th, &c.) Montjoie, "Histoire de la Révolution de France," 2nd part, ch. xxi. p. 5.

and in a condition to produce dangerous diseases; nevertheless, most of the small consumers are reduced to the hard necessity of using this spoilt grain." At Villeneuve-le-Roi, writes the mayor, "the rye of the two lots last sent is so black and poor that it cannot be retailed without wheat." At Sens the barley "tastes musty" to such an extent that buyers of it throw the detestable bread which it makes in the face of the subdelegate. At Chevreuse the barley has sprouted and smells bad; the "poor wretches," says an employé, "must be hard pressed with hunger to put up with it." At Fontainebleau "the barley, half eaten away, produces more bran than flour, and to make bread of it, one is obliged to work it over several times." This bread, such as it is, is an object of savage greed; "it has come to this, that it is impossible to distribute it except through wickets"; those, again, who thus obtain their ration, "are often attacked on the road and robbed of it by the more vigorous of the famished people." At Nangis "the magistrates prohibit the same person from buying more than two bushels in the same market." In short, provisions are so scarce that there is a difficulty in feeding the soldiers; the minister dispatches two letters one after another to order the cutting down of 250,000 bushels of rye before the harvest.[6] Paris thus, in a perfect state of tranquillity, appears like a famished city put on rations at the end of a long siege, and the dearth will not be greater nor the food worse in December, 1870, than in July, 1789.

"The nearer the 14th of July approached," says an eye-witness,[7] "the more did the dearth increase. Every baker's shop was surrounded by a crowd, to which bread was distributed with the most grudging economy. . . . This bread was generally blackish, earthy, and bitter, producing inflammation of the throat and pain in the

6. Roux and Buchez, *ibid.* "It is very unfortunate," writes the Marquis d'Autichamp, "to be obliged to cut down the standing crops ready to be gathered in; but it is dangerous to let the troops die of hunger."

7. Montjoie, "Histoire de la Révolution de France," ch. xxix. v. 37. De Goncourt, "La Société Française pendant la Révolution," p. 53. Deposition of Maillard (Criminal Inquiry of the Châtelet concerning the events of October 5th and 6th).

bowels. I have seen flour of detestable quality at the military school and at other depôts. I have seen portions of it yellow in colour, with an offensive smell; some forming blocks so hard that they had to be broken into fragments by repeated blows of a hatchet. For my own part, wearied with the difficulty of procuring this poor bread, and disgusted with that offered to me at the tables d'hôte, I avoided this kind of food altogether. In the evening I went to the Café du Caveau, where, fortunately, they were kind enough to reserve for me two of those rolls which are called *flutes,* and this is the only bread I have eaten for a week at a time." But this resource is only for the rich. As for the people, to get bread fit for dogs, they must stand in a line for hours. And here they fight for it; "they snatch food from one another." There is no more work to be had; "the work-rooms are deserted"; often, after waiting a whole day, the workman returns home empty-handed, and when he does bring back a four-pound loaf it costs him 3 francs 12 sous; that is, 12 sous for the bread, and 3 francs for the lost day. In this long line of unemployed, excited men, swaying to and fro before the shop-door, dark thoughts are fermenting: "if the bakers find no flour to-night to bake with, we shall have nothing to eat tomorrow." An appalling idea—in presence of which the whole power of the Government is not too strong; for to keep order in the midst of famine nothing avails but the sight of an armed force, palpable and threatening. Under Louis XIV. and Louis XV. there had been even greater hunger and misery; but the outbreaks, which were roughly and promptly put down, were only partial and passing disorders. Some rioters were at once hung, and others were sent to the galleys: the peasant or the workman, convinced of his impotence, at once returned to his stall or his plough. When a wall is too high one does not even think of scaling it.—But now the wall is cracking—all its custodians, the clergy, the nobles, the Third-Estate, men of letters, the politicians, and even the Government itself, making the breach wider. The wretched, for the first time, discover an issue: they dash through it, at first in driblets, then in a mass, and rebellion becomes as universal as resignation was formerly.

II

It is because through this opening hope steals like a beam of light, and gradually finds its way down to the depths below. For the last fifty years it has been rising, and its rays, which first illuminated the upper class in their splendid apartments in the first story, and next the middle class in their entresol and on the ground floor, have now for two years penetrated to the cellars where the people toil, and even to the deep sinks and obscure corners where rogues and vagabonds and malefactors, a foul and swarming herd, crowd and hide themselves from the persecution of the law. To the first two provincial assemblies instituted by Necker in 1778 and 1779, Loménie de Brienne has in 1778 just added nineteen others; under each of these are assemblies of the *arrondissement;* under each assembly of the *arrondissement* are parish assemblies.[8] Thus the whole machinery of administration has been changed. It is the new assemblies which assess the taxes and superintend their collection; which determine upon and direct all public works; and which form the court of final appeal in regard to matters in dispute. The intendant, the subdelegate, the *élu,*[9] thus lose three-quarters of their authority. Conflicts arise, consequently, between rival powers whose frontiers are not clearly defined; command shifts about, and obedience is diminished. The subject no longer feels on his shoulders the commanding weight of the one hand which, without possibility of interference or resistance, held him in, urged him forward, and made him move on. Meanwhile, in each assembly of the parish *arrondissement,* and even of the province, plebeians, "husbandmen,"[10] and oftentimes common farmers, sit by the side of lords and prelates. They listen to and

8. De Tocqueville, "L'Ancien Régime et la Révolution," 272–290. De Lavergne, "Les Assemblées provinciales," 109. *Procès-verbaux* des assemblées provinciales, *passim.*

9. A magistrate who gives judgment in a lower court in cases relative to taxation. These terms are retained because there are no equivalents in English.

10. "*Laboureurs*"—this term, at this epoch, is applied to those who till their own land.

remember the vast figure of the taxes which are paid exclusively, or almost exclusively, by them—the *taille* and its accessories, the poll-tax and road dues, and assuredly on their return home they talk all this over with their neighbour. These figures are all printed; the village attorney discusses the matter with his clients, the artisans and rustics, on Sunday as they leave the mass, or in the evening in the large public room of the tavern. These little gatherings, moreover, are sanctioned, encouraged by the powers above. In the earliest days of 1788 the provincial assemblies order a board of inquiry to be held by the syndics and inhabitants of each parish. Knowledge is wanted in detail of their grievances—what part of the revenue is chargeable to each impost, what the cultivator pays and how much he suffers, how many privileged persons there are in the parish; the amount of their fortune, whether they are residents, what their exemptions amount to; and, in the replies, the attorney who holds the pen, names and points out with his finger each privileged individual, criticizes his way of living, and estimates his fortune, calculates the injury done to the village by his immunities, inveighs against the taxes and the tax-collectors. On leaving these assemblies the villager broods over what he has just heard. He sees his grievances no longer singly as before, but in mass, and coupled with the enormity of evils under which his fellows suffer. Besides this, they begin to disentangle the causes of their misery: the King is good—why then do his collectors take so much of our money? This or that canon or nobleman is not unkind—why then do they make us pay in their place?—Suppose a beast of burden to which a sudden gleam of reason should reveal the equine species contrasted with the human species; and imagine, if you can, what his first ideas would be in relation to the postillions and drivers who bridle and whip him, and again in relation to the good-natured travellers and sensitive ladies who pity him, but who to the weight of the vehicle add their own and that of their luggage.

So, in the mind of the peasant, athwart his perplexed broodings, a new idea, slowly, little by little, is unfolded—that of an oppressed multitude of which he makes one, a vast herd scattered far beyond the visible horizon, everywhere ill used, starved, and fleeced. Towards the end of 1788 we begin to detect in the correspondence of the intendants and military commandants the dull universal muttering of coming wrath. Men's characters seem to change; they become suspicious and restive.—And just at this moment, the Government, dropping the reins, calls upon them to direct themselves.[11] In the month of November, 1787, the King declared that he would convoke the States-General. On the 5th of July, 1788, he calls for memorials on this subject from every competent person and body. On the 8th of August he fixes the date of the session. On the 5th of October he convokes the notables, in order to consider the subject with them. On the 27th of December he grants a double representation to the Third-Estate, because "its cause is allied with generous sentiments, and it will always obtain the support of public opinion." The same day he introduces into the electoral assemblies of the clergy a majority of curés, "because good and useful pastors are daily and closely associated with the indigence and relief of the people," from which it follows "that they are much more familiar with their sufferings" and necessities. On the 24th January, 1789, he prescribes the procedure and method of the meetings. After the 7th of February writs of summons are sent out one after the other. Eight days after, each parish assembly begins to draw up its memorial of grievances, and becomes excited over the detailed enumeration of all the miseries which it sets down in writing.—All these appeals and all these acts are so many strokes which reverberate in the popular imagination. "It is the desire of His Majesty," says the order issued, "that every one, from the extremities of his kingdom, and from the most obscure of its hamlets, should be certain of his wishes and protests reaching him." Thus, it is all quite true: there can be no mistake about it, the thing is sure. The people are invited to speak out, they are summoned, they are consulted. There is a disposition to relieve them; henceforth their misery shall be less; better times are coming. This is all they know about it. A few months after, in July,[12] the only

11. Duvergier, "Collection des lois et décrets," i. 1 to 23, and particularly p. 15.

12. Arthur Young, July 12th, 1789 (in Champagne).

answer a peasant girl can make to Arthur Young is, "something was to be done by some great folks for such poor ones, but she did not know who nor how"; the thing is too complicated, beyond the reach of a stupefied and mechanical brain. One idea alone emerges—the hope of immediate relief, the persuasion that right is on their side, the resolution to aid it with every possible means; and, consequently, an anxious waiting, a ready impulse, a tension of the will which simply stays for the opportunity to relax and launch forth like a resistless arrow towards the unknown end which will reveal itself all of a sudden. It is hunger that so suddenly marks out for them this aim: the market must be supplied with grain; the farmers and owners must bring it; wholesale buyers, whether the Government or individuals, must not transport it elsewhere; it must be sold at a low price; the price must be cut down and fixed, so that the baker can sell bread at two sous the pound; grain, flour, wine, salt, and provisions must pay no more duties; seignorial dues and claims, ecclesiastical tithes, and royal or municipal taxes must no longer exist. On the strength of this idea disturbances broke out on all sides in March, April, and May; contemporaries "do not know what to think of such a scourge;[13] they cannot comprehend how such a vast number of criminals, without visible leaders, agree amongst themselves everywhere to commit the same excesses just at the time when the States-General are going to begin their sittings." The reason is that, under the ancient régime, the conflagration was smouldering in a closed chamber; the great door is suddenly opened, the air enters, and immediately the flame breaks out.

III

At first there are only intermittent, isolated fires, which are extinguished or go out of themselves; but, a moment after, in the same place, or very near it, the sparks again appear, and their number, like their recurrence, shows the vastness, depth, and heat of the combustible matter which is about to explode. In the four months which precede the taking of the Bastille, over three hundred out-

13. Montjoie, 1st part, 102.

breaks may be counted in France. They take place from month to month, and from week to week, in Poitou, Brittany, Touraine, Orléanais, Normandy, Ile-de-France, Picardy, Champagne, Alsace, Burgundy, Nivernais, Auvergne, Languedoc, and Provence. On the 28th of May the parliament of Rouen announces robberies of grain, "violent and bloody tumults, in which men on both sides have fallen," throughout the province, at Caen, Saint-Lô, Mortain, Granville, Evreux, Bernay, Pont-Andemer, Elboeuf, Louviers, and in other sections besides. On the 20th of April, Baron de Bezenval, military commander in the central provinces, writes: "I once more lay before M. Necker a picture of the frightful condition of Touraine and of Orléanais. Every letter I receive from these two provinces is the narrative of three or four riots, which are put down with difficulty by the troops and constabulary"[14]—and throughout the whole extent of the kingdom a similar state of things is seen.

The women, as is natural, are generally at the head of these outbreaks. It is they who, at Montlhéry, rip open the sacks of grain with their scissors. On learning each week, on market-day, that the price of a loaf of bread advances three, four, or seven sous, they break out into shrieks of rage: at this rate for bread, with the small salaries of the men, and when work fails,[15] how can a family be fed? Crowds gather around the sacks of flour and the doors of the bakers; amidst outcries and reproaches some one in the crowd makes a push; the proprietor or dealer is hustled and knocked down, the shop is invaded, the commodity is in the hands of the buyers and of the famished, each one grabbing for himself, pay or no pay, and running away with the booty.—Sometimes a party is made up beforehand.[16] At Bray-sur-Seine, on the 1st of May, the villagers for four leagues around, armed with stones, knives, and cudgels, to the number of

14. Floquet, "Histoire du Parlement de Normandie," vii. 508.—"Archives Nationales," H. 1453.

15. Arthur Young, June 29th (at Nangis).

16. "Archives Nationales," H. 1453. Letter of the Duc de Mortemart, Seigneur of Bray, May 4th; of M. de Ballainvilliers, intendant of Languedoc, April 15th.

four thousand, compel the husbandmen and farmers who have brought grain with them to sell it at 3 livres, instead of 4 livres 10 sous the bushel; and threaten to do the same thing on the following market-day. The farmers will not come again, the storehouse will be empty, and soldiers must be at hand, or the inhabitants of Bray will be pillaged. At Bagnols, in Languedoc, on the 1st and 2nd of April, the peasants, armed with cudgels and assembled by tap of drum, "traverse the town, threatening to burn and destroy everything if flour and money are not given to them": they go to private houses for grain, divide it amongst themselves at a reduced price, "promising to pay when the next crop comes round," and force the consuls to put bread at two sous the pound, and to increase the day's wages four sous.—Indeed this is now the regular thing; it is not the people who obey the authorities, but the authorities who obey the people. Consuls, sheriffs, mayors, municipal officers, town-clerks, become confused and hesitating in the face of this huge clamour; they feel that they are likely to be trodden under foot or thrown out of the windows. Others, with more firmness, are aware that a riotous crowd is mad, and scruple to spill blood; at least, they yield for the time, hoping that at the next market-day there will be more soldiers and better precautions taken. At Amiens, "after a very violent outbreak,"[17] they decide to take the wheat belonging to the Jacobins, and, protected by the troops, to sell it to the people at a third below its value. At Nantes, where the town-hall is attacked, they are forced to lower the price of bread one sou per pound. At Angoulême, to avoid a recourse to arms, they request the Comte d'Artois to renounce his dues on flour for two months, reduce the price of bread, and compensate the bakers. At Cette they are so maltreated they let everything take its course; the people sack their dwellings and get the upper hand; they announce by sound of trumpet that all their demands are granted. On other occasions, the mob

17. "Archives Nationales," H. 1453. Letter of the intendant, M. d'Agay, April 30th; of the municipal officers of Nantes, January 9th; of the intendant, M. Mealan d'Ablois, June 22nd; of M. de Ballainvilliers, April 15th.

dispenses with their services and acts for itself. If there happens to be no grain on the market-place, the people go after it wherever they can find it—to proprietors and farmers who are unable to bring it for fear of pillage; to convents, which by royal edict are obliged always to have one year's crop in store; to granaries where the Government keeps its supplies; and to convoys which are dispatched by the intendants to the relief of famished towns. Each for himself—so much the worse for his neighbour. The inhabitants of Fougères beat and drive out those who come from Ernée to buy in their market; like violence is shown at Vitré to the inhabitants of Maine.[18] At Sainte-Léonard the people stop the grain started for Limoges; at Bost that intended for Aurillac; at Saint-Didier that ordered for Moulins; and at Tournus that dispatched to Macon. In vain are escorts added to the convoys; troops of men and women, armed with hatchets and guns, put themselves in ambush in the woods along the road, and seize the horses by their bridles; the sabre has to be used to secure any advance. In vain are arguments and kind words offered, "and in vain even is wheat offered for money; they refuse, shouting out that the convoy shall not go on." They have taken a stubborn stand, their resolution being that of a bull planted in the middle of the road and lowering his horns. Since the wheat is in the district, it is theirs; whoever carries it off or withholds it is a robber. This fixed idea cannot be driven out of their minds. At Chantenay, near Mans,[19] they prevent a miller from carrying that which he had just bought to his mill; at Montdragon, in Languedoc, they stone a dealer in the act of sending his last waggon-load elsewhere; at Thiers, workmen go in force to gather wheat in the fields; a proprietor with whom some is found is nearly killed; they drink wine

18. "Archives Nationales," H. 1453. Letter of the Count de Langeron, July 4th; of M. de Meulan d'Ablois, June 5th; "*Procès-verbal* de la Maréchaussée de Bost," April 29th. Letters of M. de Chazerat, May 29th; of M. de Bezenval, June 2nd; of the intendant, M. Amelot, April 25th.

19. "Archives Nationales," H. 1453. Letter of M. de Bezenval, May 27th; of M. de Ballainvilliers, April 25th; of M. de Foullonde, April 19th.

in the cellars, and leave the taps running. At Nevers, the bakers not having put bread on their counters for four days, the populace force the granaries of private persons, of dealers and religious communities. "The frightened corn-dealers part with their grain at any price; most of it is stolen in the face of the guards," and, in the tumult of these domiciliary visits, a number of houses are sacked.—In these days woe to all who are concerned in the acquisition, commerce, and manipulation of grain! Popular imagination requires living beings to whom it may impute its misfortunes, and on whom it may gratify its resentments. To it, all such persons are monopolists, and, at any rate, public enemies. Near Angers the Benedictine establishment is invaded, and its fields and woods are devastated.[20] At Amiens "the people are arranging to pillage and perhaps burn the houses of two merchants, who have built labour-saving mills"; restrained by the soldiers, they confine themselves to breaking windows; but other "groups come to destroy or plunder the houses of two or three persons whom they suspect of being monopolists." At Nantes, a *sieur* Geslin, being deputed by the people to inspect a house, and finding no wheat, a shout is set up that he is a receiver, an accomplice! The crowd rush at him, and he is wounded and almost cut in pieces.—It is very evident that there is no more security in France; property, even life, is in danger. The first of all property, that of provisions, is violated in hundreds of places, and everywhere is menaced and precarious. The intendants and subdelegates everywhere call for aid, declare the constabulary incompetent, and demand regular troops. And mark how public authority, everywhere inadequate, disorganized, and tottering, finds stirred up against it not only the blind madness of hunger, but, in addition, the evil instincts which profit by every disorder and the inveterate lusts which every political commotion frees from restraint.

20. "Archives Nationales," H. 1453. Letter of the intendant, M. d'Aine, March 12th; of M. d'Agay, April 30th; of M. Amelot, April 25th; of the municipal authorities of Nantes, January 9th, &c.

IV

We have seen how numerous the smugglers, dealers in contraband salt, poachers, vagabonds, beggars, and escaped convicts[21] have become, and how a year of famine increases the number. All are so many recruits for the mobs, and whether in a disturbance or by means of a disturbance each one of them fills his pouch. Around Caux,[22] even up to the environs of Rouen, at Roncherolles, Quévrevilly, Préaux, Saint-Jacques, and in all the surrounding neighbourhood bands of armed ruffians force their way into the houses, particularly the parsonages, and lay their hands on whatever they please. To the south of Chartres "three or four hundred woodcutters, from the forests of Bellème, chop away everything that opposes them, and force grain to be given up to them at their own price." In the vicinity of Étampes, fifteen bandits enter the farmhouses at night and put the farmer to ransom, threatening him with a conflagration. In Cambrésis they pillage the abbeys of Vauchelles, of Verger, and of Guillemans, the chateau of the Marquis de Besselard, the estate of M. Doisy, two farms, the waggons of wheat passing along the road to Saint-Quentin, and, besides this, seven farms in Picardy. "The seat of this revolt is in some villages bordering on Picardy and Cambrésis, familiar with smuggling operations and to the license of that pursuit." The peasants allow themselves to be enticed away by the bandits. Man slips rapidly down the incline of dishonesty; one who is half-honest, and takes part in a riot inadvertently or in spite of himself, repeats the act, allured on by impunity or by gain. In fact, "it is not dire necessity which impels them"; they make a speculation of cupidity, a new sort of illicit trade. An old

21. "The Ancient Régime," pp. 380–389.

22. Floquet, vii. 508 (Report of February 27th). Hippeau, "Le Gouvernement de Normandie," iv. 377. (Letter of M. Perrot, June 23rd.)—"Archives Nationales," H. 1453. Letter of M. de Sainte-Suzanne, April 29th. *Ibid.* F[7], 3,250. Letter of M. de Rochambeau, May 16th. *Ibid.* F[7], 3,185. Letter of the Abbé Duplaquet, Deputy of the Third-Estate of Saint-Quentin, May 17th. Letter of three husbandmen in the environs of Saint-Quentin, May 14th.

carabinier, sabre in hand, a forest-keeper, and "about eight persons sufficiently lax, put themselves at the head of four or five hundred men, go off each day to three or four villages, and force everybody who has any wheat to give it to them at 24 livres," and even at 18 livres, the sack. Those among the band who say that they have no money carry away their portion without payment. Others, after having paid what they please, resell at a profit, which amounts to even 45 livres the sack; a good business, and one in which greed takes poverty for its accomplice. At the next harvest the temptation will be similar: "they have threatened to come and do our harvesting for us, and also to take our cattle and sell the meat in the villages at the rate of two sous the pound."—In every important insurrection there are similar evil-doers and vagabonds, enemies to the law, savage, prowling desperadoes, who, like wolves, roam about wherever they scent a prey. It is they who serve as the directors and executioners of public or private malice. Near Usès twenty-five masked men, with guns and clubs, enter the house of a notary, fire a pistol at him, beat him, wreck the premises, and burn his registers along with the title-deeds and papers which he has in keeping for the Count de Rouvres: seven of them are arrested, but the people are on their side, and fall on the constabulary and free them.[23]—They are known by their acts, by their love of destruction for the sake of destruction, by their foreign accent, by their savage faces and their rags. Some of them come from Paris to Rouen, and, for four days, the town is at their mercy;[24] the stores are forced open, train waggons are discharged, wheat is wasted, and convents and seminaries are put to ransom; they invade the dwelling of the attorney-general, who has begun proceedings against them, and want to tear him to pieces; they break his mirrors and his furniture, leave the premises laden with booty, and go into the town and its outskirts to pillage the manufactories and break up or burn all the machinery.—Henceforth

23. "Archives Nationales," H. 1453. Letter of the Count de Perigord, military commandant of Languedoc, April 22nd.

24. Floquet, vii. 511 (from the 11th to the 14th July).

these constitute the new leaders: for in every mob it is the boldest and least scrupulous who march ahead and set the example in destruction. The example is contagious: the beginning was the craving for bread, the end is murder and incendiarism; the savagery which is unchained adding its unlimited violence to the limited revolt of necessity.

V

Bad as it is, this savagery might, perhaps, have been overcome, in spite of the dearth and of the brigands; but what renders it irresistible is the belief of its being authorised, and that by those whose duty it is to repress it. Here and there words and actions of a brutal frankness break forth, and reveal beyond the sombre present a more threatening future.—After the 9th of January, 1789, among the populace which attacks the Hôtel-de-Ville and besieges the bakers' shops of Nantes, "shouts of *Vive la Liberté!*[25] mingled with those of *Vive le Roi!* are heard." A few months later, around Ploërmel, the peasants refuse to pay tithes, alleging that the memorial of their seneschal's court demands their abolition. In Alsace, after March, there is the same refusal "in many places"; many of the communities even maintain that they will pay no more taxes until their deputies to the States-General shall have fixed the precise amount of the public contributions. In Isère it is decided, by proceedings, printed and published, that "personal dues" shall no longer be paid, while the landowners who are affected by this dare not prosecute in the tribunals. At Lyons, the people have come to the conclusion "that all levies of taxes are to cease," and, on the 29th of June, on hearing of the meeting of the three orders, "astonished by the illuminations and signs of public rejoicing," they believe that the good time has

25. "Archives Nationales," H. 1453. Letter of the municipal authorities of Nantes, January 9th; of the subdelegate of Ploërmel, July 4th; *ibid.* F^7, 2,353. Letter of the intermediary commission of Alsace, September 8th; *ibid.* F^7, 3,227. Letter of the intendant, Caze de la Bove, June 16th; *ibid.* H. 1453. Letter of Terray, intendant of Lyons, July 4th; of the *prévot des échevins,* July 5th and 7th.

come; "they think of forcing the delivery of meat to them at four sous the pound, and wine at the same rate. The publicans insinuate to them the prospective abolition of *octrois,* and that, meanwhile, the King, in favour of the reassembling of the three orders, has granted three days' freedom from all duties at Paris, and that Lyons ought to enjoy the same privilege." Upon this the crowd, rushing off to the barriers, to the gates of Sainte-Claire and Perrache, and to the Guillotière bridge, burn or demolish the bureaux, destroy the registers, sack the lodgings of the clerks, carry off the money and pillage the wine on hand in the depôt. In the mean time a rumour has circulated all round through the country that there is free entrance into the town for all provisions, and during the following days the peasantry stream in with enormous files of waggons loaded with wine and drawn by several oxen, so that, in spite of the reestablished guard, it is necessary to let them enter all day without paying the dues; it is only on the 7th of July that these can again be collected.—The same thing occurs in the southern provinces, where the principal imposts are levied on provisions. There also the collections are suspended in the name of public authority. At Agde,[26] "the people, considering the so-called will of the King as to equality of classes, are foolish enough to think that they are everything and can do everything"; thus do they interpret in their own way and in their own terms the double representation which is accorded to the Third-Estate. They threaten the town, consequently, with general pillage if the prices of all provisions are not reduced, and if the duties of the province on wine, fish, and meat are not suppressed; again, "they wish to nominate consuls who have sprung up out of their body," and the bishop, the lord of the manor, the mayor and the notables, against whom they forcibly stir up the peasantry in the country, are obliged to proclaim by sound of trumpet that their demands shall be granted. Three days afterwards they exact a diminution of one-half of the tax on grinding, and go in quest of the bishop who owns

26. "Archives Nationales," H. 1453. Letter of the mayor and councils of Agde, April 21st; of M. de Perigord, April 19th, May 5th.

the mills. The prelate, who is ill, sinks down in the street, and seats himself on a stone; they compel him forthwith to sign an act of renunciation, and hence "his mill, valued at 15,000 livres, is reduced to 7,500 livres."—At Limoux, under the pretext of searching for grain, they enter the houses of the comptroller and tax contractors, carry off their registers, and throw them into the water along with the furniture of their clerks.—In Provence it is worse; for most unjustly, and through inconceivable imprudence, the taxes of the towns are all levied on flour; it is therefore to this impost that the dearness of bread is directly attributed; hence the fiscal agent becomes a manifest enemy, and revolts on account of hunger are transformed into insurrections against the State.

VI

Here, again, political novelties are the spark that ignites the mass of gunpowder; everywhere, the uprising of the people takes place on the very day on which the electoral assembly meets; from forty to fifty riots occur in the provinces in less than a fortnight. Popular imagination, like that of a child, goes straight to its mark; the reforms having been announced, people think them accomplished, and, to make sure of them, steps are at once taken to carry them out; now that we are to have relief, let us relieve ourselves. "This is not an isolated riot as usual," writes the commander of the troops;[27] "here the faction is united and governed by uniform principles; the same errors are diffused through all minds. . . . The principles impressed on the people are that the King desires equality; no more bishops or lords, no more distinctions of rank, no tithes, and no seignorial

27. "Archives Nationales," H. 1453. Letters of M. de Caraman, March 23rd, 26th, 27th, 28th; of the seneschal Missiessy, March 24th; of the mayor of Hyères, March 25th, &c.; *ibid.* H. 1274; of M. de Montmayran, April 2nd; of M. de Caraman, March 18th, April 12th; of the intendant, M. de la Tour, April 2nd; of the *procureur-général,* M. d'Antheman, April 17th, and the report of June 15th; of the municipal authorities of Toulon, April 11th; of the subdelegate of Manosque, March 14th; of M. de Saint-Tropez, March 21st.—*Procés-verbal,* signed by 119 witnesses, of the insurrection at Aix, March 5th, &c.

privileges. Thus, these misguided people fancy that they are exercising their rights, and obeying the will of the King." The effect of sonorous phrases is apparent; the people have been told that the States-General were to bring about the "regeneration of the kingdom"; the inference is "that the date of their assembly was to be one of an entire and absolute change of conditions and fortunes." Hence, "the insurrection against the nobles and the clergy is as active as it is widespread." "In many places it was distinctly announced that there was a *sort of war declared against landowners and property,*" and "in the towns as well as in the rural districts the people persist in declaring that *they will pay nothing, neither taxes, duties, nor debts.*"—Naturally, the first assault is against the *piquet,* or meal-tax. At Aix, Marseilles, Toulon, and in more than forty towns and market-villages, this is summarily abolished; at Aupt and at Luc nothing remains of the weighing-house but the four walls; at Marseilles the house of the slaughter-house contractor, at Brignolles that of the director of the leather excise, are sacked: the determination is "to purge the land of excise-men."—This is only a beginning; bread and other provisions must become cheap, and that without delay. At Arles, the corporation of sailors, presided over by M. de Barras, consul, had just elected its representatives: by way of conclusion to the meeting, they pass a resolution insisting that M. de Barras should reduce the price of all comestibles, and, on his refusal, they "open the window, exclaiming, 'We hold him, and we have only to throw him into the street for the rest to pick him up.'" Compliance is inevitable. The resolution is proclaimed by the town-criers, and at each article which is reduced in price the crowd shout, "Vive le Roi, vive M. Barras!"—One must yield to brute force. But the inconvenience is great; for, through the suppression of the meal-tax, the towns have no longer a revenue; and, on the other hand, as they are obliged to indemnify the butchers and bakers, Toulon, for instance, incurs a debt of 2,500 livres a day.

In this state of disorder, woe to those who are under suspicion of having contributed, directly or indirectly, to the evils which the people endure! At Toulon a demand is made for the head of the mayor, who signs the tax-list, and of the keeper of the records; they are trodden under foot, and their houses are ransacked. At Manosque, the Bishop of Sisteron, who is visiting the seminary, is accused of favouring a monopolist; on his way to his carriage, on foot, he is hooted and menaced: he is first pelted with mud, and then with stones. The consuls in attendance, and the subdelegate who come to his assistance, are mauled and repulsed. Meanwhile, some of the most furious begin, before his eyes, "to dig a ditch to bury him in." Protected by five or six brave fellows, he succeeds in reaching his carriage, amidst a volley of stones, wounded on the head and on many parts of his body, and is finally saved only because the horses, which are likewise stoned, run away. Foreigners, Italians, bandits, are mingled with the peasants and artisans, and expressions are heard and acts are seen which indicate a jacquerie.[28] "The most excited said to the bishop, 'We are poor and you are rich, and we mean to have all your property.'"[29] Elsewhere, "the seditious mob exacts contributions from all people in good circumstances. At Brignolles, thirteen houses are pillaged from top to bottom, and thirty others half-pillaged.—At Aupt, M. de Montferrat, in defending himself, is killed and "hacked to pieces."—At La Seyne, the populace, led by a peasant, assemble by beat of drum; some women fetch a bier, and set it down before the house of a leading bourgeois, telling him to prepare for death, and that "they will have the honour of burying him." He escapes; his house is pillaged, as well as the bureau of the meal-tax; and, the following day, the chief of the band "obliges the principal inhabitants to give him a sum of money to indemnify, as he states it, the peasants who have abandoned their work," and devoted the day to serving the public.—At Peinier, the Président de Peinier, an octogenarian, is "besieged in his chateau by a band of a hundred and fifty artisans and peasants," who bring with them

28. A rising of the peasants. The term is used to indicate a country mob in contradistinction to a city or town mob.—Tr.

29. "Archives Nationales," H. 1274. Letter of M. de la Tour, April 2nd (with a detailed memorial and depositions).

a consul and a notary. Aided by these two functionaries, they force the president "to pass an act by which he renounces his seignorial rights of every description."—At Sollier they destroy the mills belonging to M. de Forbin-Janson, sack the house of his business agent, pillage the chateau, demolish the roof, chapel, altar, railings, and escutcheons, enter the cellars, stave in the casks, and carry away everything that can be carried, "the transportation taking two days"; all of which is a damage of a hundred thousand crowns for the marquis.—At Riez they surround the episcopal palace with fagots, threatening to burn it, "and compromise with the bishop on a promise of fifty thousand livres," and want him to burn his archives.—In short, the sedition is *social,* for it singles out for attack all who profit by, or stand at the head of, the established order of things.

Seeing them act in this way, one would say that the theory of the *Contrat-Social* had been instilled into them. They treat magistrates as domestics, promulgate laws, conduct themselves like sovereigns, exercise public power, and establish, summarily, arbitrarily, and brutally, whatever they think to be in conformity with natural right.—At Peinier they exact a second electoral assembly, and, for themselves, the right of suffrage.—At Saint-Maximin they themselves elect new consuls and officers of justice.—At Solliez they oblige the judge's lieutenant to give in his resignation, and they break his staff of office.—At Barjols "they use consuls and judges as their town servants, announcing that they are masters and that they will themselves administer justice."—In fact, they do administer it as they understand it—that is to say, through many exactions and robberies! One man has wheat; he must share it with him who has none. Another has money; he must give it to him who has not enough to buy bread with. On this principle, at Barjols, they tax the Ursuline nuns 1,800 livres, carry off fifty loads of wheat from the Chapter, eighteen from one poor artisan, and forty from another, and constrain canons and beneficiaries to give acquittances to their farmers. Then, from house to house, with club in hand, they oblige some to hand over money, others to abandon their claims on their debtors, "one to desist from criminal proceedings, another to nullify a decree obtained, a third to reimburse the expenses of a lawsuit gained years before, a father to give his consent to the marriage of his son."—All their grievances are brought to mind, and we all know the tenacity of a peasant's memory. Having become the master, he redresses wrongs, and especially those of which he thinks himself the object. There must be a general restitution; and first, of the feudal dues which have been collected. They take of M. de Montmeyan's business agent all the money he has as compensation for that received by him during fifteen years as a notary. A former consul of Brignolles had, in 1775, inflicted penalties to the amount of 1,500 or 1,800 francs, which had been given to the poor; this sum is taken from his strong box. Moreover, if consuls and law officers are wrongdoers, the title-deeds, rent-rolls, and other documents by which they do their business are still worse. To the fire with all old writings—not only office registers, but also, at Hyères, all the papers in the town-hall and those of the principal notary.—In the matter of papers none are good but new ones—those which convey some discharge, quittance, or obligation to the advantage of the people. At Brignolles the owners of the grist-mills are constrained to execute a contract of sale by which they convey their mills to the commune in consideration of 5,000 francs per annum, payable in ten years without interest—an arrangement which ruins them. On seeing the contract signed the peasants shout and cheer, and so great is their faith in this piece of stamped paper that they at once cause a mass of thanksgiving to be celebrated in the Cordeliers. Formidable omens, these! which mark the inward purpose, the determined will, the coming deeds of this rising power. If it prevails, its first work will be to destroy all ancient documents, all title-deeds, rent-rolls, contracts, and claims to which force compels it to submit. By force likewise it will draw up others to its own advantage, and the scribes who do it will be its own deputies and administrators whom it holds in its rude grasp.

Those who are in high places are not alarmed; they even find that there is some good in the revolt, inasmuch as it compels the towns to suppress unjust taxation.[30] The new Marseilles guard, formed of young men, is allowed to march to Aubagne, "to insist that *M. le lieutenant criminel* and *M. l'avocat du Roi* release the prisoners." The disobedience of Marseilles, which refuses to receive the magistrates sent under letters patent to take testimony, is tolerated. And better still, in spite of the remonstrances of the parliament of Aix, a general amnesty is proclaimed; "no one is excepted but a few of the leaders, to whom is allowed the liberty of leaving the kingdom." The mildness of the King and of the military authorities is admirable. It is admitted that the people are children, that they err only through ignorance, that faith must be had in their repentance, and, as soon as they return to order, they must be received with paternal effusions.—The truth is, that the child is a blind Colossus, exasperated by sufferings. Hence whatever it takes hold of is shattered—not only the local wheels of the provinces, which, if temporarily deranged, may be repaired, but even the mainspring at the centre which puts the rest in motion, and the destruction of which will throw the whole machinery into confusion.

30. "Archives Nationales," H. 1274. Letter of M. de Caraman, April 22nd:—"One real benefit results from this misfortune. . . . The well-to-do class is brought to sustain that which exceeded the strength of the poor daily labourers. We see the nobles and people in good circumstances a little more attentive to the poor peasants: they are now habituated to speaking to them with more gentleness." M. de Caraman was wounded, as well as his son, at Aix, and if the soldiery, who were stoned, at length fired on the crowd, he did not give the order.—*Ibid.* Letter of M. d'Anthéman, April 17th; of M. de Barentin, June 11th.

CHAPTER II

Paris up to the 14th of July— I. *Mob recruits in the environs—Entry of vagabonds—The number of paupers*— II. *Excitement of the press and of opinion—The people take part*— III. *The Réveillon affair*— IV. *The Palais-Royal—Popular gatherings become a political power—Pressure on the Assembly*— V. *Defection of the soldiery*— VI. *July 13th and 14th*— VII. *Murders of Foulon and Berthier*— VIII. *Paris in the hands of the people.*

INDEED it is in the centre that the convulsive shocks are strongest. Nothing is lacking to aggravate the insurrection—neither the most lively provocations to stimulate it, nor the most numerous bands to carry it out. The environs of Paris all furnish recruits for it; nowhere are there so many miserable wretches, so many of the famished, and so many rebellious beings. Robberies of grain take place everywhere—at Orleans, at Cosne, at Rambouillet, at Jouy, at Pont-Saint-Maxence, at Bray-sur-Seine, at Sens, at Nangis.[1] Wheaten flour is so scarce at Meudon, that every purchaser is ordered to buy at the same time an equal quantity of barley. At Viroflay, thirty women, with a rear guard of men, stop on the main road vehicles which they suppose to be loaded with grain. At Montlhéry seven brigades of the police are dispersed by stones and clubs: an immense throng of

1. "Archives Nationales," H. 1453. Letter of M. Miron, lieutenant of police, April 26th; of M. Joly de Fleury, *procureur-général,* May 29th; of MM. Marchais and Berthier, April 18th and 27th, March 23rd, April 5th, May 5th.—Arthur Young, June 10th and 29th. "Archives Nationales," H. 1453. Letter of the sub-delegate of Montlhéry, April 14th.

eight thousand persons, women and men, provided with bags, fall upon the grain exposed for sale, force the delivery to them of wheat worth 40 francs at 24 francs, pillaging the half of it and conveying it off without payment. "The constabulary is disheartened," writes the subdelegate; "the determination of the people is wonderful; I am frightened at what I have seen and heard."—After the 13th of July, 1788, the day of the hailstorm, "despair" seized the peasantry; well disposed as the proprietors may have been, it was impossible to assist them; "not a workshop is open;[2] the noblemen and the bourgeois, obliged to grant delays in the payment of their incomes, can give no work." Accordingly, "the famished people are on the point of risking life for life," and, publicly and boldly, they seek food wherever it can be found. At Conflans-Saint-Honorine, Eragny, Neuville, Chenevières, at Cergy, Pontoise, Ile-Adam, Presle, and Beaumont, men, women, and children, the whole parish, range the country, set snares, and destroy the burrows. "The rumour is current that the Government, informed of the damage done by the game to cultivators, allows its destruction . . . and really the hares ravaged about a fifth of the crop." At first an arrest is made of nine of these poachers; but they are released, "taking circumstances into account," and therefore, for two months, there is a slaughter on the property of the Prince de Conti and of the Ambassador Mercy d'Argenteau; in default of bread they eat rabbits.—Along with the abuse of property they are led, by a natural impulse, to attack property itself. Near Saint-Denis the woods belonging to the abbey are devastated; "the farmers of the neighbourhood carry away loads of wood, drawn by four and five horses"; the inhabitants of the villages of Ville-Parisis, Tremblay, Vert-Galant, Villepinte, sell it publicly, and threaten the wood-rangers with a beating: on the 15th of June the damage is already estimated at 60,000 livres.—It makes little dif-

2. "Archives Nationales," H. 1453. Letter of the subdelegate Gobert, March 17th; of the officers of police, June 15th: "On the 12th, 13th, 14th, and 15th of March the inhabitants of Conflans generally rebelled against the game law in relation to the rabbit."

ference whether the proprietor has been benevolent, like M. de Talaru,[3] who had supported the poor on his estate at Issy the preceding winter. The peasants destroy the dyke which conducts water to his communal mill; condemned by the parliament to restore it, they declare that not only will they not obey, but that if M. de Talaru rebuilds it they will return, to the number of three hundred armed men, and tear it away the second time.

For those who are most compromised Paris is the nearest refuge; for the poorest and most exasperated, the door of nomadic life stands wide open. Bands rise up around the capital, just as in countries where human society has not yet been formed, or has ceased to exist. During the first two weeks in May,[4] near Villejuif, a band of five or six hundred vagabonds strive to force Bicêtre and approach Saint-Cloud. They arrive from thirty, forty, and sixty leagues off, from Champagne, from Lorraine, from the whole circuit of country devastated by the hailstorm. All hover around Paris and are there engulfed as in a sewer, the unfortunate along with criminals, some to find work, others to beg and to rove about under the injurious promptings of hunger and the rumours of the public thoroughfares. During the last days of April,[5] the clerks at the toll-houses note the entrance of "a frightful number of poorly clad men of sinister aspect." During the first days of May a change in the appearance of the crowd is remarked; there mingle in it "a number of foreigners, from all countries, most of them in rags, armed with big sticks, and whose very aspect announces what is to be feared from them." Already, before this final influx, the public sink is full to overflowing. Think of the extraordinary and rapid increase of population in Paris,

3. Montjoie, 2nd part, ch. xxi. p. 14 (the first week in June). Montjoie is a party man; but he gives dates and details, and his testimony, when it is confirmed elsewhere, deserves to be admitted.

4. Montjoie, 1st part, 92–101. "Archives Nationales," H. 1453. Letter of the officer of police of Saint-Denis: "A good many workmen arrive daily from Lorraine as well as from Champagne," which increases the famine.

5. De Bezenval, "Mémoires," i. 353. Cf. "The Ancient Régime," p. 388. Marmontel, ii. 252 and following pages. De Ferrières, i. 407.

the multitude of artisans brought there by recent demolitions and constructions, all the craftsmen whom the stagnation of manufactures, the augmentation of *octrois,* the rigour of winter, and the dearness of bread have reduced to extreme distress. Remember that in 1786 "two hundred thousand persons are enumerated whose property, all told, has not the intrinsic worth of fifty crowns"; that, from time immemorial, they are at war with the city watchmen; that in 1789 there are twenty thousand poachers in the capital; that, to provide them with work, it is found necessary to establish national workshops; "that twelve thousand are kept uselessly occupied digging on the hill of Montmartre, and paid twenty sous per day; that the wharfs and quays are covered with them, that the Hôtel-de-Ville is invested by them, and that, around the palace, they seem to be a reproach to the inactivity of disarmed justice"; that daily they grow bitter and excited around the doors of the bakeries, where, kept waiting a long time, they are not sure of obtaining bread: you may anticipate the fury and the force with which they will storm any obstacle to which their attention may be directed.

II

This obstacle has been pointed out to them for a couple of years: the Ministry, the Court, the Government, the ancient régime. Whoever protests against it in favour of the people is sure to be followed as far, and farther, than he chooses to lead. The moment the Parliament of a large city refuses to register fiscal edicts it finds a riot at its service. On the 7th of June, 1788, at Grenoble, tiles rain down on the heads of the soldiery, and the military force is powerless. At Rennes an army is necessary to put down the rebellious city, and after this a permanent camp, four regiments of infantry and two of cavalry, under the command of a Marshal of France.[6] The following year, when the Parliaments turn over to the side of the privileged class, the disturbance again begins, but this time against the Parliaments. In February, 1789, at Besançon and at Aix, the magistrates

6. Arthur Young, September 1st, 1788.

are hooted at, chased in the streets, besieged in the town-hall, and obliged to conceal themselves or take to flight.—If such is the disposition in the provincial capitals, what must it be in the capital of the kingdom? To begin—in the month of August, 1788, after the dismissal of Brienne and Lamoignon, the mob, collected on the Place Dauphine, constitutes itself judge, burns both ministers in effigy, disperses the watch, and resists the troops: no sedition, as bloody as this, had been seen for a century. Two days later, the riot bursts out a second time; the people are seized with a resolve to go and burn the residences of the two ministers and that of Dubois, the lieutenant of police.

Clearly a new leaven has been infused among the ignorant and brutal masses, and the new ideas are producing their effect. They have been insensibly filtering for a long time from layer to layer, and after having gained over the aristocracy, the whole of the lettered portion of the Third-Estate, the lawyers, the schools, all the young, they have insinuated themselves drop by drop and by a thousand fissures into the class which supports itself by the labour of its own hands. Noblemen, at their toilettes, have scoffed at Christianity, and affirmed the rights of man before their valets, hairdressers, purveyors, and all those that are in attendance upon them. Men of letters, lawyers, and attorneys have repeated, in the bitterest tone, the same diatribes and the same theories in the coffee-houses and in the restaurants, on the promenades and in all public places. They have spoken out before the lower class as if it were not present, and, from all this eloquence poured out without precaution, some bubbles besprinkle the brain of the artisan, the publican, the messenger, the shopkeeper, and the soldier.

Hence it is that a year suffices to convert mute discontent into political passion. From the 5th of July, 1787, on the invitation of the King, who convokes the States-General and demands advice from everybody, both speech and the press alter in tone.[7] Instead of gen-

7. Barrère, "Mémoires," i. 234.

eral conversation of a speculative turn there is preaching, with a view to practical effect, sudden, radical, and close at hand, preaching as shrill and thrilling as the blast of a trumpet. Revolutionary pamphlets appear in quick succession: "Qu'est-ce que le Tiers?" by Sieyès; "Mémoire pour le Peuple Français," by Cerutti; "Considérations sur les Intérêts des Tiers-Etat," by Rabtau Saint-Etienne; "Ma Pétition," by Target; "Les Droits des Etats généraux," by M. d'Entraigues, and, a little later, "La France libre," by Camille Desmoulins, and others by hundreds and thousands,[8] all of which are repeated and amplified in the electoral assemblies, where new-made citizens come to declaim and increase their own excitement.[9] The unanimous, universal, and daily shout rolls along from echo to echo, into barracks and into faubourgs, into markets, workshops, and garrets. In the month of February, 1789, Necker avows "that obedience is not to be found anywhere, and that even the troops are not to be relied on." In the month of May, the fisherwomen, and next the fruiterers of the Halle come to recommend the interests of the people to the bodies of electors, and to sing rhymes in honour of the Third-Estate. In the month of June pamphlets are in all hands; "even lackeys are poring over them at the gates of hotels." In the month of July, as the King is signing an order, a patriotic valet becomes alarmed and reads it over his shoulder.—There is no illusion here; it is not merely the bourgeoisie which ranges itself against the legal authorities and against the established régime, but the whole people, the craftsmen, the shopkeepers and the domestics, workmen of every kind and degree, the populace underneath the people, the vagabonds, street rovers, and mendicants, the whole multitude, which, bound down by anxiety for its daily bread, had never lifted its eyes to look at the great social order of which it is the lowest stratum, and the whole weight of which it bears.

8. See, in the National Library, the long catalogue of those which have survived.

9. Malouet, i. 255. Bailly, i. 43 (May 9th and 19th).—D'Hezecques, "Souvenirs d'un page de Louis XVI." 293.—De Bezenval, i. 368.

III

Suddenly it stirs, and the superposed scaffolding totters. It is the movement of a brute nature exasperated by want and maddened by suspicion. Have paid hands, which are invisible, goaded it on from beneath? Contemporaries are convinced of this, and it is probably the case.[10] But the uproar made around the suffering brute would alone suffice to make it shy, and explain its sudden start.—On the 21st of April the Electoral Assemblies have begun in Paris; they are held in each quarter for the clergy, the nobles, and the Third-Estate. Every day, for almost a month, files of electors are seen passing along the streets. Those of the first degree continue to meet after having nominated those of the second: the nation must needs watch its mandatories and maintain its imprescriptible rights. If this exercise of their rights has been delegated to them, they still belong to the nation, and it reserves to itself the privilege of interposing when it pleases. A pretension of this kind travels fast; immediately after the Third-Estate of the Assemblies it reaches the Third-Estate of the streets. Nothing is more natural than the desire to lead one's leaders: the first time any dissatisfaction occurs, they lay hands on those who halt and make them march on as directed. On a Saturday, April 25th,[11] a rumour is current that Réveillon, an elector and manufacturer of wall-paper, Rue Saint-Antoine, and Lérat, a commissioner, have "spoken badly" at the Electoral Assembly of Sainte-Marguerite. To speak badly means to speak badly of the people. What has Réveillon said? Nobody knows, but popular imagination, with its ter-

10. Marmontel, ii. 249.—Montjoie, 1st part, p. 92.—De Bezenval, i. 387: "These spies added that persons were seen exciting the tumult and were distributing money."

11. "Archives Nationales," Y. 11441. Interrogatory of the Abbé Roy, May 5th. Y. 11033, Interrogatory (April 28th and May 4th) of twenty-three wounded persons brought to the Hôtel-Dieu. These two documents are of prime importance in presenting the true aspect of the insurrection; to these must be added the narrative of M. de Bezenval, who was commandant at this time with M. du Châtelet. Almost all other narratives are amplified or falsified through party spirit.

rible powers of invention and precision, readily fabricates or welcomes a murderous phrase. He said that "a working-man with a wife and children could live on fifteen sous a day." Such a man is a traitor, and must be disposed of at once; "all his belongings must be put to fire and sword." The rumour, it must be noted, is false.[12] Réveillon pays his poorest workman twenty-five sous a day, is the means of supporting three hundred and fifty, and, in spite of a dull season the previous winter, he kept all on at the same rate of wages. He himself was once a workman, and obtained a medal for his inventions, and is benevolent and respected by all respectable persons. All this avails nothing; bands of vagabonds and foreigners, who have just passed through the barriers, do not look so closely into matters, while the journeymen, the carters, the cobblers, the masons, the braziers, and the stone-cutters whom they entice in their lodgings are just as ignorant as they are. When irritation has accumulated, it breaks out at haphazard.

Just at this time the clergy of Paris renounce their privileges in the way of imposts,[13] and the people, taking friends for adversaries, add in their invectives the name of the clergy to that of Réveillon.

During the whole of the day, and also during the leisure moments of Sunday, the fermentation increases; on Monday the 27th, another day of idleness and drunkenness, the bands begin to move. Certain witnesses encounter one of these in the Rue Saint-Sévérin, "armed with clubs," and so numerous as to bar the passage. "Shops and doors are closed on all sides, and the people cry out, 'There's the revolt!' " The seditious crowd belch out curses and invectives against the clergy, "and, catching sight of an abbé, shout 'Priest!' " Another band parades an effigy of Réveillon decorated with the ribbon of the order of St. Michael, which undergoes the parody of a sentence and is burnt on the Place de Grève, after which they threaten his house. Driven back by the guard, they invade that of a manufacturer of saltpetre, who is his friend, and burn and smash his effects and

12. De Ferrières, vol. iii. note A. (justificatory explanation by Réveillon).

13. Bailly, i. 25 (April 26th).

furniture.[14] It is only towards midnight that the crowd is dispersed and the insurrection is supposed to have ended. On the following day it begins again with greater violence; for, besides the ordinary stimulants of misery[15] and the craving for license, they have a new stimulant in the idea of a cause to defend, the conviction that they are fighting "for the Third-Estate." In a cause like this each one should help himself, and all should help each other. "We should be lost," one of them exclaimed, "if we did not sustain each other." Strong in this belief, they sent deputations three times into the Faubourg Saint-Marceau to obtain recruits, and on their way, with uplifted clubs they enrol, willingly or unwillingly, all they encounter. Others, at the Porte Saint-Antoine, arrest people who are returning from the races, demanding of them if they are for the nobles or for the Third-Estate, and force women to descend from their vehicles and to cry "Vive le Tiers-Etat!"[16] Meanwhile the crowd has increased before Réveillon's dwelling; the thirty men on guard are unable to resist; the house is invaded and sacked from top to bottom; the furniture, provisions, clothing, registers, waggons, even the poultry in the back-yard, all is cast into blazing bonfires lighted in three different places; five hundred louis d'or, the ready money, and the silver plate are stolen. Several roam through the cellars, drink liquor or varnish at haphazard until they fall down dead drunk or expire in convulsions. Against this howling horde, a corps of the watch, mounted and on foot, is seen approaching;[17] also a hundred cavalry

14. Hippeau, iv. 377 (Letters of M. Perrot, April 29th).

15. Letter to the King by an inhabitant of the Faubourg Saint-Antoine:—"Do not doubt, sire, that our recent misfortunes are due to the dearness of bread."

16. Dammartin, "Evénements qui se sont passés sous mes yeux," &c. i. 25:—"We turned back and were arrested by small bands of scoundrels, who insolently proposed to us to shout 'Vive Necker! Vive le Tiers-Etat!'" His two companions were knights of St. Louis, and their badges seemed an object of "increasing hatred." "The badge excited coarse mutterings, even on the part of persons who appeared superior to the agitators."

17. Dammartin, *ibid.* i. 25:—"I was dining this very day at the Hôtel d'Ecquevilly, in the Rue Saint-Louis." He leaves the house on foot and witnesses

of the "Royal Croats," the French Guards, and later on the Swiss Guards. "Tiles and chimneys are rained down on the soldiers," who fire back four files at a time. The rioters, drunk with brandy and rage, defend themselves desperately for several hours; more than two hundred are killed, and nearly three hundred are wounded; they are only put down by cannon, while the mob keeps active until far into the night. Towards eight in the evening, in the Rue Vieille du Temple, the Paris Guard continue to make charges in order to protect the doors which the miscreants try to force. Two doors are forced at half-past eleven o'clock in the Rue Saintonge and in the Rue de Bretagne, that of a pork-dealer and that of a baker.—Even to this last wave of the outbreak which is subsiding we can distinguish the elements which have produced the insurrection, and which are about to produce the Revolution. Starvation is one of these: in the Rue de Bretagne the troop which rifles the baker's shop carries bread off to the women staying at the corner of the Rue Saintonge. Brigandage is another: in the middle of the night M. du Châtelet's spies, gliding alongside of a ditch, "see a group of ruffians" assembled beyond the Barrière du Trône, their leader, mounted on a little knoll, urging them to begin again; and the following days, on the highways, vagabonds are saying to each other, "We can do no more at Paris, because they are too sharp on the look-out; let us go to Lyons!" There are, finally, the patriots: on the evening of the insurrection, between the Pont-au-Change and the Pont-Marie, the half-naked ragamuffins, besmeared with dirt, bearing along their hand-barrows, are fully alive to their cause; they beg alms in a loud tone of voice, and stretch out their hats to the passers, saying, "Take pity on this poor Third-Estate!"—The starving, the ruffians, and the patriots, all form one body, and henceforth misery, crime, and public

---

the disturbance. "Fifteen to sixteen hundred wretches, the excrement of the nation, degraded by shameful vices, covered with rags, and gorged with brandy, presented the most disgusting and revolting spectacle. More than a hundred thousand persons of both sexes and of all ages and conditions interfered greatly with the operations of the troops. The firing soon commenced and blood flowed: two innocent persons were wounded near me."

spirit unite to provide an ever-ready insurrection for the agitators who desire to raise one.

IV

But the agitators are already in permanent session. The Palais-Royal is an open-air club where, all day and even far into the night, one excites the other and urges on the crowd to blows. In this enclosure, protected by the privileges of the House of Orleans, the police dare not enter. Speech is free, and the public who avail themselves of this freedom seem purposely chosen to abuse it.—The public and the place are adapted to each other.[18] The Palais-Royal, the centre of prostitution, of play, of idleness, and of pamphlets, attracts the whole of that unrooted population which floats about in a great city, and which, without occupation or home, lives only for curiosity or for pleasure—the frequenters of the coffee-houses, the runners for gambling hells, adventurers, and social outcasts, the overplus or forlorn hope of literature, arts, and the bar, attorneys' clerks, students of the schools, cockneys, loungers, strangers, and the occupants of furnished lodgings, amounting, it is said, to forty thousand in Paris. They fill the garden and the galleries; "one would hardly find here one of what were called the "Six Bodies,"[19] a bourgeois settled down and occupied with his own affairs, a man whom business and family cares render serious and influential. There is no place here for industrious and orderly bees; it is the rendezvous of political and literary drones. They flock into it from every quarter of Paris, and the tumultuous, buzzing swarm covers the ground like an overturned hive. "Ten thousand people," writes Arthur Young,[20] "have been all this day in the Palais-Royal"; the press is so great that an apple thrown from a balcony on the moving floor of heads would not

18. De Goncourt, "La Société Française pendant la Révolution." Thirty-one gambling-houses are enumerated here, while a pamphlet of the day is entitled "Pétition des deux mille cent filles du Palais-Royal."

19. Montjoie, 2nd part, 144. Bailly, ii. 130.

20. Arthur Young, June 24th, 1789. Montjoie, 2nd part, 69.

reach the ground. The condition of these heads may be imagined; they are emptier of ballast than any in France, the most inflated with speculative ideas, the most excitable and the most excited. In this pell-mell of improvised politicians no one knows who is speaking; nobody is responsible for what he says. Each is there as in the theatre, unknown among the unknown, requiring sensational impressions and transports, a prey to the contagion of the passions around him, borne along in the whirl of sounding phrases, of ready-made news, growing rumours, and other exaggerations by which fanatics keep outdoing each other. There are shoutings, tears, applause, stamping, and clapping, as at the performance of a tragedy; one or another individual becomes so inflamed and hoarse that he dies on the spot with fever and exhaustion. In vain has Arthur Young been accustomed to the tumult of political liberty; he is dumbfounded at what he sees.[21] According to him, the excitement is "incredible. . . . We think sometimes that Debrett's or Stockdale's shops at London are crowded; but they are mere deserts compared to Desenne's and some others here, in which one can scarcely squeeze from the door to the counter. . . . Every hour produces its pamphlet; thirteen came out today, sixteen yesterday, and ninety-two last week. Nineteen-twentieths of these productions are in favour of liberty"; and by liberty is meant the extinction of privileges, numerical sovereignty, the application of the *Contrat-Social*, "the Republic," and more besides, a universal levelling, permanent anarchy, and even the jacquerie. Camille Desmoulins, one of the orators commonly there, announces it and urges it in precise terms: "Now that the animal is entrapped, let him be knocked on the head. . . . Never will the victors have a richer prey. *Forty thousand palaces, mansions, and chateaux, two-fifths of the property of France, will be the recompense of valour.* Those who pretend to be the conquerors will be conquered in turn. The nation shall be *purged.*" Here, in advance, is the programme of the Reign of Terror.

21. Arthur Young, June 9th, 24th, and 26th. "La France libre," *passim,* by C. Desmoulins.

Now all this is not only read, but declaimed, amplified, and turned to practical account. In front of the coffee-houses "those who have stentorian lungs relieve each other every evening."[22] "The coffee-houses . . . present astonishing spectacles . . . expectant crowds are at the doors and windows, listening *à gorge déployée* to certain orators, who from chairs or tables harangue each his little audience; the eagerness with which they are heard, and the thunder of applause they receive for every sentiment of more than common hardiness or violence against the present Government, cannot easily be imagined." "Three days ago a child of four years, well taught and intelligent, was promenaded around the garden, in broad daylight, at least twenty times, borne on the shoulders of a street porter, crying out, 'Verdict of the French people: Polignac exiled one hundred leagues from Paris; Condé the same; Conti the same; Artois the same; the Queen—I dare not write it.'" A hall made of boards in the middle of the Palais-Royal is always full, especially of young men, who carry on their deliberations in parliamentary fashion: in the evening the president invites the spectators to come forward and sign motions passed during the day, and of which the originals are placed in the Café Foy.[23] They count on their fingers the enemies of the country; "and first two Royal Highnesses (Monsieur and the Count d'Artois), three Most Serene Highnesses (the Prince de Condé, Duc de Bourbon, and the Prince de Conti), one favourite (Madame de Polignac), MM. de Vandreuil, de la Trémoille, du Châtelet, de Villedeuil, de Barentin, de la Galaisière, Vidaud de la Tour, Berthier, Foulon, and also M. Linguet." Placards are posted demanding the pillory on the Pont-Neuf for the Abbé Maury. One orator proposes "to burn the house of M. d'Espréménil, his wife, children, furniture, and himself: this is passed unanimously."—No opposition is tolerated. One of those present having manifested some

22. C. Desmoulins, letters to his father, and Arthur Young, June 9th.

23. Montjoie, 2nd part, 69, 77, 124, 144. C. Desmoulins, letters of June 24th and the following days.

horror at such sanguinary motions, "is seized by the collar, obliged to kneel down, to make an apology, and to kiss the ground; the punishment inflicted on children is given to him; he is ducked repeatedly in one of the fountain-basins, after which they hand him over to the populace, who roll him in the mud." On the following day an ecclesiastic is trodden under foot, and flung from hand to hand. A few days after, on the 22nd of June, there are two similar inflictions. The sovereign mob exercises all the functions of sovereign authority—with those of the legislator those of the judge, and those of the judge with those of the executioner. Its idols are sacred; if any one fails to show them respect he is guilty of *lèse-majesté*, and at once punished. In the first week of July, an abbé who speaks ill of Necker is flogged; a woman who insults the bust of Necker is stripped by the fishwomen, and beaten until she is covered with blood. War is declared against suspicious uniforms. "On the appearance of a hussar," writes Desmoulins, "they shout, 'There goes Punch!' and the stone-cutters fling stones at him. Last night two officers of the hussars, MM. de Sombreuil and de Polignac, came to the Palais-Royal . . . chairs were flung at them, and they would have been knocked down if they had not run away. The day before yesterday they seized a spy of the police and gave him a ducking in the fountain. They ran him down like a stag, hustled him, pelted him with stones, struck him with canes, forced one of his eyes out of its socket, and finally, in spite of his entreaties and cries for mercy, plunged him a second time in the fountain. His torments lasted from noon until half-past five o'clock, and he had about ten thousand executioners."—Consider the effect of such a focal centre at a time like this. A new power has sprung up side by side with legal powers, a legislature of the highways and public squares—anonymous, irresponsible, without restraint, driven onward by coffee-house theories, by transports of the brain and the vehemence of mountebanks, while the bare arms which have just accomplished the work of destruction in the Faubourg Saint-Antoine, form its body-guard and ministerial cabinet.

V

This is the dictatorship of a mob, and its proceedings, conforming to its nature, consist in acts of violence; wherever it finds resistance, it strikes.—The people of Versailles, in the streets and at the doors of the Assembly, daily "come and insult those whom they call *aristocrats*."[24] On Monday, June 22nd, "d'Espréménil barely escapes being knocked down; the Abbé Maury . . . owes his escape to the strength of a curé, who takes him up in his arms and tosses him into the carriage of the Archbishop of Arles." On the 23rd, "the Archbishop of Paris and the Keeper of the Seals are hooted, railed at, scoffed at, and derided, until they almost sink with shame and rage," and so formidable is the tempest of vociferation with which they are greeted, that Passeret, the King's secretary, who accompanies the minister, dies of the excitement that very day. On the 24th, the Bishop of Beauvais is almost knocked down by a stone which strikes him on the head. On the 25th, the Archbishop of Paris is saved only by the speed of his horses, the multitude pursuing him and pelting him with stones; his hotel is besieged, the windows are all shattered, and, notwithstanding the intervention of the French Guards, the peril is so great that he is obliged to promise that he will join the deputies of the Third-Estate. This is the way in which the rude hand of the people effects a reunion of the Orders. It bears as heavily on its own representatives as on its adversaries. "Although our hall was closed to the public," says Bailly, "there were always more than six hundred spectators";[25] not respectful and silent, but active and noisy, mingling with the deputies, raising their hands to vote in all cases, taking part in the deliberations by their applause and hisses: a col-

24. Etienne Dumont, "Souvenirs," p. 72. C. Desmoulins, letter of June 24th. Arthur Young, June 25th. Roux and Buchez, ii. 28.

25. Bailly, i. 227 and 179. Monnier, "Recherches sur les causes," &c., i. 289, 291; ii. 61. Malouet, i. 209; ii. 10. "Actes des Apôtres," v. 43 (Letter of M. de Guillermy, July 31st, 1790). Marmontel, i. 28: "The people came even into the Assembly, to encourage their partisans, to select and indicate their victims, and to terrify the feeble with the dreadful trial of open balloting."

lateral Assembly which often imposes its own will on the other. They take note of and put down the names of their opponents, which names, transmitted to chair-bearers in attendance at the entrance of the hall, and from them to the populace waiting for the departure of the deputies, are from that time regarded as the names of public enemies.[26] Lists are made out and printed, and, at the Palais-Royal in the evening, they become the lists of the proscribed.—It is under this brutal pressure that many decrees are passed, and, among them, that by which the commons declare themselves the National Assembly and assume supreme power. The night before, Malouet had proposed to ascertain, by a preliminary vote, on which side the majority was: the noes instantly gathered around him to the number of three hundred, "upon which a man springs out from the galleries, falls upon him and takes him by the collar exclaiming, 'Hold your tongue, you false citizen!' " Malouet is released and the guard comes forward, "but terror has spread through the hall, threats are uttered against opponents, and the next day we were only ninety." Moreover, the lists of their names had been circulated; some of them, deputies from Paris, went to see Bailly that very evening: one amongst them, "a very honest man and good patriot," had been told that his house was to be set on fire; now his wife had just given birth to a child, and the slightest tumult before the house would have been fatal. Such arguments are decisive. Consequently, three days afterwards, at the Tennis-court, but one deputy, Martin d'Auch, dares to write the word "opposant" after his name. Insulted by many of his colleagues, "at once denounced to the people who had collected at the entrance of the building, he is obliged to escape by a side door to avoid being cut to pieces," and, for several days, to keep away from the meetings.[27] Owing to this intervention of the

26. Manuscript letters of M. Boullé, deputy, to the municipal authorities of Pontivy, from May 1st, 1789, to September 4th, 1790 (communicated by M. Rosenzweig, archivist at Vannes). June 16th, 1789: "The crowd gathered around the hall . . . was, during these days, from 3,000 to 4,000 persons."

27. Letters of M. Boullé, June 23rd. "How sublime the moment, that in which we enthusiastically bind ourselves to the country by a new oath! . . .

galleries the radical minority, numbering about thirty,[28] lead the majority, and they do not allow them to free themselves. On the 28th of May, Malouet, having demanded a secret session to discuss the conciliatory measures which the King had proposed, the galleries hoot at him, and a deputy, M. Bouche, addresses him in very plain terms. "You must know, sir, that we are deliberating here in the presence of our masters, and that we must account to them for our opinions." This is the doctrine of the *Contrat-Social,* and, through timidity, fear of the Court and of the privileged class, through optimism and faith in human nature, through enthusiasm and the necessity of adhering to previous actions, the deputies, who are novices, provincial, and given up to theories, neither dare nor know how to escape from the tyranny of the prevailing dogma. Henceforth it becomes the law. All the Assemblies, the Constituent, the Legislative, the Convention, submit to it entirely. The public in the galleries are the admitted representatives of the people, under the same title, and even under a higher title, than the deputies. Now, this public is that of the Palais-Royal, consisting of strangers, idlers, lovers of novelties, Paris romancers, leaders of the coffee-houses, the future pillars of the clubs—in short, the wild enthusiasts among the middle class, just as the crowd which threatens doors and throws stones is recruited from among the wild enthusiasts of the lowest class. Thus by an involuntary selection, the faction which constitutes itself a public power is composed of nothing but violent minds and violent hands. Spontaneously and without previous concert dangerous fanatics are joined with dangerous brutes, and in the increasing discord between the legal authorities this is the illegal league which is certain to overthrow all.

Why should this moment be selected by one of our number to dishonour himself? His name is now blasted throughout France. And the unfortunate man has children! Suddenly overwhelmed by public contempt he leaves, and falls fainting at the door, exclaiming, 'Ah! this will be my death!' I do not know what has become of him since. What is strange is, he had not behaved badly up to that time, and he voted for the Constitution."

28. De Ferrières, i. 168. Malouet, i. 298 (according to him the faction did not number more than ten members), and ix. 10. Dumont, 250.

When a commanding general sits in council with his staff-officers and his counsellors, and discusses the plan of a campaign, the chief public interest is that discipline should remain intact, and that intruders, soldiers, or menials, should not throw the weight of their turbulence and thoughtlessness into the scales which have to be cautiously and firmly held by their chiefs. This was the express demand of the Government;[29] but the demand was not regarded; and against the persistent usurpation of the multitude nothing is left to it but the employment of force. But force itself is slipping from its hands, while growing disobedience, like a contagion, after having gained the people is spreading among the troops. From the 23rd of June,[30] two companies of the French Guards refused to do duty. Confined to their barracks, they on the 27th break out, and henceforth "they are seen every evening entering the Palais-Royal, marching in double file." They know the place well; it is the general rendezvous of the abandoned women whose lovers and parasites they are.[31] "The patriots all gather around them, treat them to ice cream and wine, and debauch them in the face of their officers." To this, moreover, must be added the fact that their colonel, M. du Châtelet, has long been odious to them, that he has fatigued them with forced drills, worried them and diminished the number of their sergeants; that he suppressed the school for the education of the children of their musicians; that he uses the stick in punishing the men, and picks quarrels with them about their appearance, their board, and their clothing. This regiment is lost to discipline: a secret society has been formed in it, and the soldiers have pledged themselves to their ensigns not to act against the National Assembly.

29. Declaration of June 23rd, article 15.

30. Montjoie, 2nd part, 118. C. Desmoulins, letters of June 24th and the following days. A faithful narrative by M. de Sainte-Fêre, formerly an officer in the French Guard, p. 9. De Bezenval, iii. 413. Roux and Buchez, ii. 35. Manuscript souvenirs of M. X.

31. Peuchet ("Encyclopédie Méthodique," 1789, quoted by Parent Duchâtelet): "Almost all of the soldiers of the Guard belong to that class (the bullies of public women): many, indeed, only enlist in the corps that they may live at the expense of these unfortunates."

Thus the confederation between them and the Palais-Royal is established.

On the 30th of June, eleven of their leaders, taken off to the Abbaye, write to claim their assistance: a young man mounts a chair in front of the Café Foy and reads their letter aloud; a band sets out on the instant, forces the gate with a sledge-hammer and iron bars, brings back the prisoners in triumph, gives them a feast in the garden and mounts guard around them to prevent their being retaken.— When disorders of this kind go unpunished, order cannot be maintained; in fact, on the morning of the 14th of July, five out of six battalions had gone over to the people. As to the other corps, they are no better and are also seduced. "Yesterday," Desmoulins writes, "the artillery regiment followed the example of the French Guards, overpowering the sentinels and coming over to mingle with the patriots in the Palais-Royal. . . . We see nothing but the rabble attaching themselves to soldiers whom they chance to encounter. 'Allons, Vive le Tiers-Etat!' and they lead them off to a tavern to drink the health of the Commons." Dragoons tell the officers who are marching them to Versailles: "We obey you, but you may tell the ministers on our arrival that if we are ordered to use the least violence against our fellow-citizens, the first shot shall be for you." At the Invalides twenty men, ordered to remove the cocks and ramrods from the guns stored in a threatened arsenal, devote six hours to rendering twenty guns useless; their object is to keep them intact for plunder and for the arming of the people.

In short, the largest portion of the army has deserted. However kind a superior officer might be, the fact of his being a superior officer secures for him the treatment of an enemy. The governor, "M. de Sombreuil, against whom these people could utter no reproach," will soon see his cannoneers point their guns at his apartment, and will just escape being hung on the iron-railings by their own hands. Thus the force which is brought forward to suppress insurrection only serves to furnish it with recruits. And even worse, for the display of arms which was relied on to restrain the mob, furnished the instigation to rebellion.

VI

The fatal moment has arrived: it is no longer a government which falls that it may give way to another; it is all government which ceases to exist in order to make way for an intermittent despotism, for factions blindly impelled on by enthusiasm, credulity, misery, and fear.[32] Like a tame elephant suddenly become wild again, the populace throws off its ordinary driver, and the new guides whom it tolerates perched on its neck are there simply for show; in future it will move along as it pleases, freed from control, and abandoned to its own feelings, instincts, and appetites. Apparently, there was no desire to do more than anticipate its aberrations. The King has forbidden all violence; the commanders order the troops not to fire;[33] but the excited and wild animal takes all precautions for insults; in future, it intends to be its own conductor, and, to begin, it treads its guides under foot.

On the 12th of July, near noon,[34] on the news of the dismissal of Necker, a cry of rage arises in the Palais-Royal; Camille Desmoulins, mounted on a table, announces that the Court meditates "a St. Bartholomew of patriots." The crowd embrace him, adopt the green cockade which he has proposed, and oblige the dancing-saloons and theatres to close in sign of mourning: they hurry off to the residence of Curtius, and take the busts of the Duke of Orleans and of Necker and carry them about in triumph. Meanwhile, the dragoons of the Prince de Lambesc, drawn up on the Place Louis-Quinze, find a barricade of chairs at the entrance of the Tuileries, and are greeted with a shower of stones and bottles.[35] Elsewhere, on the Boulevard,

32. Gouverneur Morris. Liberty is now the general cry; authority is a name and no longer a reality. (Correspondence with Washington, July 19th.)

33. Bailly, i. 302. "The King was very well-disposed; his measures were intended only to preserve order and the public peace. . . . Du Châtelet was forced by facts to acquit M. de Bezenval of attempts against the people and the country." Cf. Marmontel, iv. 183; Mounier, ii. 40.

34. C. Desmoulins, letter of the 16th July. Roux and Buchez, ii. 83.

35. Trial of the Prince de Lambesc (Paris, 1790), with the eighty-three depo-

before the Hôtel Montmorency, some of the French Guards, escaped from their barracks, fired on a loyal detachment of the "Royal Allemand." The tocsin is sounding on all sides, the shops where arms are sold are pillaged, and the Hôtel-de-Ville is invaded; fifteen or sixteen well-disposed electors, who meet there, order the districts to be assembled and armed.—The new sovereign, the people in arms and in the street, has declared himself.

The dregs of society at once come to the surface. During the night between the 12th and 13th of July,[36] "all the barriers, from the Faubourg Saint-Antoine to the Faubourg Saint-Honoré, besides those of the Faubourgs Saint-Marcel and Saint-Jacques, are forced and set on fire." There is no longer an *octroi;* the city is without a revenue just at the moment when it is obliged to make the heaviest expenditures; but this is of no consequence to the populace, which, above all things, wants to have cheap wine. "Ruffians, armed with pikes and sticks, proceed in several parties to give up to pillage the

---

sitions and the discussion of the testimony. It is the crowd which began the attack. The troops fired in the air. But one man, a *sieur* Chauvel, was wounded slightly by the Prince de Lambesc. (Testimony of M. Carboire, p. 84, and of Captain de Reinack, p. 101.) "M. le Prince de Lambesc, mounted on a grey horse with a grey saddle without holsters or pistols, had scarcely entered the garden when a dozen persons jumped at the mane and bridle of his horse and made every effort to drag him off. A small man in grey clothes fired at him with a pistol. . . . The prince tried hard to free himself, and succeeded by making his horse rear up and by flourishing his sword; without, however, up to this time, wounding any one. . . . He deposes that he saw the prince strike a man on the head with the flat of his sabre who was trying to close the turning-bridge, which would have cut off the retreat of his troops. The troops did no more than try to keep off the crowd which assailed them with stones, and even with firearms, from the top of the terraces." The man who tried to close the bridge had seized the prince's horse with one hand; the wound he received was a scratch about 23 lines long, which was dressed and cured with a bandage soaked in brandy. All the details of the affair prove that the patience and humanity of the officers were extreme. Nevertheless "on the following day, the 13th, some one posted a written placard on the *carrefour* Bussy recommending the citizens of Paris to seize the prince and quarter him at once."—(Deposition of M. Cosson, p. 114.)

36. Bailly, i. 336. Marmontel, iv. 310.

houses of those who are regarded as enemies to the public welfare." "They go from door to door crying, 'Arms and bread!' During this fearful night, the bourgeoisie kept themselves shut up, each trembling at home for himself and those belonging to him." On the following day, the 13th, the capital appears to be given up to bandits and the lowest of the low. One of the bands hews down the gate of the Lazarists, destroys the library and clothes-presses, the pictures, the windows and laboratory, and rushes to the cellars, where it staves in the casks and gets drunk: twenty-four hours after this, about thirty of them are found dead and dying, drowned in wine, men and women, one of these being at the point of childbirth. In front of the house[37] the street is full of the wreck, and of ruffians who hold in their hands, "some, eatables, others a jug, forcing the passers-by to drink, and pouring out wine to all comers. Wine runs down into the gutter, and the scent of it fills the air"; it is a drinking bout: meanwhile they carry away the grain and flour which the monks kept on hand according to law, fifty-two loads of it being taken to the market. Another troop comes to La Force, to deliver those imprisoned for debt; a third breaks into the Garde Meuble, carrying away valuable arms and armour. Mobs assemble before the hotel of Madame de Breteuil and the Palais-Bourbon, which they intend to ransack, in order to punish their proprietors. M. de Crosne, one of the most liberal and most respected men of Paris, but, unfortunately for himself, a lieutenant of the police, is pursued, escaping with difficulty, and his hotel is sacked. During the night between the 13th and 14th of May, the baker's shops and the wine shops are pillaged; "men of the vilest class, armed with guns, pikes, and turnspits, make people open their doors and give them something to eat and drink,

37. Montjoie, part 3, 86. "I talked with those who guarded the chateau of the Tuileries. They did not belong to Paris. . . . A frightful physiognomy and hideous apparel." Montjoie, not to be trusted in many places, merits consultation for little facts of which he was an eye-witness. Morellet, "Mémoires," i. 374. Dussaulx, "L'oeuvre des sept jours," 352. "Revue Historique," March, 1876. Interrogatory of Desnot. His occupation during the 13th of July (published by Guiffrey).

as well as money and arms." Vagrants, ragged men, several of them "almost naked," and "most of them armed like savages, and of hideous appearance"—they are "such as one does not remember to have seen in broad daylight"; many of them are strangers, come from nobody knows where.[38] It is stated that there were fifty thousand of them, and that they had taken possession of the principal guard-houses.

During these two days and nights, says Bailly, "Paris ran the risk of being pillaged, and was only saved from the marauders by the National Guard." Already, in the open street,[39] "these creatures tore off women's shoes and earrings," and the robbers were beginning to have full sway.—Fortunately the militia organized itself, and the principal inhabitants and gentlemen enrol themselves; 48,000 men are formed into battalions and companies; the bourgeoisie buy guns of the vagabonds for three livres apiece, and sabres or pistols for twelve sous. At last, some of the offenders are hung on the spot, and others disarmed, and the insurrection again becomes political. But, whatever its object, it remains always wild, because it is in the hands of the populace. Dussaulx, its panegyrist, confesses[40] that "he thought he was witnessing the total dissolution of society." There is no leader, no management. The electors who have converted themselves into the representatives of Paris seem to command the crowd, but it is the crowd which commands them. One of them, Legrand, to save the Hôtel-de-Ville, has no other resource but to send for six barrels of gunpowder, and to declare to the assailants that he is about to blow everything into the air. The commandant whom they themselves have chosen, M. de Salles, has twenty bayonets at his breast during a quarter of an hour, and, more than once,

38. Mathieu Dumas, "Mémoires," i. 531. "Peaceable people fled at the sight of these groups of strange, frantic vagabonds. Everybody closed their houses. . . . When I reached home, in the Saint-Denis quarter, several of these brigands caused great alarm by firing off guns in the air."

39. Dussaulx, 379.

40. Dussaulx, 359, 360, 361, 288, 336. "In effect their entreaties resembled commands, and, more than once, it was impossible to resist them."

the whole committee is near being massacred. Let the reader imagine, on the premises where the discussions are going on, and petitions are being made, "a concourse of fifteen hundred men pressed by a hundred thousand others who are forcing an entrance," the wainscoting cracking, the benches upset one over another, the enclosure of the bureau pushed back against the president's chair, a tumult such as to bring to mind "the day of judgment," the death-shrieks, songs, yells, and "people beside themselves, for the most part not knowing where they are nor what they want."

Each district is also a petty centre, while the Palais-Royal is the main centre. Propositions, "accusations, and deputations" travel to and fro from one to the other, along with the human torrent which is obstructed or rushes ahead with no other guide than its own inclination and the chances of the way. One wave gathers here and another there, their stategy consisting in pushing and in being pushed. Yet, their entrance is effected only because they are let in. If they get into the Invalides it is owing to the connivance of the soldiers.—At the Bastille, firearms are discharged from ten in the morning to five in the evening against walls forty feet high and thirty feet thick, and it is by chance that one of their shots reaches an *invalide* on the towers. They are treated the same as children whom one wishes to hurt as little as possible. The governor, on the first summons to surrender, orders the cannon to be withdrawn from the embrasures; he makes the garrison swear not to fire if it is not attacked; he invites the first of the deputations to lunch; he allows the messenger dispatched from the Hôtel-de-Ville to inspect the fortress; he receives several discharges without returning them, and lets the first bridge be carried without firing a shot.[41] When, at length, he does fire, it is at the last extremity, to defend the second bridge, and after having notified the assailants that he is going to do so. In short, his forbearance and patience are excessive, in conformity with the humanity of the times. The people, in turn, are infat-

41. Dussaulx, 447 (Deposition of the *invalides*). "Revue Rétrospective," iv. 282 (Narrative of the commander of the thirty-two Swiss Guards).

uated with the novel sensations of attack and resistance, with the smell of gunpowder, with the excitement of the contest; all they can think of doing is to rush against the mass of stone, their expedients being on a level with their tactics. A brewer fancies that he can set fire to this block of masonry by pumping over it spikenard and poppy-seed oil mixed with phosphorus. A young carpenter, who has some archaeological notions, proposes to construct a catapult. Some of them think that they have seized the governor's daughter, and want to burn her in order to make the father surrender. Others set fire to a projecting mass of buildings filled with straw, and thus close up the passage. "The Bastille was not taken by main force," says the brave Elie, one of the combatants; "it surrendered before even it was attacked,"[42] by capitulation, on the promise that no harm should be done to anybody. The garrison, being perfectly secure, had no longer the heart to fire on human beings while themselves risking nothing,[43] and, on the other hand, they were unnerved by the sight of the immense crowd. Eight or nine hundred men only[44] were concerned in the attack, most of them workmen or shopkeepers belonging to the faubourg, tailors, wheelwrights, mercers, and wine-dealers, mixed with the French Guards. The Place de la Bastille, however, and all the streets in the vicinity, were crowded with the curious who came to witness the sight; "among them," says a witness,[45] "were a number of fashionable women of very good appear-

42. Marmontel, iv. 317.

43. Dussaulx, 454. "The soldiers replied that they would accept whatever happened rather than cause the destruction of so great a number of their fellow-citizens."

44. Dussaulx, 447. The number of combatants, maimed, wounded, dead, and living, is 825. Marmontel, iv. 320. "To the number of victors, which has been carried up to 800, people have been added who were never near the place."

45. Souvenirs Manuscrits de M. X., an eye-witness. He leaned against the fence of the Beaumarchais garden and looked on, with Mademoiselle Contat, the actress, at his side, who had left her carriage in the Place-Royale.—Marat, "L'ami du peuple," No. 530. "When an unheard-of conjunction of circumstances had caused the fall of the badly defended walls of the Bastille, under the efforts of a handful of soldiers and of a troop of unfortunate creatures, most of them

ance, who had left their carriages at some distance." To the hundred and twenty men of the garrison looking down from their parapets it seemed as though all Paris had come out against them. It is they, also, who lower the drawbridge and introduce the enemy: everybody has lost his head, the besieged as well as the besiegers, the latter more completely because they are intoxicated with the sense of victory. Scarcely have they entered when they begin the work of destruction, and the latest arrivals shoot at random those that come earlier; "each one fires without heeding where or on whom his shot tells." Sudden omnipotence and the liberty to kill are a wine too strong for human nature; giddiness is the result; men *see red*, and their frenzy ends in ferocity.

For the peculiarity of a popular insurrection is that nobody obeys anybody; the bad passions are free as well as the generous ones; heroes are unable to restrain assassins. Elie, who is the first to enter the fortress, Cholat, Hulin, the brave fellows who are in advance, the French Guards who are cognizant of the laws of war, try to keep their word of honour; but the crowd pressing on behind them know not whom to strike, and they strike at random. They spare the Swiss soldiers who have fired at them, and who, in their blue smocks, seem to them to be prisoners; on the other hand, by way of compensation, they fall furiously on the *invalides* who opened the gates to them; the man who prevented the governor from blowing up the fortress has his wrist severed by the blow of a sabre, is twice pierced with a sword and is hung, and the hand which had saved one of the districts of Paris is promenaded through the streets in triumph. The officers are dragged along and five of them are killed, with three soldiers, on the spot, or on the way. During the long hours of firing, the murderous instinct has become aroused, and the wish to kill, changed into a fixed idea, spreads afar among the crowd which has hitherto remained inactive. It is convinced by its own clamour; a hue and cry is all that it now needs; the moment one strikes, all

---

Germans and almost all provincials, the Parisians presented themselves before the fortress, curiosity alone having led them there."

want to strike. "Those who had no arms," says an officer, "threw stones at me;[46] the women ground their teeth and shook their fists at me. Two of my men had already been assassinated behind me. I finally got to within some hundreds of paces of the Hôtel-de-Ville, amidst a general cry that I should be hung, when a head, stuck on a pike, was presented to me to look at, while at the same moment I was told that it was that of M. de Launay," the governor. The latter, on going out, had received the cut of a sword on his right shoulder; on reaching the Rue Saint-Antoine "everybody pulled his hair out and struck him." Under the arcade of Saint-Jean he was already "severely wounded." Around him, some said, "his head ought to be struck off"; others, "let him be hung"; and others, "he ought to be tied to a horse's tail." Then, in despair, and wishing to put an end to his torments, he cried out, "Kill me," and, in struggling, kicked one of the men who held him in the lower abdomen. On the instant he is pierced with bayonets, dragged in the gutter, and, striking his corpse, they exclaim, "He's a scurvy wretch (*galeux*) and a monster who has betrayed us; *the nation* demands his head to exhibit to the public," and the man who was kicked is asked to cut it off. This man, a cook out of place, a simpleton who "went to the Bastille to see what was going on," thinks that as it is the general opinion, the act is *patriotic,* and even believes that he "deserves a medal for destroying a monster." Taking a sabre which is lent to him, he strikes the bare neck, but the dull sabre not doing its work, he takes a small black-handled knife from his pocket, and, "as in his capacity of cook he knows how to cut meat," he finishes the operation successfully. Then, placing the head on the end of a three-pronged pitchfork, and accompanied by over two hundred armed men, "not counting the populace," he marches along, and, in the Rue Saint-Honoré, he has two inscriptions attached to the head, to indicate without mistake whose head it is. They grow merry

46. Narrative of the commander of the thirty-two Swiss. Narrative of Cholat, wine-dealer, one of the victors. Examination of Desnot (who cut off the head of M. de Launay).

over it: after filing alongside of the Palais-Royal, the procession arrives at the Pont-Neuf, where, before the statue of Henry IV., they bow the head three times, saying, "Salute thy master!"—This ends the mockery: some of it is found in every triumph, and beneath the butcher the buffoon becomes apparent.

VII

Meanwhile, at the Palais-Royal, other buffoons, who with the levity of gossips sport with lives as freely as with words, have drawn up, during the night between the 13th and 14th of July, a list of proscriptions, copies of which are hawked about: care is taken to address one of them to each of the persons designated, the Comte d'Artois, Marshal de Broglie, the Prince de Lambesc, Baron de Bezenval, MM. de Breteuil, Foulon, Berthier, Maury, d'Espréménil, Lefèvre d'Amécourt, and others besides;[47] a reward is promised to whoever will bring their heads to the Café de Caveau. Here are names for the unchained multitude; all that now is necessary is that some band should encounter a man who is denounced; he will go as far as the lamp at the street corner, but not beyond it. Throughout the day of the 14th, this improvised tribunal holds a permanent session, and follows up its decisions with its actions. M. de Flesselles, provost of the merchants and president of the electors at the Hôtel-de-Ville, having shown himself somewhat lukewarm,[48] the Palais-Royal declares him a traitor and sends him off to be hung; on the way a young man fells him with a pistol-shot, others fall upon his body, while his head, borne upon a pike, goes to join that of M. de Launay. Equally deadly accusations and of equally speedy execution float in the air and from every direction. "On the slightest pretext," says an elector, "they denounced to us those whom they thought opposed to the Revolution—which already signified the same as enemies of

47. Montjoie, part 3, 85. Dussaulx, 357, 287, 368.

48. Nothing more. No witness states that he had seen the pretended note to M. de Launay. According to Dussaulx, he could not have had either the time or the means to write it.

the State. With no other examination, nothing less was spoken of then but the seizure of their persons, the ruin of their houses, and the levelling of their hotels. One young man exclaimed: 'Follow me this moment, let us start off at once to Bezenval's!'" Their brains are so scared, and their minds so distrustful, that at every step in the streets "one's name has to be given, one's profession declared, one's residence, and one's intentions. . . . One can neither enter nor leave Paris without being suspected of treason." The Prince de Montbarrey, advocate of the new ideas, and his wife, are stopped in their carriage at the barrier, and are on the point of being cut to pieces. A deputy of the nobles, on his way to the National Assembly, is seized in his cab and conducted to the Place de Grève; the corpse of M. de Launay is shown to him, and he is told that he is to be treated in the same fashion. Every life hangs by a thread, and, on the following days, when the King had sent away his troops, dismissed his Ministers, recalled Necker, and granted everything, the danger remains just as great. The multitude, abandoned to the revolutionists and to itself, continues to perform the same bloody antics, while the municipal chiefs[49] whom it has elected, Bailly, Mayor of Paris, and Lafayette, commandant of the national guard, are obliged to use cunning, to implore, to throw themselves between the multitude and the unfortunates whom they wish to destroy.

On the 15th of July, in the night, a woman disguised as a man is arrested in the court of the Hôtel-de-Ville, and so maltreated that she faints away; Bailly, in order to save her, is obliged to feign anger against her and have her sent immediately to prison. From the 14th to the 22nd of July, Lafayette, at the risk of his life, saves with his own hand seventeen persons in different quarters.[50] On the 22nd of

49. Bailly, ii. 32, 74, 88, 90, 95, 108, 117, 137, 158, 174. "I gave orders which were neither obeyed nor listened to. . . . They gave me to understand that I was not safe." (July 15th.) "In these sad times one enemy and one calumnious report sufficed to excite the multitude. All who had formerly held power, all who had annoyed or restrained the insurrectionists, were sure of being arrested."

50. M. de Lafayette, "Mémoires," iii. 264. Letters of July 16th, 1789. "I have already saved the lives of six persons whom they were hanging in different quarters."

July, upon the denunciations which multiply around Paris like trains of gunpowder, two administrators of high rank, M. Foulon, Councillor of State, and M. Berthier, his son-in-law, are arrested, one near Fontainebleau, and the other near Compiègne. M. Foulon, a strict master,[51] but intelligent and useful, expended sixty thousand francs the previous winter on his estate in giving employment to the poor. M. Berthier, an industrious and capable man, had officially surveyed and valued Ile-de-France, to equalise the taxes, and had reduced the overcharged quotas first one-eighth and then a quarter. But both of these gentlemen have arranged the details of the camp against which Paris has risen; both are publicly proscribed for eight days previously by the Palais-Royal, and, with a people frightened by disorder, exasperated by hunger, and stupefied by suspicion, an accused person is a guilty one. With regard to Foulon, as with Réveillon, a story is made up, coined in the same mint, a sort of currency for popular circulation, and which the people itself manufactures by casting into one tragic expression the sum of its sufferings and rankling memories:[52] "He said that we were worth no more than his horses, and that if we had no bread we had only to eat grass."—The old man of seventy-four is brought to Paris, with a truss of hay on his head, a collar of thistles around his neck, and his mouth stuffed with hay. In vain does the electoral bureau order his imprisonment that he may be saved; the crowd yells out: "Sentenced and hung!" and, authoritatively, appoints the judges. In vain does Lafayette insist and entreat three several times that the judgment be regularly rendered, and that the accused be sent to the Abbaye; a new wave of people comes up, and one man, "well dressed," cries out: "What is the need of a sentence for a man who has been condemned for thirty years?" Foulon is carried off, dragged across the square, and hung to the

51. Poujoulat, "Histoire de la Révolution Française," p. 100 (with supporting documents). *Procès-verbaux* of the Provincial Assembly, Ile-de-France (1787), p. 127.

52. For instance: "He is severe with his peasants." "He gives them no bread, and he wants them then to eat grass." "He wants them to eat grass like horses." "He has said that they could very well eat hay, and that they are no better than horses." The same story is found in many of the contemporary jacqueries.

lantern; the cord breaks twice, and twice he falls upon the pavement; rehung with a fresh cord and then cut down, his head is severed from his body and placed on the end of a pike.[53] Meanwhile, Berthier, sent away from Compiègne by the municipality, afraid to keep him in his prison where he was constantly menaced, arrives in a cabriolet under escort. The people carry placards around him filled with opprobrious epithets; in changing horses they threw hard black bread into the carriage, exclaiming, "There, wretch, see the bread you made us eat!" On reaching the church of Saint-Merry, a fearful storm of insults burst forth against him: he is called a monopolist, "although he had never bought or sold a grain of wheat"; in the eyes of the multitude, who must needs account for the evil by some evildoer, he is the author of the famine. Conducted to the Abbaye, his escort is dispersed and he is pushed on to the lantern. Then, seeing that all is lost, he snatches a gun from one of his murderers and bravely defends himself. A soldier of the "Royal Croats" gives him a cut with his sabre across the stomach, and another tears out his heart. As the cook, who had cut off the head of M. de Launay, happens to be on the spot, they hand him the heart to carry while the soldiers take the head, and both go to the Hôtel-de-Ville to show their trophies to M. de Lafayette. On their return to the Palais-Royal, and while they are seated at table in a tavern, the people demand these two remains; they throw them out of the window and finish their supper, whilst the heart is marched about below in a bouquet of white carnations.—Such are the spectacles which this garden presents where, a year before, "good society in full dress" came on leaving the Opera to chat, often until two o'clock in the morning, under the mild light of the moon, listening now to the violin of Saint-Georges, and now to the charming voice of Garat.

VIII

Henceforth it is clear that no one is safe: neither the new militia nor the new authorities suffice to enforce respect for the law. "They did

53. Bailly, ii. 108. "The people, less enlightened and as imperious as despots, recognise no positive signs of good administration but success."

not dare," says Bailly,[54] "oppose the people who, eight days before this, had taken the Bastille." In vain, after the last two murders, do Bailly and Lafayette indignantly threaten to withdraw—they are forced to remain; their protection, such as it is, is all that is left, and, if the National Guard is unable to prevent every murder, it prevents some of them. People live as they can under the constant expectation of fresh popular violence. "*To every impartial man,*" says Malouet, "*the Terror dates from the 14th of July.*" On the 17th, before setting out for Paris, the King attends communion and makes his will in anticipation of assassination. From the 16th to the 18th, twenty personages of high rank, among others most of those on whose heads a price is set by the Palais-Royal, leave France—the Count d'Artois, Marshal de Broglie, the Princes de Condé, de Conti, de Lambesc, de Vaudemont, the Countess de Polignac, and the Duchesses de Polignac and de Guiche. The day following the two murders, M. de Crosne, M. Doumer, M. Sureau, the most zealous and most valuable members of the committee on subsistences, all those appointed to make purchases and to take care of the storehouses, conceal themselves or fly. On the eve of the two murders, the notaries of Paris, being menaced with a riot, had to advance 45,000 francs which were promised to the workmen of the Faubourg Saint-Antoine; while the public treasury, almost empty, is drained of 30,000 livres per day to diminish the cost of bread. Persons and possessions, great and small, private individuals and public functionaries, the Government itself, all is in the hands of the mob. "From this moment," says a deputy,[55] "liberty did not exist even in the National Assembly . . . France stood dumb before thirty factious persons. The Assembly became in their hands a passive instrument, which they forced to serve them in the execution of their projects." They themselves do not lead, although they seem to lead. The great brute, which has taken the bit in its mouth, holds on to it, and its plunging becomes more violent; for not only do both spurs which maddened it—I mean the desire for innovation and the daily scarcity of food—continue to

54. Bailly, ii. 95, 108. Malouet, i. 14.
55. De Ferrières, i. 168.

prick it on, but also the political hornets which, increasing by thousands, buzz around its ears, while the license in which it revels for the first time, joined to the applause lavished upon it, urges it forward more violently each day. The insurrection is glorified. Not one of the assassins is sought out. It is against the conspiracy of Ministers that the Assembly institutes an enquiry. Rewards are bestowed upon the conquerors of the Bastille; it is declared that they have saved France. All honours are awarded to the people—to their good sense, their magnanimity, their justice. Adoration is paid to the new sovereign: he is publicly and officially told, in the Assembly and by the press, that he possesses every virtue, all rights and all powers. If he spills blood it is inadvertently, on provocation, and always with an infallible instinct. Moreover, says a deputy, "this blood, was it so pure?" The greater number of people prefer the theories of their books to the experience of their eyes; they persist in the idyl which they have fashioned for themselves. At the worst their dream, driven out from the present, takes refuge in the future. Tomorrow, when the Constitution is complete, the people, made happy, will again become wise: let us endure the storm which leads us on to so noble a harbour.

Meanwhile, beyond the King, inert and disarmed, beyond the Assembly, disobeyed or submissive, appears the real monarch, the people—that is to say, the mob of a hundred, a thousand, a hundred thousand beings gathered together haphazard, on an impulse, on an alarm, suddenly and irresistibly made legislators, judges, and executioners: a formidable power, undefined and destructive, on which no one has any hold, and which, with its mother, howling and misshapen Liberty, sits at the threshold of the Revolution like Milton's two spectres at the gates of Hell.

> "The one seemed woman to the waist, and fair,
> But ended foul in many a scaly fold,
> Voluminous and vast, a serpent armed
> With mortal sting. About her middle round
> A cry of hell-hounds never ceasing bark'd

With wide Cerberean mouths full loud, and rung
A hideous peal: and yet, when they list, would creep,
If aught disturb'd their noise, into her womb,
And kennel there; yet there still bark'd and howl'd
Within unseen. . . .
. . . The other shape,
If shape it might be called, that shape had none
Distinguishable in member, joint, or limb,
Or substance might be call'd that shadow seem'd,
For each seem'd either; black it stood as night,
Fierce as ten furies, terrible as hell,
And shook a dreadful dart; what seem'd his head
The likeness of a kingly crown had on.

* * * * * *

The monster moving onward came as fast,
With horrid strides."

CHAPTER III

I. *Anarchy from July 14th to October 6th, 1789—Destruction of the Government—To whom does real power belong?*— II. *The Provinces—Destruction of old Authorities—Incompetency of new Authorities*— III. *Disposition of the People—Famine*— IV. *Panic—General arming*— V. *Attacks on public individuals and public property—At Strasbourg—At Cherbourg—At Maubeuge—At Rouen—At Besançon—At Troyes*— VI. *Taxes are no longer paid—Devastation of the Forests—The new game laws*— VII. *Attacks upon private individuals and private property—Aristocrats denounced to the people as their enemies—Effect of news from Paris—Influence of the village attorneys—Isolated acts of violence—A general rising of the peasantry in the east—War against the chateaux, feudal estates, and property—Preparations for other jacqueries.*

I

HOWEVER bad a particular government may be, there is something still worse, and that is the suppression of all government. For, it is owing to government that human wills form a harmony instead of a chaos. It serves society as the brain serves a living being. Incapable, inconsiderate, extravagant, engrossing, it often abuses its position, overstraining or misleading the body for which it should care, and which it should direct. But, taking all things into account, whatever it may do, more good than harm is done, for through it the body stands erect, marches on and guides its steps. Without it there is no organized deliberate action, serviceable to the whole body. In it alone do we find the comprehensive views, knowledge of the members of which it consists and of their aims, an idea of outward relationships, full and accurate information, in short, the superior intelligence which conceives what is best for the common interests, and adapts means to ends. If it falters and is no longer obeyed, if it is forced and pushed from without by a violent pressure, it ceases to control public affairs, and the social organization retrogrades by many steps. Through the dissolution of society, and the isolation of individuals, each man returns to his original feeble state, while power is vested in passing aggregates which spring up like whirling vortices amongst the human dust.—One may divine how this power, which the most competent find it difficult to apply properly, is exercised by bands of men starting up from the ground. The question is of provisions, their possession, price, and distribution; of taxation, its proportion, apportionment, and collection; of private property, its varieties, rights, and limitations; of public authority, its province and its limits; of all those delicate cog-wheels which, working into each other, constitute the great economic, social, and political machine. Each band in its own canton lays its rude hands on the wheels within its reach, wrenching or breaking them haphazard, under the impulse of the moment, heedless and indifferent to consequences, even when the reaction of tomorrow crushes them in the ruin which they cause today. Thus do unchained negroes, each pulling and hauling his own way, undertake to manage a ship of which they have just obtained the mastery.—In such a state of things white men are hardly worth more than black ones; for, not only is the band, whose aim is violence, composed of those who are most destitute, most wildly enthusiastic, and most inclined to destructiveness and to license, but also, as this band tumultuously carries out its violent action, each individual the most brutal, the most irrational, and most corrupt, descends lower than himself, even to the darkness, the madness, and the savagery of the dregs of society. In fact, a man who in the interchange of blows, would resist the excitement of murder, and not use his strength like a savage, must be familiar with arms, accustomed to danger, cool-blooded, alive to the sentiment of honour, and, above all, sensitive to that stern military code which, to the imagination of the soldier, ever holds out to him the provost's gibbet to which he is sure to rise, should he strike one blow too many. All these restraints, inward as well as outward, are wanting to the man who plunges into insurrection. He is a novice in the acts of violence which he carries out. He has no fear of the law, because he abolishes it. The action begun carries him further than he intended to go. His anger is exasperated by peril and resistance. He catches the fever from contact with those who are fevered, and follows robbers who have become his comrades.[1] Add to this the clamours, the drunkenness, the spectacle of destruction, the nervous tremor of the body strained beyond its powers of endurance, and we can comprehend how, from the peasant, the labourer, and the bourgeois, pacified and tamed by an old civilisation, we see all of a sudden spring forth the barbarian, and, still worse, the primitive animal, the grinning, sanguinary, wanton baboon, who chuckles while he slays, and gambols over the ruin he has accomplished. Such is the actual government to which France is given up, and after eighteen months' experience, the best qualified, most judicious, and profoundest observer of the Revolution will find nothing to compare to it but the invasion of the Roman Empire in the fourth century.[2] "The Huns, the Heruli, the Vandals, and the Goths will come neither from the north nor from the Black Sea; they are in our very midst."

II

When in a building the principal beam gives way, cracks follow and multiply, and the secondary joists fall in one by one for lack of the prop which supported them. In a similar manner the authority of

1. Dussaulx, 374. "I remarked that if there were a few among the people at that time who dared commit crime, there were several who wished it, and that every one permitted it."—"Archives Nationales," D. xxix. 3. (Letter of the municipal authorities of Crémieux, Dauphiny, November 3, 1789.) "The care taken to lead them first to the cellars and to intoxicate them, can alone give a conception of the incredible excesses of rage to which they gave themselves up in the sacking and burning of the chateaux."

2. *Mercure de France,* January 4, 1792. ("Revue politique de l'année 1791," by Mallet-Dupan.)

the King being broken, all the powers which he delegated fall to the ground.[3] Intendants, parliaments, military commands, grand provosts, administrative, judicial, and police functionaries in every province, and of every branch of the service, who maintain order and protect property, taught by the murder of De Launay, the imprisonment of Bezenval, the flight of Marshal de Broglie, the assassinations of Foulon and Berthier, know what it costs to perform their duties, and, lest this should be forgotten, local insurrections intervene, and keep them in mind of it.

The officer in command in Burgundy is a prisoner at Dijon, with a guard at his door; and he is not allowed to speak with any one without permission, and without the presence of witnesses.[4] The Commandant of Caen is besieged in the old palace and capitulates. The Commandant of Bordeaux surrenders Château-Trompette with its guns and equipment. The Commandant at Metz, who remains firm, suffers the insults and the orders of the populace. The Commandant of Brittany wanders about his province "like a vagabond," while at Rennes his people, furniture, and plate are kept as pledges; as soon as he sets foot in Normandy he is surrounded, and a sentinel is placed at his door. The Intendant of Besançon takes to flight; that of Rouen sees his dwelling sacked from top to bottom, and escapes amid the shouts of a mob demanding his head. At Rennes, the Dean of the Parliament is arrested, maltreated, kept in his room with a guard over him, and then, although ill, sent out of the town under an escort. At Strasbourg, "thirty-six houses of magistrates are marked for pillage."[5] At Besançon, the President of the Parliament is con-

3. Albert Babeau, i. 206. (Letter of the deputy Camuzet de Belombre, August 22, 1789.) "The executive power is absolutely gone today." Gouverneur Morris, letter of July 31, 1789: "This country is now as near in a state of anarchy as it is possible for a community to be without breaking up."

4. "Archives Nationales," H. 1453. Letter of M. Amelot, July 24th; H. 784, of M. de Langeron, October 16th and 18th.—KK. 1105. Correspondence of M. de Thiard, October 7th and 30th, September 4th.—Floquet, vii. 527, 555.—Guadet, "Histoire des Girondins" (July 29, 1789).

5. M. de Rochambeau, "Mémoires," i. 353 (July 18th).—Sauzay, "Histoire de la Persécution Révolutionnaire dans le Département du Doubs," i. 128 (July

strained to let out of prison the insurgents arrested in a late outbreak, and to publicly burn the whole of the papers belonging to the prosecution. In Alsace, since the beginning of the troubles, the provosts were obliged to fly; the bailiffs and manorial judges hid themselves; the forest-inspectors ran away, and the houses of the guards were demolished: one man, sixty years of age, is outrageously beaten and marched about the village, the people, meanwhile, pulling out his hair; nothing remains of his dwelling but the walls and a portion of the roof; all his furniture and effects are broken up, burnt, or stolen; he is forced to sign, along with his wife, an act by which he binds himself to refund all penalties inflicted by him, and to abandon all claims for damages for the injuries to which he has just been subjected. In Franche-Comté the authorities dare not condemn delinquents, and the police do not arrest them; the military commandant writes that "crimes of every kind are on the increase, and that he has no means of punishing them." Insubordination is permanent in all the provinces; one of the provincial commissions states with sadness: "When all powers are in confusion and annihilated, when public force no longer exists, when all ties are sundered, when every individual considers himself relieved from all kinds of obligation, when public authority no longer dares make itself felt, and it is a crime to have been clothed with it, what can be expected of our efforts to restore order?"[6] All that remains of this great demolished State is forty thousand knots of men, each separated and isolated,

---

19th.)— "Archives Nationales" F[7], 3,253. (Letter of the deputies of the provincial commission of Alsace, September 8th.) D. xxix. I. note of M. de Latour-du-Pin, October 28, 1789.—Letter of M. de Langeron, September 3rd; of Breitman, *garde-marteau*, Val Saint-Amarin (Upper Alsace), July 26th.

6. Léonce de Lavergne, 197. (Letter of the intermediate commission of Poitou, the last month in 1789.)—Cf. Brissot (*Le patriote français*, August, 1789). "General insubordination prevails in the provinces because the restraints of executive power are no longer felt. What were but lately the guarantees of that power? The intendants, tribunals, and the army. The intendants are gone, the tribunals are silent, and the army is against the executive power and on the side of the people. Liberty is not an aliment which all stomachs can digest without some preparation for it."

in towns and small market-villages where municipal bodies, elected committees, and improvised national guards strive to prevent the worst excesses.—But these local chiefs are novices; they are human, and they are timid. Chosen by acclamation they believe in popular rights; in the midst of riots they feel themselves in danger. Hence, they generally obey the crowd. "Rarely," says one of the provincial commissions' reports, "do the municipal authorities issue a summons; they allow the greatest excesses rather than enter upon prosecutions for which, sooner or later, they may be held responsible by their fellow-citizens. . . . Municipal bodies have no longer the power to resist anything." Especially in the rural districts the mayor or syndic, who is a farmer, makes it his first aim to make no enemies, and would resign his place if it were to bring him any "unpleasantness" with it. His rule in the towns, and especially in large cities, is almost as lax and more precarious, because explosive material is accumulated here to a much larger extent, and the municipal officers, in their arm-chairs at the town-hall, sit over a mine which may explode at any time. Tomorrow, perhaps, some resolution passed at a tavern in the suburbs, or some incendiary newspaper just received from Paris, will furnish the spark.—No other defence against the populace is at hand than the sentimental proclamations of the National Assembly, the useless presence of troops who stand by and look on, and the uncertain help of a National Guard which will arrive too late. Occasionally these townspeople, who are now the sovereigns, utter a cry of distress from under the hands of the sovereigns of the street who grasp them by the throat. At Puy-en-Velay,[7]

7. "Archives Nationales," D. xxix. I. (Letter of the clergy, consuls, *présidial*-councillors, and principal merchants of Puy-en-Velay, September 16, 1789.)—H. ix. 53 (letter of the Intendant of Alençon, July 18th). "I must not leave you in ignorance of the multiplied outbreaks we have in all parts of my jurisdiction. The impunity with which they flatter themselves, because the judges are afraid of irritating the people by examples of severity, only emboldens them. Mischief-makers, confounded with honest folks, spread false reports about particular persons whom they accuse of concealing grain, or of not belonging to the Third-

a town of twenty thousand inhabitants, the *présidial,*[8] the committee of twenty-four commissioners, a body of two hundred dragoons, and eight hundred men of the guard of burgesses, are "paralyzed, and completely stupefied, by the vile populace. A mild treatment only increases its insubordination and insolence." This populace proscribes whomsoever it pleases, and six days ago a gibbet, erected by its hands, has announced to the new magistrates the fate that awaits them. "What will become of us this winter," they exclaim, "in our impoverished country, where bread is not to be had! We shall be the prey of wild beasts!"

III

These people, in truth, are hungry, and, since the Revolution, their misery has increased. Around Puy-en-Velay the country is laid waste, and the soil broken up by a terrible tempest, a fierce hailstorm, and a deluge of rain. In the south, the crop proved to be moderate and even insufficient. "To trace a picture of the condition of Languedoc," writes the intendant,[9] "would be to give an account of calamities of every description. The panic which prevails in all communities, and which is stronger than all laws, stops traffic, and would cause famine even in the midst of plenty. Commodities are enormously high, and there is a lack of cash. Communities are ruined by the enormous outlays to which they are exposed—the payment of the deputies to the seneschal's court, the establishment of the burgess guards, guardhouses for this militia, the purchase of arms, uniforms, and outlays in forming communes and permanent councils; printing of all kinds, for the publication of the most unessential deliberations; the loss of time due to disturbances occasioned by these circumstances; the utter stagnation of manufactures and of

---

Estate, and, under this pretext, they pillage their houses, taking whatever they can find, the owners only avoiding death by flight."

8. A body of magistrates forming one of the lower tribunals.—[Tr.]

9. "Archives Nationales," H. 942. (Observations of M. de Ballainvilliers, October 30, 1789.)

trade"—all these causes combined "have reduced Languedoc to the last extremity."—In the centre, and in the north, where the crops are good, provisions are not less scarce, because wheat is not allowed a circulation, and is kept concealed. "For five months," writes the municipal assembly of Louviers,[10] "not a farmer has made his appearance in the markets of this town. Such a circumstance was never known before, although, from time to time, high prices have prevailed to a considerable extent. On the contrary, the markets were always well supplied in proportion to the high price of grain." In vain the municipality orders the surrounding forty-seven parishes to provide them with wheat; they pay no attention to the mandate; each for himself and each for his own house; the intendant is no longer present to compel local interests to give way to public interests. "In the wheat districts around us," says a letter from one of the Burgundy towns, "we cannot rely on being able to make free purchases. Special regulations, supported by the burgess militia, prevent grain from being sent out, and put a stop to its circulation. The adjacent markets are of no use to us. Not a sack of grain has been brought into our market for about eight months."—At Troyes, bread costs four sous per pound; at Bar-sur-Aube, and in the vicinity, four and a half sous per pound. The artisan who is out of work now earns twelve sous a day at the relief works, and, on going into the country, he sees that the grain crop is good. What conclusion can he come to but that the dearth is due to the monopolists, and that, if he should die of hunger, it would be because those scoundrels have starved him?—By virtue of this reasoning whoever has to do with these provisions, whether proprietor, farmer, merchant, or administrator, all are considered traitors. It is plain that there is a plot against the people: the government, the Queen, the clergy, the nobles are all parties to it; and likewise the magistrates and the wealthy

10. "Archives Nationales," D. xxix. I. Letter of the municipal assembly of Louviers, the end of August, 1789. Letter of the communal assembly of Saint-Bris (bailiwick of Auxerre), September 25th.—Letter of the municipal officers of Ricey-Haut, near Bar-sur-Seine, August 25th; of the Chevalier d'Allouville, September 8th.

amongst the bourgeoisie and the rich. A rumour is current in the Ile-de-France that sacks of flour are thrown into the Seine, and that the cavalry horses are purposely made to eat grain in the stalk. In Brittany, it is maintained that grain is exported and stored up abroad. In Touraine, it is certain that this or that wholesale dealer allows it to sprout in his granaries rather than sell it. At Troyes, a story prevails that another has poisoned his flour with alum and arsenic, commissioned to do so by the bakers.—Conceive the effect of suspicions like these upon a suffering multitude! A wave of hatred ascends from the empty stomach to the morbid brain. The people are everywhere in quest of their imaginary enemies, plunging forward with closed eyes no matter on whom or on what, not merely with all the weight of their mass, but with all the energy of their fury.

IV

From the earliest of these weeks they were already alarmed. Accustomed to being led, the human herd is scared at being left to itself; it misses its leaders whom it has trodden under foot; in throwing off their trammels it has deprived itself of their protection. It feels lonely, in an unknown country, exposed to dangers of which it is ignorant, and against which it is unable to guard itself. Now that the shepherds are slain or disarmed, suppose the wolves should unexpectedly appear!—And there are wolves—I mean vagabonds and criminals—who have but just issued out of the darkness. They have robbed and burned, and are to be found at every insurrection. Now that the police force no longer puts them down, they show themselves instead of keeping themselves concealed. They have only to lie in wait and come forth in a band, and both life and property will be at their mercy.—Deep anxiety, a vague feeling of dread, spreads through both town and country: towards the end of July the panic, like a blinding, suffocating whirl of dust, suddenly sweeps over hundreds of leagues of territory. The brigands are coming! they are firing the crops! they are only six leagues off, and then only two—it is proved by the fugitives who are escaping in confusion.

On the 28th of July, at Angoulême,[11] the tocsin is heard about three o'clock in the afternoon; the drums beat to arms, and cannon are mounted on the ramparts; the town has to be put in a state of defence against 15,000 bandits who are approaching; and from the walls a cloud of dust on the road is discovered with terror. It proves to be the post-waggon on its way to Bordeaux. After this the number of brigands is reduced to 1,500, but there is no doubt that they are ravaging the country. At nine o'clock in the evening 20,000 men are under arms, and thus they pass the night, always listening without hearing anything. Towards three o'clock in the morning there is a fresh alarm with the tocsin, and the people form themselves in battle array; it is certain that the brigands have burned Ruffec, Verneuil, La Rochefoucauld, and other places. The next day countrymen flock in to give their aid against bandits who are still absent. "At nine o'clock," says a witness, "we had 40,000 men in the town, to whom we had to be grateful." As the bandits do not show themselves, it must be because they are concealed; a hundred horsemen, a large number of men on foot, start out to search the forest of Braçonne, and to their great surprise they find nothing. But the terror is not allayed; "during the following days a guard is kept mounted, and companies are enrolled among the burgesses," while Bordeaux, duly informed, dispatches a courier to offer the support of 20,000 men and even 30,000. "What is surprising," adds the narrator, "is that at ten leagues off in the neighbourhood, in each parish, a similar disturbance took place, and at about the same hour."—That a girl returning to the village at night should meet two men who do not belong to the neighbourhood is sufficient to give rise to these panics. The case is the same in Auvergne. Whole parishes, on the strength of this, betake themselves at night to the woods, abandoning their houses, and carrying away their furniture; "the fugitives trod down and destroyed their own crops; pregnant

11. "Archives Nationales," D. xxix. I. Letter of M. Briand-Delessart (Angoulême, August 1st).—Of M. Bret, Lieutenant-General of the provostship of Mardogne, September 5th.—Of the Chevalier de Castellas (Auvergne), September 15th (relating to the night between the 2nd and 3rd of August).—Madame Campan, ii. 65.

women were injured in the forests, and others lost their wits." Fear lends them wings. Two years after this, Madame Campan was shown a rocky peak on which a woman had taken refuge, and from which she was obliged to be let down with ropes.—The people at last return to their homes, and their lives seem to resume the even tenor of their way. But such large masses are not unsettled with impunity; a tumult like this is, in itself, a fruitful source of alarm: as the country did rise, it must have been on account of threatened danger; and if the peril was not due to brigands, it must have come from some other quarter. Arthur Young, at Dijon and in Alsace,[12] hears at the public dinner-tables that the Queen had formed a plot to undermine the National Assembly and to massacre all Paris. Later on he is arrested in a village near Clermont, and examined because he is evidently conspiring with the Queen and the Comte d'Entraigues to blow up the town and send the survivors to the galleys.

No argument, no experience has any effect against the multiplying phantoms of an overexcited imagination. Henceforth every commune, and every man, provide themselves with arms and keep them ready for use. The peasant searches his hoard, and "finds from ten to twelve francs for the purchase of a gun." "A national militia is found in the poorest village." Burgess guards and companies of volunteers patrol all the towns. Military commanders deliver arms, ammunition, and equipments, on the requisition of municipal bodies, while, in case of refusal, the arsenals are pillaged, and, voluntarily or by force, four hundred thousand guns thus pass into the hands of the people in six months.[13] Not content with this they must have

12. Arthur Young, "Voyages in France," July 24th and 31st, August 13th and 19th.

13. D. Bouillé, 108.—"Archives Nationales," KK. 1105. Correspondence of M. de Thiard, September 20, 1789 (apropos of one hundred guns given to the town of Saint-Brieuc). "They are not of the slightest use, but this passion for arms is a temporary epidemic which must be allowed to subside of itself. People are determined to believe in brigands and in enemies, whereas neither exist." September 25th, "Vanity alone impels them, and the pride of having cannon is their sole motive."

cannon. Brest having demanded two, every town in Brittany does the same thing; their *amour-propre* is excited, and also the need of feeling themselves strong. They lack nothing now to render themselves masters. All authority, all force, every means of constraint and of intimidation is in their hands, and in theirs alone; and these sovereign hands have nothing to guide them in this actual interregnum of all legal powers, but the wild or murderous suggestions of hunger or distrust.

V

It would take too much space to recount all the violent acts which were committed—convoys arrested, grain pillaged, millers and corn-merchants hung, decapitated, slaughtered, farmers called upon under threats of death to give up even the seed reserved for sowing, proprietors ransomed and houses sacked.[14] These outrages, unpunished, tolerated, and even excused or badly suppressed, are constantly repeated, and are, at first, directed against public men and public property. As is commonly the case, the rabble head the march and stamp the character of the whole insurrection.

On the 19th of July, at Strasbourg, on the news of Necker's return to office, it interprets after its own fashion the public joy which it witnesses. Five or six hundred beggars,[15] their numbers soon in-

14. "Archives Nationales," H. 1453. Letters of M. Amelot, July 17th and 24th. "Several wealthy private persons of the town (Auxonne) have been put to ransom by this band, of which the largest portion consists of ruffians."—Letter of nine cultivators of Breteuil (Picardy), July 23rd (their granaries were pillaged up to the last grain the previous evening). "They threaten to pillage our crops and set our barns on fire as soon as they are full. M. Tassard, the notary, has been visited in his house by the populace, and his life has been threatened." Letter of Moreau, Procureur du Roi at the Seneschal's Court at Bar-le-Duc, September 15, 1789, D. xxix. I. "On the 27th of July the people rose and most cruelly assassinated a merchant trading in wheat. On the 27th and 28th his house and that of another were sacked," &c.

15. Chronicle of Dominick Schmutz ("Revue d'Alsace," v. iii. 3rd series). These are his own expressions: *Gesindel, Lumpen-gesindel.*—De Rochambeau, "Mémoires," i. 353. Arthur Young (an eye-witness), July 21st. Of Dammartin

creased by the petty tradesmen, rush to the town-hall, the magistrates only having time to fly through a back door. The soldiers, on their part, with arms in their hands, allow all these things to go on, while several of them spur the assailants on. The windows are dashed to pieces under a hailstorm of stones, the doors are forced with iron crow-bars, and the populace enter amid a burst of acclamations from the spectators. Immediately, through every opening in the building, which has a façade frontage of eighty feet, "there is a shower of shutters, sashes, chairs, tables, sofas, books and papers, and then another of tiles, boards, balconies and fragments of woodwork." The public archives are thrown to the wind, and the surrounding streets are strewed with them; the letters of enfranchisement, the charters of privileges, all the authentic acts which, since Louis XIV., have guaranteed the liberties of the town, perish in the flames. Some of the rabble in the cellars stave in casks of precious wine; fifteen thousand measures of it are lost, making a pool five feet deep in which several are drowned. Others, loaded with booty, go away under the eyes of the soldiers without being arrested. The havoc continues for three days; a number of houses belonging to some of the magistrates "are sacked from garret to cellar." When the honest burgesses at last obtain arms and restore order, they are content with the hanging of one of the robbers; although, in order to please the people, the magistrates are changed and the price of bread and meat is reduced. It is not surprising that after such tactics, and with such rewards, the riot should spread through the neighbourhood far and near: in fact, starting from Strasbourg it overruns Alsace, while in the country as in the city, there are always drunkards and rascals found to head it.

No matter where—be it in the east, in the west, or in the north—

(eye-witness), i. 105. M. de Rochambeau shows the usual indecision and want of vigour: whilst the mob are pillaging houses and throwing things out of the windows, he passes in front of his regiments (8,000 men) drawn up for action, and says, "My friends, my good friends, you see what is going on. How horrible! Alas! these are your papers, your titles and those of your parents." The soldiers smile at this sentimental prattle.

the instigators are always of this stamp. At Cherbourg, on the 21st of July,[16] the two leaders of the riot are "highway robbers," who place themselves at the head of women of the suburbs, foreign sailors, the populace of the harbour, and it includes soldiers in workmen's smocks. They force the delivery of the keys of the grain warehouses, and wreck the dwellings of the three richest merchants, also that of M. de Garantot, the subdelegate: "All records and papers are burnt; at M. de Garantot's alone the loss is estimated at more than 100,000 crowns at least."—The same instinct of destruction prevails everywhere—a sort of envious fury against all who possess, command, or enjoy anything. At Maubeuge, on the 27th of July, at the very moment of the assembly of the representatives of the commune,[17] the rabble interferes directly in its usual fashion. A band of nail- and gun-makers takes possession of the town-hall, and obliges the mayor to reduce the price of bread. Almost immediately after this another band follows uttering cries of death, and smashes the windows, while the garrison, which has been ordered out, quietly contemplates the damage done. Death to the mayor, to all rulers, and to all employés! The rioters force open the prisons, set the prisoners free, and attack the tax-offices. The *octroi* offices are demolished from top to bottom: they pull down the harbour offices and throw the scales and weights into the river. All the custom and excise stores are carried off, and the officials are compelled to give acquittances. The houses of the registrar and of the sheriff, that of the revenue comptroller, two hundred yards outside the town, are sacked; the doors and the windows are smashed, the furniture and linen is torn to shreds, and the plate and jewellery is thrown into the wells. The same havoc is committed in the mayor's town-house, also in his country-house a league off. "Not a window, not a door, not one article or eatable" is preserved; their work, moreover, is

16. Dumouriez (an eye-witness), book iii. ch. 3. The trial was begun and judgment given by twelve lawyers and an assessor, whom the people, in arms, had themselves appointed. Hippeau, iv. 382.

17. "Archives Nationales," F^7, 3,248. (Letter of the mayor, M. Poussiaude de Thierri, September 11th.)

conscientiously done, without stopping a moment, "from ten in the evening up to ten in the morning on the following day." In addition to this the mayor, who has served for thirty-four years, resigns his office at the solicitation of the well-disposed but terrified people, and leaves the country.—At Rouen, after the 24th of July,[18] a written placard shows, by its orthography and its style, what sort of intellects composed it and what kind of actions are to follow it: "Nation, you have here four heads to strike off—those of Pontcarry (the first president), Maussion (the intendant), Godard de Belboeuf (the attorney-general), and Durand (the attorney of the King in the town). Without this we are lost, and if you do not do it, people will take you for a heartless nation." Nothing could be more explicit. The municipal body, however, to whom the Parliament denounces this list of proscriptions, replies, with its forced optimism, that "no citizen should consider himself or be considered as proscribed; he may and must believe himself to be safe in his own dwelling, satisfied that there is not a person in the city who would not fly to his rescue." This is equal to telling the populace that it is free to do as it pleases. On the strength of this the leaders of the riot work on in security for ten days. One of them is a man named Jourdain, a lawyer of Lisieux, and, like most of his brethren, a demagogue in principles; the other is a strolling actor from Paris named Bordier, famous in the part of harlequin,[19] a bully in a house of ill-fame, "a night-rover and drunkard, and who, fearing neither God nor devil," has taken up patriotism, and comes down into the provinces to play tragedy, and that, tragedy in real life. The fifth act begins on the night of the 3rd of August, with Bordier and Jourdain as the principal actors, and behind them the rabble along with several companies of fresh volunteers. A shout is heard, "Death to the monopolists! death to Maussion! we must have his head!" They pillage his hotel: many of them become intoxicated and fall asleep in his cellar. The revenue offices, the toll-gates of the town, the excise office, all buildings in

18. Floquet, vii. 551.

19. De Goncourt, "La Société Française pendant la Révolution," 37.

which the royal revenue is collected, are wrecked. Immense bonfires are lighted in the streets and on the old market square; furniture, clothes, papers, kitchen utensils, are all thrown in pell-mell, while carriages are dragged out and tumbled into the Seine. It is only when the town-hall is attacked that the national guard, beginning to be alarmed, makes up its mind to seize Bordier and some others. The following morning, however, at the shout of *Carabo,* and led by Jourdain, the prison is forced, Bordier set free, and the intendant's residence, with its offices, is sacked a second time. When, finally, the two rascals are taken and led to the scaffold, the populace is so strongly in their favour as to require the pointing of loaded cannon on them to keep them down.—At Besançon,[20] on the 13th of August, the leaders consist of the servant of an exhibitor of wild animals, two gaol-birds of whom one has already been branded in consequence of a riot, and a number of "inhabitants of ill-repute," who, towards evening, spread through the town along with the soldiers. The gunners insult the officers they meet, seize them by the throat, and want to throw them into the Doubs. Others go to the house of the commandant, M. de Langeron, and demand money of him; on his refusing to give it they tear off their cockades and exclaim, "We too belong to the Third-Estate!" in other words, that they are the masters: subsequently they demand the head of the intendant, M. de Caumartin, forcibly enter his dwelling and break up his furniture. On the following day the rabble and the soldiers enter the coffee-houses, the convents, and the inns, and demand to be served with wine and eatables as much as they want, and then, heated by drink, they burn the excise offices, force open several prisons, and set free all the smugglers and deserters. To put an end to this saturnalia a grand banquet in the open air is suggested, in which the National Guard is to fraternize with the whole garrison; but the banquet turns into a drinking-bout, entire companies remaining under the tables dead drunk; other companies carry away with them four hogsheads

20. "Archives Nationales," D. xxix. I. Letter of the officers of the bailiwick of Dôle, August 24th. Sauzay i. 128.

of wine, and the rest, finding themselves left in the lurch, are scattered abroad outside the walls in order to rob the cellars of the neighbouring villages. The next day, encouraged by the example set them, a portion of the garrison, accompanied by a number of workmen, repeat the expedition in the country. Finally, after four days of this orgy, to prevent Besançon and its outskirts from being indefinitely treated as a conquered country, the burgess guard, in alliance with the soldiers who have remained loyal, rebel against the rebellion, go in quest of the marauders, and hang two of them that same evening.—Such is insurrection![21] an irruption of brute force which, turned loose on the habitations of men, can do nothing but gorge itself, waste, break, destroy, and do damage to itself; and if we follow the details of local history, we see how, in these days, similar outbreaks of violence might be expected at any time.

At Troyes,[22] on the 18th of July, a market-day, the peasants refuse to pay the entrance duties; the *octroi* having been suppressed at Paris, it ought also to be suppressed at Troyes. The populace, excited by this first disorderly act, gather into a mob for the purpose of dividing the grain and arms amongst themselves, and the next day the town-hall is invested by seven or eight thousand men, armed with clubs and stones. The day after, a band, recruited in the surrounding villages, armed with flails, shovels, and pitch-forks, enters under the leadership of a joiner who marches at the head of it with a drawn sabre; fortunately, "all the honest folks among the burgesses" immediately form themselves into a national guard, and this first attempt at a jacquerie is put down. But the agitation continues, and

21. There is a similar occurrence at Strasbourg, a few days after the sacking of the town-hall. The municipality having given each man of the garrison twenty sous, the soldiers abandon their post, set the prisoners free at the Pont-Couvert, feast publicly in the streets with the women taken out of the penitentiary, and force innkeepers and the keepers of drinking-places to give up their provisions. The shops are all closed, and, for twenty-four hours, the officers are not obeyed. (De Dammartin, i. 105.)

22. Albert Babeau, i. 187, 273.—*Moniteur*, ii. 379. (Extract from the provost's verdict of November 27, 1789.)

false rumours constantly keep it up. On the 29th of July, on the report being circulated that five hundred "brigands" had left Paris and were coming to ravage the country, the tocsin sounds in the villages, and the peasants go forth armed.—Henceforth, a vague idea of some impending danger fills all minds; the necessity of defence and of guarding against enemies is maintained. The new demagogues avail themselves of this to keep their hold on the people, and when the time comes, to use it against their chiefs. It is of no use to assure the people that the latter are patriots; that only recently they welcomed Necker with enthusiastic shouts; that the priests, the monks, and canons were the first to adopt the national cockade; that the nobles of the city and its environs are the most liberal in France; that, on the 20th of July, the burgess guard saved the town; that all the wealthy give to the national workshops; that Mayor Huez, "a venerable and honest magistrate," is a benefactor to the poor and to the public. All the old leaders are objects of distrust.—On the 8th of August, a mob demands the dismissal of the dragoons, arms for all volunteers, bread at two sous the pound, and the freedom of all prisoners. On the 19th of August the National Guard rejects its old officers as aristocrats, and elects new ones. On the 27th of August, the crowd invade the town-hall and distribute the arms amongst themselves. On the 5th of September, two hundred men, led by Truelle, president of the new committee, force the salt depôt and have salt delivered to them at six sous per pound.—Meanwhile, in the lowest quarters of the city, a story is concocted to the effect that if wheat is scarce it is because Huez, the mayor, and M. de St. Georges, the old commandant, are monopolists, and now they say of Huez what they said five weeks before of Foulon, that "he wants to make the people eat hay." The many-headed brute growls fiercely and is about to spring. As usual, instead of restraining him, they try to manage him. "You must put your authority aside for a moment," writes the deputy of Troyes to the sheriffs, "and act towards the people as to a friend; be as gentle with them as you would be with your equals, and rest assured that they are capable of responding to it." Thus does Huez act, and he even does more, paying no attention to their menaces, refusing to provide for his own safety and almost offering himself as a sacrifice. "I have wronged no one," he exclaimed; "why should any one bear me ill-will?" His sole precaution is to provide something for the unfortunate poor when he is gone: he bequeaths in his will 18,000 livres to the poor, and, on the eve of his death, sends 100 crowns to the bureau of charity. But what avail self-abnegation and beneficence against blind, insane rage! On the 9th of September, three loads of flour proving to be unsound, the people collect and shout out, "Down with the flour-dealers! Down with machinery! Down with the mayor! Death to the mayor, and let Truelle be put in his place!"—Huez, on leaving his courtroom, is knocked down, murdered by kicks and blows, throttled, dragged to the reception hall, struck on his head with a *sabot,* and pitched down the grand staircase. The municipal officers strive in vain to protect him; a rope is put around his neck and they begin to drag him along. A priest, who begs to be allowed at least to save his soul, is repulsed and beaten. A woman jumps on the prostrate old man, stamps on his face and repeatedly thrusts her scissors in his eyes. He is dragged along with the rope around his neck up to the Pont de la Selle, and thrown into the neighbouring ford, and then drawn out, again dragged through the streets and in the gutters, with a bunch of hay crammed in his mouth.[23]

In the meantime, his house as well as that of the lieutenant of police, that of the notary Guyot, and that of M. de Saint-Georges, are sacked; the pillaging and destruction lasts four hours; at the notary's house, six hundred bottles of wine are consumed or carried off; objects of value are divided, and the rest, even down to the iron balcony, is demolished or broken; the rioters cry out, on leaving,

23. *Moniteur, ibid.* Picard, the principal murderer, confessed "that he had made him suffer a great deal; that the said *sieur* Huez did not die until they came near the Chaudron Inn; that he nevertheless intended to make him suffer more by stabbing him in the neck at the corner of each street, (and) by contriving it so that he might do it often, as long as there was life in him; that the day on which M. Huez died yielded him ten francs, together with the neck-buckle of M. Huez, found on him when he was arrested in his flight."

that they have still to burn twenty-seven houses, and to take twenty-seven heads. "No one at Troyes went to bed that fatal night."—During the succeeding days, for nearly two weeks, society seems to be dissolved. Placards posted about the streets proscribe municipal officers, canons, divines, privileged persons, prominent merchants, and even ladies of charity; the latter are so frightened that they throw up their office, while a number of persons move off into the country; others barricade themselves in their dwellings and only open their doors with sabre in hand. Not until the 26th does the orderly class rally sufficiently to resume the ascendancy and arrest the miscreants.—Such is public life in France after the 14th of July: the magistrates in each town feel that they are at the mercy of a band of savages and sometimes of cannibals. Those of Troyes had just tortured Huez after the fashion of Hurons, while those of Caen did worse; Major de Belzance, not less innocent, and under sworn protection,[24] was cut to pieces like Laperouse in the Fiji Islands, and a woman ate his heart.

VI

We can divine, under such circumstances, whether taxes come in, and whether municipalities that sway about in every popular breeze have the power of keeping up odious revenue rights.—Towards the end of September,[25] I find a list of thirty-six committees or municipal bodies which, within a radius of fifty leagues around Paris, refuse to ensure the collection of taxes. One of them tolerates the sale of contraband salt, in order not to excite a riot. Another takes the precaution to disarm the employés in the excise department. In a third the municipal officers were the first to provide themselves with contraband salt and contraband tobacco.

24. *Mercure de France,* September 26, 1789. Letters of the officers of the Bourbon regiment and of members of the general committee of Caen.—Floquet, vii. 545.

25. "Archives Nationales," H. 1453. *Ibid.* D. xxix. I. Note of M. de la Tour-du-Pin, October 28th.

At Peronne and at Ham, the order having come to restore the toll-houses, the people destroy the soldiers' quarters, conduct all the employés to their homes, and order them to leave within twenty-four hours, under penalty of death. After twenty months' resistance Paris will end the matter by forcing the National Assembly to give in and by obtaining the final suppression of its *octroi*.[26]—Of all the creditors whose hand each one felt on his shoulders, that of the exchequer was the heaviest, and now it is the weakest; hence this is the first whose grasp is to be shaken off; there is none which is more heartily detested or which receives harsher treatment. Especially against collectors of the salt-tax, custom-house officers, and excise-men the fury is universal. These, everywhere,[27] are in danger of their lives and are obliged to fly. At Falaise, in Normandy, the people threaten to "cut to pieces the director of the excise." At Baignes, in Saintonge, his house is devastated and his papers and effects are burned; they put a knife to the throat of his son, a child six years of age, saying, "Thou must perish that there may be no more of thy race." For four hours the clerks are on the point of being torn to pieces; through the entreaties of the lord of the manor, who sees scythes and sabres aimed at his own head, they are released only on the condition that they "abjure their employment."—Again, for two months following the taking of the Bastille, insurrections break out by hundreds, like a volley of musketry, against indirect taxation. From the 23rd of July the Intendant of Champagne reports that "the

26. Decree, February 1, 1789, enforced May 1 following.

27. "Archives Nationales," D. xxix. I. Letter of the Count de Montausier, August 8th, with notes by M. Paulian, director of the excise (an admirable letter, modest and liberal, and ending by demanding a pardon for people led astray). H. 1453. Letter of the attorney of the election district of Falaise, July 17th, &c. *Moniteur,* I. 303, 387, 505 (sessions of August 7th and 27th and of September 23rd). "The royal revenues are diminishing steadily." Roux and Buchez, III. 219 (session of October 24, 1789). Discourse of a deputation from Anjou: "Sixty thousand men are armed; the barriers have been destroyed, the clerks' horses have been sold by auction; the employés have been told to withdraw from the province within eight days. The inhabitants have declared that they will not pay taxes so long as the salt-tax exists."

uprising is general in almost all the towns under his generalship." On the following day the Intendant of Alençon writes that, in his province, "the royal dues will no longer be paid anywhere." On the 7th of August, M. Necker states to the National Assembly that in the two intendants' districts of Caen and Alençon it has been necessary to reduce the price of salt one-half; that "in an infinity of places" the collection of the excise is stopped or suspended; that the smuggling of salt and tobacco is done by "convoys and by open force" in Picardy, in Lorraine, and in the Trois-Evêchés; that the indirect tax does not come in, that the receivers-general and the receivers of the *taille* are "at bay" and can no longer keep their engagements. The public income diminishes from month to month; in the social body, the heart, already so feeble, faints; deprived of the blood which no longer reaches it, it ceases to propel to the muscles the vivifying current which restores their waste and adds to their energy.

"All controlling power is slackened," says Necker, "everything is a prey to the passions of individuals." Where is the power to constrain them and to secure to the State its dues? The clergy, the nobles, wealthy townsmen, and certain brave artisans and farmers, undoubtedly pay, and even sometimes give spontaneously. But in society those who possess intelligence, who are in easy circumstances and conscientious, form a small select class—the great mass is egotistic, ignorant, and needy, and lets its money go only under constraint; there is but one way to collect the taxes, and that is to extort them. From time immemorial, direct taxes in France have been collected only by bailiffs and seizures; which is not surprising, as they take away a full half of the net income. Now that the peasants of each village are armed and form a band, let the collector come and make seizures if he dare!—"Immediately after the decree on the equality of the taxes," writes the provincial commission of Alsace,[28] "the people generally refused to make any payments, until those who were exempt and privileged should have been inscribed on the

28. "Archives Nationales," F^7, 3,253 (Letter of September 8, 1789).

local lists." In many places the peasants threaten to obtain the reimbursement of their instalments, while in others they insist that the decree should be retrospective and that the new rate-payers should pay for the past year. "No collector dare send an official to distrain; none that are sent dare fulfil their mission."—"It is not the good bourgeois" of whom there is any fear, "but the rabble who make the latter and every one else afraid of them"; resistance and disorder everywhere come from "people that have nothing to lose."—Not only do they shake off taxation, but they usurp property, and declare that, being the Nation, whatever belongs to the Nation belongs to them. The forests of Alsace are laid waste, the seignorial as well as communal, and wantonly destroyed with the wastefulness of children or of maniacs. "In many places, to avoid the trouble of removing the woods, they are burnt, and the people content themselves with carrying off the ashes."—After the decrees of August 4th, and in spite of the law which licenses the proprietor only to hunt on his own grounds, the impulse to break the law becomes irresistible. Every man who can procure a gun begins operations;[29] the crops which are still standing are trodden under foot, the lordly residences are invaded, and the palings are scaled; the King himself at Versailles is wakened by shots fired in his park. Stags, fawns, deer, wild boars, hares, and rabbits, are slain by thousands, cooked with stolen wood, and eaten up on the spot. There is a constant discharge of musketry throughout France for more than two months, and, as on an American prairie, every living animal belongs to him who kills it. At Choiseul, in Champagne, not only are all the hares and partridges of the barony exterminated, but the ponds are exhausted

29. Arthur Young, September 30th. "One would think that every rusty gun in Provence is at work, killing all sorts of birds; the shot has fallen five or six times in my chaise and about my ears," Beugnot, I. 141. "Archives Nationales," D. xxix. I. Letter of the Chevalier d'Allonville, September 8, 1789 (environs of Bar-sur-Aube). "The peasants go in armed bands into the woods belonging to the Abbey of Trois-Fontaines, which they cut down. They saw up the oaks and transport them on waggons to Pont-Saint-Dizier, where they sell them. In other places they fish in the ponds and break the embankments."

of fish; the court of the chateau even is entered, to fire on the pigeon-house and destroy the pigeons, and then the pigeons and fish, of which they have too many, are offered to the proprietor for sale.—It is "the patriots" of the village with "smugglers and bad characters" belonging to the neighbourhood who make this expedition; they are seen in the front ranks of every act of violence, and it is not difficult to foresee that, under their leadership, attacks on public persons and public property will be followed by attacks on private persons and private property.

VII

Indeed, a proscribed class already exists, and a name has been found for it: it is the "aristocrats." This deadly term, applied at first to the nobles and prelates in the States-General who declined to take part in the reunion of the three orders, is extended so as to embrace all whose titles, offices, alliances, and manner of living distinguish them from the multitude. That which entitled them to respect is that which marks them out as objects of ill-will; while the people, who, though suffering from their privileges, did not regard them personally with hatred, are taught to consider them as their enemies. Each, on his own estate, is held accountable for the evil designs attributed to his brethren at Versailles, and, on the false report of a plot at the centre, the peasants range themselves on the side of the conspirators.[30] Thus does the peasant jacquerie commence, and the wild enthusiasts who have fanned the flame in Paris are likewise fanning the flame in the provinces. "You wish to know the authors of the agitations," writes

30. "Archives Nationales," D. xxix. I. Letter of the assessor of the police of Saint-Flour, October 3, 1789. On the 31st of July, a report is spread that the brigands are coming. On the 1st of August the peasants arm themselves. "They amuse themselves by drinking, awaiting the arrival of the brigands; the excitement increases to such an extent as to make them believe that M. le Comte d'Espinchal had arrived in disguise the evening before at Massiac, that he was the author of the troubles disturbing the province at this time, and that he was concealed in his chateau." On the strength of this shots are fired into the windows, and there are searches, &c.

a sensible man to the committee of investigation; "you will find them amongst the deputies of the Third-Estate," and especially among the attorneys and advocates. "These dispatch incendiary letters to their constituents, which letters are received by municipal bodies alike composed of attorneys and of advocates. . . . they are read aloud in the public squares, while copies of them are distributed among all the villages. In these villages, if any one knows how to read besides the priest and the lord of the manor, it is the legal practitioner," the born enemy of the lord of the manor, whose place he covets, vain of his oratorical powers, embittered by his poverty, and never failing to blacken everything.[31] It is highly probable that he is the one who composes and circulates the placards calling on the people, in the King's name, to resort to violence.—At Secondigny, in Poitou, on the 23rd of July,[32] the labourers in the forest receive a letter "which summons them to attack all the country gentlemen round about, and to massacre without mercy all those who refuse to renounce their privileges . . . promising them that not only will their crimes go unpunished, but that they will even be rewarded." M. Despretz-Montpezat, correspondent of the deputies of the nobles, is seized, and dragged with his son to the dwelling of the procurator-fiscal, to force him to give his signature; the inhabitants are forbidden to render him assistance "on pain of death and fire." "Sign," they exclaim, "or we will tear out your heart, and set fire to this house!" At this moment the neighbouring notary, who is doubtless an accomplice, appears with a stamped paper, and says to him, "Monsieur, I have just come from Niort, where the Third-

31. "Archives Nationales," K. xxix. I. Letter of Etienne Fermier, Naveinne, September 18th (it is possible that the author, for the sake of caution, took a fictitious name). The manuscript correspondence of M. Boullé, deputy of Pontivy, to his constituents, is a type of this declamatory and incendiary writing. Letter of the consuls, priests, and merchants of Puy-en-Velay, September 16th.—"The Ancient Régime," p. 396.

32. "Archives Nationales," D. xxix. I. Letter of M. Despretz-Montpezat, a former artillery officer, July 24th (with several other signatures). On the same day the tocsin is sounded in fifty villages on the rumour spreading that 7,000 brigands, English and Breton, were invading the country.

Estate has done the same thing to all the gentlemen of the town; one, who refused, was cut to pieces before our eyes."—"We are compelled to sign renunciations of our privileges, and give our assent to one and the same taxation, as if the nobles had not already done so." The band gives notice that it will proceed in the same fashion with all the chateaux in the vicinity, and terror precedes or follows them. "Nobody dares write," M. Despretz sends word; "I attempt it at the risk of my life."—Nobles and prelates become objects of suspicion everywhere; village committees open their letters, and they have to suffer their houses to be searched.[33] They are forced to adopt the new cockade: to be a gentleman, and not wear it, is to deserve hanging. At Mamers, in Maine, M. de Beauvoir refuses to wear it, and is at the point of being put into the pillory and at once knocked on the head. Near La Flèche, M. de Brissac is arrested, and a message is sent to Paris to know if he shall be taken there, "or be beheaded in the meantime." Two deputies of the nobles, MM. de Montesson and de Vassé, who had come to ask the consent of their constituents to their joining the Third-Estate, are recognised near Mans; their honourable scruples and their pledges to the constituents are considered of no importance, nor even the step that they are now taking to fulfil them; it suffices that they voted against the Third-Estate at Versailles; the populace pursues them and breaks up their carriages, and pillages their trunks.—Woe to the nobles, especially if they have taken any part in local rule, and if they are opposed to popular panics! M. Cureau, deputy-mayor of Mans,[34] had issued orders during the famine, and, having retired to his chateau of Nouay, had

33. "Archives Nationales," D. xxix. I. Letter of Briand-Delessart, August 1st (domiciliary visits to the Carmelites of Angoulême where it is pretended that Mme. de Polignac has just arrived.—Beugnot, I. 140.—Arthur Young, July 20th, &c.—Roux and Buchez, iv. 166, Letter of Mamers, July 24th; of Mans, July 26th.

34. Montjoie, ch. lxii. p. 93 (according to acts of legal procedure). There was a soldier in the band who had served under M. de Montesson and who wanted to avenge himself for the punishments he had undergone in the regiment.

told the peasants that the announcement of the coming of brigands was a false alarm; he thought that it was not necessary to sound the tocsin, and all that was necessary was that they should remain quiet. Accordingly he is set down as being in league with the brigands, and besides this he is a monopolist, and a buyer of standing crops. The peasants lead him off, along with his son-in-law, M. de Montesson, to the neighbouring village, where there are judges. On the way "they dragged their victims on the ground, pummelled them, trampled on them, spit in their faces, and besmeared them with filth." M. de Montesson is shot, while M. Cureau is killed by degrees; a carpenter cuts off the two heads with a double-edged axe, and children bear them along to the sound of drums and violins. Meanwhile, the judges of the place, brought by force, draw up an official report stating the finding of thirty louis and several bills of the Banque d'Escompte in the pockets of M. de Cureau, on the discovery of which a shout of triumph is set up: this evidence proves that they were going to buy up the standing wheat!—Such is the course of popular justice. Now that the Third-Estate has become the nation, every mob thinks that it has the right to pronounce sentences, which it carries out, on lives and on possessions.

These explosions are isolated in the western, central, and southern provinces: the conflagration, however, is universal in the east, on a strip of ground from thirty to fifty leagues broad, extending from the extreme north down to Provence. Alsace, Franche-Comté, Burgundy, Mâconnais, Beaujolais, Auvergne, Viennois, Dauphiny—the whole of this territory resembles a continuous mine which explodes at the same time. The first column of flame which shoots up is on the frontiers of Alsace and Franche-Comté, in the vicinity of Belfort and Vésoul—a feudal district, in which the peasant, overburdened with taxes, bears the heavier yoke with greater impatience. An instinctive argument is going on in his mind without his knowing it. "The good Assembly and the good King want us to be happy—suppose we help them! They say that the King has already relieved us of the taxes—suppose we relieve ourselves of paying rents! Down with the nobles! They are no better than the tax-collectors!"—On the 16th of July, the chateau of Sancy, belonging to the Princesse de Beaufremont, is sacked, and on the 18th those of Lure, Bithaine, and Molans.[35] On the 29th, an accident which occurs with some fireworks at a popular festival at the house of M. de Memmay, leads the lower class to believe that the invitation extended to them was a trap, and that there was a desire to get rid of them by treachery.[36] Seized with rage they set fire to the chateau, and during the following week[37] destroy three abbeys, ruin eleven chateaux, and pillage others; "all records are destroyed, the registers and court-rolls are carried off, and the deposits violated."—Starting from this spot, "the hurricane of insurrection" stretches over the whole of Alsace from Huningue to Landau.[38] The insurgents display placards, signed *Louis*, stating that for a certain lapse of time they shall be permitted to exercise justice themselves, and, in Sundgau, a well-dressed weaver, decorated with a blue belt, passes for a prince, the King's second son. They begin by falling on the Jews, their hereditary leeches; they sack their dwellings, divide their money among themselves, and hunt them down like so many fallow-deer. At Bâle alone, it is said that twelve hundred of these unfortunate fugitives arrived with their families.—The distance between the Jew creditor and the Christian proprietor is not great, and this is soon cleared. Remiremont is only saved by a detachment of dragoons. Eight hundred men attack the chateau of Uberbrünn. The abbey of Neubourg is taken by storm. At Guebwiller, on the 31st of July, five hundred peasants, subjects of the abbey of Murbach, make a descent on the abbot's palace and on the house of the canons. Cupboards, chests,

35. *Mercure de France,* August 20th (Letter from Vésoul, August 13th).

36. M. de Memmay proved his innocence later on, and was rehabilitated by a public decision after two years' proceedings (session of June 4, 1791; *Mercure* of June 11th).

37. *Journal des Débats et Décrees,* i. 258. (Letter of the municipality of Vésoul, July 22nd.—Discourse of M. de Toulougeon, July 29th.)

38. De Rochambeau, "Mémoires," i. 353. "Archives Nationales," F^7, 3,253. (Letter of M. de Rochambeau, August 4th.)—Chronicle of Schmutz (*ibid.*), p. 284. "Archives Nationales," D. xxix. i. (Letter of Mme. Ferrette, of Remiremont, August 9th.)

beds, windows, mirrors, frames, even the tiles of the roof and the hinges of the casements are hacked to pieces: "They kindle fires on the beautiful inlaid floors of the apartments, and there burn up the library and the title-deeds." The abbot's superb carriage is so broken up that not a wheel remains entire. "Wine streams through the cellars. One cask of sixteen hundred measures is half lost; the plate and the linen are carried off."—Society is evidently being overthrown, while with the power, property is changing hands.

These are their very words. In Franche-Comté[39] the inhabitants of eight communes come and declare to the Bernardins of Grâce-Dieu and of Lieu-Croissant "that, being of the Third-Estate, it is time now for the people to rule over abbots and monks, considering that the domination of the latter has lasted too long," and thereupon they carry off all the titles to property and to rentals belonging to the abbey in their commune. In Upper Dauphiny, during the destruction of M. de Murat's chateau, a man named Ferréol struck the furniture with a big stick, exclaiming, "Hey, so much for you, Murat; you have been master a good while, now it's our turn!"[40] Those who rifle houses, and steal like highway robbers, think that they are defending a cause, and reply to the challenge, "Who goes there?" "We are for the brigand Third-Estate!"—Everywhere the belief prevails that they are clothed with authority, and they conduct themselves like a conquering horde under the orders of an absent general. At Remiremont and at Luxeuil they produce an edict, stating that "all this brigandage, pillage, and destruction" is permitted. In Dauphiny, the leaders of the bands say that they possess the King's orders. In Auvergne, "they follow imperative orders, being advised that such is his Majesty's will." Nowhere do we see that an insurgent village exercises personal vengeance against its lord. If the people fire on the nobles they encounter, it is not through personal hatred.

39. Sauzay, i. 180. (Letters of monks, July 22nd and 26th.)

40. "Archives Nationales," D. xxix. I. (Letter of M. de Bergeron, attorney to the *présidial* of Valence, August 28th, with the details of the verdict stated.) Official report of the militia of Lyons, sent to the president of the National Assembly, August 10th. (Expedition to Serrière, in Dauphiny, July 31st.)

They are destroying the class, and do not pursue individuals. They detest feudal privileges, holders of charters, the cursed parchments by virtue of which they are made to pay, but not the nobleman who, when he resides at home, is of humane intentions, compassionate, and even often beneficent. At Luxeuil, the abbot, who is forced with uplifted axe to sign a relinquishment of his seignorial rights over twenty-three estates, has dwelt among them for forty-six years, and has been wholly devoted to them.[41] In the canton of Crémieu, "where the havoc is immense," all the nobles, write the municipal officers, are "patriots and benevolent." In Dauphiny, the engineers, magistrates, and prelates, whose chateaux are sacked, were the first to espouse the cause of the people and of public liberties against the ministers. In Auvergne, the peasants themselves "manifest a good deal of repugnance to act in this way against such kind masters." But it must be done; the only concession which can be made in consideration of the kindness which had been extended to them is, not to burn the chateau of the ladies of Vanes, who had been so charitable; but they burn all their title-deeds, and torture the business agent at three different times by fire, to force him to deliver a document which he does not possess; they then only withdraw him from the fire half-broiled, because the ladies, on their knees, implore mercy for him.—They are like the soldiers on a campaign who execute orders with docility, for which necessity is the only plea, and who, without regarding themselves as brigands, commit acts of brigandage.

But here the situation is more tragical, for it is war in the midst of peace, a war of the brutal and barbarised multitude against the highly cultivated, well-disposed, and confiding, who had not antic-

41. Letter of the Count of Courtivron, deputy substitute (an eye-witness).—"Archives Nationales," D. xxix. I. Letter of the municipal officers of Crémieu (Dauphiny), November 3rd. Letter of the Vicomte de Carbonnière (Auvergne), August 3rd.—Arthur Young, July 30th (Dijon) says, apropos of a noble family which escaped almost naked from its burning chateau, "they were esteemed by the neighbours; their virtues ought to have commanded the love of the poor, for whose resentment there was no cause."

ipated anything of the kind, who had not even dreamt of defending themselves, and who had no protection. The Comte de Courtivron, with his family, was staying at the watering-place of Luxeuil with his uncle, the Abbé of Clermont-Tonnerre, an old man of seventy years. On the 19th of July, fifty peasants from Fougerolle break into and demolish everything in the houses of an usher and a collector of the excise. Thereupon the mayor of the place intimates to the nobles and magistrates who are taking the waters, that they had better leave the house in twenty-four hours, as "he had been advised of an intention to burn the houses in which they were staying," and he did not wish to have Luxeuil exposed to this danger on account of their presence there. The following day, the guard, as obliging as the mayor, allows the band to enter the town and to force the abbey; the usual events follow—renunciations are extorted, records and cellars are ransacked, plate and other effects are stolen. M. de Courtivron escaping with his uncle during the night, the tocsin is sounded and they are pursued, and with difficulty obtain refuge in Plombières. The bourgeoisie of Plombières, however, for fear of compromising themselves, oblige them to depart. On the road two hundred insurgents threaten to kill their horses and to smash their carriage, and they only find safety at last at Porentruy, outside of France. On his return, M. de Courtivron is shot at by the band which has just pillaged the abbey of Lure, and they shout out at him as he passes, "Let's massacre the nobles!" Meanwhile, the chateau of Vauvilliers, to which his sick wife had been carried, is devastated from top to bottom; the mob search for her everywhere, and she only escapes by hiding herself in a hay-loft. Both are anxious to fly into Burgundy, but word is sent them that at Dijon "the nobles are blockaded by the people," and that, in the country, they threaten to set their houses on fire.—There is no asylum to be had, either in their own homes nor in the homes of others, nor in places along the roads, fugitives being stopped in all the small villages and market-towns. In Dauphiny[42] "the Abbess of St. Pierre de Lyon, one of the

42. "Archives Nationales," xxix. 1. (Letter of the commission of the States of Dauphiny, July 31st.)

nuns, M. de Perrotin, M. de Bellegarde, the Marquis de la Tour-du-Pin, and the Chevalier de Moidieu, are arrested at Champier by the armed population, led to the Côte Saint-André, confined in the town-hall, whence they send to Grenoble for assistance," and, to have them released, the Grenoble Committee is obliged to send commissioners. Their only refuge is in the large cities, where some semblance of a precarious order exists, and in the ranks of the City Guards, which march from Lyons, Dijon, and Grenoble, to keep the inundation down. Throughout the country scattered chateaux are swallowed up by the popular tide, and, as the feudal rights are often in plebeian hands, it insensibly rises beyond its first overflow.—There is no limit to an insurrection against property. This one extends from abbeys and chateaux to the "houses of the bourgeoisie."[43] The grudge at first was confined to the holders of charters; now it is extended to all who possess anything. Well-to-do farmers and priests abandon their parishes and fly to the towns. Travellers are put to ransom. Thieves, robbers, and returned convicts, at the head of armed bands, seize whatever they can lay their hands on. Cupidity becomes inflamed by such examples; on domains which are deserted and in a state of confusion, where there is nothing to indicate a master's presence, all seems to lapse to the first comer. A small farmer of the neighbourhood has carried away wine and returns the following day in search of hay. All the furniture of a chateau in Dauphiny is removed, even to the hinges of the doors, by a large reinforcement of carts.—"It is the war of the poor against the rich," says a deputy, "and, on the 3rd of August, the Committee on Reports declares to the National Assembly "that no kind of property has been spared." In Franche-Comté, "nearly forty chateaux and sei-

43. "Désastres du Mâconnais," by Puthod de la Maison-Rouge (August, 1789). "Ravages du Mâconnai"—Arthur Young, July 27th. Roux and Buchez, iv. 211, 214. Arthur Young, July 27th.—*Mercure de France*, September 12, 1789. (Letter by a volunteer of Orleans.) "On the 15th of August, eighty-eight ruffians, calling themselves reapers, present themselves at Bascon, in Beauce, and, the next day, at a chateau in the neighbourhood, where they demand within an hour the head of the son of the lord of the manor, M. Tassin, who can only redeem himself by a contribution of 1,600 livres and the pillaging of his cellars.

gnorial mansions have been pillaged or burnt."[44] From Langres to Gray about three out of five chateaux are sacked. In Dauphiny twenty-seven are burned or destroyed; five in the small district of Viennois, and, besides these, all the monasteries—nine at least in Auvergne, seventy-two, it is said, in Mâconnais and Beaujolais, without counting those of Alsace. On the 31st of July, Lally-Tollendal, on entering the tribune, has his hands full of letters of distress, with a list of thirty-six chateaux burnt, demolished, or pillaged, in one province, and the details of still worse violence against persons:[45] "in Languedoc, M. de Barras, cut to pieces in the presence of his wife who is about to be confined, and who is dead in consequence; in Normandy, a paralytic gentleman left on a burning pile and taken off from it with his hands burnt; in Franche-Comté, Madame de Bathilly compelled, with an axe over her head, to give up her title-deeds and even her estate; Madame de Listenay forced to do the same, with a pitchfork at her neck and her two daughters in a swoon at her feet; Comte de Montjustin, with his wife, having a pistol at his throat for three hours; and both dragged from their carriage to be thrown into a pond, where they are saved by a passing regiment of soldiers; Baron de Montjustin, one of the twenty-two popular noblemen, suspended for an hour in a well, listening to a discussion whether he shall be dropt down or whether he should die in some other way; the Chevalier d'Ambly, torn from his chateau and dragged naked into the village, placed on a dung-heap after having his eyebrows and all his hair pulled out, while the crowd kept on dancing around him."

44. Letter of the Count de Courtivron.—Arthur Young, July 31st.—Roux and Buchez, ii. 543.—*Mercure de France,* August 15, 1789 (sitting of the 8th, discourse of a deputy).—Mermet, "Histoire de la Ville de Vienne," 445.—"Archives Nationales," *ibid.* (Letter of the Commission of the States of Dauphiny, July 31st.) "The list of burnt or devastated chateaux is immense." The committee already cites sixteen of them. Puthod de la Maison-Rouge, *ibid.:* "Were all devastated places to be mentioned, it would be necessary to cite the whole province" (Letter from Mâcon). "They have not the less destroyed most of the chateaux and bourgeois dwellings, at one time burning them and at another tearing them down."

45. Lally-Tollendal, "Second Letter to my Constituents," 104.

In the midst of a disintegrated society, under the semblance only of a government, it is manifest that an invasion is under way, an invasion of barbarians which will complete by terror that which it has begun by violence, and which, like the invasions of the Normans in the tenth and eleventh centuries, ends in the conquest and dispossession of an entire class. In vain the National Guard and the other troops that remain loyal succeed in stemming the first torrent; in vain does the Assembly hollow out a bed for it and strive to bank it in by fixed boundaries. The decrees of the 4th of August and the regulations which follow are but so many spiders' webs stretched across a torrent. The peasants, moreover, putting their own interpretation on the decrees, convert the new laws into authority for continuing in their course or beginning over again. No more rents, however legitimate, however legal! "Yesterday,"[46] writes a gentleman of Auvergne, "we were notified that the fruit-tithe (*percières*) would no longer be paid, and that the example of other provinces was only being followed which no longer, even by royal order, pay tithes." In Franche-Comté "numerous communities are satisfied that they no longer owe anything either to the King or to their lords. . . . The villages divide amongst themselves the fields and woods belonging to the nobles."—It must be noted that charter-holding

46. Doniol, "La Revolution et la Féodalité," p. 60 (a few days after the 4th of August).—"Archives Nationales," H. 784. Letters of M. de Langeron, military commander at Besançon, October 16th and 18th. *Ibid.,* D. xxix. 1. Letter of the same, September 3rd. Arthur Young (in Provence, at the house of Baron de la Tour-d'Aignes). "The baron is an enormous sufferer by the Revolution; a great extent of country which belonged in absolute right to his ancestors, has been granted for quit-rents, *ceus,* and other feudal payments, so that there is no comparison between the lands retained and those thus granted by his family. . . . The solid payments which the Assembly have declared to be redeemable are every hour falling to nothing, without a shadow of recompense. . . . The situation of the nobility in this country is pitiable; they are under apprehensions that nothing will be left them, but simply such houses as the mob allows to stand unburnt; that the small farmers will retain their farms without paying the landlord his half of the produce; and that, in case of such a refusal, there is actually neither law nor authority in the country to prevent it. This chateau, splendid even in ruins, with the fortune and lives of the owners, is at the mercy of an armed rabble."

and feudal titles are still intact in three-fourths of France, that it is the interest of the peasant to ensure their disappearance, and that he is always armed. To secure a new outbreak of jacqueries, it is only necessary that central control, already thrown into disorder, should be withdrawn. This is the work of Versailles and of Paris; and there, at Paris as well as at Versailles, some, through lack of foresight and infatuation, and others, through blindness and indecision—the latter through weakness and the former through violence—all are labouring to accomplish it.

CHAPTER IV

I. *Paris—Powerlessness and discords of the authorities—The people, King—* II. *Their distress—The dearth and the lack of work—How men of executive ability are recruited—* III. *The new popular leaders—Their ascendency—Their education—Their sentiments—Their situation—Their councils—Their denunciations—* IV. *Their interference with the Government—Their pressure on the Assembly—* V. *The 5th and 6th of October—* VI. *The Government and the nation in the hands of the revolutionary party.*

I

THE powerlessness, indeed, of the heads of the Government, and the lack of discipline among all its subordinates, are much greater in the capital than in the provinces.—Paris possesses a mayor, Bailly; but "from the first day, and in the easiest manner possible,"[1] his municipal council, that is to say, "the assembly of the representatives of the commune, has accustomed itself to carry on the government alone, overlooking him entirely."—There is a central administration—the municipal council, presided over by the mayor; but, "at this time, authority is everywhere except where the preponderating authority should be; the districts have delegated it and at the same time retained it"; each of them acts as if it were alone and supreme. There are secondary powers—the district-committees, each with its president, its clerk, its offices, and commissioners; but the mobs of

1. Bailly, "Mémoires," ii. 195, 242.

the street march on without awaiting their orders; while the people, shouting under their windows, impose their will on them; in short, says Bailly again, "everybody knew how to command, but nobody knew how to obey."

"Imagine," writes Loustalot himself, "a man whose feet, hands, and limbs possessed intelligence and a will, whose one leg would wish to walk when the other one wanted to rest, whose throat would close when the stomach demanded food, whose mouth would sing when the eyelids were weighed down with sleep; and you will have a striking picture of the condition of things in the capital."

There are "sixty Republics" in Paris; each district is an independent, isolated power, which receives no order without criticizing it, always in disagreement and often in conflict with the central authority or with the other districts. It receives denunciations, orders domiciliary visits, sends deputations to the National Assembly, passes resolutions, posts its bills, not only in its own quarter but throughout the city, and sometimes even extends its jurisdiction outside of Paris. Everything comes within its province, and particularly that which ought not to do so.—On the 18th of July, the district of Petits-Augustins[2] "decrees in its own name the establishment of justices of the peace," under the title of tribunes, and proceeds at once to elect its own, nominating the actor Molé. On the 30th, that of the Oratoire annuls the amnesty which the representatives of the commune in the Hôtel-de-Ville had granted, and orders two of its members to go to a distance of thirty leagues to arrest M. de Bezenval. On the 19th of August, that of Nazareth issues commissions to seize and bring to Paris the arms deposited in strong places. From the beginning each assembly sent to the Arsenal in its own name, and "obtained as many cartridges and as much powder as it desired." Others claim the right of keeping a watchful eye over the Hôtel-de-Ville and of reprimanding the National Assembly. The Oratoire decides that the representatives of the commune shall be invited to deliberate in public. Saint-Nicholas des Champs deliberates on the

2. Bailly, ii. 74, 174, 242, 261, 282, 345, 392.

veto and begs the Assembly to suspend its vote.—It is a strange spectacle, that of these various authorities each contradicting and destroying the other. Today the Hôtel-de-Ville appropriates five loads of cloth which have been dispatched by the Government, and the district of Saint-Gervais opposes the decision of the Hôtel-de-Ville. Tomorrow Versailles intercepts grain destined for Paris, while Paris threatens, if it is not restored, to march on Versailles. I omit the incidents that are ridiculous:[3] anarchy in its essence is both tragic and grotesque, and, in this universal breaking up of things, the capital, like the kingdom, resembles a bear-garden when it does not resemble a Babel.

But behind all these discordant authorities the real sovereign, who is the mob, is very soon apparent. On the 15th of July it undertakes the demolition of the Bastille of its own accord, and this popular act is sanctioned; for it is necessary that appearances should be kept up; even to give orders after the blow is dealt, and to follow when it is impossible to lead.[4] A short time after this the collection of the *octroi* at the barriers is ordered to be resumed; forty armed individuals, however, present themselves in their district and say, that if guards are placed at the *octroi* stations, "they will resist force with force, and even make use of their cannon." On the false rumour that arms are concealed in the Abbey of Montmartre, the abbess, Madame de Montmorency, is accused of treachery, and twenty thousand persons invade the monastery.—The commander of the National Guard and the mayor are constantly expecting a riot; they hardly dare absent themselves a day to attend the King's *fête* at Versailles. As soon as the multitude can assemble in the streets, an explosion is imminent. "On rainy days," says Bailly, "I was quite at my ease."—It is under this constant pressure that the Government is carried on; and the

3. Such as domiciliary visits and arrests apparently made by lunatics. ("Archives de la Préfecture de Police de Paris.")—And Montjoie, ch. lxx. p. 67. Expedition of the National Guard against imaginary brigands who are cutting down the crops at Montmorency and the volley fired in the air.—Conquest of Ile-Adam and Chantilly.

4. Bailly, ii. 46, 95, 232, 287, 296.

elect of the people, the most esteemed magistrates, those who are in best repute, are at the mercy of the throng who clamour at their doors. In the district of St. Roch,[5] after many useless refusals, the General Assembly, notwithstanding all the reproaches of its conscience and the resistance of its reason, is obliged to open letters addressed to Monsieur, to the Duke of Orleans, and to the Ministers of War, of Foreign Affairs, and of the Marine. In the committee on subsistences, M. Serreau, who is indispensable and who is confirmed by a public proclamation, is denounced, threatened, and constrained to leave Paris. M. de la Salle, one of the strongest patriots among the nobles, is on the point of being murdered for having signed an order for the transport of gunpowder;[6] the multitude, in pursuit of him, attach a rope to the nearest street-lamp, ransack the Hôtel-de-Ville, force every door, mount into the belfry, and seek for the traitor even under the carpet of the bureau and between the legs of the electors, and are only stayed in their course by the arrival of the National Guard.

The people not only sentence but they execute, and, as is always the case, blindly. At Saint-Denis, Chatel, the mayor's lieutenant, whose duty it is to distribute flour, had reduced the price of bread at his own expense: on the 3rd of August his house is forced open at two o'clock in the morning, and he takes refuge in a steeple; the mob follow him, cut his throat and drag his head along the streets.—Not only do the people execute, but they pardon—and with equal discernment. On the 11th of August, at Versailles, as a parricide is about to be broken on the wheel, the crowd demand his release, fly at the executioner, and set the man free.[7] Veritably this is sovereign

5. "Archives de la Préfecture de Police," *procès-verbal* of the section of Butte des Moulins, October 5, 1789.

6. Bailly, ii. 224.—Dussaulx, 418, 202, 257, 174, 158. The powder transported was called *poudre de traite* (transport); the people understood it as *poudre de traître* (traitor). M. de la Salle was near being killed through the addition of an *r*. It is he who had taken command of the National Guard on the 13th of July.

7. Floquet, vii. 54. There is the same scene at Granville, in Normandy, on

power like that of the oriental sovereign who arbitrarily awards life or death! A woman who protests against this scandalous pardon is seized and comes near being hung; for the new monarch considers as a crime whatever is offensive to his new majesty. Again, he receives public and humble homage. The Prime Minister, on imploring the pardon of M. de Bezenval at the Hôtel-de-Ville, in the presence of the electors and of the public, has said in set terms: "It is before the most unknown, the obscurest citizen of Paris that I prostrate myself, at whose feet I kneel." A few days before this, at Saint-Germain-en-Laye, and at Poissy, the deputies of the National Assembly not only kneel down in words, but actually, and for a long time, on the pavement in the street, and stretch forth their hands, weeping, to save two lives of which only one is granted to them.—Behold the monarch by these brilliant signs! Already do the young, who are eager imitators of all actions that are in fashion, ape them in miniature; during the month which follows the murder of Berthier and Foulon, Bailly is informed that the *gamins* in the streets are parading about with the heads of two cats stuck on the ends of two poles.[8]

II

A pitiable monarch, whose recognised sovereignty leaves him more miserable than he was before! Bread is always scarce, and before the baker's doors the row of waiting people does not diminish. In vain Bailly passes his nights with the committee on supplies; they are always in a state of terrible anxiety. Every morning for two months there is only one or two days' supply of flour, and often, in the evening, there is not enough for the following morning.[9] The life

---

the 16th of October. A woman had assassinated her husband, while a soldier who was her lover is her accomplice; the woman was about to be hung and the man broken on the wheel, when the populace shout, "The nation has the right of pardon," overset the scaffold, and save the two assassins.

8. Bailly, ii. 274 (August 17th).

9. Bailly, ii. 83, 202, 230, 235, 283, 299.

of the capital depends on a convoy which is ten, fifteen, twenty leagues off, and which may never arrive: one convoy of twenty carts is pillaged on the 18th of July, on the Rouen road; another, on the 4th of August, in the vicinity of Louviers. Were it not for Salis' Swiss regiment, which, from the 14th of July to the end of September, marches day and night as an escort, not a boat-load of grain would reach Paris from Rouen.[10]—The commissaries charged with making purchases or with supervising the expeditions are in danger of their lives. Those who are sent to Provins are seized, and a column of four hundred men with cannon has to be dispatched to deliver them. The one who is sent to Rouen learns that he will be hung if he dares to enter the place. At Mantes a mob surrounds his cabriolet, the people regarding whoever comes there for the purpose of carrying away grain as a public pest; he escapes with difficulty out of a back door and returns on foot to Paris.—From the very beginning, according to a universal rule, the fear of a short supply helps to augment the famine. Every one lays in a stock for several days; on one occasion sixteen loaves of four pounds each are found in an old woman's garret. The bakings, consequently, which are estimated according to the quantity needed for a single day, become inadequate, and the last of those who wait at the bakers' shops for bread return home empty-handed.—On the other hand the appropriations made by the city and the State to diminish the price of bread simply serve to lengthen the rows of those who wait for it; the countrymen flock in thither, and return home loaded to their villages. At Saint-Denis, bread having been reduced to two sous the pound, none is left for the inhabitants. To this constant anxiety add that of a slack season. Not only is there no certainty of there being bread at the bakers' during the coming week, but many know that they will not have money in the coming week with which to buy bread. Now that security has disappeared and the rights of property are shaken, work is wanting. The rich, deprived of their feudal dues, and, in addition thereto of their rents, have reduced their expenditure; many of them,

10. *Mercure de France*, the number for September 26th. De Goncourt p. 111.

threatened by the committee of investigation, exposed to domiciliary visits, and liable to be informed against by their servants, have emigrated. In the month of September M. Necker laments the delivery of six thousand passports in fifteen days to the wealthiest inhabitants. In the month of October ladies of high rank, refugees in Rome, send word that their domestics should be discharged and their daughters placed in convents. Before the end of 1789 there are so many fugitives in Switzerland that a house, it is said, brings in more rent than it is worth as capital. With this first emigration, which is that of the chief spendthrifts—Count d'Artois, Prince de Conté, Duc de Bourbon, and so many others—the opulent foreigners have left, and, at the head of them, the Duchesse de l'Infantado, who spent 800,000 livres a year. There are only three Englishmen in Paris.

It was a city of luxury, the European hot-house of costly and refined pleasures: the glass once broken, the amateurs leave and the delicate plants perish; there is no employment now for the innumerable hands which cultivated them. Fortunate are they who at the relief works obtain a miserable sum by handling a pick-axe! "I saw," says Bailly, "mercers, jewellers, and merchants implore the favour of being employed at twenty sous the day." Enumerate, if you can, in one or two recognised callings, the hands which are doing nothing:[11] 1,200 hair-dressers keep about 6,000 journeymen; 2,000 others follow the same calling in private houses; 6,000 lackeys do but little else than this work. The body of tailors is composed of 2,800 masters, who have under them 5,000 workmen. "Add to these the number privately employed—the refugees in privileged places like the abbeys of Saint-Germain and Saint-Marcel, the vast enclosure of the Temple, that of Saint-John the Lateran, and the Faubourg Saint-Antoine, and you will find at least 12,000 persons cutting, fitting, and sewing." How many in these two groups are now idle! How many others are walking the streets, such as upholsterers, lace-makers, embroiderers, fan-makers, gilders, carriage-makers, binders, engravers, and all the other producers of Parisian nick-nacks! For

11. Mercier, "Tableau de Paris," i. 58; x. 151.

those who are still at work how many days are lost at the doors of bakers' shops and in patrolling as National Guards! Gatherings are formed in spite of the prohibitions of the Hôtel-de-Ville,[12] and the crowd openly discuss their miserable condition: 3,000 journeymen-tailors near the Colonnade, as many journeymen-shoemakers in the Place Louis XV., the journeymen-hair-dressers in the Champs-Elysées, 4,000 domestics without places on the approaches to the Louvre—and their propositions are on a level with their intelligence. Servants demand the expulsion from Paris of the Savoyards who enter into competition with them. Journeymen-tailors demand that a day's wages be fixed at forty sous, and that the old-clothes dealers shall not be allowed to make new ones. The journeymen-shoemakers declare that those who make shoes below the fixed price shall be driven out of the kingdom. Each of these irritated and agitated crowds contains the germ of an outbreak—and, in truth, these germs are found on every pavement in Paris: at the relief works, which at Montmartre collect 17,000 paupers; in the Market, where the bakers want to "lantern" the flour commissioners, and at the doors of the bakers, of whom two, on the 14th of September and on the 5th of October, are conducted to the street-lamp and barely escape with their lives.—In this suffering, mendicant crowd, enterprising men become more numerous every day: they consist of deserters, and from every regiment; they reach Paris in bands, often 250 in one day. There, "caressed and fed to the top of their bent,"[13] having received from the National Assembly 50 livres each, maintained by the King in the enjoyment of their advance-money, regaled by the

12. De Ferrières, i. 178.—Roux and Buchez, ii. 311, 316.—Bailly, ii. 104, 174, 207, 246, 257, 282.

13. *Mercure de France,* September 5th, 1789. Horace Walpole's Letters, September 5, 1789.—M. de Lafayette, "Mémoires," i. 272. During the week following the 14th of July, 6,000 soldiers deserted and went over to the people, besides 400 and 500 Swiss Guards and six battalions of the French Guards, who remain without officers and do as they please. Vagabonds from the neighbouring villages flock in, and there are more than "30,000 foreigners and vagrants" in Paris.

districts, of which one alone incurs a debt of 14,000 livres for wine and sausages furnished to them, "they accustom themselves to greater expense," to greater license, and are followed by their companions. "During the night of the 31st of July the French Guards on duty at Versailles abandon the custody of the King and betake themselves to Paris, without their officers, but with their arms and baggage," that "they may take part in the cheer which the city of Paris extends to their regiment." At the beginning of September, 16,000 deserters of this stamp are counted.[14] Now, among those who commit murder these are in the first rank; and this is not surprising when we take the least account of their antecedents, education, and habits. It was a soldier of the "Royal Croat" who tore out the heart of Berthier. They were three soldiers of the regiment of Provence who forced the house of Chatel at Saint-Denis, and dragged his head through the streets. It is Swiss soldiers who, at Passy, knock down the commissioners of police with their guns. Their headquarters are at the Palais-Royal, amongst women whose instruments they are, and amongst agitators from whom they receive the word of command. Henceforth, all depends on this word, and we have only to contemplate the new popular leaders to know what it will be.

III

Administrators and members of district assemblies, agitators of barracks, coffee-houses, clubs, and public thoroughfares, writers of pamphlets, penny-a-liners are multiplying as fast as buzzing insects are hatched on a sultry night. After the 14th of July thousands of places have presented themselves to unrestrained ambitions; "attorneys, notaries' clerks, artists, merchants, shopmen, comedians, and especially advocates;[15] each wants to be either an officer, a director,

14. Bailly, ii. 282. The crowd of deserters was so great that Lafayette was obliged to place a guard at the barriers to keep them from entering the city. "Without this precaution the whole army would have come in."

15. De Ferrières, i. 103.—De Lavalette, i. 39.—Bailly, i. 53 (on the lawyers). "It may be said that the success of the Revolution is due to this class." Marmontel, ii. 243. "Since the first elections of Paris, in 1789, I remarked," he says,

a councillor, or a minister of the new reign; while the journals, which are established by dozens,[16] form a permanent tribune, where orators come to court the people to their personal advantage." Philosophy, fallen into such hands, seems to parody itself, and nothing equals its emptiness, unless it be its mischievousness and success. Lawyers, in the sixty assembly districts, roll out the high-sounding dogmas of the revolutionary catechism. This or that one, passing from the question of a party wall to the constitution of empires, becomes the improvised legislator, so much the more inexhaustible and the more applauded as his flow of words, showered upon his hearers, proves to them that every capacity and every right are naturally and legit-

---

"this species of restless intriguing men, contending with each other to be heard, impatient to make themselves prominent. . . . It is well known what interest this body (the lawyers) had to change Reform into Revolution, the Monarchy into a Republic; the object was to organize for itself a perpetual aristocracy."—Roux and Buchez, ii. 358 (article by C. Desmoulins). "In the districts everybody exhausts his lungs and his time in trying to be president, vice-president, secretary, or vice-secretary."

16. Eugène Hatin, "Histoire de la Presse," vol. v.—*Le Patriote français,* by Brissot, July 28, 1789.—*L'Ami du Peuple,* by Marat, September 12, 1789.—*Annales patriotiques et littéraires,* by Carra and Mercier, October 5, 1789.—*Les Révolutions de Paris,* chief editor Loustalot, July 17, 1789.—*Le Tribun du Peuple,* letters by Fauchet (middle of 1789).—*Révolutions de France et de Brabant,* by C. Desmoulins, November 28, 1789; his *France libre* (I believe of the month of August, and his *Discours de la Lanterne,* of the month of September). The *Moniteur* does not make its appearance until November 24, 1789. In the seventy numbers which follow, up to February 3, 1790, the debates of the Assembly were afterwards written out, amplified, and put in a dramatic form. All numbers anterior to February 3, 1790, are the result of a compilation executed in the year iv. The narrative part during the first six months of the Revolution is of no value. The report of the sittings of the Assembly is more exact, but should be revised sitting by sitting and discourse by discourse for a detailed history of the National Assembly. The principal authorities which are really contemporary are, *Le Mercure de France, Le Journal de Paris, Le Point du Jour,* by Barrère, the *Courrier de Versailles,* by Gorsas, the *Courrier de Provence,* by Mirabeau, the *Journal des Débats et Décrets,* the official reports of the National Assembly, the *Bulletin de l'Assemblée Nationale,* by Marat, besides the newspapers above cited for the period following the 14th of July, and the speeches, which are printed separately.

imately theirs. "When that man opened his mouth," says a cool-blooded witness, "we were sure of being inundated with quotations and maxims, often apropos of lanterns, or of the stall of a herb-dealer. His stentorian voice made the vaults ring; and after he had spoken for two hours, and his breath was completely exhausted, the admiring and enthusiastic shouts which greeted him amounted almost to phrensy. Thus the orator fancied himself a Mirabeau, while the spectators imagined themselves the Constituent Assembly, deciding the fate of France." The journals and pamphlets are written in the same style. Every brain is filled with the fumes of conceit and of big words; the leader of the crowd is he who raves the most, and he guides the wild enthusiasm which he increases.

Let us consider the most popular of these chiefs; they are the green or the dry fruit of literature, and of the bar. The newspaper is the shop which every morning offers them for sale, and if they suit the overexcited public it is simply owing to their acid or bitter flavour. Their empty, unpractised minds are wholly void of political conceptions; they have no capacity or practical experience. Desmoulins is twenty-nine years of age, Loustalot twenty-seven, and their intellectual ballast consists of college reminiscences, souvenirs of the law schools, and the common-places picked up in the houses of Raynal and his associates. As to Brissot and Marat, who are ostentatious humanitarians, their knowledge of France and of foreign countries consists in what they have seen through the dormer windows of their garrets, and through utopian spectacles. To minds of this class, empty or led astray, the *Contrat-Social* could not fail to be a gospel; for it reduces political science to a strict application of an elementary axiom which relieves them of all study, and hands society over to the caprice of the people, or, in other words, delivers it into their own hands.—Hence they demolish all that remains of social institutions, and push on equalisation until everything is brought down to a dead level. "With my principles," writes Desmoulins,[17] "is associated the satisfaction of putting myself where I

17. C. Desmoulins, letters of September 20th and of subsequent dates. (He

belong, of showing my strength to those who have despised me, of lowering to my level all whom fortune has placed above me: my motto is that of all honest people—No superiors!" Thus, under the great name of Liberty, each vain spirit seeks its revenge and finds its nourishment. What is sweeter and more natural than to justify passion by theory, to be factious in the belief that this is patriotism, and to cloak the interests of ambition with the interests of humanity?

Let us picture to ourselves these directors of public opinion as we find them three months before this: Desmoulins, a briefless barrister, living in furnished lodgings with petty debts, and on a few louis extracted from his relations. Loustalot, still more unknown, was admitted the previous year to the Parliament of Bordeaux, and has landed at Paris in search of a career. Danton, another second-rate lawyer, coming out of a hovel in Champagne, borrowed the money to pay his expenses, while his stinted household is kept up only by means of a louis which is given to him weekly by his father-in-law, who is a coffee-house keeper. Brissot, a strolling Bohemian, formerly employé of literary pirates, has roamed over the world for fifteen years, without bringing back with him either from England or America anything but a coat out at elbows and false ideas; and, finally, Marat—a writer that has been hissed, an abortive scholar and philosopher, a misrepresenter of his own experiences, caught by the natural philosopher Charles in the act of committing a scientific fraud, and fallen from the top of his inordinate ambition to the subordinate post of doctor in the stables of the Comte d'Artois. At the present time, Danton, President of the Cordeliers, can arrest any one he pleases in his district, and his violent gestures and thundering voice secure to him, till something better turns up, the government of his section of the city. A word of Marat's has just caused Major Belzunce at Caen to be assassinated. Desmoulins announces, with a smile of triumph, that "a large section of the capital regards him as

---

quotes a passage from Lucan in the sense indicated.)—Brissot, "Mémoires," *passim.*—Biography of Danton by Robinet. (See the testimony of Madame Roland and of Rousselin de Saint-Albin.)

one among the principal authors of the Revolution, and that many even go so far as to say that he is *the* author of it." Is it to be supposed that, borne so high by such a sudden jerk of fortune, they wish to put on the drag and again descend? and is it not clear that they will aid with all their might the revolt which hoists them towards the loftiest summits? Moreover the brain reels at a height like this; suddenly launched in the air and feeling as if everything was tottering around them, they utter exclamations of indignation and terror, they see plots on all sides, imagine invisible cords pulling in an opposite direction, and they call upon the people to cut them. With the full weight of their inexperience, incapacity, and improvidence, of their fears, credulity, and dogmatic obstinacy, they urge on popular attacks, and their newspaper articles or discourses are all summed up in the following phrases: "Fellow-citizens, you, the people of the lower class, you who listen to me, you have enemies in the Court and the aristocracy. The Hôtel-de-Ville and the National Assembly are your servants. Seize your enemies with a strong hand, and hang them, and let your servants know that they must quicken their steps!"

Desmoulins styles himself "Solicitor-General of the Lantern,"[18] and if he at all regrets the murders of Foulon and Berthier, it is because this too expeditious judgment has allowed the proofs of conspiracy to perish, thereby saving a number of traitors: he himself mentions twenty of them haphazard, and little does he care whether he makes mistakes. "We are in the dark, and it is well that faithful dogs should bark, even at all who pass by, so that there may be no fear of robbers."

From this time forth Marat[19] denounces the King, the ministers,

18. "Discours de la Lanterne." See the epigraph of the engraving.

19. Roux and Buchez, iii. 55; article of Marat, October 1st. "Sweep all the suspected men out of the Hôtel-de-Ville. . . . Reduce the deputies of the communes to fifty; do not let them remain in office more than a month or six weeks, and compel them to transact business only in public." And ii. 412, another article by Marat.—*Ibid.* iii. 21. An article by Loustalot.—C. Desmoulins, "Discours de la Lanterne," *passim.*—Bailly, ii. 326.

the administration, the bench, the bar, the financial system, and the academies, all as "suspicious"; at all events the people only suffer on their account. "The Government is monopolizing grain, so as to force us to buy bread which poisons us for its weight in gold." The Government, again, through a new conspiracy is about to blockade Paris, so as to starve it with greater ease. Utterances of this kind, at such a time, are firebrands thrown upon fear and hunger to kindle the flames of rage and cruelty. To this frightened and fasting crowd the agitators and newspaper writers continue to repeat that it must act, and act alongside of the authorities, and, if need be, against them. In other words, We will do as we please; we are the sole legitimate masters; "*in a well-constituted government, the people as a body are the real sovereign:* our delegates are appointed only to execute our orders; what right has the clay to rebel against the potter?"

On the strength of such principles, the tumultuous club which occupies the Palais-Royal substitutes itself for the Assembly at Versailles. Has it not all the titles for this office? The Palais-Royal "saved the nation" on the 12th and 13th of July. The Palais-Royal, "through its spokesmen and pamphlets," has made everybody and even the soldiers "philosophers." It is the house of patriotism, "the rendezvous of the select among the patriotic," whether provincials or Parisians, of all who possess the right of suffrage, and who cannot or will not exercise it in their own district. "It saves time to come to the Palais-Royal. There is no need there of appealing to the President for the right to speak, or to wait one's time for a couple of hours. The orator proposes his motion, and, if it finds supporters, mounts a chair. If he is applauded, it is put into proper shape. If he is hissed, he goes away. This was the way of the Romans." Behold the veritable National Assembly! It is superior to the other semi-feudal affair, encumbered with "six hundred deputies of the clergy and nobility," who are so many intruders and who "should be sent out into the galleries."—Hence the pure Assembly rules the impure Assembly, and "the Café Foy lays claim to the government of France."

IV

On the 13th of July, the harlequin who led the insurrection at Rouen having been arrested, "it is openly proposed at the Palais-Royal to go in a body and demand his release."[20] On the 1st of August, Thouret, whom the moderate party of the Assembly have just made President, is obliged to resign; the Palais-Royal threatens to send a band and murder him along with those who voted for him, and lists of proscriptions, in which several of the deputies are inscribed, begin to be circulated.—From this time forth, on all great questions—the abolition of the feudal system, the suppression of tithes, a declaration of the rights of man, the dispute about the Chambers, the King's power of veto[21]—the pressure from without inclines the balance: in this way the Declaration of Rights, which is rejected in secret session by twenty-eight bureaus out of thirty, is forced through by the tribunes in a public sitting and passed by a majority.—Just as before the 14th of July, and to a still greater extent, two kinds of compulsion influence the votes, and it is always the ruling faction which employs both its hands to throttle its opponents. On the one hand this faction takes post on the galleries in knots composed nearly always of the same persons, "five or six hundred permanent actors," who yell according to understood signals and at the word of command.[22]

20. Mounier, "Des causes qui ont empêché les Français d'être libre," i. 59.—Lally-Tollendal, second letter, 104.—Bailly, ii. 203.

21. De Bouillé, 207.—Lally-Tollendal, *ibid.*, 141, 146.—Mounier, *ibid.*, 41, 60.

22. *Mercure de France,* October 2, 1790 (article of Mallet-Dupan: "I saw it"). Criminal proceedings at the Châtelet on the events of October 5th and 6th. Deposition of M. Feydel, a deputy, No. 178.—De Montlosier, i. 259.—Desmoulins (*La Lanterne*). "Some members of the communes are gradually won over by pensions, by plans for making a fortune, and by caresses. Happily, the incorruptible galleries are always on the side of the patriots. *They represent the tribunes of the people seated on a bench in attendance on the deliberations of the Senate* (in Rome) *and who had the veto.* They represent the capital, and, fortunately, *it is under the batteries of the capital that the constitution is being framed.*" (C. Desmoulins, who is a *naif* politician, always lets the cat out of the bag.)

Many of these are French Guards, in citizen's dress, and who relieve each other: previously they have asked of their favourite deputy "at what hour they must come, whether all goes on well, and whether he is satisfied with those fools of parsons (*calotins*) and the aristocrats." Others consist of low women under the command of Théroigne de Méricourt, a virago courtesan, who assigns them their positions and gives them the signal for hooting or for applause. Publicly and in full session, on the occasion of the debate on the veto, "the deputies are applauded or insulted by the galleries according as they utter the word 'suspensive,' or the word 'indefinite.'" "Threats," (says one of them) "circulated; I heard them on all sides around me." These threats are repeated on going out: "Valets dismissed by their masters, deserters, and women in rags," threaten the "lantern" to the refractory, "and thrust their fists in their faces. In the hall itself, and much more accurately than before the 14th of July, their names are taken down, and the lists, handed over to the populace," travel to the Palais-Royal, from where they are dispatched in correspondence and in newspapers to the provinces.[23]—Thus we see the second means of compulsion; each deputy is answerable for his vote, at Paris, with his own life, and, in the province, with those of his family. Members of the former Third-Estate avow that they abandon the idea of two Chambers, because "they are not disposed to get their wives' and children's throats cut." On the 30th of August, Saint-Hurugue, the most noisy of the Palais-Royal barkers, marches off to Versailles, at the head of 1,500 men, to complete the conversion of the Assembly. This garden club indeed, from the heights of its great learning, integrity, and immaculate reputation, decides that "the ignorant, corrupt, and doubtful deputies must be got rid of." That they are such cannot be questioned, because they defend the royal sanction; there are over 600 and more, 120 being

23. "Procédure du Châtelet," *ibid.* Deposition of M. Malouet (No. 111). "I received every day, as well as MM. Lally and Mounier, anonymous letters and lists of proscriptions on which we were inscribed. These letters announced a prompt and violent death to every deputy that advocated the authority of the King."

deputies of the commons, who must be expelled to begin with, and then must be brought to judgment.[24] In the meantime they are informed, as well as the Bishop of Langres, President of the National Assembly, that "15,000 men are ready to *light up* their chateaux and in particular yours, sir." To avoid all mistake, the secretaries of the Assembly are informed in writing that "2,000 letters" will be sent into the provinces to denounce to the people the conduct of the malignant deputies: "Your houses are held as a surety for your opinions: keep this in mind, and save yourselves!" At last, on the morning of the 1st of August, five deputations from the Palais-Royal, one of them led by Loustalot, march in turn to the Hôtel-de-Ville, insisting that the drums should be beaten and the citizens be called together for the purpose of changing the deputies, or their instructions, and of ordering the National Assembly to suspend its discussion on the veto until the districts and provinces could give expression to their will: the people, in effect, alone being sovereign, and alone competent, always has the right to dismiss or instruct anew its servants, the deputies. On the following day, August 2nd, to make matters plainer, new delegates from the same Palais-Royal suit gestures to words; they place two fingers on their throats, on being introduced before the representatives of the commune, as a hint that, if the latter do not obey, they will be hung.

After this it is vain for the National Assembly to make any show of indignation, to declare that it despises threats, and to protest its independence; the impression is already produced. "More than 300 members of the communes," says Mounier, "had decided to support the absolute veto." At the end of ten days most of these had gone over, several of them through attachment to the King, because they were afraid of "a general uprising," and "were not willing to jeopardise the lives of the royal family." But concessions like these only provoke fresh extortions. The politicians of the street now know by experience the effect of brutal violence on legal authority. Embold-

24. Roux and Buchez, i. 368, 376.—Bailly, ii. 326, 341.—Mounier, *ibid.*, 62, 75.

ened by success and by impunity, they reckon up their strength and the weakness of the latter. One blow more, and they are undisputed masters. Besides, the issue is already apparent to clear-sighted men. When the agitators of the public thoroughfares, and the porters at the street-corners, convinced of their superior wisdom, impose decrees by the strength of their lungs, of their fists, and of their pikes, at that moment experience, knowledge, good sense, cool-blood, genius, and judgment, disappear from human affairs, and things revert back to chaos. Mirabeau, in favour of the veto for life, saw the crowd imploring him with tears in their eyes to change his opinion: "Monsieur le Comte, if the King obtains this veto, what will be the use of a National Assembly? We shall all be slaves!"[25] Outbursts of this description are not to be resisted, and all is lost. Already, near the end of September, the remark applies which Mirabeau makes to the Comte de la Marck: "Yes, all is lost; the King and Queen will be swept away, and you will see the populace trampling on their lifeless bodies." Eight days after this, on the 5th and 6th of October, it breaks out against both King and Queen, against the National Assembly and the Government, against all government present and to come; the violent party which rules in Paris obtains possession of the chiefs of France to hold them under strict surveillance, and to justify its intermittent outrages by one permanent outrage.

V

Two distinct currents again combine in one torrent to hurry the crowd onward to a common end. On the one hand are the cravings of the stomach, and women excited by the famine: "Now that bread cannot be had in Paris, let us go to Versailles and demand it there; once we have the King, Queen, and Dauphin in the midst of us, they will be obliged to feed us"; we will bring back "the Baker, the Bakeress, and the Baker's boy." On the other hand, there is fanaticism, and men who are pushed on by the lust of dominion. "Now

25. Etienne Dumont, 145.—Correspondence between Comte de Mirabeau and Comte de la Marck.

that our chiefs yonder disobey us, let us go and make them obey us forthwith; the King is quibbling over the Constitution and the Rights of Man—let him give them his sanction; his guards refuse to wear our cockade—let them accept it; they want to carry him off to Metz—let him come to Paris; here, under our eyes and in our hands, he, and the lame Assembly too, will march straight on, and quickly, whether they like it or not, and always on the right road."—Under this confluence of ideas the expedition is arranged.[26] Ten days before this, it is publicly alluded to at Versailles. On the 4th of October, at Paris, a woman proposes it at the Palais-Royal; Danton roars at the Cordeliers; Marat, "alone, makes as much noise as the four trumpets on the Day of Judgment." Loustalot writes that "a second revolutionary paroxysm is necessary." "The day passes," says Desmoulins, "in holding councils at the Palais-Royal, and in the Faubourg Saint-Antoine, on the ends of the bridges, and on the quays . . . in pulling off the cockades of but one colour. . . . These are torn off and trampled under foot with threats of the lantern, in case of fresh offence; a soldier who is trying to refasten his, changes his mind on seeing a hundred sticks raised against him."[27] These are the pre-

26. "Procédure criminelle du Châtelet," Deposition 148.—Roux and Buchez, iii. 67, 65. (Narrative of Desmoulins, article of Loustalot.) *Mercure de France,* number for September 5, 1789. "Sunday evening, August 30, at the Palais-Royal, the expulsion of several deputies of every class was demanded, and especially some of those from Dauphiny. . . . They spoke of bringing the King to Paris as well as the Dauphin. All virtuous citizens, every incorruptible patriot, was exhorted to set out immediately for Versailles."

27. These acts of violence were not reprisals; nothing of the kind took place at the banquet of the body-guards (October 1st). "Amidst the general joy," says an eye-witness, "I heard no insults against the National Assembly, nor against the popular party, nor against anybody. The only cries were '*Vive le Roi! Vive la Reine!* We will defend them to the death!'" (Madame de Larochejacquelein, p. 40. *Ibid.* Madame Campan, another eye-witness.) It appears to be certain, however, that the younger members of the National Guard at Versailles turned their cockades so as to be like other people, and it is also probable that some of the ladies distributed white cockades. The rest is a story made up before and after the event to justify the insurrection. Cf. Leroi, "Histoire de Versailles," ii. 20–107. *Ibid.* p. 141. "As to that proscription of the national cockade, all

monitory symptoms of a crisis; a huge ulcer has formed in this feverish, suffering body, and it is about to break.

But, as is usually the case, it is a purulent concentration of the most poisonous passions and the foulest motives. The vilest of men and women were engaged in it. Money was freely distributed. Was it done by intriguing subalterns who, playing upon the aspirations of the Duke of Orleans, extracted millions from him under the pretext of making him lieutenant-general of the kingdom? Or is it due to the fanatics who, from the end of April, clubbed together to debauch the soldiery, and stir up a body of ruffians for the purpose of levelling and destroying everything around them?[28] There are always Machiavellis of the highways and of houses of ill-fame ready to excite the foul and the vile of both sexes. On the first day that the Flemish regiment goes into garrison at Versailles an attempt is made to corrupt it with money and women. Sixty abandoned women are sent from Paris for this purpose, while the French Guards come and treat their new comrades. The latter have been regaled at the Palais-Royal, while three of them, at Versailles, exclaim, showing some crown pieces of six livres, "What a pleasure it is to go to Paris! one always comes back with money!" In this way, resistance is overcome beforehand. As to the attack, women are to be the advanced guard, because the soldiers will scruple to fire at them; their ranks, however, will be reinforced by a number of men disguised as women. On looking closely at them they are easily recognised, notwithstanding their rouge, by their badly-shaven beards, and by their voices and gait.[29] No difficulty has been found in obtaining men and women

---

witnesses deny it." The originator of the calumny is Gorsas, editor of the *Courrier de Versailles.*

28. "Procédure Criminelle du Châtelet." Depositions 88, 110, 120, 126, 127, 140, 146, 148.—Marmontel, "Mémoires," a conversation with Champfort, in May, 1789.—Morellet, "Mémoires," i. 398. (According to the evidence of Garat, Champfort gave all his savings, 3,000 livres, to defray the expenses of manoeuvres of this description.)—Malouet (ii. 2) knew four of the deputies "who took direct part in this transaction."

29. "Procédure Criminelle du Châtelet." 1st. On the Flemish soldiers. Depo-

among the prostitutes of the Palais-Royal and the military deserters who serve them as bullies. It is probable that the former lent their lovers the cast-off dresses they had to spare. At night all will meet again at the common rendezvous, on the benches of the National Assembly, where they are quite as much at home as in their own houses.[30]—In any event, the first band which marches out is of this stamp, displaying the finery and the gaiety of the profession; "most of them young, dressed in white, with powdered hair and a sprightly air"; many of them "laughing, singing, and drinking," as they would do at setting out for a picnic in the country. Three or four of them are known by name—one brandishing a sword, and another, the notorious Théroigne. Madeleine Chabry Louison, who is selected to address the King, is a pretty grisette who sells flowers, and something else doubtless, at the Palais-Royal. Some appear to belong to the first rank in their calling, and to have tact and the manners of society—suppose, for instance, that Champfort and Laclos sent their mistresses. To these must be added washerwomen, beggars, barefooted women, and fishwomen, enlisted for several days before and paid accordingly. This is the first nucleus, and it keeps on growing; for, by compulsion or consent, the troop incorporates into it, as it passes along, all the women it encounters—seamstresses, portresses, housekeepers, and even respectable females, whose dwellings are entered with threats of cutting off their hair if they do not fall in. To these must be added vagrants, street-rovers, ruffians, and robbers—the lees of Paris, which accumulate and come to the surface every time agitation occurs: they are to be found already at the first hour, behind the troop of women at the Hôtel-de-Ville. Others are

---

sitions 17, 20, 24, 35, 87, 89, 98.—2nd. On the men disguised as women. Depositions 5, 10, 14, 44, 49, 59, 60, 110, 120, 139, 145, 146, 148. The prosecutor designates six of them to be seized.—3rd. On the condition of the women of the expedition. Depositions 35, 83, 91, 98, 146, and 24.—4th. On the money distributed. Depositions 49, 56, 71, 82, 110, 126.

30. "Procédure Criminelle du Châtelet." Deposition 61. "During the night scenes, not very decent, occurred among these people, which the witness thought it useless to relate."

to follow during the evening and in the night. Others are waiting at Versailles. Many, both at Paris and Versailles, are under pay: one, in a dirty whitish vest, chinks gold and silver coin in his hand.—Such is the foul scum which, both in front and in the rear, rolls along with the popular tide; whatever is done to stem the torrent, it widens out and will leave its mark at every stage of its overflow.

The first troop, consisting of four or five hundred women, begin operations by forcing the guard of the Hôtel-de-Ville, which is unwilling to make use of its bayonets. They spread through the rooms and try to burn all the written documents they can find, declaring that there has been nothing but scribbling since the Revolution began.[31] A crowd of men follow after them, bursting open doors, and pillaging the magazine of arms. Two hundred thousand francs in Treasury notes are stolen or disappear; several of the ruffians set fire to the building, while others hang an abbé. The abbé is cut down, and the fire extinguished only just in time: such are the interludes of the popular drama. In the meantime, the crowd of women increases on the Place de Grève, always with the same unceasing cry, "Bread!" and "To Versailles!" One of the conquerors of the Bastille, the usher Maillard, offers himself as a leader. He is accepted, and taps his drum; on leaving Paris, he has seven or eight thousand women with him, and, in addition, some hundreds of men; by dint of remonstrances, he succeeds in maintaining some kind of order amongst this rabble as far as Versailles.—But it is a rabble notwithstanding, and consequently so much brute force, at once anarchical and imperious. On the one hand, each, and the worst among them, does what he pleases—which will be quite evident this very evening. On the other hand, its ponderous mass crushes all authority and overrides all rules and regulations—which is at once apparent on reaching Versailles. Admitted into the Assembly, at first in small

31. "Procédure Criminelle du Châtelet." Depositions 35, 44, 81.—Roux and Buchez, iii. 120. (*Procès-verbal* of the Commune, October 5th.) *Journal de Paris*, October 12th. A few days after, M. Pic, clerk of the prosecutor, brought "a package of 100,000 francs which he had saved from the enemies' hands," and another package of notes was found thrown, in the hubbub, into a receipt-box.

numbers, the women crowd against the door, push in with a rush, fill the galleries, then the hall, the men along with them, armed with clubs, halberds, and pikes, all pell-mell, side by side with the deputies, taking possession of their benches, voting along with them, and gathering about the President, who, surrounded, threatened, and insulted, finally abandons the position, while his chair is taken by a woman.[32] A fishwoman commands in a gallery, and about a hundred women around her shout or keep silence at her bidding, while she interrupts and abuses the deputies: "Who is that spouter? Silence that babbler; he does not know what he is talking about. The question is how to get bread. Let papa Mirabeau speak—we want to hear him." A decree on subsistences having been passed, the leaders demand something in addition; they must be allowed to enter all places where they suspect any monopolizing to be going on, and the price of "bread must be fixed at six sous the four pounds, and meat at six sous per pound." "You must not think that we are children to be played with. We are ready to strike. Do as you are bidden."—All their political injunctions emanate from this central idea. "Send back the Flemish regiment—it is a thousand men more to feed, and they take bread out of our mouths." "Punish the aristocrats, who hinder the bakers from baking." "Down with the skull-cap—the priests are the cause of our trouble!" "Monsieur Mounier, why did you advocate that villainous veto? Beware of the lantern!" Under this pressure, a deputation of the Assembly, with the President at its head, sets out on foot, in the mud, through the rain, and watched by a howling escort of women and men armed with pikes: after five hours of waiting and entreaty, it wrings from the King, besides the decree on subsistences, about which there was no difficulty, the acceptance, pure and simple, of the Declaration of Rights, and his sanction to the constitutional articles.—Such is the independence of the King and the Assembly.[33] Thus are the new principles of justice

32. "Procédure Criminelle du Châtelet." Depositions 61, 77, 81, 148, 154.—Dumont, 181.—Mounier, "Exposé justificatif," *passim*.

33. "Procédure Criminelle du Châtelet." Deposition 168. The witness sees

established, the grand outlines of the Constitution, the abstract axioms of political truth under the dictation of a crowd which extorts not only blindly, but which is half-conscious of its blindness. "Monsieur le Président," some among the women say to Mounier, who returns with the Royal sanction, "will it be of any real use to us? will it give poor folks bread in Paris?"

Meanwhile, the scum has been bubbling up around the chateau; and the abandoned women subsidised in Paris are pursuing their calling.[34] They slip through into the lines of the regiment drawn up on the square, in spite of the sentinels. Théroigne, in an Amazonian red vest, distributes money among them. "Side with us," some say to the men; "we shall soon beat the King's Guards, strip off their fine coats and sell them." Others lie sprawling on the ground, alluring the soldiers, and make such offers as to lead one of them to exclaim, "We are going to have a jolly time of it!" Before the day is over, the regiment is seduced; the women have, according to their own idea, acted for a good motive. When a political idea finds its way into such heads, instead of ennobling them, it becomes degraded there; its only effect is to let loose vices which a remnant of modesty still keeps in subjection, and full play is given to luxurious or ferocious instincts under cover of the public good.—The passions, moreover, become intensified through their mutual interaction; crowds, clamour, disorder, longings, and fasting, end in a state of phrensy, from which nothing can issue but dizzy madness and rage.—This phrensy began to show itself on the way. Already, on setting out, a woman had exclaimed, "We shall bring back the Queen's head on the end of a pike!"[35] On reaching the Sèvres bridge others added, "Let us cut her throat, and make cockades of her entrails!" Rain is falling; they are cold, tired, and hungry, and get

---

on leaving the King's apartment "several women dressed as fish-dealers, one of whom, with a pretty face, has a paper in her hand, and who exclaims as she holds it up, 'Heh! we forced him to sign.' "

34. "Procédure Criminelle du Châtelet." Depositions 89, 91, 98. "Promising all, even raising their petticoats before them."

35. "Procédure Criminelle du Châtelet." Depositions 9, 20, 24, 30, 49, 61, 82, 115, 149, 155.

nothing to eat but a bit of bread, distributed at a late hour, and with difficulty, on the Place d'Armes. One of the bands cuts up a slaughtered horse, roasts it, and consumes it half raw, after the manner of savages. It is not surprising that, under the names of patriotism and "justice," savage ideas spring up in their minds against "members of the National Assembly who are not with the principles of the people," against "the Bishop of Langres, Mounier, and the rest." One man in a ragged old red coat declares that "he must have the head of the Abbé Maury to play nine-pins with." But it is especially against the Queen, who is a woman, and in sight, that the feminine imagination is the most aroused. "She alone is the cause of the evils we endure . . . she must be killed, and quartered."—Night advances; there are acts of violence, and violence engenders violence. "How glad I should be," says one man, "if I could only lay my hand on that she-devil, and strike off her head on the first curbstone!" Towards morning, some cry out, "Where is that cursed cat? We must eat her heart out. . . . We'll take off her head, cut her heart out, and fry her liver!"—With the first murders the appetite for blood has been awakened; the women from Paris say that "they have brought tubs to carry away the stumps of the Royal Guards," and at these words others clap their hands. Some of the riff-raff of the crowd examine the rope of the lantern in the court of the National Assembly, and judging it not to be sufficiently strong, are desirous of supplying its place with another "to hang the Archbishop of Paris, Maury, and d'Espréménil."—This murderous, carnivorous rage penetrates even among those whose duty it is to maintain order, one of the National Guard being heard to say that "the body-guards must be killed to the last man, and their hearts torn out for a breakfast."

Finally, towards midnight, the National Guard of Paris arrives; but it only adds one insurrection to another, for it has likewise mutinied against its chiefs.[36] "If M. de Lafayette is not disposed to accompany us," says one of the grenadiers, "we will take an old

36. "Procédure Criminelle du Châtelet." Depositions 7, 30, 35, 40.—Cf. Lafayette, "Mémoires," and Madame Campan, "Mémoires."

grenadier for our commander." Having come to this decision, they go after the general at the Hôtel-de-Ville, while delegates of six of the companies make known their orders to him. "General, we do not believe that you are a traitor, but we think that the Government is betraying us. . . . The committee on subsistences is deceiving us, and must be removed. We want to go to Versailles to exterminate the body-guard and the Flemish regiment who have trampled on the national cockade. If the King of France is too feeble to wear his crown, let him take it off; we will crown his son and things will go better." In vain Lafayette refuses, and harangues them on the Place de Grève; in vain he resists for hours, now addressing them and now imposing silence. Armed bands, coming from the Faubourgs Saint-Antoine and Saint-Marceau, swell the crowd; they take aim at him; others prepare the lantern. He then dismounts and endeavours to return to the Hôtel-de-Ville, but his grenadiers bar the way: "*Morbleu,* General, you will stay with us; you will not abandon us!" Being their chief it is pretty plain that he must follow them; which is also the sentiment of the representatives of the commune at the Hôtel-de-Ville, who send him their authorisation, and even the order to march, "seeing that it is impossible for him to refuse."

Fifteen thousand men thus reach Versailles, and in front of and along with them thousands of ruffians, protected by the darkness. On this side the National Guard of Versailles, posted around the chateau, together with the people of Versailles, who bar the way against vehicles, have closed up every outlet.[37] The King is prisoner in his own palace, he and his, with his ministers and his court, and with no defence. For, with his usual optimism, he has confided the outer posts of the chateau to Lafayette's soldiers, and, through a humanitarian obstinacy which he is to maintain up to the last,[38] he

37. "Procédure Criminelle du Châtelet." Deposition 24. A number of butcher-boys run after the carriages issuing from the *Petite-Ecurie* shouting out, "Don't let the curs escape!"

38. "Procédure Criminelle du Châtelet." Depositions 101, 91, 89, and 17. M. de Miomandre, a body-guard, mildly says to the ruffians mounting the staircase: "My friends, you love your King, and yet you come to annoy him even in his palace!"

has forbidden his own guards to fire on the crowd, so that they are only there for show. With common right in his favour, the law, and the oath which Lafayette had just obliged his troops to renew, what could he have to fear? What could be more effective with the people than trust in them and prudence? And by playing the sheep one is sure of taming brutes!

From five o'clock in the morning they prowl around the palace-railings. Lafayette, exhausted with fatigue, has taken an hour's repose,[39] which hour suffices for them.[40] A populace armed with pikes and clubs, men and women, surrounds a squad of eighty-eight National Guards, forces them to fire on the King's Guards, bursts open a door, seizes two of the guards, and chops their heads off. The executioner, who is a studio model, with a heavy beard, stretches out his blood-stained hands and glories in the act; and so great is the effect on the National Guard that they move off, through sensibility, in order not to witness such sights: such is the resistance! In the meantime the crowd invade the staircases, beat down and trample on the guards they encounter, and burst open the doors with imprecations against the Queen. The Queen runs off, just in time, in her underclothes; she takes refuge with the King and the rest of the royal family, who have in vain barricaded themselves in the Oeil-de-Boeuf, a door of which is broken in: here they stand, awaiting death, when Lafayette arrives with his grenadiers and saves all that can be saved—their lives, and nothing more. For, from the crowd huddled in the marble court the shout rises, "To Paris with the King!" a command to which the King submits.

Now that the great hostage is in their hands, will they deign to accept the second one? This is doubtful. On the Queen approaching

39. Malonet, II. 2. "I felt no distrust," says Lafayette in 1798; "the people promised to remain quiet."

40. "Procédure Criminelle du Châtelet." Depositions 9, 16, 60, 128, 129, 130, 139, 158, 168, 170. M. du Repaire, body-guard, being sentry at the railing from two o'clock in the morning, a man passes his pike through the bars saying, "You embroidered ———, your turn will come before long." M. du Repaire, "retires within the sentry-box without saying a word to this man, considering the orders that have been issued not to act."

the balcony with her son and daughter, a howl arises of "No children!" She is the one they want to cover with their guns—and this she comprehends. At this moment M. de Lafayette, throwing the shield of his popularity over her, appears on the balcony at her side and respectfully kisses her hand. The reaction is instantaneous in this overexcited crowd. Both man and woman, in such a state of nervous tension, readily jump from one extreme to another, rage bordering on tears. A portress, who is a companion of Maillard's,[41] imagines that she hears Lafayette promise in the Queen's name "to love her people and be as much attached to them as Jesus Christ to his Church." People sob and embrace each other; the grenadiers shift their caps to the heads of the body-guard. The good time has come: "the people have got back their King." Nothing is to be done now but to rejoice; and the cortège moves on. The royal family and a hundred deputies, in carriages, form the centre, and then comes the artillery, with a number of women bestriding the cannons; next, a convoy of flour. Round about are the King's Guards, each with a National Guard mounted behind him; then comes the National Guard of Paris, and after them men with pikes and women on foot, on horseback, in cabs, and on carts; in front is a band bearing two severed heads on the ends of two poles, which halts at a hair-dresser's, in Sèvres, to have these heads powdered and curled;[42] they are made to bow by way of salutation, and are daubed all over with cream; there are jokes and shouts of laughter; the people stop to eat and drink on the road, and oblige the guards to clink glasses with them; they shout and fire salvos of musketry; men and women hold each other's hands and sing and dance about in the mud.—Such is

41. "Procédure Criminelle du Châtelet." Depositions 82, 170.—Madame Campan, ii. 87.—De Lavalette, i. 33.—Cf. Bertrand de Molleville, "Mémoires."

42. Duval, "Souvenirs de la Terreur," i. 78. (Doubtful in almost everything, but here he is an eye-witness. He dined opposite the hair-dresser's, near the railing of the Park of Saint-Cloud.) M. de Lally-Tollendal's second letter to a friend. "At the moment the King entered his capital with two bishops of his council with him in the carriage, the cry was heard, "Off to the lantern with the bishops!"

the new fraternity—a funeral procession of legal and legitimate authorities, a triumph of brutality over intelligence, a murderous and political Mardi gras, a formidable masquerade which, preceded by the insignia of death, drags along with it the heads of France, the King, the ministers, and the deputies, that it may constrain them to rule according to its phrensy, that it may hold them under its pikes until it is pleased to slaughter them.

VI

This time there can be no mistake: the Reign of Terror is fully and firmly established. On this very day the mob stops a vehicle, in which it hopes to find M. de Virieu, and declares, on searching it, that "they are looking for the deputy to massacre him, as well as others of whom they have a list."[43] Two days afterwards the Abbé Grégoire tells the National Assembly that not a day passes without ecclesiastics being insulted in Paris, and pursued with "horrible threats." Malouet is advised that "as soon as guns are distributed among the militia, the first use made of them will be to get rid of those deputies who are bad citizens," and among others of the Abbé Maury. "The moment I stepped out into the streets," writes Mounier, "I was publicly followed. It was a crime to be seen in my company. Wherever I happened to go, along with two or three of my companions, it was stated that an assembly of aristocrats was forming. I had become such an object of terror that they threatened to set fire to a country-house where I had passed twenty-four hours; and, to relieve their minds, a promise had to be given that neither myself nor my friends should be again received into it." In one week five or six hundred deputies have their passports[44] made out, and hold themselves ready to depart. During the following month one hun-

43. De Montlosier, I. 303.—*Moniteur,* sessions of the 8th, 9th, and 10th of October.—Malouet, ii. 9, 10, 20.—Mounier, "Recherches sur les Causes, etc.," and "Addresse aux Dauphinois."

44. De Ferrières, i. 346. (On the 9th of October, 300 members have already taken their passports.) *Mercure de France,* No. of the 17th October. Correspondence of Mirabeau and M. de la Marck, i. 116, 126, 364.

dred and twenty give in their resignations, or no longer appear in the Assembly. Mounier, Lally-Tollendal, the Bishop of Langres, and others besides, quit Paris, and afterwards France. Mallet-Dupan writes, "Opinion now dictates its judgment with steel in hand. *Believe or die* is the anathema which vehement spirits pronounce, and this in the name of Liberty. Moderation has become a crime." After the 7th of October, Mirabeau says to the Comte de la Marck: "If you have any influence with the King or the Queen, persuade them that they and France are lost if the royal family does not leave Paris. I am busy with a plan for getting them away." He prefers everything to the present situation, "even civil war"; for "war, at least, invigorates the soul," while here, "under the dictatorship of demagogues, we are being drowned in slime." Given up to itself, Paris, in three months, "will certainly be a hospital, and, perhaps, a theatre of horrors." Against the rabble and its leaders, it is essential that the King should at once coalesce "with his people," that he should go to Rouen, appeal to the provinces, provide a centre for public opinion, and, if necessary, resort to armed resistance. Malouet, on his side, declares that "the Revolution, since the 5th of October, "horrifies all sensible men, and every party, but that it is complete and irresistible." Thus the three best minds that are associated with the Revolution—those whose verified prophecies attest genius or good sense; the only ones who, for two or three years, and from week to week, have always predicted wisely, and who have employed reason in their demonstrations—these three, Mallet-Dupan, Mirabeau, Malouet, agree in their estimate of the event, and in measuring its consequences. The nation is gliding down a declivity, and no one possesses the means or the force to arrest it. The King cannot do it: "undecided and weak beyond all expression, his character resembles those oiled ivory balls which one vainly strives to keep together."[45] And as for the Assembly, blinded, violated, and impelled on by the theory it proclaims, and by the faction which supports it, each of its grand decrees only renders its fall the more precipitate.

45. Correspondence of Mirabeau and M. de la Marck, i. 175. (The words of Monsieur to M. de la Marck.)

BOOK II

The Constituent Assembly, and the Result of its Labours

CHAPTER I

The Constituent Assembly—Conditions required for the framing of good laws— I. *These conditions absent in the Assembly—Causes of disorder and irrationality—The place of meeting—The large number of deputies—Interference of the galleries—Rules of procedure wanting, defective, or disregarded—The parliamentary leaders—Susceptibility and overexcitement of the Assembly—Its paroxysms of enthusiasm—Its tendency to emotion—It encourages theatrical display—Changes which these displays introduce in its good intentions—* II. *Inadequacy of its information—Its composition—The social standing and culture of the larger number—Their incapacity—Their presumption—Fruitless advice of competent men—Deductive politics—Parties—The minority; its faults—The majority; its dogmatism—* III. *Ascendancy of the revolutionary party—Theory in its favour—The constraint thus imposed on men's minds—Appeal to the passions—Brute force on the side of the party—It profits by this—Oppression of the minority—* IV. *Refusal to supply the ministry—Effects of this mistake—Misconception of the situation—The committee of investigation—Constant alarms—Effects of ignorance and fear on the work of the Constituent Assembly.*

If there is any work in this world difficult to achieve it is a constitution, and especially a complete one. To replace the old forms in which a great nation has lived by others that are different, appropriate, and enduring; to fit a mould of a hundred thousand compartments to the life of twenty-six millions of men; to fashion this so harmoniously, adapt it so well, so closely, with such an exact appreciation of their needs and faculties, that they may enter it of themselves and move about in it without collisions, and that their spontaneous activity should at once find the ease of old routine—is a prodigious undertaking, and probably beyond the powers of the human mind. In any event, the mind requires all its powers to carry the undertaking out, and it cannot too carefully guard itself against all sources of disturbance and error. An Assembly, and especially a Constituent Assembly, requires, outwardly, security and independence, inwardly, silence and order, and generally, calmness, good sense, practical ability, and discipline under competent and recognised leaders. Do we find anything of all this in the Constituent Assembly?

I

We have only to look at it outwardly to have some doubts about it. At Versailles, and then at Paris, the sessions are held in an immense hall capable of seating 2,000 persons, in which the most powerful voice must be strained in order to be heard. It is not calculated for the moderate tone suitable for the discussion of business; the speaker is obliged to shout, and the strain on the voice communicates itself to the mind; the place itself suggests declamation; and this all the more readily because the assemblage consists of 1,200—that is to say, a crowd, and almost a mob. At the present day, in our Assemblies of five or six hundred deputies, there are constant interruptions and an incessant buzz; there is nothing so rare as self-control, and the firm resolve to give an hour's attention to a discourse opposed to the opinions of the hearers. What can be done here to compel silence and patience? Arthur Young on different occasions sees "a hundred members on the floor at once," shouting and gesticulating. "Gentlemen, you are killing me!" says Bailly, one day, sinking with exhaustion. Another president exclaims in despair, "Two hundred speaking at the same time cannot be heard; will you make it impossible then to restore order in the Assembly?" The rumbling, discordant din is farther increased by the uproar of the galleries.[1] "In the British Parliament," writes Mallet-Dupan, "I saw the galleries

1. Arthur Young, June 15, 1789.—Bailly, *passim.*—*Moniteur,* iv. 522 (June 2, 1790).—*Mercure de France* (Feb. 11, 1792).

cleared in a trice because the Duchess of Gordon happened unintentionally to laugh too loud." Here, the thronging crowd of spectators, the newsmongers of the pavement, the delegates from the Palais-Royal, the soldiers disguised as citizens, and the prostitutes who are collected and marshalled, applaud, clap their hands, stamp, and hoot, at their pleasure. This is carried to so great an extent that M. de Montlosier ironically proposes "to give the galleries a voice in the deliberations."[2] Another member wishes to know whether the representatives are so many actors, whom the nation sends there to endure the hisses of the Paris public. Interruptions, in fact, take place as in a theatre, and, frequently, if the members do not give satisfaction, they are forced to desist. On the other hand, the deputies who are popular with this energetic audience, on which they keep an eye, are actors before the footlights: they involuntarily yield to its influence, and exaggerate their ideas as well as their words to be in unison with it. Tumult and violence, under such circumstances, become a matter of course, and the chances of an Assembly acting wisely are diminished by one-half; on becoming a club of agitators, it ceases to be a conclave of legislators.

Let us enter and see how this one proceeds. Thus encumbered, thus surrounded and agitated, does it take at least those precautions without which no assembly of men can govern itself? When several hundred persons assemble together for deliberation, it is evident that some sort of an internal police is necessary; first of all, some code of accepted usages, some written precedents, by which its acts may be prepared and defined, considered in detail, and properly passed. The best of these codes is ready to hand: at the request of Mirabeau, Romilly has sent over the standing orders of the English House of Commons.[3] But, with the presumption of novices, they pay no attention to this code; they imagine it is needless for them; they will

2. *Moniteur,* v. 631 (Sep. 12, 1790), and September 8th (what is said by the Abbé Maury).—Marmontel, book xiii. 237.—Malouet, i. 261.—Bailly, i. 227.

3. Sir Samuel Romilly, "Mémoires," i. 102, 354.—Dumont, 158. (The official rules bear date July 29, 1789.)

borrow nothing from foreigners; they accord no authority to experience, and, not content with rejecting the forms it prescribes, "it is with difficulty they can be made to follow any rule whatever." They leave the field open to the impulsiveness of individuals; any kind of influence, even that of a deputy, even of one elected by themselves, is suspected by them; hence their choice of a new president every fortnight. They submit to no constraint or control, neither to the legal authority of a parliamentary code, nor to the moral authority of parliamentary chiefs. They are without any such; they are not organized in parties; neither on one side nor on the other is a recognised *leader* found who fixes the time, arranges the debate, draws up the motion, assigns parts, and gives the rein to or restrains his supporters. Mirabeau is the only one capable of obtaining this ascendancy; but, on the opening of the Assembly, he is discredited by the notoriety of his vices, and, towards the last, is compromised by his connection with the Court. No other is of sufficient eminence to have any influence; there is too much of average and too little of superior talent. Self-esteem, moreover, is as yet too vigorous an element to allow of concessions. Each of these improvised legislators has come satisfied with his own system, and to break him in under a leader to whom he would intrust his political conscience, to make of him what three out of four of these deputies should be, a voting machine, would require an apprehension of danger, some painful experience, an enforced surrender which he is far from realising.[4] For this reason, save in the violent party, each acts as his own chief, according to the impulse of the moment, and the confusion may be imagined. Strangers who witness it, lift their hands in pity and astonishment. "They *discuss* nothing in their Assembly," writes Gouverneur Morris.[5] "One large half of the time is spent in hallooing and bawling. . . . Each member comes to retail the result of his lucubrations" amidst this noise, taking his turn as inscribed, without reply-

4. Cf. Ferrières, i. 3. His repentance is affecting.

5. Letter to Washington, January 24, 1790.—Dumont, 125.—Garat, letter to Condorcet.

ing to his predecessor, or being replied to by his successor, without ever meeting argument by argument; so that while the firing is interminable, "all their shots are fired in the air." Before this "frightful clatter" can be reported, the papers of the day are obliged to make all sorts of excisions, to prune away "nonsense," and reduce the "inflated and bombastic style." Chatter and clamour, that is the whole substance of most of these famous sittings. "You would hear," says a journalist, "more yells than speeches; the sittings seemed more likely to end in fights than in decrees. . . . Twenty times I said to myself, on leaving, that if anything could arrest and turn the tide of the Revolution, it would be a picture of these meetings traced without caution or adaptation. . . . All my efforts were therefore directed to represent the truth, without rendering it repulsive. Out of what had been merely a row, I concocted a scene. . . . I gave all the sentiments, but not always in the same words. I translated their yells into words, their furious gestures into attitudes, and when I could not inspire esteem, I endeavoured to rouse the emotions."

There is no remedy for this evil; for, besides the absence of discipline, there is an inward and fundamental cause for the disorder. These people are *too susceptible.* They are Frenchmen, and Frenchmen of the eighteenth century; brought up in the amenities of the utmost refinement, accustomed to deferential manners, to constant kind attentions and mutual obligations, so thoroughly imbued with the instinct of good breeding that their conversation seems almost insipid to strangers.[6] All at once they are transported to the thorny soil of politics, exposed to insulting debates, flat contradictions, venomous denunciation, constant detraction, and open invective; engaged in a battle in which every species of weapon peculiar to a parliamentary life is employed, and in which the hardiest veterans

6. Arthur Young, i. 46. "Tame and elegant, uninteresting and polite, the mingled mass of communicated ideas has power neither to offend nor instruct. . . . All vigour of thought seems excluded from expression. . . . Where there is much polish of character there is little argument."—Cabinet des Estampes. See engravings of the day by Moreau, Prieur, Monet, representing the opening of the States-General. All the figures have a graceful, elegant, and genteel air.

are scarcely able to keep cool. Judge of the effect of all this on inexperienced, highly strung nerves, on men of the world accustomed to the accommodations and amiabilities of universal urbanity. They are at once beside themselves.—And all the more so because they never anticipated a battle; but, on the contrary, a festival, a grand and charming idyl, in which everybody, hand in hand, would assemble in tears around the throne and save the country amid mutual embraces. Necker himself arranges, like a theatre, the chamber in which the sessions of the Assembly are to be held.[7] "He was not disposed to regard the Assemblies of the States-General as anything but a peaceful, imposing, solemn, august spectacle, which the people would enjoy"; and when the idyl suddenly changes into a drama, he is so frightened that it seems to him as if a landslip had occurred that threatened, during the night, to break down the framework of the building.—At the time of the meeting of the States-General, everybody is delighted; all imagine that they are about to enter the promised land. During the procession of the 4th of May, "tears of joy," says the Marquis de Ferrières, "filled my eyes. . . . In a state of transport . . . I beheld France supported by Religion" exhorting us all to concord. "The sacred ceremonies, the music, the incense, the priests in their sacrificial robes, that dais, that orb radiant with precious stones. . . . I called to my mind the words of the prophet. . . . My God, my country, and my countrymen, all were one with myself!" This susceptibility repeatedly breaks out in the course of the session, and carries decrees which had never been dreamt of. "Sometimes,"[8] writes the American ambassador, "an orator gets up in the midst of a deliberation, makes a fine discourse on a different subject, and closes with a nice little resolution which is carried with a huzzah. Thus, in considering the plan of a national bank proposed by M. Necker, one of them took it into his head to

7. Marmontel, book xiii. 237.—Malouet, i. 261.—Ferrières, i. 19.

8. Gouverneur Morris, January 24, 1790.—Likewise (De Ferrières, i. 71) the decree on the abolition of nobility was not the order of the day, and was carried by surprise.

move that every member should give his silver buckles—which was agreed to at once, and the honourable mover laid his upon the table, after which the business went on again." Thus, overexcited, they do not know in the morning what they will do in the afternoon, and they are at the mercy of every surprise. When they are seized with these fits of enthusiasm, infatuation spreads over all the benches; prudence gives way, all foresight disappears, and every objection is stifled. During the night of the 4th of August,[9] "nobody is master of himself . . . the Assembly presents the spectacle of an inebriated crowd in a shop of valuable furniture, breaking and smashing at will whatever they can lay their hands on." "That which would have required a year of care and reflection," says a competent foreigner, "was proposed, deliberated over, and passed by general acclamation. The abolition of feudal rights, of titles, of the privileges of the provinces, three articles which alone embraced a whole system of jurisprudence and statesmanship, were decided with ten or twelve other measures in less time than is required in the English Parliament for the first reading of an important bill." "Such are our Frenchmen," says Mirabeau again, "they spend a month in disputes about syllables, and overthrow, in a single night, the whole established system of the Monarchy!"[10] The truth is, they display the nervousness of women, and, from one end of the Revolution to the other, this excitability keeps on increasing.

Not only are they excited, but the pitch of excitement must be maintained, and, like the drunkard who, once stimulated, has recourse again to strong waters, one would say that they carefully try to expel the last remnants of calmness and common sense from their brains. They delight in pompous phrases, in high-sounding rhetoric, in declamatory sentimental strokes of eloquence: this is the style of nearly all their speeches, and so strong is their taste, they are not

9. Ferrières, i. 189.—Dumont, 146.

10. Letter of Mirabeau to Sieyès, June 11, 1790. "Our nation of monkeys with the throats of parrots."—Dumont, 146.—"Sieyès and Mirabeau always entertained a contemptible opinion of the Constituent Assembly."

satisfied with the orations made amongst themselves. Lally and Necker, having made "affecting and sublime" speeches at the Hôtel-de-Ville, the Assembly wish them to be repeated before them:[11] this being the heart of France, it is proper for it to answer to the noble emotions of all Frenchmen. Let this heart throb on, and as strongly as possible, for that is its office, and day by day it receives fresh impulses. Almost all sittings begin with the reading of flattering addresses or of threatening denunciations. The petitioners frequently appear in person, and read their enthusiastic effusions, their imperious advice, their doctrines of dissolution. Today it is Danton, in the name of Paris, with his bull visage and his voice that seems a tocsin of insurrection; tomorrow, the vanquishers of the Bastille, or some other troop, with a band of music which continues playing even into the hall. The meeting is not a conference for business, but a patriotic opera, where the eclogue, the melodrama, and sometimes the masquerade, mingle with the cheers and the clappings of hands.[12]—A serf of the Jura is brought to the bar of the Assembly aged one hundred and twenty years, and one of the members of the cortège, "M. Bourbon de la Crosnière, director of a patriotic school, asks permission to take charge of the august old man, that he may be waited on by the young people of all ranks, and especially by the

11. *Moniteur,* 256, 431 (July 16 and 31, 1789).—*Journal des Débats et Décrets,* i. 105, July 16th. "A member demands that M. de Lally repeats his discourse, which is seconded by the whole Assembly."

12. *Moniteur* (March 11, 1790). "A nun of St. Mandé, brought to the bar of the house, thanks the Assembly for the decree by which the cloisters are opened, and denounces the tricks, intrigues, and even violence exercised in the convents to prevent the execution of the decree."—*Ibid.* March 29, 1790. See the various addresses which are read. "At Lagnon, the mother of a family assembled her ten children, and swore with them and for them to be loyal to the nation and to the King."—*Ibid.* June 5, 1790. "M. Chambroud reads the letter of the collector of customs of Lannion, in Brittany, to a priest, a member of the National Assembly. He implores his influence to secure the acceptance of his civic oath and that of *all his family, ready to wield either the censer, the cart, the scales, the sword, or the pen.*" On reading a number of these addresses the Assembly appears to be a supplement of the *Petites Affiches* (a small advertising journal in Paris).

children of those whose fathers were killed in the attack on the Bastille."[13] Great is the hubbub and excitement. The scene seems to be in imitation of Berquin,[14] with the additional complication of a mercenary consideration.

But small matters are not closely looked into, and the Assembly, under the pressure of the galleries, stoops to shows, such as are held at fairs. Sixty vagabonds who are paid twelve francs a head, in the costumes of Spaniards, Dutchmen, Turks, Arabs, Tripolitans, Persians, Hindoos, Mongols, and Chinese, conducted by the Prussian Anacharsis Clootz, enter, under the title of Ambassadors of the Human Race, to declaim against tyrants, and they are admitted to the honours of the sitting. On this occasion the masquerade is a stroke devised to hasten and extort the abolition of nobility.[15] At other times, there is little or no object in it; its ridiculousness is inexpressible, for the farce is played out as seriously and earnestly as in a village award of prizes. For three days, the children who have taken their first communion before the constitutional bishop have been promenaded through the streets of Paris; at the Jacobin club they recite the nonsense they have committed to memory; and, on the fourth day, admitted to the bar of the Assembly, their spokesman, a poor little thing of twelve years old, repeats the parrot-like tirade. He winds up with the accustomed oath, upon which all the others cry out in their piping, shrill voices, "We swear!" As a climax, the President, Treilhard, a sober lawyer, replies to the little *gamins* with perfect gravity in a similar strain, employing metaphors, personifications, and everything else belonging to the stock-in-trade of a pedant on his platform: "You merit a share in the glory of the founders of liberty, prepared as you are to shed your blood in her behalf." Immense applause from the "left" and the galleries, and a

13. *Moniteur,* October 23, 1789.

14. A well-known writer of children's stories.—[Tr.]

15. Ferrières, ii. 65 (June 10, 1790).—De Montlosier, i. 402. "One of these masqueraders came the following day to get his money of the Comte de Billancourt, mistaking him for the Duc de Liancourt. 'Monsieur,' says he, 'I am the man who played the Chaldean yesterday.' "

decree ordering the speeches of both president and children to be printed. The children, probably, would rather have gone out to play; but, willingly or unwillingly, they receive or endure the honours of the sitting.[16]

Such are the tricks of the stage and of the platform by which the managers here move their political puppets. Emotional susceptibility, once recognised as a legitimate force, thus becomes an instrument of intrigue and constraint. The Assembly, having accepted theatrical exhibitions when these were sincere and earnest, is obliged to tolerate them when they become mere sham and buffoonery. At this vast national banquet, over which it meant to preside, and to which, throwing the doors wide open, it invited all France, its first intoxication was due to wine of a noble quality; but it has touched glasses with the populace, and by degrees, under the pressure of its associates, it has descended to adulterated and burning drinks, to a grotesque unwholesome inebriety which is all the more grotesque and unwholesome, because it persists in believing itself to be reason.

II

If reason could only resume its empire during the lucid intervals! But reason must exist before it can govern, and in no French Assembly, except the two following this, have there ever been fewer political intellects. Strictly speaking, with careful search, there could undoubtedly be found in France, in 1789, five or six hundred experienced men, such as the intendants and military commanders of every province; next to these the prelates, administrators of large dioceses, the members of the local "*parlements*," whose courts gave them influence, and who, besides judicial functions, possessed a portion of administrative power; and finally, the principal members of the Provincial Assemblies, all of them influential and sensible people who had exercised control over men and affairs, at once humane, liberal, moderate, and capable of understanding the difficulty, as well as the necessity, of a great reform; indeed, their correspondence, full

16. Roux and Buchez, x. 118 (June 16, 1791).

of facts, stated with precision and judgment, when compared with the doctrinaire rubbish of the Assembly, presents the strongest possible contrast. But most of these lights remain under a bushel; only a few of them get into the Assembly; these burn without illuminating, and are soon extinguished in the tempest. The venerable Machault is not there, nor Malesherbes; there are none of the old ministers or the marshals of France. Not one of the intendants is there, except Malouet—and by the superiority of this man, the most judicious of the Assembly, one can judge the services which his colleagues would have rendered. Out of two hundred and ninety-one members of the clergy,[17] there are indeed forty-eight bishops or archbishops and thirty-five abbots or canons, but, being prelates and with large endowments, they excite the envy of their order, and are generals without any soldiers. We have the same spectacle among the nobles. Most of them, the gentry of the provinces, have been elected in opposition to the grandees of the Court. Moreover, neither the grandees of the Court, devoted to worldly pursuits, nor the gentry of the provinces, confined to private life, are practically familiar with public affairs. A small group among them, twenty-eight magistrates and about thirty superior officials who have held command or have been connected with the administration, probably have some idea of the peril of society; but it is precisely for this reason that they seem to be behind the age and remain without influence. In the Third-Estate, out of five hundred and seventy-seven members, only ten have exercised any important functions, those of intendant, councillor of state, receiver-general, lieutenant of police, director of the mint, and others of the same category. The great majority is composed of unknown lawyers and people occupying inferior positions in the profession, notaries, royal attorneys, register-commissaries, judges and assessors of the *présidial,* bailiffs and lieutenants of the bailiwick, simple practitioners confined from their youth to the narrow circle of an inferior jurisdiction or to a routine

17. See the printed list of deputies, with the indication of their *baillage* or *sénéchaussée,* quality, condition, and profession.

of scribbling, with no escape but philosophical excursions in imaginary space under the guidance of Rousseau and Raynal. There are three hundred and seventy-three of this class, to whom may be added thirty-eight farmers and husbandmen, fifteen physicians, and, among the manufacturers, merchants, and capitalists, some fifty or sixty who are their equals in education and in political capacity. Scarcely one hundred and fifty proprietors are here from the middle class.[18] To these four hundred and fifty deputies, whose condition, education, instruction, and mental range qualified them for being good clerks, prominent men in a commune, honourable fathers of a family, or, at best, provincial academicians, add two hundred and eight curés, their equals; this makes six hundred and fifty out of eleven hundred and eighteen deputies, forming a positive majority, which, again, is augmented by about fifty philosophical nobles, leaving out the weak who follow the current, and the ambitious who range themselves on the strong side. We may divine what a chamber thus made up can do, and those who are familiar with such matters prophesy what it *will* do.[19] "There are some able men in the National Assembly," writes the American minister, "yet the best heads among them would not be injured by experience, and, unfortunately, there are great numbers who, with much imagination, have little knowledge, judgment, or reflection." It would be just as sensible to select eleven hundred notables from an inland province and intrust to them the repair of an old frigate. They would conscientiously break the vessel up, and the frigate they would construct in its place would founder before it left port.

If they would only consult the pilots and professional shipbuilders! There are several of such to be found around them, whom they cannot suspect, for most of them are foreigners, born in free countries, impartial, sympathetic, and, what is more, unanimous.

18. De Bouillé, 75. When the King first saw the list of the deputies, he exclaimed, "What would the nation have said if I had made up my council or the *Notables* in this way?" (Roux and Buchez, iv. 39.)

19. Gouverneur Morris, July 31, 1789.

The Minister of the United States writes, two months before the convocation of the States-General:[20] "I, a republican, and just, as it were, emerged from that Assembly which has formed one of the most republican of republican constitutions—I preach incessantly respect for the prince, attention to the rights of the nobility, and moderation, not only in the object, but also in the pursuit of it." Jefferson, a democrat and radical, expresses himself no differently. At the time of the oath of the Tennis Court, he redoubles his efforts to induce Lafayette and other patriots to make some arrangement with the King to secure freedom of the press, religious liberty, trial by jury, the habeas corpus, and a national legislature—*things which he could certainly be made to adopt*—and then to retire into private life, and let these institutions act upon the condition of the people until they had rendered it capable of further progress, with the assurance that there would be no lack of opportunity for them to obtain still more. "This was all," he continues, "that I thought your countrymen able to bear soberly and usefully." Arthur Young, who studies the moral life of France so conscientiously, and who is so severe in depicting old abuses, cannot comprehend the conduct of the Commons. "To set aside practice for theory . . . in establishing the interests of a great kingdom, in securing freedom to 25,000,000 of people, seems to me the very acme of imprudence, the very quintessence of insanity." Undoubtedly, now that the Assembly is all-powerful, it is to be hoped that it will be reasonable: "I will not allow myself to believe for a moment that the representatives of the people can ever so far forget their duty to the French nation, to humanity, and their own fame, as to suffer any inordinate and impracticable views—any visionary or theoretic systems— . . . to turn aside their exertions from that security which is in their hands, to place on the chance and hazard of public commotion and civil war the invaluable blessings which are certainly in their power. I will not conceive it possible that men who have eternal fame within their

20. Gouverneur Morris, February 25, 1789.—Lafayette, "Mémoires," v. 492. Letter of Jefferson, February 14, 1815.—Arthur Young, June 27 and 29, 1789.

grasp *will place the rich inheritance on the cast of a die, and, losing the venture, be damned among the worst and most profligate adventurers that ever disgraced humanity.*" As their plan becomes more definite the remonstrances become more decided, and all the expert judges point out to them the importance of the wheels which they are wilfully breaking. "As they have[21] hitherto felt severely the authority exercised over them in the name of their princes, every limitation of that authority seems to them desirable. Never having felt the evils of too weak an executive, the disorders to be apprehended from anarchy make as yet no impression. . . . They want an American Constitution,[22] with the exception of a King instead of a President, without reflecting that they have not American citizens to support that Constitution. . . . If they have the good sense to give the nobles, as nobles, some portion of the national power, this free constitution will probably last. But otherwise it will degenerate either into a pure monarchy, or a vast republic, or a democracy. Will the latter last? I doubt it. I am sure that it will not, unless the whole nation is changed." A little later, when they renounce a parliamentary monarchy to put in its place "a royal democracy," it is at once explained to them that such an institution applied to France can produce nothing but anarchy, and finally end in despotism. "Nowhere[23] has liberty proved to be stable without a sacrifice of its excesses, without some barrier to its own omnipotence. . . . Under this miserable government . . . the people, soon weary of storms, and abandoned without legal protection to their seducers or to their oppressors, will shatter the helm, or hand it over to some audacious hand that stands ready to seize it." Events occur from month to month in fulfilment of these predictions, and the predictions grow gloomier and more gloomy. It is a flock of wild birds:[24] "It is very difficult to guess whereabouts the flock will settle when it flies so wild. . . . This unhappy country,

21. Morris, July 1, 1789.
22. July 4, 1789.
23. Mallet-Dupan, *Mercure,* September 26, 1789.
24. Gouverneur Morris, January 24, 1790; November 22, 1790.

bewildered in the pursuit of metaphysical whims, presents to our moral view a mighty ruin. The Assembly, at once master and slave, new in power, wild in theory, raw in practice, engrossing all functions without being able to exercise any, has taken from that fierce, ferocious people every restraint of religion and respect. . . . Such a state of things cannot last. . . . The glorious opportunity is lost, and for this time, at least, *the Revolution has failed.*"

We see, from the replies of Washington, that he is of the same opinion. On the other side of the Channel, Pitt, the ablest practician, and Burke, the ablest theorist, of political liberty, express the same judgment. Pitt, after 1789, declares that the French have overleaped freedom. After 1790, Burke, in a work which is a prophecy as well as a masterpiece, points to military dictation as the termination of the Revolution, "the most completely arbitrary power that has ever appeared on earth."

Nothing is of any effect. With the exception of the small powerless group around Malouet and Mounier, the warnings of Morris, Jefferson, Romilly, Dumont, Mallet-Dupan, Arthur Young, Pitt, and Burke, all of them men who have experience of free institutions, are received with indifference or repelled with disdain. Not only are our new politicians incapable, but they think themselves the contrary, and their incompetence is aggravated by their infatuation. "I often used to say," writes Dumont,[25] "that if a hundred persons were stopped at haphazard in the streets of London, and a hundred in the streets of Paris, and a proposal were made to them to take charge of the Government, ninety-nine would accept it in Paris and ninety-nine would refuse it in London. . . . The Frenchman thinks that all difficulties can be overcome by a little quickness of wit. Mirabeau accepted the post of reporter to the Committee on Mines without having the slightest tincture of knowledge on the subject." In short, most of them enter on politics "like the gentleman who, on being asked if he knew how to play on the harpsichord, replied, 'I cannot tell, I never tried, but I will see.'" "The Assembly had so high an

25. Dumont, 33, 58, 62.

opinion of itself, especially *the left side of it,* that it would willingly have undertaken the framing of the Code of Laws for all nations. . . . Never had so many men been seen together, fancying that they were all legislators, and that they were there to correct all the errors of the past, to remedy all mistakes of the human mind, and ensure the happiness of all ages to come. Doubt had no place in their minds, and infallibility always presided over their contradictory decrees."—This is because they have a theory, and because, according to their notion, this theory renders special knowledge unnecessary. Herein they are thoroughly sincere, and it is of set purpose that they reverse all ordinary modes of procedure. Up to this time a constitution used to be organized or repaired like a ship. Experiments were made from time to time, or a model was taken from vessels in the neighbourhood; the first aim was to make the ship sail; its construction was subordinated to its work; it was fashioned in this or that way according to the materials on hand; a beginning was made by examining these materials, and trying to estimate their rigidity, weight, and strength.—All this is behind the age; the Assembly is too enlightened to follow in a rut. In conformity with the fashion of the time it works by *deduction,* after the method of Rousseau, according to an abstract notion of right, of the State, and of the social compact.[26]

According to this process, by virtue of political geometry alone, the ship is to be ideal, and since it is ideal it is certain that it will sail, and much better than any empirical craft. They carry out their legislative hobbies according to this principle, and it is easy to divine

26. S. Romilly, "Memoirs," i. 102. "It was their constant course first, *décréter le principe,* and leave the drawing up of what they had so resolved (or, as they called it, *la rédaction*) for a subsequent operation. It is astonishing how great an influence it had on their debates and measures."—*Ibid.* i. 354. Letter by Dumont, June 2, 1789. "They prefer their own folly to all the results of British experience. They revolt at the idea of borrowing anything from your government, which is scoffed at here as one of the iniquities of human reason; although they admit that you have two or three good laws; but that you should presume to have a Constitution is not to be sustained."

the nature of their discussions. There are no convincing facts, no pointed arguments; nobody would ever imagine that the speakers were gathered together to conduct real business. Through speech after speech, strings of hollow abstractions are endlessly renewed as in a meeting of students in rhetoric for the purpose of practice, or in a society of old bookworms for their own amusement. On the question of the veto "each orator in turn, armed with his portfolio, reads a dissertation which has no bearing whatever" on the preceding one, which makes "a sort of academical session," a succession of pamphlets[27] fresh every morning for several days. On the question of the Rights of Man fifty-four orators are placed on the list. "I remember," says Dumont, "that long discussion, which lasted for weeks, as a period of mortal ennui—vain disputes over words, a metaphysical jumble, and most tedious babble; the Assembly was turned into a Sorbonne lecture-room," and this while chateaux were burning, while town-halls were being sacked, and courts dared no longer hold assize, while the distribution of wheat was stopped, and while society was in course of dissolution. In the same manner the theologians of the Lower Empire kept up their wrangles about the uncreated light of Mount Tabor while Mahomet II was battering the walls of Constantinople with his cannon.—Ours, of course, are another sort of men, juvenile in feeling, sincere, enthusiastic, even generous, and further, more devoted, laborious, and in some cases endowed with rare talent. But neither zeal, nor labour, nor talent are of any use when not employed in the service of a sound idea; and if in the service of a false one, the greater they are the more mischief they do.

Towards the end of the year 1789, there can be no doubt of this; and the parties now formed reveal the measure of their presumption, improvidence, incapacity, and obstinacy. "This Assembly," writes the American ambassador, "may be divided into three parties: one, called the aristocrats, consists of the high clergy, the parliamentary judges, and such of the nobility as think they ought to form a sepa-

27. Dumont, 138, 151.

rate order." This is the party which offers resistance to follies and errors, but with follies and errors almost equally great. In the beginning "the prelates,[28] instead of conciliating the curés, kept them at a humiliating distance, affecting distinctions, exacting respect," and, in their own chamber, "ranging themselves apart on separate benches." The nobles, on the other hand, the more to alienate the commons, began by charging these with "revolt, treachery, and treason," and by demanding the use of military force against them. Now that the victorious Third-Estate has again overcome them and overwhelms them with numbers, they become still more maladroit, and conduct the defence much less efficiently than the attack. "In the Assembly," says one of them, "they do not listen, but laugh and talk aloud"; they take pains to embitter their adversaries and the galleries by their impertinence. "They leave the chamber when the President puts the question and invite the deputies of their party to follow them, or cry out to them not to take part in the deliberation: through this desertion, the clubbists become the majority, and decree whatever they please." It is in this way that the appointment of judges and bishops is withdrawn from the King and assigned to the people. Again, after the return from Varennes, when the Assembly finding out that the result of its labours is impracticable is disposed to render it less democratic, the whole of the right side will refuse to share in the debates, and, what is worse, will vote with the revolutionists to exclude members of the Constituent from the Legislative Assembly. Thus, not only does it abandon its own cause, but it commits self-destruction, and its desertion ends in suicide.—A second party remains, "the middle party,"[29] which consists of well-intentioned people from every class, sincere partisans of a good government; but, unfortunately, they have acquired their ideas of government from books, and are admirable on paper. But as it happens that the men who live in the world are very different from imaginary men who

28. Marmontel, xii. 265.—Ferrières, i. 48; ii. 50, 58, 126.—Dumont, 74.

29. Gouverneur Morris, January 24, 1790. According to Ferrières this party comprised about three hundred members.

dwell in the heads of philosophers, it is not to be wondered at if the systems taken out of books are fit for nothing but to be upset by another book. Intellects of this stamp are the natural prey of utopians. Lacking the ballast of experience they are carried away by pure logic and serve to enlarge the flock of theorists.—The latter form the third party, which is called the "enragés" (the wild men), and who, at the expiration of six months, find themselves "the most numerous of all." "It is composed," says Morris, "of that class which in America is known by the name of pettifogging lawyers, together with a host of curates and many of those persons who in all revolutions throng to the standard of change because they are not satisfied with their present situation. This last party is in close alliance with the populace, and derives from this circumstance very great authority." All powerful passions are on its side, not merely the irritation of the people tormented by misery and suspicion, not merely the ambition and self-esteem of the bourgeois, in revolt against the ancient régime, but also the inveterate bitterness and fixed ideas of so many suffering minds and so many factious intellects, Protestants, Jansenists, economists, philosophers, men who, like Fréteau, Rabout Saint-Etienne, Volney, Sieyès, are hatching out a long arrear of resentments or hopes, and who only await the opportunity to impose their system with all the intolerance of dogmatism and of faith. To minds of this stamp the past is a dead letter; example is no authority; realities are of no account; they live in their own Utopia. Sieyès, the most important of them all, judges that "the whole English constitution is charlatanism, designed for imposing on the people;"[30] he regards the English "as children in the matter of a constitution," and thinks that he is capable of giving France a much better one. Dumont, who sees the first committees at the houses of Brissot and Clavières, goes away with as much anxiety as "disgust." "It is impossible," he says, "to depict the confusion of ideas, the license of the imagination, the burlesque of popular notions. One would think that they saw before them the world on the

30. Dumont, 33, 58, 62.

day after the creation." They seem to think, indeed, that human society does not exist, and that they are appointed to create it. Just as well might ambassadors "of hostile tribes, and of diverse interests, set themselves to arrange their common lot as if nothing had previously existed." There is no hesitation. They are satisfied that the thing can be easily done, and that, with two or three axioms of political philosophy, the first man that comes may make himself master of it. Overweening conceit of this kind among men of experience would seem ridiculous; in this assembly of novices it is a power. A flock which has lost its way follows those who go in front; they are the most irrational but they are the most confident, and in the Chamber as in the nation it is the breakneck-riders who become its leaders.

III

Two advantages give this party the ascendancy, and these advantages are of such importance that henceforth whoever possesses them is sure of being master.—In the first place the prevailing theory is on the side of the revolutionists, and they alone are determined thoroughly to apply it. This party, therefore, is the only one which is consistent and popular in the face of adversaries who are unpopular and inconsequent. Nearly all of the latter, indeed, defenders of the ancient régime, or partisans of a limited monarchy, are likewise imbued with abstract principles and philosophical speculation. The most refractory nobles have advocated the rights of man in their memorials. Mounier, the principal opponent of the demagogues, was the leader of the commons when they proclaimed themselves to be the National Assembly.[31] That is enough: they have entered the narrow defile which leads to the abyss. They had no idea of it at the first start, but one step leads to another, and, willing or unwilling,

31. De Lavergne, "Les Assemblées Provinciales," 384. Deliberations of the States of Dauphiny, drawn up by Mounier and signed by two hundred gentlemen (July, 1788). "The rights of man are derived from nature alone, and are independent of human conventions."

they march on, or are pushed on. When the abyss comes in sight it is too late; they have been driven there by the logical results of their own concessions; they can do nothing but wax eloquent and indignant; having abandoned their vantage-ground, they find no halting-place remaining.—There is an enormous power in general ideas, especially if they are simple, and appeal to the passions. None are simpler than these, since they are reducible to the axiom which assumes the rights of man, and subordinate to them every institution, old or new. None are better calculated to inflame the sentiments, since the doctrine enlists human pride in its service, and, in the name of justice, consecrates all the demands of independence and domination. Consider three-fourths of the deputies, immature and prejudiced, possessing no information but a few formulas of the current philosophy, with no thread to guide them but pure logic, abandoned to the declamation of lawyers, to the wild utterances of the newspapers, to the promptings of self-esteem, to the hundred thousand tongues which, on all sides, at the bar of the Assembly, at the tribune, in the clubs, in the streets, in their own breasts, repeat unanimously to them, and every day, the same flattery: "You are sovereign and omnipotent. Right is vested in you alone. The King exists only to execute your will. Every order, every corporation, every power, every civil or ecclesiastical association is illegitimate and null the moment you declare it to be so. You may even transform religion. You are the fathers of the country. You have saved France, you will regenerate humanity. The whole world looks on you in admiration; finish your glorious work—forward, always forward." Superior good sense and rooted convictions could alone stand firm against this flood of seductions and solicitations; but vacillating and ordinary men are carried away by it. In the harmony of applause which rises, they do not hear the crash of the ruins they produce. In any case, they stop their ears, and shun the cries of the oppressed; they refuse to admit that their work could possibly bring about evil results; they accept the sophisms and untruths which justify it; they allow the assassinated to be calumniated in order to excuse the assassins; they listen to Merlin de Douay, who, after three or four jacqueries, when pillaging, incendiarism, and murder are going on in all the provinces, has just declared in the name of the Committee on Feudalism[32] that "a law must be presented to the people, the justice of which may enforce silence on the feudatory egotists who, for the past six months, so indecently protest against spoliation; the wisdom of which may restore to a sense of duty the peasant who has been led astray for a moment by his resentment of a long oppression." And when Raynal, the surviving patriarch of the philosophic party, one day, for a wonder, takes the plain truth with him into their tribune, they resent his straightforwardness as an outrage, and excuse it solely on the ground of his imbecility. An omnipotent legislator cannot depreciate himself; like a king he is condemned to self-admiration in his public capacity. "There were not thirty deputies amongst us," says a witness, "who thought differently from Raynal," but "in each other's presence the credit of the Revolution, the perspective of its blessings, was an article of faith which had to be believed in"; and, against their own reason, against their conscience, the moderates, caught in the net of their own acts, join the revolutionists to complete the Revolution.

Had they refused, they would have been compelled; for, to obtain the power, the Assembly has, from the very first, either tolerated or solicited the violence of the streets. But, in accepting insurrectionists for its allies, it makes them masters, and henceforth, in Paris as in the provinces, illegal and brutal force becomes the principal power of the State. "The triumph was accomplished through the people; it was impossible to be severe with them";[33] hence, when insurrections were to be put down, the Assembly had neither the courage nor the force necessary. "They blame for the sake of decency; they frame their deeds by expediency," and in turn justly undergo the pressure which they themselves have sanctioned against others. Only three or four times do the majority, when the insurrection becomes too daring—after the murder of the baker François, the insurrection of

32. "Rapport de Merlin de Douay," February 8, 1790, p. 2. Malouet, ii. 51.
33. Dumont, 133. De Monblosier, i. 355, 361.

the Swiss Guard at Nancy, and the outbreak of the Champ de Mars—feel that they themselves are menaced, vote for and apply martial law, and repel force with force. But, in general, when the despotism of the people is exercised only against the royalist minority, they allow their adversaries to be oppressed, and do not consider themselves affected by the violence which assails the party of the "right": they are enemies, and may be given up to the wild beasts. In accordance with this, the "left" has made its arrangements; its fanaticism has no scruples; it is principle, it is absolute truth that is at stake; this must triumph at any cost. Besides, can there be any hesitation in having recourse to the people in the people's own cause? A little compulsion will help along the good cause, and hence the siege of the Assembly is continually renewed. This was the practice already at Versailles before the 6th of October, while now, at Paris, it is kept up more actively and with less disguise.

At the beginning of the year 1790,[34] the band under pay comprises seven hundred and fifty effective men, most of them deserters or soldiers drummed out of their regiments, who are at first paid five francs and then forty sous a day. It is their business to make or support motions in the coffee-houses and in the streets, to mix with the spectators at the sittings of the sections, with the groups at the Palais-Royal, and especially in the galleries of the National Assembly, where they are to hoot or applaud at a given signal. Their leader

34. Bertrand de Molleville, ii. 221 (according to a police report).—Schmidt, "Tableaux de la Révolution," i. 215. (Report of the agent Dutard, May 13, 1793.)—Lacretelle, "Dix Ans d'Épreuves," p. 35. "It was about midnight when we went out in the rain, sleet, and snow, in the piercing cold, to the church of the Feuillants, to secure places for the galleries of the Assembly, which we were not to occupy till noon on the following day. We were obliged, moreover, to contend for them with a crowd animated by passions, and even by interests, very different from our own. We were not long in perceiving that a considerable part of the galleries was under pay, and that the scenes of cruelty which gave pain to us were joy to them. I cannot express the horror I felt on hearing those women, since called *tricoteuses,* take a delight in the already homicidal doctrines of Robespierre, enjoying his sharp voice and feasting their eyes on his ugly face, the living type of envy." (The first months of 1790.)

is a Chevalier de Saint-Louis, to whom they swear obedience, and who receives his orders from the Committee of Jacobins. His first lieutenant at the Assembly is a M. Saule, "a stout, small, stunted old fellow, formerly an upholsterer, then a charlatan hawker of four-penny boxes of grease—made from the fat of those that had been hung—for the cure of diseases of the kidneys, and all his life a sot . . . who, by means of a tolerably shrill voice, which was always well moistened, has acquired some reputation in the galleries of the Assembly." In fact, he has forged admission tickets; he has been turned out; he has been obliged to resume "the box of ointment, and travel for one or two months in the provinces with a man of letters for his companion." But on his return, "through the protection of a groom of the Court, he obtained a piece of ground for a coffee-house against the wall of the Tuileries garden, almost alongside of the National Assembly," and now it is at home in his coffee-shop behind his counter that the hirelings of the galleries "come to him to know what they must say, and to be told the order of the day in regard to applause." Besides this, he is there himself; "it is he who for three years is to regulate public sentiment in the galleries confided to his care, and, for his useful and satisfactory services, the Constituent Assembly will award him a recompense," to which the Legislative Assembly will add "a pension of six hundred livres, besides a lodging in an apartment of the Feuillants."

We can divine how men of this stamp, thus compensated, do their work. From the top of the galleries[35] they drown the demands of the "right" by the force of their lungs; this or that decree, as, for instance, the abolition of titles of nobility, is carried, "not by shouts, but by terrific howls."[36] On the arrival of the news of the sacking

35. *Moniteur,* v. 237 (July 26, 1790); v. 594 (September 8, 1790); v. 631 (September 12, 1790); vi. 310 (October 6, 1790). (Letter of the Abbé Peretti.)

36. De Ferrières, ii. 75.—*Moniteur,* vi. 373, 374 (September 6, 1790).—M. de Virieu. "Those who insult certain members and hinder the freedom of debate by hooting or applause must be silenced. Is it the three hundred spectators who are to be our judges, or the nation?" M. Chasset, President: "Monsieur the Deputy voting, I call you to order. You speak of hindrances to a free vote; there has never been anything of the kind in this Assembly."

of the Hôtel de Castries by the populace, they applaud. On the question coming up as to the decision whether the Catholic faith shall be dominant, "they shout out that the aristocrats must all be hung, and then things will go on well." Their outrages not only remain unpunished, but are encouraged: this or that noble who complains of their hooting is called to order, while their interference and vociferations, their insults and their menaces, are from this time introduced as one of the regular wheels of legislative operations. Their pressure is still worse outside the Chamber.[37] The Assembly is obliged several times to double its guard. On the 27th of September, 1790, there are 40,000 men around the building to extort the dismissal of the Ministers, and "motions for assassination" are made under the windows. On the 4th of January, 1791, whilst on a call of the house the ecclesiastical deputies pass in turn to the tribune, to take or refuse the oath to the civil constitution of the clergy, a furious clamour ascends in the Tuileries, and even penetrates into the Chamber. "To the lantern with all those who refuse!" On the 27th of September, 1790, M. Dupont, economist, having spoken against the *assignats,* is surrounded on leaving the Chamber and hooted at, hustled, pushed against the basin of the Tuileries, into which he was being thrown when the guard rescued him. On the 21st of June, 1790, M. de Cazalès just misses "being torn to pieces by the people."[38] Deputies of the "right" are threatened over and over again by gestures in the streets and in the coffee-houses; effigies of them with ropes about the neck are publicly displayed. The Abbé Maury is several times on the point of being hung: he saves himself once by presenting a pistol. Another time the Vicomte de Mirabeau is

37. Sauzay, i. 140. Letter of M. Lompré, liberal deputy, to M. Séguin, *chanoine* (towards the 2nd of November, 1789). "The service becomes more difficult every day; we have become objects of popular fury, and, when no other resource was left to us to avoid the tempest but to get rid of the endowments of the clergy, we yielded to force. It had become a pressing necessity, and I should have been sorry to have had you still here, exposed to the outrages and violence with which I have been repeatedly threatened."

38. *Mercure de France,* Nos. of January 15, 1791; October 2, 1790; May 14, 1791. Roux and Buchez, v. 343 (April 13, 1790); vii. 76 (September 2, 1790); x. 225 (June 21, 1791).—De Montlosier, i. 357.—*Moniteur,* iv. 427.

obliged to draw his sword. M. de Clermont-Tonnerre, having voted against the annexation of the Comtat to France, is assailed with chairs and clubs in the Palais-Royal, pursued into a porter's room and from thence to his dwelling; the howling crowd break in the doors, and are only repelled with great difficulty. It is impossible for the members of the "right" to assemble together; they are "stoned" in the church of the Capucins, then in the Salon Français in the Rue Royale, and then, to crown the whole, an ordinance of the new judges shuts up their hall, and punishes them for the violence which they have to suffer.[39] In short, they are at the mercy of the mob. The most moderate, the most liberal, and the most manly both in heart and head, Malouet, declares that "in going to the Assembly he rarely forgot to carry his pistols with him."[40] "For two years," he says, "after the King's flight, we never enjoyed one moment of freedom and security." "On going into a slaughter-house," writes another deputy, "you see some animals at the entrance which still have a short time to live, until the hour comes to despatch them. Such was the impression which the assemblage of nobles, bishops, and parliamentarians[41] on the right side made on my mind every time I entered the Assembly, the executioners of the left side permitting them to breathe a little longer." They are insulted and outraged even upon their benches; "placed between peril within and peril without, between the hostility of the galleries"[42] and that of the howlers at the entrance, "between personal insults and the abbey of Saint-Germain, between shouts of laughter celebrating the burning of their chateaux and the clamours which, thirty times in a quarter of an hour, cry down their opinions," they are given over and denounced "to the ten thousand Cerberuses" of the journals and of the streets, who pursue them with their yells and "cover them with

39. Archives of the Police, exposed by the Committee of the district of Saint-Roch. Judgment of the Police Tribunal, May 15, 1790.

40. Malouet, ii. 68.—De Montlosier, ii. 217, 257 (Speech of M. Lavie, September 18, 1791).

41. *I.e.,* members of the old local *parlements.*

42. *Mercure,* October 1, 1791. (Article by Mallet-Dupan.)

their slaver." Any expedient is good enough for putting down their opposition, and, at the end of the session, in full Assembly, they are threatened with "a recommendation to the departments," which means the excitement of riots and of the permanent jacquerie of the provinces against them in their own houses.—Parliamentary strategy of this sort, employed uninterruptedly for twenty-nine months, finally produces its effect. Many of the weak are gained over;[43] even on characters of firm temper fear has a hold; he who would march under fire with head erect shuddered at the idea of being dragged in the gutter by the rabble; the brutality of the populace always exercises a material ascendancy over finely strung nerves. On the 12th of July, 1791,[44] the call of the house decreed against the absentees proves that one hundred and thirty-two deputies no longer appear in their places. Eleven days before, among those who still attend, two hundred and seventy announced that they would take no further part in the proceedings. Thus, before the completion of the Constitution, the whole of the opposition, more than four hundred members, over one-third of the Assembly, is reduced to flight or to silence. By dint of oppression, the revolutionary party has got rid of all resistance, while the violence which gave to it ascendancy in the streets, now gives to it equal ascendancy within the walls of Parliament.

IV

Generally in an omnipotent assembly, when a party takes the lead and forms a majority, it furnishes the Ministry; and this fact suffices to give, or to bring back to it, some glimpse of common sense. For its leaders, with the Government in their own hands, become responsible for it, and when they propose or pass a law, they are obliged to anticipate its effect. Rarely will a Secretary of War or of the Navy adopt a military code which goes to establish permanent

43. Malouet, ii. 66. "Those only who were not intimidated by insults or threats, nor by actual blows could come forward as opponents."

44. Roux and Buchez, x. 432, 465.

disobedience in the army or in the navy. Rarely will a Secretary of the Treasury propose an expenditure for which there is not a sufficient revenue, or a system of taxation that provides no returns. Placed where full information can be procured, daily advised of every detail, surrounded by skilful counsellors and expert clerks, the chiefs of the majority, who thus become heads of the administration, immediately drop theory for practice; and the fumes of political speculation must be pretty dense in their minds if they exclude the multiplied rays of light which experience constantly sheds upon them. Let the stubbornest of theorists take his stand at the helm of a ship, and, whatever be the obstinacy of his principles or his prejudices, he will never, unless he is blind or led by the blind, persist in steering always to the right or always to the left. Just so after the flight to Varennes, when the Assembly, in full possession of the executive power, directly controls the Ministry, it comes to recognise for itself that its constitutional machine will not work, except in the way of destruction; and it is the principal revolutionists, Barnave, Duport, the Lameths, Chapelier, and Thouret,[45] who undertake to make alterations in the mechanism so as to lessen its friction. This source of knowledge and judgment, however, to which they are induced to resort for a moment, in spite of themselves and too late, has been closed up by themselves from the very beginning. On the 6th of November, 1789, in deference to principle and in dread of corruption, the Assembly had declared that none of its members should hold ministerial office. We see it in consequence deprived of all the instruction which comes from direct contact with affairs, surrendered without any counterpoise to the seductions of theory, reduced by its own decision to a mere academy of legislation.

Nay, still worse, through another effect of the same error, it condemns itself by its own act to constant fits of panic. For, having allowed the power which it was not willing to assume to slip into lukewarm or suspicious hands, it is always uneasy, and all its decrees bear an uniform stamp, not only of the wilful ignorance to which it

45. Malouet, ii. 153.

shuts itself up, but also of the exaggerated or chimerical fears in which its life is passed.—Imagine a ship conveying a company of lawyers, literary men, and other passengers, who, supported by a mutinous and poorly fed crew, take full command, but refuse to select one of their own number for a pilot or for the officer of the watch. The former captain continues to nominate them; through very shame, and because he is a good sort of man, his title is left to him, and he is retained for the transmission of orders. If these orders are absurd, so much the worse for him; if he resists them, a fresh mutiny forces him to yield; and even when they cannot be executed, he has to answer for their being carried out. In the meantime, in a room between decks, far away from the helm and the compass, our club of amateurs discuss the equilibrium of floating bodies, decree a new system of navigation, have the ballast thrown overboard, crowd on all sail, and are astonished to find that the ship heels over on its side. The officer of the watch and the pilot must, evidently, have managed the manoeuvre badly. They are accordingly dismissed and others put in their place, while the ship heels over farther yet and begins to leak in every joint. Enough: it is the fault of the captain and the old staff of officers. They are not well-disposed; for a beautiful system of navigation like this ought to work well; and if it fails to do so, it is because some one interferes with it. It is positively certain that some of those people belonging to the former régime must be traitors, who would rather have the ship go down than submit; they are public enemies and monsters. They must be seized, disarmed, put under surveillance, and punished.—Such is the reasoning of the Assembly. Evidently, to reassure it, a message from the Minister of the Interior chosen by the Assembly, to the lieutenant of police whom he had appointed, to come to his hotel every morning, would be all that was necessary. But it is deprived of this simple resource by its own act, and has no other expedient than to appoint a committee of investigation to discover crimes of "treason against the nation."[46] What could be more vague than such

46. Decrees of July 23rd and 28th, 1789.—"Archives Nationales." Papers

a term? What could be more mischievous than such an institution? Renewed every month, deprived of special agents, composed of credulous and inexperienced deputies, this committee, set to perform the work of a Lenoir or a Fouché, makes up for its incapacity by violence, and its proceedings anticipate those of the Jacobin inquisition.[47] Alarmist and suspicious, it encourages accusations, and, for lack of plots to discover, it invents them. Inclinations, in its eyes, stand for actions, and floating projects become accomplished outrages. On the denunciation of a domestic who has listened at a door, on the gossip of a washerwoman who has found a scrap of paper in a dressing-gown, on the false interpretation of a letter, on vague indications which it completes and patches together by the strength of its imagination, it forges a *coup d'état*, makes examinations, domiciliary visits, nocturnal surprises, and arrests;[48] it exaggerates, blackens, and comes in public session to denounce the whole affair to the National Assembly. First comes the plot of the Breton nobles to deliver Brest to the English;[49] then the plot for hiring brigands to destroy the crops; then the plot of the 14th of July to burn Paris; then the plot of Favras to murder Lafayette, Necker, and Bailly; then the plot of Augeard to carry off the King—with others from week to week, not counting those which swarm in the brains of the journalists, and which Desmoulins, Fréron, and Marat reveal with a flourish of trumpets in each of their publications. "All these alarms are cried daily in the streets like cabbages and turnips, the good

---

of the Committee of Investigation, *passim*. Among other affairs see that of Madame de Persan (*Moniteur*, v. 611, sitting of September 9, 1790), and that of Malouet ("Mémoires," ii. 12).

47. Roux and Buchez, iv. 56 (Report of Garan de Coulon); v. 49 (Decision of the Committee of Investigation, December 28, 1789).

48. The arrests of M. de Riolles, M. de Bussy, &c., of Madame de Jumilhac, of two other ladies, one at Bar-le-Duc and the other at Nancy, &c.

49. Sitting of July 28, 1789, the speeches of Duport and Rewbell, &c.—*Mercure*, No. of January 1, 1791 (article by Mallet-Dupan).—Roux and Buchez, v. 146. "Behold five or six successive conspiracies—that of the sacks of flour, that of the sacks of money, &c." (Article by Camille Desmoulins.)

people of Paris inhaling them along with the pestilential vapours of our mud."[50]

Now, in this aspect, as well as in a good many others, the Assembly is the people; satisfied that it is in danger,[51] it makes laws as the former make their insurrections, and protects itself by strokes of legislation as the former protects itself by blows with pikes. Failing to take hold of the motor spring by which it might direct the machine, it distrusts all the old and all the new wheels. The old ones seem to it an obstacle, and, instead of utilising them, it breaks them one by one—parliaments, provincial states, religious orders, the church, the nobles, and royalty. The new ones are suspicious, and instead of harmonizing them, it puts them out of gear in advance—the executive power, administrative powers, judicial powers, the police, the gendarmerie, and the army.[52] Thanks to these precautions

50. "Archives de la Préfecture de Police." Extract from the registers of the deliberations of the Conseil-Général of the district of Saint-Roch, October 10, 1789: *Arrêté:* to request *Messieurs de la Commune* to devote themselves, with all the prudence, activity, and force of which they are capable, to the discovery, exposure, and publication of the horrible plots and infernal treachery which are constantly meditated against the inhabitants of the capital; to denounce to the public the authors, abettors, and adherents of the said plots, whatever their rank may be; to secure their persons and ensure their punishment with all the rigour which outrages of this kind call for." The commandant of the battalion and the district captains come daily to consult with the committee. "While the alarm lasts, the first story of each house is to be lighted with lamps during the night: all citizens of the district are requested to be at home by ten o'clock in the evening at the latest, unless they should be on duty. . . . All citizens are invited to communicate whatever they may learn or discover in relation to the abominable plots which are secretly going on in the capital."

51. Letter of M. de Guillermy, July 31, 1790 ("Actes des Apôtres," v. 56). "During these two nights (July 13th and 14th, 1789) that we remained in session I heard one deputy try to get it believed that an artillery corps had been ordered to point its guns against our hall; another, that it was undermined, and that it was to be blown up; another went so far as to declare that he smelt powder, upon which M. le Comte de Virieu replied that powder had no odour until it was burnt."

52. Dumont, 351. "Each constitutional law was a party triumph."

it is impossible for any of them to be turned against itself; but, also, thanks to these precautions, none of them can perform their functions.

In building, as well as in destroying, the Assembly had two bad counsellors, on the one hand fear, on the other hand theory; and on the ruins of the old machine which it has demolished without discernment, the new machine, which it has constructed without forecast, will work only to its own ruin.

CHAPTER II

Destruction— I. *Two principal vices of the ancient régime—Two principal reforms proposed by the King and the privileged classes—They suffice for actual needs—Impracticable if carried further*— II. *Nature of societies, and the principle of enduring constitutions*— III. *The classes which form a State—Political aptitude of the aristocracy—Its disposition in 1789—Special services which it might have rendered—The principle of the Assembly as to original equality—Rejection of an Upper Chamber—The feudal rights of the aristocracy—How far and why they were worthy of respect—How they should have been transformed—Principle of the Assembly as to original liberty—Distinction established by it in feudal dues; application of its principle—The lacunae of its law—Difficulties of redemption—Actual abolition of all feudal liens—Abolition of titles and territorial names—Growing prejudice against the aristocracy—Its persecutions—The emigration*— IV. *The corporations of a State—Abuse and lukewarmness in 1789 in the ecclesiastical bodies—How the State used its right of overseeing and reforming them—Social usefulness of corporations—The sound part in the monastic institution—Zeal and services of nuns—How ecclesiastical possessions should be employed—Principle of the Assembly as to private communities and mortmain—Disestablishment and disendowment of all corporations—Uncompensated suppression of tithes—Confiscation of ecclesiastical possessions—Effect on the Treasury and on disendowed services—The civil constitution of the clergy—Rights of the Church in relation to the State—Certainty and effects of a conflict—Priests considered as State-functionaries—Principal stipulations of the law—Obligations of the oath—The majority of priests refuse to take it—The majority of believers on their side—Persecution of believers and of priests.*

I

In the structure of the old society there were two fundamental vices which called for two reforms of corresponding importance.[1] In the first place, those who were privileged having ceased to render the services for which the advantages they enjoyed constituted their compensation, their privileges were no longer anything but a gratuitous charge imposed on one portion of the nation for the benefit of the other, and hence the necessity for suppressing them. In the second place, the Government, being absolute, made use of public resources as if they were its own private property, arbitrarily and wastefully; it was therefore necessary to impose upon it some efficacious and regular restraints. To render all citizens equal before taxation, to put the purse of the tax-payers into the hands of their representatives, such was the twofold operation to be carried out in 1789; and the privileged class as well as the King willingly lent themselves to it. Not only, in this respect, were the memorials of nobles and clergy in perfect harmony, but the monarch himself, in his declaration of the 23rd of June, 1789, decreed the two articles. Henceforth, every tax or loan was to obtain the consent of the States-General; this consent was to be renewed at each new meeting of the States; the public estimates were to be annually published, discussed, specified, apportioned, voted on, and verified by the States; there were to be no arbitrary assessments or use of public funds; allowances were to be specially assigned for all separate services, the household of the King included. In each province or district-general, there was to be an elected Provincial Assembly, one-half composed of ecclesiastics and nobles, and the other half of members of the Third-Estate, to apportion general taxes, to manage local affairs, to decree and direct public works, to administer hospitals, prisons, workhouses, and to continue its function, in the interval of the sessions, through an intermediary commission chosen by itself; so that, besides the principal control of the centre, there were to be thirty

1. Cf. "The Ancient Régime," books i. and v.

subordinate controlling powers at the extremities. There was to be no more exemption or distinction in the matter of taxation; the road-tax (*corvée*) was to be abolished, also the right of *franc-fief*[2] imposed on plebeians, the rights of mortmain,[3] subject to indemnity, and internal customs-duties. There was to be a reduction of the captainries, a modification of the salt-tax and of the excise, the transformation of civil justice, too costly for the poor, and of criminal justice, too severe for the humbler classes. Here we have, besides the principal reform, equalization of taxes, the beginning and inducement of the more complete operation which is to strike off the last of the feudal manacles. Moreover, six weeks later, on the 4th of August, the privileged, in an outburst of generosity, come forward of their own accord to cut off or undo the whole of them. This double reform thus encountered no obstacles, and, as Arthur Young reported to his friends, it merely required one vote to have it adopted.[4]

This was enough; for all real necessities were now satisfied. On the one hand, through the abolition of privileges in the matter of taxation, the burden on the peasant and, in general, on the small tax-payer was diminished one-half, and perhaps two-thirds; instead of paying fifty-three francs on one hundred francs of net income, he paid no more than twenty-five or even sixteen;[5] an enormous relief, and one which, with the proposed revisal of the excise and

2. A special tax paid by a plebeian on acquiring real estate.

3. A tax imposed on the inheritance of property.

4. Arthur Young, i. 209, 223. "If the communes steadily refuse what is now held out to them, they put immense and certain benefits to the chance of fortune, to that hazard which may make posterity curse instead of bless their memories as real patriots who had nothing in view but the happiness of their country."

5. According to valuations by the Constituent Assembly, the tax on real property ought to produce 240,000,000 francs, and provide one-fifth of the net revenue of France, estimated at 1,200,000,000. The personal (*mobilière*) tax, which replaced the *capitation,* ought to produce, besides, 60,000,000. Total for direct taxation, 300,000,000, or one-fourth—that is to say, twenty-five per cent. of the net revenue. If the direct taxation had been maintained up to the rate of the ancient régime (190,000,000, according to Necker's report in May, 1789), this impost would only have provided one-sixth of the net revenue, or sixteen per cent.

salt duties, made a complete change in his condition. Add to this the gradual redemption of ecclesiastical and feudal dues, and at the end of twenty years the peasant, already proprietor of a fifth of the soil, was in the way of attaining, without the violent procedure of the Revolution, a degree of independence and well-being which he has only achieved by passing through it. On the other hand, through the annual vote on the taxes, not only were waste and arbitrariness in the employment of the public funds put a stop to, but also the foundations of the parliamentary system of government were laid: whoever holds the purse-strings is, or becomes, master of the rest; henceforth in the maintenance or establishment of any service, the assent of the States was to be necessary. Now, in the three Chambers which the three orders were thenceforward to form, there were two in which the plebeians predominated. Public opinion, moreover, was on their side, while the King, the true constitutional monarch, far from possessing the imperious inflexibility of a despot, did not now possess the initiative of an ordinary person. Thus the preponderance fell to the communes, and they could legally, without any collision, execute, multiply, and complete, with the aid of the prince and through him, all useful reforms.[6] This was enough; for human society, like a living body, is seized with convulsions when it is subjected to operations on too great a scale, and these, although restricted, were probably all that France in 1789 could endure. To equitably reorganize afresh the whole system of direct and indirect taxation; to revise, recast, and transfer to the frontiers the customs-tariffs; to suppress, through negotiations and with indemnity, feudal and ecclesiastical claims, was an operation of the greatest magnitude, and as complex as it was delicate. Things could be satisfactorily arranged only through minute inquiries, verified calculations, prolonged essays, and mutual concessions. In England, in our day, a

6. Dumont, 267. (The words of Mirabeau three months before his death.) "Ah, my friend, how right we were at the start when we wanted to prevent the commons from declaring themselves the National Assembly! That is the source of the evil. They wanted to rule the King, instead of ruling through him."

quarter of a century has been required to bring about a lesser reform, the transformation of tithes and manorial-rights; and time likewise was necessary for our Assemblies to perfect their political education,[7] to get rid of their theories, to learn, by contact with practical business, and in the study of details, the distance which separates speculation from practice; to discover that a new system of institutions works well only through a new system of habits, and that to decree a new system of habits is tantamount to attempting *to build an old house*. Such, however, is the work they undertake. They reject the King's proposals—the limited reforms, the gradual transformations. According to them, it is their right and their duty to remake society from top to bottom. Such is the command of pure reason, which has discovered the Rights of Man and the conditions of the Social Contract.

II

Apply the Social Contract, if you like, but apply it only to those for whom it was drawn up. These consist of human abstractions, men of no age and of no country, pure entities hatched under the divining rod of metaphysics. In reality they are formed by eliminating the differences which distinguish one man from another[8]—a Frenchman from a Papuan, a modern Englishman from a Briton in the time of Caesar—and by retaining only the part which is common to all. The essence thus obtained is a prodigiously meagre one, an infinitely curtailed extract of human nature, that is, in the phraseology of the day, "a being with a desire to be happy and the faculty of reasoning," no more and no less. Millions of individuals, all precisely alike, are fashioned according to this pattern, while, through a second simplification, as extraordinary as the first one, they are all supposed to be free and all equal, without a past, without kindred, without re-

7. Gouverneur Morris, April 29, 1789 (on the principles of the future constitution), "One generation at least will be required to render the public familiar with them."

8. Cf. "The Ancient Régime," book iii.

sponsibility, without traditions, without customs, like so many mathematical units, all separable and all equivalent, and then it is imagined that, assembled together for the first time, these proceed to make their primitive bargain. From the nature they are supposed to possess and the situation in which they are placed, no difficulty is found in deducing their interests, their wills, and the contract between them. But if this contract suits them, it does not follow that it suits others. On the contrary, it follows that it does not suit others; the inconvenience becomes extreme on its being imposed on a living society; the measure of that inconvenience will be the immensity of the distance which divides a hollow abstraction, a philosophical phantom, an empty unsubstantial image from the real and complete man.

In any event an entity, man so reduced and mutilated as to be only the minimum of man, is not now the subject in hand; but, on the contrary, Frenchmen of the year 1789. It is for them alone that the constitution is being made: it is therefore they alone who should be considered; they are manifestly men of a particular species, having their peculiar temperament, their special aptitudes, their own inclinations, their religion, their history, a complete mental and moral organization, hereditary and deeply rooted, bequeathed to them by the primitive race, and to which every great event, each political or literary era for twenty centuries, has brought an accretion, a metamorphosis or convolution. It is like some tree of a unique species whose trunk, thickened by age, preserves in its annual rings and in its knots, branchings, and curvatures, the deposits which its sap has made and the imprint of the innumerable seasons through which it has passed. Philosophic definitions, so vague and trite, applied to such an organism are meaningless labels which teach us nothing. And all the more because extreme diversities and inequalities show themselves on this exceedingly elaborate and complicated background—those of age, education, faith, class, and fortune; and these must be taken into account, for these contribute to the formation of interests, passions, and dispositions. To take only the most important of these, it is clear that, according to the average of human life,[9] one-half of the population is composed of children, and, besides this, one-half of the adults are women. In every twenty inhabitants eighteen are Catholic, of whom sixteen are believers, at least through habit and tradition. Twenty-five out of twenty-six millions of Frenchmen cannot read, one million at the most being able to do so; and in political matters only five or six hundred are competent. As to the condition of each class, its ideas, its sentiments, its kind and degree of culture, we should have to devote a large volume to a mere sketch of them.

There is still another feature and the most important of all. These men who are so different from each other are far from being independent, or from contracting together for the first time. They and their ancestors for eight hundred years form a national body, and it is because they belong to this body that they live, multiply, labour, make acquisitions, become enlightened and civilised, and accumulate the vast heritage of comforts and intelligence which they now enjoy. Each in this community is like the cell of an organized body: undoubtedly the body is only an accumulation of cells, but the cell is born, subsists, develops, and attains its individual ends only by the healthy condition of the whole body. Its chief interest, accordingly, is the prosperity of the whole organism, and the fundamental requirement of all the little fragmentary lives, whether they know it or not, is the conservation of the great total life in which they are comprised as musical notes in a concert. Not only is this a necessity for them, but it is also a duty. Each individual that comes into the world is indebted to the State, and this debt keeps on increasing up to maturity, for it is with the cooperation of the State, under the guardianship of its laws, and protected by the public power, that his ancestors, and after them his parents, have transmitted to him life, property, and education. His faculties, his ideas, his sentiments, his

9. According to Voltaire ("L'Homme aux Quarante Écus"), the average duration of human life was only twenty-three years.

whole moral and physical being, are products to which the community has nearly or remotely contributed, at least as tutor and guardian. By virtue of this the State is his creditor, just as a destitute father is of his able-bodied son; it is entitled to food, to services, and, in all the powers or resources at his disposal it justly lays claim to a certain portion. This he knows and feels; the idea of country is deeply implanted within him, and when occasion calls for it, it will show itself in ardent emotions, prolonged sacrifices, and heroic actions.—Such are veritable Frenchmen, and we at once see how different they are from the simple, indistinguishable, detached monads which the philosophers insist on substituting for them. Their association need not be created, for it already exists; for eight centuries they have had a "common weal" (*la chose publique*). The safety and prosperity of this common weal is at once their interest, their need, their duty, and even their most secret wish. If it is possible to speak here of a contract, their quasi-contract is made and settled for them beforehand. The first article, at all events, is stipulated for, and this overrides all the others. The State is not to be disintegrated. Public powers must, accordingly, exist, and these must be respected. If there are a number of these, they must be so defined and so balanced as to be of mutual assistance, instead of neutralising each other by their opposition. Whatever government is adopted, it must place matters in the hands best qualified to conduct them. The law must not exist for the advantage of the minority, nor for that of the majority, but for the entire community.—In regard to this first article no one must derogate from it—neither the minority nor the majority, neither the Assembly elected by the nation, nor the nation itself, even if unanimous. It has no right arbitrarily to dispose of the common weal, to put it in peril according to its caprice, to subordinate it to the application of a theory or to the interests of a single class, even if this class is the most numerous. For, that which is the common weal does not belong to it, but to the whole community, past, present, and to come. Each generation is simply the temporary manager and responsible trustee of a precious and glorious patrimony which it has received from the former generation, and which it has to transmit to the one that comes after it. In this perpetual endowment, to which all Frenchmen from the first days of France have brought their offerings, there is no doubt about the intentions of countless benefactors; they have made their gifts conditionally, that is, on the condition that the endowment should remain intact, and that each successive beneficiary should merely serve as the administrator of it. Should any of the beneficiaries, through presumption or levity, through rashness or one-sidedness, compromise the charge intrusted to them, they wrong all their predecessors whose sacrifices they invalidate, and all their successors whose hopes they frustrate. Accordingly, before undertaking to frame a constitution, let the whole community be considered in its entirety, not merely in the present but in the future, as far as the eye can reach. The interest of the public, viewed in this far-sighted manner, is the end to which all the rest must be subordinate, and for which a constitution provides. A constitution, whether oligarchical, monarchical, or aristocratic, is simply an instrument, good if it attains this end, and bad if it does not attain it, and which, to attain it, must, like every species of mechanism, vary according to the ground, materials, and circumstances. The most ingenious is illegitimate if it dissolves the State, while the clumsiest is legitimate if it keeps the State intact. There is none that springs out of an anterior, universal, and absolute right. According to the people, the epoch, and the degree of civilisation, according to the outer or inner condition of things, all civil or political equality or inequality may, in turn, be or cease to be beneficial or hurtful, and therefore justify the legislator in removing or preserving it. It is according to this superior and salutary law, and not according to an imaginary and impossible contract, that he is to organize, limit, and distribute from the centre to the extremities, through inheritance or through election, through equalisation or through privilege, the rights of the citizen and the powers of the community.

III

Was it essential as a preliminary thing to clear the ground, and was it advisable to abolish or only to reform the various orders and corporations?—Two prominent orders, the clergy and the nobles, enlarged by the ennobled plebeians who had grown wealthy and acquired titled estates, formed a privileged aristocracy side by side with the Government, whose favours it monopolized on the condition of seeking them assiduously and with due acknowledgment, privileged on its own domains, and taking advantage there of all rights belonging to the feudal chieftain without performing his duties. This abuse was evidently an enormous one and had to be ended. But, it did not follow that, because the position of the privileged class on their domains and in connection with the Government was open to abuse, they should be deprived of protection for person and property on their domains, and of influence and occupation under the Government. A favoured aristocracy, when it is unoccupied and renders none of the services which its rank admits of, when it monopolizes all honours, offices, promotions, preferences, and pensions,[10] to the detriment of others not less needy and deserving, is undoubtedly a serious evil. But when an aristocracy is subject to the common law, when it is occupied, especially when its occupation is in conformity with its aptitudes, and more particularly when it is available for the formation of an upper elective chamber or an hereditary peerage, it is of vast service.—In any case it cannot be irreversibly suppressed; for, although it may be abolished by law, it is reconstituted by facts. The legislator must necessarily choose between two systems, that which lets it lie fallow, or that which enables it to be productive, that which drives it away from, or that which rallies it round, the public service. In every society which has lived

10. *Mercure,* July 6, 1790. According to the report of Camus (sitting of July 2nd), the official total of pensions amounted to thirty-two millions; but if we add the gratuities and allowances out of the various treasuries, the actual total was fifty-six millions.

for any length of time, a nucleus of families always exists whose fortunes and importance are of ancient date. Even when, as in France in 1789, this class seems to be exclusive, each half century introduces into it new families such as members of the parliaments, intendants, capitalists who have risen to the top of the social ladder through the wealth they have acquired or through the important offices they have filled; and here, in the medium thus constituted, the statesman and wise counsellor of the people, the independent and able politician is most naturally developed.—On the one hand, thanks to his fortune and his rank, a man of this class is above all vulgar ambitions and temptations. He is able to give his services gratuitously; he is not obliged to concern himself about money or about providing for his family and making his way in the world. A political mission is no interruption to his career; he is not obliged, like the engineer, merchant, or physician, to sacrifice either his business, his advancement, or his clients. He can resign his post without injury to himself or to those dependent on him, follow his own convictions, resist the noisy deleterious opinions of the day, and be the loyal servant, not the low flatterer of the public. Whilst, consequently, in the inferior or average conditions of life, the mainspring is self-interest, with him the grand motive is pride. Now, amongst the deeper feelings of man there is none which is more adapted for transformation into probity, patriotism, and conscientiousness; for, the first requisite of the high-spirited man is self-respect, and to obtain that he is induced to deserve it. Compare, from this point of view, the gentry and nobility of England with the "politicians" of the United States.—On the other hand, with equal talents, a man who belongs to this sphere of life enjoys opportunities for acquiring a better comprehension of public affairs than a poor man of the lower classes. The information he requires is not the erudition obtained in libraries and in private study. He must be familiar with living men, and, besides these, with agglomerations of men, and even more with human organizations, with States, with Governments, with parties, with administrative systems, at home and abroad, in full operation and on the spot. There is but one way to reach this end, and that is to see for himself, with his own eyes, at once in general outline and in detail, by intercourse with the heads of departments, with eminent men and specialists, in whom are gathered up the information and the ideas of a whole class. Now the young do not frequent society of this description, either at home or abroad, except on the condition of possessing a name, family, fortune, education, and a knowledge of social observances. All this is necessary to enable a young man of twenty to find doors everywhere open to him, to be received everywhere on an equal footing, to be able to speak and to write three or four living languages, to make long, expensive, and instructive sojourns in foreign lands, to select and vary his position in the different branches of the public service, without pay or nearly so, and with no object in view but that of his political culture. Thus brought up a man, even of common capacity, is worthy of being consulted. If he is of superior ability, and there is employment for him, he may become a statesman before thirty; he may acquire ripe capacities, become Prime Minister, the sole pilot, alone able, like Pitt, Canning, or Peel, to steer the ship of State between the reefs, or give in the nick of time the touch to the helm which will save the ship. Such is the service to which an upper class is adapted. There is no other but this special stock-breeding system which can furnish a regular supply of racers, and, now and then, the favourite winner that distances all his competitors in the European field.

But in order that they may prepare themselves for this career and take to it naturally, the way must be clear, and a man must not be compelled to travel too repulsive a road. If rank, inherited fortune, personal dignity, and refined manners are sources of disfavour with the people; if, to obtain their suffrages, he is forced to treat as equals electoral brokers of low character; if impudent charlatanism, vulgar declamation, and servile flattery are the sole means by which votes can be secured, then, as nowadays in the United States, and formerly in Athens, the aristocratic body will retire into private life and soon settle down into a state of idleness. A man of culture and refinement, born with an income of a hundred thousand a year, is not tempted to become either manufacturer, lawyer, or physician. For want of other occupation he loiters about, entertains his friends, chats, indulges in the tastes and hobbies of an amateur, amuses himself or dies with ennui, and accordingly is one of the great forces of the State lost to the State. In this way the best and largest acquirements of the past, the heaviest accumulations of material and of moral capital, remain unproductive. In a pure democracy the upper branches of the social tree, not only the old ones but the young ones, remain sterile. When a vigorous branch passes above the rest and reaches the top it ceases to bear fruit. The élite part of the nation is thus condemned to constant and irremediable failures because it cannot find a suitable outlet for its activity. It wants no other outlet, for in all other directions its rivals, who are born below it, can serve as usefully and as well as itself. But this one it must have, for on this side its aptitudes are superior, natural, unique, and the State which refuses to give it air resembles the gardener who in his fondness for a plane surface would repress his best shoots. Hence, in the constructions which aim to utilise the permanent forces of society and yet maintain civil equality, the aristocracy is brought to take a part in public affairs by the duration and gratuitous character of its mission, by the institution of an hereditary character, by the application of various machinery, all of which is combined so as to develop the ambition, the culture, and the political capacity of the upper class, and to place power, or the control of power, in its hands, on the condition that it shows itself worthy of exercising it.—Now, in 1789, the upper class was not unworthy of it. Members of the parliaments, the noblemen, bishops, capitalists, were the men amongst whom, and through whom, the philosophy of the eighteenth century was propagated. Never was an aristocracy more liberal, more humane, and more thoroughly converted to useful reforms;[11] many of them remain so under the knife of the guillotine. The magistrates of the superior tribunals, in particular, traditionally

11. "The Ancient Régime," p. 297, and the following pages.—"Le Duc de Broglie," by M. Guizot, p. 11. (Last words of Prince Victor de Broglie, and the opinions of M. d'Argenson.)

and by virtue of their institution, were the enemies of excessive expenditure and the critics of arbitrary acts. As to the gentry of the provinces, "they were so weary," says one of them,[12] "of the Court and the Ministers that most of them were democrats." For many years, in the Provincial Assemblies the whole of the upper class—the clergy, nobles, and Third-Estate—furnishes abundant evidence of its good disposition, of its application to business, its capacity and even generosity, while its mode of studying, discussing, and assigning the local taxation indicates what it would have done with the general budget had this been intrusted to it. It is evident that it would have protected the general taxpayer as zealously as the taxpayer of the province, and have kept as close an eye upon the public purse at Paris as on that of Bourges or of Montauban.—Thus were the materials of a good chamber ready at hand, and the only thing that had to be done was to collect them together. On having the facts presented to them, its members would have passed without difficulty from a hazardous theory to common-sense practice, and the aristocracy which had enthusiastically given an impetus to reform in its saloons would, in all probability, have carried it out effectively and with moderation in the Parliament.

Unhappily, the Assembly is not providing a Constitution for contemporary Frenchmen, but for abstract beings. Instead of seeing classes in society one placed above the other, it simply sees individuals in juxtaposition; its attention is not fixed on the advantage of the nation, but on the imaginary rights of man. As all men are equal, all must have an equal share in the government. There must be no orders in a State, no avowed or concealed political privileges, no constitutional complications or electoral combinations by which an aristocracy, however liberal and capable, can secure to itself any portion of the public power.—On the contrary, because it was once privileged to enjoy, it is now suspected as a candidate for service; and all projects which, directly or indirectly, reserve or provide a place for it, are rejected: first, the Royal Declaration, which, in

12. De Ferrières, i. p. 2.

conformity with historical precedents, maintained the three orders in three distinct chambers, and only summoned them to deliberate together "on matters of general utility"; next, the plan of the Constitutional Committee, which proposed a second Chamber, appointed for life by the King on the nomination of the Provincial Assemblies; and, finally, the project of Mounier, which confided to these same Assemblies the election of a Senate for six years, renewed by thirds every two years, composed of men of at least thirty-five years of age, and with an income in real property of 10,000 livres per annum. The instinct of equality is too powerful. A second Chamber is not wanted, even if accessible to plebeians. Through it[13] "the smaller number would control the greater"; "we should fall back on the humiliating distinctions" of the ancient régime; "we should revivify the germ of an aristocracy which must be exterminated." "Moreover, whatever recalls or revives feudal institutions is bad, and an Upper Chamber is one of its remnants." "If the English have one, it is because they have been forced to make a compromise with prejudice." The National Assembly, sovereign and philosophic, soars above their errors, their trammels, and their example. The depository of truth, it has not to receive lessons from others, but to give them, and to offer to the world's admiration the first type of a Constitution which is perfect and in conformity with principle—the most effective of any in preventing the formation of a directing class; in closing the way to public business, not only to the old noblesse, but to the aristocracy of the future; in continuing and exaggerating the work of absolute monarchy; in preparing a community of officials and administrators; in sinking the level of humanity; in reducing to sloth and brutalising or blighting the élite of the families which maintain or raise themselves; and in withering the most precious of nurseries, that in which the State recruits its statesmen.

13. *Moniteur,* sitting of September 7, 1790, i. 431–437. Speeches of MM. de Silhery, de Lanjuinais, Thouret, de Lameth, and Rabaul Saint-Etienne. Barnave wrote in 1791: "It was necessary to be content with one single Chamber; the instinct of equality required it. A second Chamber would have been the refuge of the aristocrats."

Excluded from the Government, the aristocracy is about to retire into private life: let us follow them to their estates.—Feudal rights instituted for a barbarous State are certainly a great drawback in a modern State. If appropriate in an epoch when property and sovereignty were fused together, when the Government was local, when life was militant, they form an incongruity at a time when sovereignty and property are separated, when the Government is centralized, when the régime is a pacific one, and when the necessary servitudes which, in the tenth century, reestablished security and agriculture, are, in the eighteenth century, purposeless servitudes which impoverish the soil and fetter the peasant. But, because these ancient claims are liable to abuse and injurious at the present day, it does not follow that they never were useful and legitimate, nor that it is allowable to abolish them without indemnity. On the contrary, for many centuries, and, on the whole, so long as the lord of the manor resided on his estate, this primitive contract was advantageous to both parties, and to such an extent that it has led to the modern contract. Thanks to the pressure of this tight bandage, the broken fragments of the community can be again united, and society once more recover its solidity, force, and activity.—In any event, that the institution, like all human institutions, took its rise in violence and was corrupted by abuses, is of little consequence; the State, for eight hundred years, recognised these feudal claims, and, with its own consent and the concurrence of its Courts, they were transmitted, bequeathed, sold, mortgaged, and exchanged, like any other species of property. Only two or three hundred, at most, remain in the families of the original proprietors. "The largest portion of the titled estates," says a contemporary,[14] "have become the property of capitalists, merchants, and their descendants; the fiefs, for the most part, being in the hands of the bourgeois of the towns." All the fiefs which, during two centuries past, have been bought by new men, now represent the economy and labour of their purchasers.—Moreover, whoever the actual holders may be, whether old or whether

14. "De Bouillé," p. 50: "All the old noble families, save two or three hundred, were ruined."

new men, the State is under obligation to them, not only by general right—and because, from the beginning, it is in its nature the guardian of all property—but also by a special right, because it has itself sanctioned this particular species of property. The buyers of yesterday paid their money only under its guarantee; its signature is affixed to the contract, and it has bound itself to secure to them the enjoyment of it. If it prevents them from doing so, let it make them compensation; in default of the thing promised to them, it owes them the value of it. Such is the law in cases of expropriation for public utility; in 1834, for instance, the English, for the legal abolition of slavery, paid to their planters the sum of £20,000,000.—But that is not sufficient: when, in the suppression of feudal rights, the legislator's thoughts are taken up with the creditors, he has only half performed his task; there are two sides to the question, and he must likewise think of the debtors. If he is not merely a lover of abstractions and of fine phrases, if that which interests him is men and not words, if he is bent upon the effective enfranchisement of the cultivator of the soil, he will not rest content with proclaiming a principle, with permitting the redemption of rents, with fixing the rate of redemption, and, in case of dispute, with sending parties before the tribunals. He will reflect that the peasantry, jointly responsible for the same debt, will find difficulty in agreeing among themselves; that they are afraid of litigation; that, being ignorant, they will not know how to set about it; that, being poor, they will be unable to pay; and that, under the weight of discord, distrust, indigence, and inertia, the new law will remain a dead letter, and only exasperate their cupidity or kindle their resentment. In anticipation of this disorder the legislator will come to their assistance; he will interpose commissions of arbitration between them and the lord of the manor; he will substitute a scale of annuities for a full and immediate redemption; he will lend them the capital which they cannot borrow elsewhere; he will establish a bank, rights, and a mode of procedure—in short, as in Savoy in 1771, in England in 1845,[15] and in Russia in 1861, he will relieve the poor without despoiling the rich;

15. Cf. Doniol, "La Révolution et la Féodalité."

he will establish liberty without violating the rights of property; he will conciliate interests and classes; he will not let loose a brutal jacquerie to enforce unjust confiscation; and he will terminate the social conflict not with strife but with peace.

It is just the reverse in 1789. In conformity with the doctrine of the social contract, the principle is set up that every man is born free, and that his freedom has always been inalienable. If he formerly submitted to slavery or to serfdom, it was owing to his having had a knife at his throat; a contract of this sort is essentially null and void. So much the worse for those who have the benefit of it at the present day; they are holders of stolen property, and must restore it to the legitimate owners. Let no one object that this property was acquired for cash down, and in good faith; they ought to have known beforehand that man and his liberty are not commercial matters, and that unjust acquisitions rightly perish in their hands.[16] Nobody dreams that the State which was a party to this transaction is the responsible guarantor. Only one scruple affects the Assembly; its legists and Merlin, its reporter, are obliged to yield to proof; they know that in current practice, and by innumerable ancient and modern titles, the noble in many cases is nothing but an ordinary lessor, and that if, in those cases, he collects his dues, it is simply in his capacity as a private person, by virtue of a mutual contract, because he has given a perpetual lease of a certain portion of his land; and he has given it only in consideration of an annual payment in money or produce, or services, together with another contingent claim which the farmer pays in case of the transmission of the lease. These

16. *Moniteur,* sitting of August 6, 1789. Speech of Duport: "Whatever is unjust cannot last. Similarly, no compensation for these unjust rights can be maintained."—Sitting of February 27, 1790. M. Populus: "As slavery could not spring from a legitimate contract, because liberty cannot be alienated, you have abolished without indemnity hereditary property in persons." Instructions and decree of June 15–19, 1791: "The National Assembly has recognised in the most emphatic manner that a man never could become the proprietor of another man, and consequently, that the rights which one had assumed to have over the person of the other, could not become the property of the former." Cf. the diverse reports of Merlin to the Committee of Feudality and the National Assembly.

two obligations could not be cancelled without indemnity; if it were done, more than one-half of the proprietors in France would be dispossessed in favour of the farmers. Hence the distinction which the Assembly makes in the feudal dues. On the one hand it abolishes without indemnity all those dues which the noble receives by virtue of being the local sovereign, the ancient proprietor of persons and the usurper of public powers; all those which the lessee paid as serf, subject to rights of inheritance, and as former vassal or dependent. On the other hand, it maintains and decrees as redeemable at a certain rate all those which the noble receives through his title of landed proprietor and of simple lessor; all those which the lessee pays by virtue of being a free contracting party, former purchaser, tenant, farmer, or grantee of landed estate. By this division it fancies that it has respected legitimate by overthrowing illegitimate property, and that in the feudal scheme of obligations, it has separated the wheat from the chaff.[17]

But, through the principle, the drawing up and the omissions of its law, it condemns both to a common destruction; the fire on which it has thrown the chaff necessarily burns up the wheat.—Practically both are bound up together in the same sheaf. If the noble formerly brought men under subjection by the sword, it is also by the sword that he formerly acquired possession of the soil. If the subjection of persons is invalid on account of the original stain of violence, the usurpation of the soil is invalid for the same reason. And if the sanction and guarantee of the State could not justify the first act of brigandage, they could not justify the second; and, since the rights which are derived from unjust sovereignty are abolished without indemnity, the rights which are derived from unjust proprietorship should be likewise abolished without compensation.—The Assembly, with remarkable imprudence, had declared in the preamble to its law that "it abolished the feudal system entirely," and, whatever its ulterior reservations might be, the fiat has gone forth. The forty

17. Duvergier, "Collection des Lois et Décrets." Laws of the 4–11 August, 1789; March 15–28, 1790; May 3–9, 1790; June 15–19, 1791.

thousand sovereign municipalities to which the text of the decree is read pay attention only to the first article, and the village attorney, imbued with the rights of man, easily proves to these assemblies of debtors that they owe nothing to their creditors. There must be no exceptions nor distinctions, no more annual rents, field-rents, dues on produce,[18] nor contingent rents, nor lord's dues and fines, or fifths. If these have been maintained by the Assembly, it is owing to misunderstanding, timidity, inconsistency, and on all sides, in the rural districts, the grumbling of disappointed greed or of unsatisfied necessities[19] is heard. "You thought that you were destroying feudalism, while your redemption laws have done just the contrary. . . . Are you not aware that what was called a Seigneur was simply an unpunished usurper? . . . That detestable decree of 1790 is the ruin of all lease-holders. It has thrown the villages into a state of consternation. The nobles reap all the advantage of it. . . . Never will redemption be possible. Redemption of unreal claims! Redemption of dues that are detestable!" In vain the Assembly insists, specifies, and explains by examples and by detailed instructions the mode of procedure and the conditions of redemption. Neither the mode of procedure nor the conditions are practicable. It has made no provisions for facilitating the agreement of parties and the satisfaction of feudal liens, no special arbitrators, nor bank for loans, nor system of annuities. And worse still, instead of clearing the road it has barred it by legal arrangements. The lease-holder is not to redeem his annual rent without at the same time compounding for the contingent rent: he is not allowed to redeem his quota of dues which he shares with others apart from his co-partners. Should his hoard be a small one, so much the worse for him. Not being able to redeem the whole, he is not allowed to redeem a part. Not having the money with which to relieve himself from both ground-rents and lord's

18. *Agrier percières*—terms denoting taxes paid in the shape of shares of produce. Those which follow—*lods, rentes, quint, requint*—belong to the taxes levied on real property.—[Tr.]

19. Doniol ("Nouveaux cahiers de 1790"). Complaints of the copy-holders of Rouergues and of Quercy, pp. 97–105.

dues he cannot relieve himself from ground-rents. Not having the money to liquidate the debt in full of those who are bound along with himself, he remains a captive in his ancient chains by virtue of the new law which announces to him his freedom.

In the face of these unexpected trammels the peasant becomes furious. His fixed idea, from the outbreak of the Revolution, is that he no longer owes anything to anybody, and, among the speeches, decrees, proclamations, and instructions which rumour brings to his ears, he comprehends but one phrase, and is determined to comprehend no other, and that is, that henceforth his obligations are removed. He does not swerve from this, and since the law hinders, instead of aiding him, he will break the law. In fact, after the 4th of August, 1789, feudal dues cease to be collected. The claims which are maintained are not enforced any more than those which are suppressed. Whole communities come and give notice to the lord of the manor that they will not pay any more rent. Others, with sword in hand, compel him to give them acquittances. Others again, to be more secure, break open his safe, and throw his title-deeds into the fire.[20] Public force is nowhere strong enough to protect him in his legal rights. Officers dare not serve writs, the courts dare not give judgment, administrative bodies dare not decree in his favour. He is despoiled through the connivance, the neglect, or the impotence of all the authorities which ought to defend him. He is abandoned to the peasants who fell his forests, under the pretext that they formerly belonged to the commune; who take possession of his mill, his wine-press, and his oven, under the pretext that territorial privileges are suppressed.[21] Most of the gentry of the provinces are ruined, without any resource, and have not even their daily bread; for their income consisted in seignorial rights, and in rents

20. See further on, book iii. ch. ii. § 4, also ch. iii.

21. *Moniteur,* sitting of March 2, 1700. Speech by Merlin: "The peasants have been made to believe that the destruction of the *banalités* (the obligation to use the public mill, wine-press, and oven, which belonged to the noble) carried along with it the loss to the noble of all these; the peasants regarding themselves as proprietors of them."

derived from their real property, which they had let on perpetual leases, and now, in accordance with the law, one-half of this income ceases to be paid, while the other half ceases to be paid in spite of the law. One hundred and twenty-three millions of revenue, representing two thousand millions and a half of capital in the money of that time, double, at least, that of the present day, thus passes as a gift, or through the toleration of the National Assembly, from the hands of creditors into those of their debtors. To this must be added an equal sum for revenue and capital arising from the tithes which are suppressed without compensation, and by the same stroke.—This is the commencement of the great revolutionary operation, that is to say, of the universal bankruptcy which, directly or indirectly, is to destroy all contracts, and abolish all debts in France. Violations of property, especially of private property, cannot be made with impunity. The Assembly desired to lop off only the feudal branch; but, in admitting that the State can annul, without compensation, the obligations which it has guaranteed, it put the axe to the root of the tree, and other rougher hands are already driving it in up to the haft.

Nothing now remains to the noble but his title, his territorial name, and his armorial bearings, which are innocent distinctions, since they no longer confer any jurisdiction or preeminence upon him, and which, as the law ceases to protect him, the first comer may borrow with impunity. Not only, moreover, do they do no harm, but they are even worthy of respect. With many of the nobles the title of the estate covers the family name, the former alone being made use of. If one were substituted for the other, the public would have difficulty in discovering M. de Mirabeau, M. de Lafayette, and M. de Montmorency, under the new names of M. Riquetti, M. Mottié, and M. Bouchard. Besides, it would be a wrong to the bearer of it, to whom the abolished title is a legitimate possession, often precious, it being a certificate of quality and descent, an authentic personal distinction of which he cannot be deprived without losing his position, rank, and worth, in the human world around him.—The Assembly, however, with a popular principle at stake, gives no heed to public utility, nor to the rights of individuals. The feudal system being abolished, all that remains of it must be got rid of. A decree is passed that "hereditary nobility is offensive to reason and to true liberty"; that, where it exists, "there is no political equality."[22] Every French citizen is forbidden to assume or retain the titles of prince, duke, count, marquis, chevalier, and the like, and to bear any other than the "true name of his family"; he is prohibited from making his servants wear liveries, and from having coats-of-arms on his house or on his carriage. In case of any infraction of this law a penalty is inflicted upon him equal to six times the sum of his personal taxes; he is to be struck off the register of citizens, and declared incapable of holding any civil or military office. There is the same punishment if to any contract or acquittance he affixes his accustomed signature; if, through habit or inadvertence, he adds the title of his estate to his family name—if, with a view to recognition, and to render his identity certain, he merely mentions that he once bore the former name. Any notary or public officer who shall write, or allow to be written, in any document the word *ci-devant* (formerly) is to be suspended from his functions. Not only are old names thus abolished, but an effort is made to efface all remembrance of them. In a little while, the childish law will become a murderous one. It will be but a little while and, according to the terms of this same decree, a military veteran of seventy-seven years, a loyal servant of the Republic, and a brigadier-general under the Convention, will be arrested on returning to his native village, because he has mechanically signed the register of the revolutionary committee as Montperreux instead of Vannod, and, for this infraction, he will be guillotined along with his brother and his sister-in-law.[23]

Once on this road, it is impossible to stop; for the principles which are proclaimed go beyond the decrees which are passed, and a bad law introduces a worse. The Constituent Assembly[24] had supposed that annual dues, like ground-rents, and contingent dues, like feudal

22. *Moniteur,* sitting of June 9, 1790. Speech of M. Charles de Lameth.—Duvergier (laws of June 19–23, 1790; September 27 and October 16, 1791).

23. Sauzay, v. 400–410.

24. Duvergier, laws of June 15–19, 1791; July 6, 1792; August 25–28, 1792.

duties (*lods et rentes*), were the price of an ancient concession of land, and, consequently, the proof to the contrary is to be thrown upon the tenant. The Legislative Assembly is about to assume that these same rentals are the result of an old feudal usurpation, and that, consequently, the proof to the contrary must rest with the proprietor. His rights cannot be established by possession from time immemorial, nor by innumerable and regular acquittances; he must produce the act of enfeoffment which is many centuries old, the lease which has never, perhaps, been written out, the primitive title already rare in 1720,[25] and since stolen or burnt in the recent jacqueries: otherwise he is despoiled without indemnity. All feudal claims are swept away by this act without exception and without compensation.

In a similar manner, the Constituent Assembly, setting common law aside in relation to inheritances *ab intestato,* had deprived all eldest sons and males of any advantages.[26] The Convention, suppressing the freedom of testamentary bequest, prohibits the father from disposing of more than one-tenth of his possessions; and again, going back to the past, it makes its decrees retrospective: every will opened after the 14th of July, 1789, is declared invalid if not in conformity with this decree; every succession from the 14th of June, 1789, which is administered after the same date, is redivided if the division has not been equal; every donation which has been made among the heirs after the same date is void. Not only is the feudal family destroyed in this way, but it must never be reformed. The aristocracy, being once declared a venomous plant, it is not sufficient to prune it away, but it must be extirpated, not only dug up by the

25. "Institution du Droit Français," by Argou, i. 103. (He wrote under the Regency.) "The origin of most of the feoffs is so ancient that if the seigneurs were obliged to produce the titles of the original concession, to obtain their rents, there would scarcely be one able to produce them. This deficiency is made up by common law."

26. Duvergier (laws of April 8–15, 1791; March 7–11; October 26, 1791; January 6–10, 1794). Mirabeau had already proposed to reduce the disposable portion to one-tenth.

root, but its seed must be crushed out.—A malignant prejudice is aroused against it, and this grows from day to day. The stings of self-conceit, the disappointments of ambition, and envious sentiments have prepared the way. Its hard, dry kernel consists of the abstract idea of equality. All around revolutionary fervour has caused blood to flow, has embittered tempers, intensified sensibilities, and created a painful abscess which daily irritation renders still more painful. Through steadily brooding over a purely speculative preference this has become a fixed idea, and is becoming a murderous one. It is a strange passion, one wholly of the brain, nourished by magniloquent phrases, but the more destructive, because phantoms are created out of words, and against phantoms no reasoning nor actual facts can prevail. This or that shopkeeper who, up to this time, had always formed his idea of nobles from his impressions of the members of the Parliament of his town or of the gentry of his canton, now pictures them according to the declamations of the club and the invectives of the newspapers. The imaginary figure, in his mind, has gradually absorbed the living figure: he no longer sees the calm and engaging countenance, but a grinning and distorted mask. Kindliness or indifference is replaced by animosity and distrust; they are overthrown tyrants, ancient evil-doers, and enemies of the public; he is satisfied beforehand and without further investigation that they are hatching plots. If they avoid being caught, it is owing to their address and perfidy, and they are only the more dangerous the more inoffensive they appear. Their submission is merely a feint, their resignation hypocrisy, their favourable disposition, treachery. Against these conspirators who cannot be touched the law is inadequate; let us stretch it in practice, and as they wince at equality let us try to make them bow beneath the yoke.

In fact, illegal persecution precedes legal prosecution; the privileged person who, by the late decrees, seems merely to be brought within the pale of the common law, is, in fact, driven outside of it. The King, disarmed, is no longer able to protect him; the partial Assembly repels his complaints; the committee of inquiry regards him as a culprit when he is simply oppressed. His income, his property, his repose, his freedom, his home, his life, that of his wife and of his children, are in the hands of an administration elected by the crowd, directed by clubs, and threatened or violated by the mob. He is debarred from the elections. The newspapers denounce him. He undergoes domiciliary visits. In hundreds of places his chateau is sacked; the assassins and incendiaries who depart from it with their hands full and steeped in blood are not prosecuted, or are shielded by an amnesty:[27] it is established by innumerable precedents that he may be run down with impunity. To prevent him from defending himself, companies of the National Guard come and seize his arms: he must become a prey, and an easy prey, like game kept back in its enclosure for an approaching hunt. In vain he abstains from provocations and reduces himself to the standing of a private individual. In vain does he patiently endure numerous provocations and resist only extreme violence. I have read many hundreds of investigations in the original manuscripts, and almost always I have admired the humanity of the nobles, their forbearance, their horror of bloodshed. Not only are a great many of them men of courage and all men of honour, but also, educated in the philosophy of the eighteenth century, they are mild, sensitive, and deeds of violence are repugnant to them. Military officers especially are exemplary, their great defect being their weakness: rather than fire on the crowd they surrender the forts under their command, and allow themselves to be insulted and stoned by the people. For two years,[28] "exposed to a thousand outrages, to defamation, to daily peril, persecuted by clubs and misguided soldiers," disobeyed, menaced, put under arrest by their own men, they remain at their post to prevent the ranks from being broken up; "with stoic perseverance they put up with contempt of their authority that they may preserve its semblance"; their courage is of that rarest kind which consists in remaining at the post of duty, impassive beneath both affronts and blows.

27. See farther on, book iii. ch. iii.

28. *Mercure,* September 10, 1791. Article by Mallet-Dupan.—*Ibid.* October 15, 1791.

Through a wrong of the greatest magnitude, an entire class which have no share in the favours of the Court, and which suffered as many injuries as any of the common plebeians, is confounded with the titled parasites who besiege the antechambers of Versailles. Twenty-five thousand families, "the nursery of the army and the fleet," the élite of the agricultural proprietors, also many gentlemen who look after and turn to account the little estates on which they live, and "who have not left their homes a year in their lives," become the pariahs of their canton. After 1789, they begin to feel that their position is no longer tenable.[29] "It is absolutely in opposition to the rights of man," says another letter from Franche-Comté, "to find one's self in perpetual fear of having one's throat cut by scoundrels who are daily confounding liberty with license." "I never knew anything so wearying," says another letter from Champagne, "as this anxiety about property and security. Never was there a better reason for it. A moment suffices to let loose an intractable population which thinks that it may do what it pleases, and which is carefully sustained in that error." "After the sacrifices that we have made," says a letter from Burgundy, "we could not expect such treatment. I thought that our property would be the last violated because the people owed us some return for staying at home in the country to expend among them the few resources that remain to us. . . . (Now), I beg the Assembly to repeal the decree on emigration; otherwise it may be said that people are purposely kept here to be assassinated.

29. "Archives Nationales," ii. 784. Letters of M. de Langeron, October 16 and 18, 1789.—Albert Babeau, "Histoire de Troyes," letters addressed to the Chevalier de Poterat, July, 1790.—"Archives Nationales," papers of the Committee on Reports, *liasse* 4, letter of M. le Belin-Chatellenot to the President of the National Assembly, July 1, 1791.—*Mercure,* October 15, 1791. Article by Mallet-Dupan: "Such is literally the language of these emigrants; I do not add a word."—*Ibid.* May 15, 1790. Letter of the Baron de Bois d'Aizy, April 29, 1790, demanding a decree of protection for the nobles. "We shall know (then) whether we are proscribed or are of any account in the rights of man written out with so much blood, or whether, finally, any other resource is left to us but that of bearing the remains of our property and our wretched existences under other skies."

. . . In case it should refuse to do us this justice, I should be quite as willing to have it decree an act of proscription against us, for we should not then be lulled to sleep by the protection of laws which are doubtless very wise, but which are not respected anywhere." "It is not our privileges," say several others, "it is not our nobility that we regret; but how is the persecution to which we are abandoned to be supported? There is no safety for us, for our property, or for our families. Wretches who are our debtors, the small farmers who rob us of our incomes, daily threaten us with the torch and the lantern. We do not enjoy one hour of repose; not a night that we are certain to pass through without trouble. Our persons are given up to the vilest outrages, our dwellings to an inquisition of armed tyrants; we are robbed of our rentals with impunity, and our property is openly attacked. We, being now the only people to pay imposts, are iniquitously taxed; in various places our entire incomes would not suffice to pay the quota which crushes us. We can make no complaint without incurring the risk of being massacred. The tribunals and the administrative bodies, the tools of the multitude, daily sacrifice us to its attacks. Even the Government seems afraid of compromising itself by claiming the protection of the laws on our behalf. It is sufficient to be pointed out as an aristocrat to be without any security. If our peasants, in general, have shown more honesty, consideration, and attachment toward us, every bourgeois of importance, the wild members of clubs, the vilest of men who sully a uniform, consider themselves privileged to insult us, and these wretches go unpunished and are protected! Even our religion is not free. One of our number has had his house sacked for having shown hospitality to an old curé of eighty belonging to his parish who refused to take the oath. Such is our fate. We are not so base as to endure it. Our right to resist oppression is not due to a decree of the National Assembly, but to natural law. We are going to leave, and to die if necessary. But to live under such a revolting anarchy! Should it not be broken up we shall never set foot in France again!"

The operation is successful. The Assembly, through its decrees and institutions, through the laws it enacts and the violence which it tolerates, has uprooted the aristocracy and cast it out of the country. The nobles, now the reverse of privileged, cannot remain in a country where, while respecting the law, they are really beyond its pale. Those who first emigrated on the 15th of July, 1789, along with the Prince de Condé, received at their houses the evening before they left a list of the proscribed on which their names appeared, and a reward was promised to whoever would bring their heads to the cellar of the Palais-Royal. Others, in larger numbers, left after the occurrences of the 6th of October. During the last months of the Constituent Assembly,[30] "the emigration goes on in companies composed of men of every condition. . . . Twelve hundred gentlemen have left Poitou alone; Auvergne, Limousin, and ten other provinces have been equally depopulated of their landowners. There are towns in which nobody remains but common workmen, a club, and the crowd of devouring office-holders created by the Constitution. All the nobles in Brittany have left, and the emigration has begun in Normandy, and is going on in the frontier provinces."— "More than two-thirds of the army will be without officers." On being called upon to take the new oath in which the King's name is purposely omitted, "six thousand officers send in their resignation." The example gradually becomes contagious; they are men of the sword, and their honour is at stake. Many of them join the princes at Coblentz, and subsequently do battle against France, in the belief that they are contending only against their executioners.

The treatment of the nobles by the Assembly is the same as the treatment of the Protestants by Louis XIV.[31] In both cases the oppressed are a superior class of men. In both cases France has been made uninhabitable for them. In both cases they are reduced to exile, and they are punished because they exiled themselves. In both cases it ended in a confiscation of their property, and in the penalty of

30. *Mercure,* October 15, 1791, and September 10, 1791. Read the admirable letter of the Chevalier de Mesgrigny, appointed colonel during the suspension of the King, and refusing his new rank.

31. Cf. the "Mémoires" of M. de Boustaquet, a Norman gentleman.

death to all who should harbour them. In both cases, by dint of persecution, they are driven to revolt. The insurrection of La Vendée corresponds with the insurrection of the Cévennes; and the emigrants, like the refugees of former times, will be found under the flags of Prussia and of England. One hundred thousand Frenchmen driven out at the end of the seventeenth century, and one hundred thousand driven out at the end of the eighteenth century! Mark how an intolerant democracy completes the work of an intolerant monarchy. The moral aristocracy was mowed down in the name of uniformity; the social aristocracy is mowed down in the name of equality. For the second time, an absolute principle, and with the same effect, buries its blade in the heart of a living society.

The success is complete. One of the deputies of the Legislative Assembly, early in its session, on being informed of the great increase in emigration, joyfully exclaims, "So much the better; France is being purged!" She is, in truth, being depleted of one-half of her best blood.

IV

There remained the corporate, ecclesiastic, and lay bodies, and, notably, the oldest, most opulent, and most considerable of all, the regular and secular clergy.—Grave abuses existed here also, for, the institution being founded on ancient requirements, had not accommodated itself to new necessities.[32] Too many episcopal sees, and arranged according to the Christian distribution of the population in the fourth century; a revenue still more badly apportioned—bishops and abbés with one hundred thousand livres a year, leading the lives of amiable idlers, while curés, overburdened with work, have but seven hundred; in one monastery nineteen monks instead of eighty, and in another four instead of fifty;[33] a number of mon-

32. Cf. "The Ancient Régime," books i. and ii.

33. Boivin-Champeaux, "Notice Historique sur la Revolution dans le Département de l'Eure," the grievances stated in the memorials. In 1788, at Rouen, there was not a single profession made by men. In the monastery of the Deux-

asteries reduced to three or to two inhabitants, and even to one; almost all the congregations of men going to decay, and many of them dying out for lack of novices;[34] a general lukewarmness among the members, great laxity in many establishments, and with scandals in some of them; scarcely one-third taking an interest in their calling, while the remaining two-thirds wish to go back to the world[35]—it is evident from all this that the primitive inspiration has been diverted or has cooled; that the endowment only partially fulfils its ends; that one-half of its resources are employed in the wrong way or remain sterile; in short, that there is a need of reformation in the body.—That this ought to be effected with the cooperation of the State and even under its direction is not less certain. For a corporation is not an individual like other individuals, and, in order that it may acquire or possess the privileges of an ordinary citizen, something supplementary must be added, some fiction, some expedient of the law. If the law is disposed to overlook the fact that a corporation is not a natural personage, if it gives to it a civil personality,

---

Amants the chapter convoked in 1789 consisted of two monks. "Archives Nationales," papers of the ecclesiastic committee, *passim*.

34. "Apologie de l'Etat Religieux" (1775), with statistics. Since 1768 the decline is "frightful"; "it is plainly to be seen that in ten or twelve years most of the regular bodies will be absolutely extinct, or reduced to a state of feebleness akin to death."

35. Sauzay, i. 224 (November, 1790). At Besançon, out of two hundred and sixty-six monks, "seventy-nine only showed any loyalty to their engagements or any affection for their calling." Others preferred to abandon it, especially all the Dominicans but five, all but one of the barefooted Carmelites, and all the Grand-Carmelites. The same disposition is apparent throughout the department, as, for instance, with the Benedictines of Cluny except one, all the Minimes but three, all the Capuchins but five, the Bernardins, Dominicans, and Augustins, all preferring to leave.—Montalembert, "Les Moines d'Occident," introduction, pp. 105–164. Letter of a Benedictine of Saint-Germain-des-Prés to a Benedictine of Vannes. "Of all the members of your congregation which come here to lodge, I have scarcely found one capable of edifying us. You may probably say the same of those who came to you from our place."—Cf. in the "Mémoires" of Merlin de Thionville the description of the Chartreuse of Val St. Pierre.

if it declares it to be capable of inheriting, of acquiring, and of selling, if it becomes a protected and respected proprietor, this is due to the favours of the State which places its tribunal and gendarmes at its service, and which, in exchange for this service, justly imposes conditions on it, and, among others, that of being useful and remaining useful, or at least that of never becoming hurtful. Such was the rule under the ancient régime, and especially since the Government has for the last quarter of a century gradually and efficaciously worked out a reform. Not only, in 1749, had it prohibited the Church from accepting land, either by donation, by testament, or in exchange, without royal letters-patent registered in Parliament; not only in 1764 had it abolished the order of Jesuits, closed their colleges, and sold their possessions, but also, since 1766, a permanent commission, formed by the King's order and instructed by him, had lopped off all the dying and dead branches of the ecclesiastical tree.[36] There was a revision of the primitive Constitutions; a prohibition to every institution to have more than two monasteries at Paris and more than one in other towns; a postponement of the age for taking vows—that of sixteen being no longer permitted—up to twenty-one for men and eighteen for women; an obligatory minimum of monks and nuns for each establishment, which varies from fifteen to nine according to circumstances; if this is not kept up there follows a suppression or prohibition to receive novices: owing to these measures, rigorously executed, at the end of twelve years "the Grammontins, the Servites, the Celestins, the ancient order of Saint-Bénédict, that of the Holy Ghost of Montpellier, and those of Sainte-Brigitte, Sainte-Croix-de-la-Bretonnerie, Saint-Ruff, and Saint-Antoine"—in short, nine complete congre-

36. Ch. Guerin, "Revue des Questions Historiques" (July 1, 1875; April 1, 1876). Abbé Guettée, "Histoire de l'Eglise de France," xii. 128. ("*Procès-verbal* de l'Assemblée du Clergé," in 1780.) "Archives Nationales," official reports and memorials of the States-General in 1789. The most obnoxious proceeding to the chiefs of the order is the postponement of the age at which vows may be taken, it being, in their view, the ruin of their institutions.—"The Ancient Régime," p. 403.

gations had disappeared. At the end of twenty years three hundred and eighty-six establishments had been suppressed, the number of monks and nuns had diminished one-third, the larger portion of possessions which had escheated were usefully applied, and the congregations of men lacked novices and complained that they could not fill up their ranks. If the monks were still found to be too numerous, too wealthy, and too indolent, it was merely necessary to keep on in this way; before the end of the century, merely by the application of the edict, the institution would be brought back, without brutality or injustice, within the scope of the development, the limitations of fortune, and the class of functions acceptable to a modern State.

But, because these ecclesiastical bodies stood in need of reform it does not follow that it was necessary to destroy them, nor, in general, that proprietary corporations are detrimental to a nation. Organized purposely for a public service, and possessing, nearly or remotely under the supervision of the State, the faculty of self-administration, these bodies are valuable organs and not unhealthy excrescences.—In the first place, through their institution, a great public benefit is secured without any charge upon the budget—worship, scientific research, primary or higher education, help for the poor, care of the sick—all set apart and sheltered from the retrenchments which public financial embarrassments might make necessary, and supported by the private generosity which, finding a ready receptacle at hand, collects into it from century to century its thousands of scattered rivulets: as a case in point, note the wealth, stability, and usefulness of the English and German universities. In the second place, their institution furnishes an obstacle to the omnipotence of the State; their walls afford a breakwater against the tide-level of absolute monarchy or of pure democracy. A man can here freely develop himself without donning the livery of either courtier or demagogue, acquire wealth, consideration, and authority, without being indebted to the caprices of royal or popular favour; he can maintain himself against established power or against prevailing opinions through his position in a body which is held together by a spirit of association. Such, at the present day, is a professor at Oxford, Göttingen, and Harvard. Such, under the ancient régime, were a bishop, a member of the Parliaments, and even a plain attorney. What can be worse than the universal bureaucracy, which produces mechanical and servile uniformity! Those who serve the public need not all be Government clerks; in countries where an aristocracy has perished, bodies of this kind are their last place of refuge. In the third place, through their institution, distinct original societies are formed in the midst of the great commonplace world around them, in which certain natures may find the only existence that suits them. If devout or laborious, not only do these afford an outlet for the deeper needs of conscience, of the imagination, of activity, and of discipline, but also they serve as dykes which restrain and direct them in a channel of masterly contrivance and of infinite benefit. In this way thousands of men and women execute at the least possible expense, voluntarily and gratuitously, and with the greatest possible effect, the least attractive or most repulsive of social requirements, thus fulfilling in human society the purpose of the sexless workers of an ant-hill.

Thus, at bottom, the institution was really good, and if it had to be cauterized it was merely essential to remove the inert or corrupted parts and preserve the healthy and sound parts.—Now, if we take only the monastic bodies, there were more than one-half of these entitled to respect. I omit those monks, one-third of whom remained zealous and exemplary—the Benedictines, who continue the "Gallia Christiana," with others who, at sixty years of age, labour in rooms without a fire; the Trappists, who cultivate the ground with their own hands, and the innumerable monasteries which serve as educational seminaries, bureaus of charity, hospices for shelter, and of which all the villages in their neighbourhood demand the conservation by the National Assembly.[37] I have to mention the nuns,

37. "The Ancient Régime," p. 33. Cf. Guerin: "The monastery of the Trois-Rois, in the north of Franche-Comté, founded four villages collected from foreign colonists. It is the only centre of charity and civilisation in a radius of

thirty-seven thousand in fifteen hundred convents. Here, except in the twenty-five chapters of canonesses, which are a semiworldly rendezvous for poor young girls of noble birth, fervour, frugality, and usefulness are almost everywhere incontestable. One of the members of the Ecclesiastical Committee admits in the Assembly tribunal that, in all their letters and addresses, the nuns ask to be allowed to remain in their cloisters; their entreaties, in fact, are as earnest as they are affecting.[38] One community writes, "We should prefer the sacrifice of our lives to that of our calling. . . . This is not the voice of some among our sisters, but of all. The National Assembly has established the claims of liberty—would it prevent the exercise of these by the only disinterested beings who ardently desire to be useful, and have renounced society solely to be of greater service to it?" "The little commerce we have with the world," writes another, "is the reason why our contentment is so little known. But it is not the less real and substantial. We know of no distinctions, no privileges amongst ourselves; our misfortunes and our property are in common. One in heart and one in soul . . . we protest before the nation, in the face of heaven and of earth, that it is not in the power of any being to shake our fidelity to our vows, which vows we renew with still more ardour than when we first pronounced them."[39] Many of the communities have no means of subsistence

---

three leagues. It took care of two hundred of the sick in a recent epidemic; it lodges the troops which pass from Alsace into Franche-Comté, and in the late hailstorm it supplied the whole neighbourhood with food."

38. *Moniteur,* sitting of February 13, 1790. (Speech of the Abbé de Montesquiou).—"Archives Nationales," papers of the Ecclesiastical Committee, DXIX. 6, Visitation de Limoges, DXIX. 25, Annonciades de Saint-Denis; *ibid.* Annonciades de Saint-Amour; Ursulines d'Auch, de Beaulieu, d'Eymoutier, de la Ciotat, de Pont Saint-Esprit, Hospitalières d'Ernée, de Laval; Sainte-Claire de Laval, de Marseille, &c.

39. Sauzay, i. 247. Out of three hundred and seventy-seven nuns at Doubs, three hundred and fifty-eight preferred to remain as they were, especially at Pontarlier, all the Bernardines, Annonciades, and Ursulines; at Besançon, all the Carmelites, the Visitandines, the Annonciades, the Clarisses, the Sisters of Refuge, the Nuns of the Saint-Esprit, and, save one, all the Benedictine Nuns.

other than the work of their own hands and the small dowries the nuns have brought with them on entering the convent. So great, however, is their frugality and economy, that the total expenditure of each nun does not surpass two hundred and fifty livres a year. The Annonciades of Saint-Amour say, "We, thirty-three nuns, both choristers and those of the white veil, live on four thousand four hundred livres net income, without being a charge to our families or to the public. . . . If we were living in society, our expenses would be three times as much"; and, not content with providing for themselves, they give in charity.

Among these communities several hundreds are educational establishments; a very great number give gratuitous primary instruction.—Now, in 1789, there are no other schools for girls, and were these to be suppressed, every avenue of instruction and culture would be closed to one of the two sexes, forming one-half of the French population. Fourteen thousand sisters of charity, distributed among four hundred and twenty convents, look after the hospitals, attend upon the sick, serve the infirm, bring up foundlings, provide for orphans, lying-in women, and repentant prostitutes. The "Visitation" is an asylum for "those who are not favoured by nature"—and, in those days, there were many more of the disfigured than at present, since out of every eight deaths one was caused by the small pox. Widows are received here, as well as girls without means and without protection, persons "worn out with the agitations of the world," those who are too feeble to support the battle of life, those who withdraw from it wounded or invalided, and "the rules of the order, not very strict, are not beyond the health or strength of the most frail and delicate." Some ingenious device of charity thus applies to each moral or social sore, with skill and care, the proper and proportionate dressing. And finally, far from falling off, nearly all these communities are in a flourishing state, and whilst among the establishments for men there are only nine, on the average, to each, in those for women there is an average of twenty-four. Here, at Saint-Flour, is one which is bringing up fifty boarders; another, at Beaulieu, instructs one hundred; another, in Franche-Comté, has charge of eight hundred abandoned children.[40]—Evidently, in the presence of such institutions one must pause, however little one may care for justice and the public interest; and, moreover, because it is useless to act rigorously against them: the legislator crushes them in vain, for they spring up again of their own accord; they are in the blood of every Catholic nation. In France, instead of thirty-seven thousand nuns, at the present day there are eighty-six thousand—that is to say, forty-five in every ten thousand women instead of twenty-eight.

In any case, if the State deprives them of their property, along with that of other ecclesiastical bodies, it is not the State that ought to claim the spoil.—The State is not their heir, and their land, furniture, and rentals are in their very nature devoted to a special purpose, although they have no designated proprietor. This treasure, which consists of the accumulations of fourteen centuries, has been formed, increased, and preserved, in view of a certain object. The millions of generous, repentant, or devout souls who have made a gift of it, or have managed it, did so with a certain intention. It was their desire to ensure education, beneficence, and religion, and nothing else. Their legitimate intentions should not be frustrated: the dead have rights in society as well as the living, for it is the dead who have made the society which the living enjoy, and we receive their heritage only on the condition of executing their testamentary act.—Should this be of ancient date, it is undoubtedly necessary to make a liberal interpretation of it, to supplement its scanty provisions, and to take new circumstances into consideration. The requirements for which it provided have often disappeared; for instance, after the destruction of the Barbary pirates, there were no more Christians to be ransomed; and only by transferring an endowment can it be perpetuated.—But if, in the original institution,

40. "Archives Nationales." Papers of the Ecclesiastical Committee, *passim.*—Sauzay, i. 51.—Statics of France for 1866.

several accessory and special clauses have become antiquated, there remains the one important, general intention, which manifestly continues imperative and permanent, that of providing for a distinct service, either of charity, of worship, or of instruction. Let the administrators be changed, if necessary, also the apportionment of the legacy bequeathed, but do not divert any of it to services of an alien character; it is inapplicable to any but that purpose or to others strictly analogous. The four milliards of investment in real property, the two hundred millions of ecclesiastical income, form for it an express and special endowment. This is not a pile of gold abandoned on the highway, which the exchequer can appropriate or assign to those who live by the roadside. Authentic titles to it exist, which, declaring its origin, fix its destination, and your business is simply to see that it reaches its destination. Such was the principle under the ancient régime, in spite of grave abuses, and under forced exactions. When the ecclesiastical commission suppressed an ecclesiastical order, it was not for the purpose of making its possessions over to the public treasury, but to apply these to seminaries, schools, and hospitals. In 1789, the revenues of Saint-Denis supported Saint-Cyr; those of Saint-Germain went to the Economats, and the Government, although absolute and needy, was sufficiently honest to admit that confiscation was robbery. The greater our power, the greater the obligation to be just, and honesty always proves in the end to be the best policy.—It is, therefore, both just and useful that the Church, as in England and in America, that superior education, as in England and in Germany, that special instruction, as in America, and that diverse endowments for public assistance and utility, should be unreservedly secured in the maintenance of their heritage. The State, as testamentary executor of this inheritance, strangely abuses its mandate when it pockets the bequest in order to choke the deficit of its own treasury, risking it in bad speculations, and swallowing it up in its own bankruptcy, until of this vast treasure, which has been heaped up for generations for the benefit of children, the infirm, the sick, and the poor, not enough is left to pay the salary of a school-mistress, the wages of a parish nurse, or for a bowl of broth in a hospital.[41]

The Assembly remains deaf to all these arguments, and that which stops its ears is not financial distress.—The Archbishop of Aix, M. de Boisjelin, offered, in the name of the clergy, to liquidate at once the debt of three hundred millions, which was urgent, by a mortgage-loan of four hundred millions on the ecclesiastical property, which was a very good expedient; for at this time the credit of the clergy is the only substantial one; it generally borrows at less than five per cent., and more money has always been offered to it than it wanted, whilst the State borrows at ten per cent., and, at this moment, there are no lenders.—But, to our new statesmen, the supply of a deficit is of much less consequence than the application of a principle. In conformity with the Social Contract they establish the maxim that in the State there is no need of corporate bodies: they acknowledge nothing but, on the one hand, the State, the depositary of all public powers, and, on the other hand, a dust of separate human molecules. Special associations, specific groups, collateral corporations are not wanted, even to fulfil functions which the State is incapable of fulfilling. "As soon as one enters a corporation," says an orator, "one must love it as one loves a family";[42] the affections and obedience are all to be monopolized by the State. Moreover, on entering into an order a man receives special aid and comfort from it, and whatever distinguishes one man from another, is opposed to civil equality. Hence, if men are to remain equal and become citizens they must be deprived of every rallying point that might compete with that of the State, and give to some an advantage over others. All natural or acquired ties, consequently, which bound men together through geographical position, through climate, his-

41. Felix Rocquain, "La France après le 18 Brumaire." (Reports of the Councillors of State dispatched on this service, *passim*).

42. *Moniteur,* October 24, 1789. (Speech of Dupont de Nemours.) All these speeches, often more fully reported and with various renderings, may be found in "Les Archives Parlementaires," 1st series, vols. iii. and ix.

tory, pursuits, and trade, are sundered. The old provinces, the old provincial governments, the old municipal administrations, parliaments, wardenships, and masterships, all are suppressed. The groups which spring up most naturally, those which arise through a community of interests, are all dispersed, and the broadest, most express, and most positive interdictions are promulgated against their revival under any pretext whatever.[43] France is cut up into geometrical sections like a chess-board, and, within these improvised limits, which are destined for a long time to remain artificial, nothing is allowed to subsist but isolated individuals in juxtaposition. There is no desire to spare organized bodies where the cohesion is great, and least of all that of the clergy.

"Special associations," says Mirabeau, "in the community at large, break up the unity of its principles and destroy the equilibrium of its forces. Large political bodies in a State are dangerous through the strength which results from their coalition and the resistance which is born out of their interests."—That of the clergy, besides, is inherently bad,[44] because "its system is in constant antagonism to the rights of man." An institution in which a vow of obedience is necessary is "incompatible" with the constitution. Congregations "subject to independent chiefs are out of the social pale and incompatible with public spirit." As to the right of society over these, and also over the Church, this is not doubtful. "Corporate bodies exist only through society, and, in destroying them, society merely takes back the life she has imparted to them." "They are simply instrumentalities fabricated by the law.[45] What does the workman do when

43. Duvergier, decree of June 14–17, 1791. "The annihilation of every corporation of citizens of any one condition or profession *being one of the foundation-stones of the French constitution,* it is forbidden to reestablish these *de facto* under any pretext or form whatever. Citizens of a like condition or profession, such as contractors, shopkeepers, workmen of all classes, and associates in any art whatever, shall not, on assembling together, appoint either president, or secretaries, or syndics, discuss or pass resolutions, or frame any regulations in relation to their assumed common interests."

44. *Moniteur,* sitting of February 12, 1790. Speeches of Dally d'Agier and Barnave.

45. *Moniteur,* sitting of August 10, 1789. Speech by Garat; February 12, 1790, speech by Pétion; October 30, 1789, speech by Thournet.

the tool he works with no longer suits him? He breaks or alters it."—This primary sophism being admitted the conclusion is plain. Since corporate bodies are abolished they no longer exist, and since they no longer exist, they cannot again become proprietors. "Your aim was to destroy ecclesiastical orders,[46] because their destruction was essential to the safety of the State. If the clergy preserve their property, the clerical order is not destroyed: you necessarily leave it the right of assembling; you sanction its independence." In no case must ecclesiastics hold possessions. "If they are proprietors they are independent, and if they are independent they will associate this independence with the exercise of their functions." The clergy, cost what it will, must be in the hands of the State, as simple functionaries and supported by its subsidies. It would be too dangerous for a nation "to admit in its bosom as proprietors a large body of men to whom so many sources of credit already give so great power. As religion is the property of all, its ministers, through this fact alone, should be in the pay of the nation"; they are essentially "officers of morality and instruction," and "salaried" like judges and professors. Let us fetch them back to this condition of things, which is the only one compatible with the rights of man, and ordain that "the clergy, as well as all corporations and bodies with power of inheritance, are now, and shall be for evermore, incapable of holding any personal or landed estate."[47]

Who, now, is the legitimate heir of all these vacated possessions? Through another sophism, the State, at once judge and party in the cause, assigns them to the State. "The founders presented them to the Church, that is to say, to the nation."[48] "Since the nation has

46. *Moniteur,* sitting of November 2, 1789. Speech by Chapelier; October 24, 1789, speech by Garat; October 30, 1789, speech by Mirabeau, and the sitting of August 10, 1789.

47. *Moniteur,* sitting of October 23, 1789. Speech by Thouret.

48. *Moniteur,* sitting of October 23, 1789. Speech by Treilhard; October 24th, speech by Garat; October 30, speech by Mirabeau. On the 8th of August, 1789, Al. de Lameth says in the tribune: "When an endowment was made, it is the nation which was endowed."

permitted their possession by the clergy, she may redemand that which is possessed only through her authorisation." "The principle must be maintained that every nation is solely and veritably proprietor of the possessions of its clergy." This principle, it must be noted, as it is laid down, involves the destruction of ecclesiastical and lay corporations, along with the confiscation of all their possessions, and soon we shall see appearing on the horizon the final and complete decree[49] by which the Legislative Assembly, "considering that a State truly free should not suffer any corporation within its bosom, not even those which, devoted to public instruction, deserve well of the country," not even those "which are solely devoted to the service of the hospitals and the relief of the sick," suppresses all congregations, all associations of men or of women, lay or ecclesiastical, all endowments for pious, charitable, and missionary purposes, all houses of education, all seminaries and colleges, and those of the Sorbonne and Navarre. Add to these the last sweep of the broom: under the Legislative Assembly the division of all communal property, except woods: under the Convention, the abolition of all literary societies, academies of science and of literature, the confiscation of all their property, their libraries, museums, and botanical gardens; the confiscation of all communal possessions not previously divided; and the confiscation of all the property of hospitals and other philanthropic establishments.[50]—The abstract principle, proclaimed by the Constituent Assembly, reveals, by degrees, its exterminating virtues. France now, owing to it, contains nothing but dispersed, powerless, ephemeral individuals, and confronting them, the State, the sole, the only permanent body that has devoured

49. Duvergier, laws of August 18, 1792; August 8–14, 1793; July 11, 1794; July 14, 1792; August 24, 1793.

50. *Moniteur,* sitting of July 31, 1792. Speech of M. Boistard; the property of the hospitals at this time was estimated at eight hundred millions. Already in 1791 (sitting of January 30th) M. de Larochefoucauld-Liancourt said to the Assembly: "Nothing will more readily restore confidence to the poor than to see the nation assuming the right of rendering them assistance." He proposes to decree, accordingly, that all hospitals and places of beneficence be placed under the control of the nation. (*Mercure,* February 12, 1791.)

all the others, a veritable Colossus, alone erect in the midst of these insignificant dwarfs.

Substituted for the others, it is henceforth to perform their duties, and spend the money well which they have expended badly.—In the first place, it abolishes tithes, not gradually and by means of a process of redemption, as in England, but at one stroke, and with no indemnity, on the ground that the tax, being an abusive, illegitimate impost, a private tax levied by individuals in cowl and cassock on others in smock frocks, is a vexatious usurpation, and resembles the feudal dues. It is a radical operation, and in conformity with principle. Unfortunately, the puerility of the thing is so gross as to defeat its own object. In effect, since the days of Charlemagne, all the estates in the country which have been sold and resold over and over again have always paid tithes, and have never been purchased except with this charge upon them, which amounts to about one-seventh of the net revenue of the country. Take off this tax and one-seventh is added to the income of the proprietor, and, consequently, a seventh to his capital. A present is made to him of one hundred francs if his land is worth seven hundred francs, and of one thousand if it is worth seven thousand, of ten thousand if it is worth seventy thousand, and of one hundred thousand if it is worth seven hundred thousand. Some people gain six hundred thousand francs by this act, and thirty thousand francs in income.[51] Through this gratuitous and unexpected gift, one hundred and twenty-three millions of revenue, and two milliards and a half of capital, is divided among the holders of real estate in France, and in a manner so ingenious that the rich receive the most. Such is the effect of abstract principles. To afford a relief of thirty millions a year to the peasants in wooden shoes, an assembly of democrats adds thirty millions a year to the revenue of wealthy bourgeois and thirty millions a year to opulent nobles. The first part of this operation, moreover, is but another burden to the State; for, in taking off the load from the

51. *Moniteur,* sitting of August 10, 1789. Speech by Sieyès. The figures given here are deduced from the statistics already given in the "Ancient Régime."

holders of real property, it has encumbered itself, the State henceforth, without pocketing a penny, being obliged to defray the expenses of worship in their place.—As to the second part of the operation, which consists in the confiscation of four milliards of real property, it proves, after all, to be ruinous, although promising to be lucrative. It makes the same impression on our statesmen that the inheritance of a great estate makes on a needy and sanguine parvenu. Regarding it as a bottomless well of gold, he draws upon it without stint and strives to realise all his fancies; as he can afford to pay, he is free to break as he pleases. It is thus that the Assembly suppresses and compensates magisterial offices to the amount of four hundred and fifty millions; financial securities and obligations to the amount of three hundred and twenty-one millions; the household charges of the King, Queen, and princes, fifty-two millions; military services and encumbrances, thirty-five millions; enfeoffed tithes, one hundred millions, and so on.[52] "In the month of May, 1789," says Necker, "the reestablishment of order in the finances was mere child's-play." At the end of a year, by dint of involving itself in debt, by increasing its expenses, and by abolishing or abandoning its income, the State lives now on the paper-currency it issues, eats up its new capital, and rapidly marches onward to bankruptcy. Never was such a vast inheritance so quickly reduced to nothing, and to less than nothing.

Meanwhile, we can demonstrate, from the first few months, what use the administrators will make of it, and the manner in which they will endow the service to which it binds them.—No portion of this confiscated property is reserved for the maintenance of public worship, or to keep up the hospitals, asylums, and schools. Not only do all obligations and all productive real property find their way into the great national crucible to be converted into *assignats,* but a number of buildings, all monastic personalty, and a portion of the ecclesiastical, diverted from its natural course, becomes swallowed up in the same gulf. At Besançon,[53] three churches out of eight, with their

52. *Moniteur,* v. 571, sitting of September 4, 1790. Report of the Committee on Finances—v. 675, sitting of September 17, 1790. Report by Necker.

53. Sauzay, i. 228 (from October 10, 1790, to February 20, 1791). "The total

land and treasure, the funds of the chapter, all the money of the conventual churches, the sacred vessels, shrines, crosses, reliquaries, votive offerings, ivories, statues, pictures, tapestry, sacerdotal dresses and ornaments, plate, jewels and precious furniture, libraries, railings, bells, masterpieces of art and of piety, all are broken up and melted in the Mint, or sold by auction for almost nothing. This is the way in which the intentions of the founders and donors are carried out.—How are so many communities, which are deprived of their rentals, to support their schools, hospices, and asylums? Even after the decree[54] which, exceptionally and provisionally, orders the whole of their revenue to be accounted for to them, will it be paid over now that it is collected by a local administration whose coffers are always empty, and whose intentions are almost always hostile? Every establishment for benevolent and educational purposes is evidently sinking, now that the special streams which nourished them run into and are lost in the dry bed of the public treasury.[55] Already, in 1790, there are no funds with which to pay the monks and nuns their small pensions for their maintenance. In Franche-Comté the Capuchins of Baume have no bread, and, to live, they are obliged to resell, with the consent of the district, a portion of the stores of their monastery which had been confiscated. The Ursuline nuns of Ornans live on the means furnished them by private individuals in order to keep up the only school which the town possesses. The Bernardine nuns of Pontarlier are reduced to the lowest stage of want: "We are satisfied," the district reports,

---

weight of the spoil of the monastic establishments in gold, silver, and plated ware, sent to the Mint, amounted to more than 525 kilogrammes (for the department)."

54. Duvergier, law of October 8–14.

55. *Moniteur,* sitting of June 3, 1792. Speech of M. Bernard, in the name of the Committee of Public Assistance: "Not a day passes in which we do not receive the saddest news from the departments on the penury of their hospitals."—*Mercure de France,* December 17, 1791, sitting of December 5. A number of deputies of the Department of the North demand aid for their hospitals and municipalities. Out of 480,000 livres revenue there remains 10,000 to them. "The property of the Communes is mortgaged, and no longer affords them any resources." 280,000 persons are without bread.

"that they have nothing to put into their mouths. We have to contribute something every day amongst ourselves to keep them from starving."[56] Only too thankful are they when the local administration gives them something to eat, or allows others to give them something. In many places it strives to famish them, or takes delight in annoying them. In March, 1791, the department of Doubs, in spite of the entreaties of the district, reduces the pension of the Visitant nuns to one hundred and one livres for the choristers, and fifty for the lay-sisters. Two months before this, the municipality of Besançon, putting its own interpretation on the decree which allowed nuns to dress as they pleased, enjoins them all, including even the sisters of charity, to abandon their old costume, which few among them had the means of replacing.—Helplessness, indifference, or malevolence, such are the various dispositions which are encountered among the new authorities whose duty it is to support and protect them. To let loose persecution there is now only needed a decree which puts the civil power in conflict with religious convictions. That decree is promulgated, and, on the 12th of July, 1790, the Assembly establishes the civil constitution of the clergy.

Notwithstanding the confiscation of ecclesiastical property, and the dispersion of the monastic communities, the main body of the ecclesiastical corps remains intact: seventy thousand priests ranged under the bishops, with the Pope in the centre as the commander-in-chief. There is no corporation more solid, more antipathetic, or more attacked. For, against it are opposed implacable hatreds and fixed opinions: the Gallicanism of the legists who, from St. Louis downwards, are the adversaries of ecclesiastical power; the doctrine of the Jansenists who, since Louis XIII., desire to bring back the Church to its primitive form; and the theory of the philosophers who, for sixty years, have considered Christianity as a mistake and Catholicism as a scourge. At the very least the institution of a clergy in Catholicism is condemned, and they think that they are moderate if they respect the rest. "We might change our religion," say some

56. Sauzay, I. 252 (December 3, 1790. April 13, 1791).

of the deputies in the tribune.[57] Now, the decree affects neither dogma nor worship; it is confined to a revision of matters of discipline, and on this particular domain which is claimed for the civil power, it is pretended that demolition and reconstruction may be effected at discretion without the concurrence of the ecclesiastical power.

Here there is an usurpation, for an ecclesiastical as well as civil society has the right to choose its own form, its own hierarchy, its own government.—On this point, every argument that can be advanced in favour of the former can be repeated in favour of the latter, and the moment one becomes legitimate the other becomes legitimate also. The sanction of a civil or of a religious society consists in the long series of services which, for centuries, it has rendered to its members, the zeal and success with which it discharges its functions, the feelings of gratitude they entertain for it, the importance they attribute to its offices, the need they have of it and their attachment to it, the conviction imprinted in their minds that without it they would be deprived of a benefit upon which they set more store than upon any other. This benefit, in a civil society, is the security of persons and property. In the religious society it is the eternal salvation of the soul. In all other particulars the resemblance is complete, and the titles of the Church are as good as those of the State. Hence, if it be just for one to be sovereign and free on its own domain, it is just for the other to be equally sovereign and free: if the Church encroaches when it assumes to regulate the constitution of the State, the State encroaches when it pretends to regulate the constitution of the Church: if the former claims the respect of the latter on its domain, the latter must show equal respect for the former on its ground. The boundary-line between the two territories is, undoubtedly, not clearly defined, and frequent contests arise between the two. Sometimes these may be forestalled or terminated by each shutting itself up within a wall of separation, and by their remaining as much as possible indifferent to each other, as

57. *Moniteur,* sitting of June 1, 1790. Speeches by Camus, Treilhard, &c.

is the case in America. At another, they may, by a carefully considered contract, each accord to the other specific rights on the intermediate zone, and both exercise their divided authority on that zone, which is the case in France. In both cases, however, the two powers, like the two societies, must remain distinct. It is needful for each of them that the other should be an equal with which it treats, and not a subordinate to which it prescribes conditions. Whatever the civil system may be, whether monarchical or republican, oligarchical or democratic, the Church abuses its credit when it condemns or attacks it. Whatever may be the ecclesiastical system, whether papal, episcopalian, presbyterian, or congregational, the State abuses its strength when, without the assent of the faithful, it abolishes their systems or imposes a new one upon them. Not only does it violate right, but its violence, most frequently, is fruitless. It may strike as it will, the root of the tree is beyond its reach, and, in the unjust war which it wages against an institution as vital as itself, it often ends in getting the worst of it.

Unfortunately, the Assembly, in this as in other matters, being preoccupied with principles, fails to look at practical facts, and, aiming to remove only the dead bark, it injures the living trunk. For many centuries, and especially since the Council of Trent, the vigorous element of Catholicism is much less religion itself than the Church. Theology retires into the background, while discipline has come to the front. Believers who, according to Church law, are required to regard spiritual authority as dogma, in fact attach their faith to the authority much more than to the dogma. Faith insists, in relation to discipline as well as to dogma, that if one rejects the decision of the Romish Church one ceases to be a Catholic; that spiritual authority comes from above and not from below; that without the institution of a bishop there can be no priest; that without the institution of a Pope there can be no bishop; that an illegitimate bishop or priest cannot administer valid sacraments; that a child baptized by one of these is not Christian; that a dying man thus absolved is not absolved; and that two believers thus married live in concubinage. It is a matter of fact that believers are no longer theologians or canonists; that, save a few Jansenists, they no longer read the Scriptures or the Fathers; that, if they accept the dogma, it is in a lump, without investigation, confiding in the hand which presents it; that their obedient conscience is in the keeping of this pastoral guide; that the Church of the third century is of little consequence to them; and that, as far as the true form of the actual Church goes, the doctor whose advice they follow is not St. Cyprian, of whom they know nothing, but their visible bishop and their living curé. Put these two premises together and the conclusion is self-evident: it is clear that they will not believe that they are baptized, absolved, or married but by this curé authorised by this bishop. Let others be put in their places whom they condemn, and you suppress worship, sacraments, and the most precious functions of spiritual life to twenty-four millions of French people, to all the peasantry, all the children, and to almost all the women; you stir up in rebellion against you the two greatest forces which move the soul—conscience and habit. And observe the effect. You not only convert the State into a gendarme in the service of heresy, but also, through this fruitless and tyrannous attempt of Gallican Jansenism, you bring into permanent discredit Gallican maxims and Jansenist doctrines. You cut away the last two roots by which a liberal sentiment still vegetated in orthodox Catholicism. You throw the clergy back on Rome; you attach them to the Pope from whom you wish to separate them, and deprive them of the national character which you wish to impose on them. They were French, and you render them Ultramontane. They excited ill-will and envy, and you render them sympathetic and popular. They were a divided body, and you give them unanimity. They were a straggling militia, scattered about under several independent authorities, and rooted to the soil through the possession of the ground; thanks to you, they are to become a regular, manageable army, emancipated from every local attachment, organized under one head, and always prepared to take the field at the word of command. Compare the authority of a bishop in his diocese in 1789 with that of a bishop sixty years later. In 1789, the Archbishop of Besançon, out of fifteen hundred offices and benefices, had the patronage of one hundred; in ninety-three incumbencies the selections were made by the metropolitan chapter; in eighteen it was made by the chapter of the Madeleine; in seventy parishes by the noble founder or benefactor; one abbé had thirteen incumbencies at his disposal, another thirty-four, another thirty-five, a prior nine, an abbess twenty; five communes directly nominated their own pastor, while abbeys, priories, and canonries were in the hands of the King.[58] At the present day in a diocese the bishop appoints all the curés or officiating priests, and may deprive nine out of ten of them; in the diocese above named, from 1850 to 1860, scarcely *one lay functionary* was nominated without the consent or intervention of the cardinal-archbishop.[59] To comprehend the spirit, discipline, and influence of our contemporary clergy, go back to the source of it, and you will find it in the decree of the Constituent Assembly. A natural organization cannot be broken up with impunity; it forms anew, adapting itself to circumstances, and closes up its ranks in proportion to its danger.

But if, according to the maxims of the Assembly, faith and worship are free in relation to the secular State, before the State as sovereign churches are subjects.—For these are societies, administrations, and hierarchies, and no society, administration, or hierarchy may subsist in the State without entering into its departments under the title of subordinate, delegate, or employé. A priest is essentially a salaried officer like the rest, a functionary[60] presiding over matters pertaining to worship and morality. If the State is disposed to change the number, the mode of nomination, the duties, and the posts of its engineers, it is not bound to assemble its engineers and ask their permission, least of all that of a foreign engineer established at Rome. If it wishes to change the condition of "its ecclesiastical officers," its right to do so is the same, and therefore unquestioned.

58. Sauzay, i. 168.

59. Personal knowledge, as I visited Besançon four times between 1863 and 1867.

60. *Moniteur*, sitting of May 30, 1790, and others following. (Report of Treilhard, speech by Robespierre.)

There is no need of asking anybody's consent in the exercise of this right, and it allows no interference between it and its clerks. The Assembly refuses to call a Gallican council; it refuses to negotiate with the Pope, and, on its authority alone, it recasts the whole Constitution of the Church. Henceforth this branch of the public administration is to be organized on the model of the others.[61] In the first place the diocese is to be in extent and limits the same as the department; consequently, all ecclesiastical circumscriptions are marked out anew, and forty-eight episcopal sees disappear. In the second place, the appointed bishop is forbidden "to refer to the Pope to obtain any confirmation whatever." All he can do is to write to him "in testimony of the unity of faith and of the communion which he is to maintain with him." The bishop is thus no longer installed by his canonical chief, and the Church of France becomes schismatic. In the third place, the metropolitan or bishop is forbidden to exact from the new bishops or curés "any oath other than that they profess the Catholic, Apostolic, and Roman religion." Assisted by his council he may examine them on their doctrine and habits, and refuse them canonical installation, but in this case his reasons must be given in writing, and be signed by himself and his council. His authority, in other respects, does not extend beyond this, for it is the civil tribunal which decides between contending parties. Thus is the catholic hierarchy broken up; the ecclesiastical superior has his hands tied; if he still delegates sacerdotal functions it is only as a matter of form. Between the curé and the bishop subordination ceases to exist just as it has ceased to exist between the bishop and the Pope, and the Church of France becomes Presbyterian.

The people now, in effect, choose their own ministers, as they do in the Presbyterian church; the bishop is appointed by the electors of the department, the curé by the district electors, and, what is an extraordinary aggravation, these need not be of his communion. It is of no consequence whether the electoral Assembly contains, as at

61. Duvergier, laws of July 12th–August 14th; November 14–25, 1790; January 21–26, 1791.

Nismes, Montauban, Strasbourg, and Metz, a notable proportion of Calvinists, Lutherans, and Jews, or whether its majority, furnished by the club, is notoriously hostile to Catholicism, and even to Christianity itself. The bishop and the curé must be chosen by the electoral body; the Holy Ghost dwells with it, and with the civil tribunals, and these may install its elect in spite of any resistance. To complete the dependence of the clergy, every bishop is forbidden to absent himself more than fifteen days without permission from the department; every curé the same length of time without the permission of the district, even to attend upon a dying father or to undergo the operation of lithotomy. In default of this permission his salary is suspended: as a functionary under salary, he owes all his time to his bureau, and if he desires a leave of absence he must ask for it from his chiefs in the Hôtel-de-Ville.[62] He must assent to all these innovations, not only with passive obedience, but by a solemn oath. All old or new ecclesiastics, archbishops, bishops, curés, vicars, preachers, hospital and prison chaplains, superiors and directors of seminaries, professors of seminaries and colleges, are to state in writing that they are ready to take this oath: moreover, they must take it publicly, in church, "in the presence of the general council, the commune, and the faithful," and promise "to maintain with all their power" a schismatic and Presbyterian Church. For there can be no doubt about the sense and bearing of the prescribed oath. It was all very well to incorporate it with a broader one, that of maintaining the Constitution. But the Constitution of the clergy is too clearly comprised in the general Constitution, like a chapter in a

62. *Moniteur*, sitting of May 31, 1790. Robespierre, in covert terms, demands the marriage of priests.—Mirabeau prepared a speech in the same sense, concluding that every priest and monk could contract marriage; on the priest or monk presenting himself with his bride before the curé, the latter should be obliged to give them the nuptial benediction, &c. Mirabeau wrote, June 2, 1790: "Robespierre . . . has juggled me out of my motion on the marriage of priests."—In general the germ of all the laws of the Convention is found in the Constituent Assembly. (Ph. Plan, "Un Collaborateur de Mirabeau," p. 56, 144.)

book, and to sign the book is to sign the chapter. Besides, in the formula to which the ecclesiastics in the Assembly are obliged to swear in the tribune, the chapter is precisely indicated, and no exception or reservation is allowed.[63] The Bishop of Clermont, with all those who have accepted the Constitution in full, save the decrees affecting spiritual matters, are silenced. Where the spiritual begins and where it ends the Assembly knows better than they, for it has defined this, and it imposes its definition on canonist and theologian; it is, in its turn, the Pope, and all consciences must bow to its decision. Let them take the "oath, pure and simple," or if they do not they are "refractory." The fiat goes forth, and the effect of it is immense, for, along with the clergy, the law reaches to laymen. On the one hand, all the ecclesiastics who refuse the oath are dismissed. If they continue "to interfere with public functions which they have personally or corporately exercised" they "shall be prosecuted as disturbers of the peace, and condemned as rebels against the law," deprived of all rights as active citizens, and declared incompetent to hold any public office. This is the penalty already inflicted on the nonjuring bishop who persists in considering himself a bishop, who ordains priests and who issues a pastoral letter. Such is soon to be the penalty inflicted on the nonjuring curé who presumes to hear confession or officiate at a mass.[64] On the other hand, all citizens who refuse to take the prescribed oath, all electors, municipal officers, judges, and administrative agents, shall lose their right of suffrage, have their functions revoked, and be declared incompetent for all public duties.[65] The result is that scrupulous Catholics are ex-

63. Duvergier, laws of November 27th–December 26, 1790; February 5th, March 22nd, and April 5, 1791.—*Moniteur,* sitting of November 6, 1790, and those that follow, especially that of December 27th. "I swear to maintain with all my power the French Constitution and especially the decrees relating to the Civil Constitution of the clergy."—Cf. sitting of January 2, 1791, speech by the Bishop of Clermont.

64. Duvergier, law of May 7, 1791, to maintain the right of nonjuring priests to perform mass in national or private edifices. (Demanded by Talleyrand and Sieyès.)

65. "Archives Nationales," F^7, 3,235. Letter of M. de Château-Randon,

cluded from every administrative post, from all elections, and especially from ecclesiastical elections; from which it follows that, the stronger one's faith the less one's share in the choice of a priest.[66]—What an admirable law, that which, under the pretext of reforming ecclesiastical abuses, places the faithful, lay or clerical, outside the pale of the law!

This soon becomes apparent. One hundred and thirty-four archbishops, bishops, and coadjutors refuse to take the oath; there are only four of them who do so, three of whom, MM. de Talleyrand, de Jarente, and de Brienne, are sceptical, and notorious for their licentiousness; the others are influenced by their consciences, above all, by their *esprit de corps* and a point of honour. Most of the curés rally around this staff of officers. In the diocese of Besançon,[67] out of fourteen hundred priests, three hundred take the oath, a thousand refuse it, and eighty retract. In the department of Doubs, only four consent to swear. In the department of Lozère, there are only "ten out of two hundred and fifty." "It is stated positively," writes the best informed of all observers, "that everywhere in France two-thirds of the ecclesiastics have refused the oath, or have only taken it with the same reservations as the Bishop of Clermont."

Thus, out of seventy thousand priests, forty-six thousand are turned out of office, and the majority of their parishioners are on their side. This is apparent in the absence of electors convoked to replace them: at Bordeaux only four hundred and fifty came to the poll out of nine hundred, while elsewhere the summons brings together only "a third or a quarter." In many places there are no candidates, or those elected decline to accept. They are obliged, in order to supply their places, to hunt up unfrocked monks of a questionable character. There are two parties, after this, in each parish;

---

deputy of la Lozère, May 28, 1791. After the decree of May 23rd, all the functionaries of the department handed in their resignations.

66. Duvergier, law of May 21–29, 1791.

67. Sauzay, i. 366, 538 to 593, 750.—"Archives Nationales," F^7, 3,235. Letter of M. de Chanteauredon, May 10, 1791.—*Mercure*, April 23rd, and April 16, 1791. Articles of Mallet-Dupan, letter from Bordeaux, March 20, 1791.

two faiths, two systems of worship, and permanent discord. Even when the new and the old curés are accommodating, their situations bring them into conflict. To the former the latter are "intruders." To the latter the former are "refractories." By virtue of his being a guardian of souls, the former cannot dispense with telling his parishioners that the intruder is excommunicated, that his sacraments are null or sacrilegious, and that it is a sin to attend his mass. By virtue of his being a public functionary, the latter does not fail to write to the authorities that the "refractory" entraps the faithful, excites their consciences, saps the Constitution, and that he ought to be put down by force. In other words, the former draws everybody away from the latter, while the latter sends the gendarmes against the former, and persecution begins.—Through a singular reversion of things, it is the majority which undergoes persecution, and the minority which practises it. The mass of the constitutional curé is, everywhere, deserted.[68] In La Vendée there are ten or twelve present in the church out of five or six hundred parishioners; on Sundays and holidays whole villages and market-towns travel from one to two leagues off to attend the orthodox mass, the villagers declaring that "if the old curé can only be restored to them, they will gladly pay a double tax." In Alsace, "nine-tenths, at least, of the Catholics refuse to recognise the legally sworn priests." The same spectacle presents itself in Franche-Comté, Artois, and in ten of the other provinces.—Finally, as in a chemical composition, the analysis is complete. Those who believe, or who recover their belief, are ranged around the old curé; all who, through conviction or tradition, hold to the sacraments, all who, through faith or habit, wish or feel a need to attend the mass. The auditors of the new curé consist of sceptics, deists, the indifferent, members of the clubs and of the administration, who resort to the church as to the Hôtel-de-

68. Roux and Buchez, xii. 77. Report of Gallois and Gensonné sent to La Vendée and the Deux Sèvres (July 25, 1791).—"Archives Nationales," F^7, 3,253, letter of the Directory of the Bas-Rhin (letter of January 7, 1792).—"Le District de Machecoul de 1788 à 1793," by Lallier.—"Histoire de Joseph Lebon," by Paris.—Sauzay, vol. i. and ii. in full.

Ville or to a popular meeting, not through religious but through political zeal, and who support the "intruder," in order to sustain the Constitution.

All this does not secure to him very fervent followers, but it provides him with very zealous defenders; and, in default of the faith which they do not possess, they give the force which is at their disposal. All means are proper against an intractable bishop or curé; not only the law which they aggravate through their forced interpretation of it and through their arbitrary verdicts, but also the riots which they stir up by their instigations and which they sanction by their toleration.[69] He is driven out of his parish, consigned to the county town, and kept in a safe place. The Directory of Aisne denounces him as a disturber of the public peace, and forbids him, under severe penalties, from administering the sacraments. The municipality of Cahors shuts up particular churches and orders the nonjuring ecclesiastics to leave the town in twenty-four hours. The electoral corps of Lot denounces them publicly as "ferocious brutes," incendiaries, and provokers of civil war. The Directory of the Bas-Rhin banishes them to Strasbourg or to fifteen leagues from the frontier. At Saint-Léon the bishop is forced to fly. At Auch the archbishop is imprisoned; at Lyons M. de Boisboissel, grand vicar, is confined in Pierre-Encize, for having preserved an archepiscopal mandate in his house; brutality is everywhere the minister of intolerance. A certain curé of Aisne who, in 1789, had fed two thousand poor, having presumed to read from his pulpit a pastoral charge concerning the observance of Lent, the mayor seizes him by the collar and prevents him from going to the altar; "two of the National Yeomanry" draw their sabres on him, and forthwith lead him away bareheaded, not allowing him to return to his house, and drive him to a distance of two leagues by beat of drum and under escort. At

69. *Mercure,* January 15th, April 23rd, May 16th and 30th, November 23, 1791.—"Le District de Machecoul," by Lallier, 173.—Sauzay, i. 295.—Lavirotte, "Annales d'Arnay-le Duc (February 5, 1792).—"Archives Nationales," F^7, 3,223. Petition of a number of the inhabitants of Montpellier, November 17, 1791.

Paris, in the church of Saint-Eustache, the curé is greeted with outcries, a pistol is pointed at his head, he is seized by the hair, struck with fists, and only reaches the sacristy through the intervention of the National Guard. In the church of the Théatins, rented by the orthodox with all legal formality, a furious band disperses the priests and their assistants, upsets the altar, and profanes the sacred vessels. A placard, posted up by the department, calls upon the people to respect the law. "I saw it," says an eye-witness, "torn down amidst imprecations against the department, the priests, and the devout. One of the chief haranguers, standing on the steps . . . terminated his speech by stating that schism ought to be stopped at any cost, that no worship but his should be allowed, that women should be whipped and priests knocked on the head." And, in fact, "a young lady accompanied by her mother is whipped on the steps of the church." Elsewhere nuns are the sufferers, even the sisters of Saint-Vincent de Paul; and, from April, 1791, onward, the same outrages on modesty and against life are propagated from town to town. At Dijon, rods are nailed fast to the gates of all the convents; at Montpellier, two or three hundred ruffians, armed with large iron-bound sticks, murder the men and outrage the women.—Nothing remains but to put the male-factors under the shelter of an amnesty, which is done by the Constituent Assembly, and to legally sanction the animosity of local administrations, which is done by the Legislative Assembly.[70] Henceforth the nonjuring ecclesiastics are deprived of their sustenance; they are declared "suspected of revolt against the law and of evil intentions against the country."—Thus, says a contemporary Protestant, "on the strength of these *suspicions* and these *intentions*, a Directory, to which the law interdicts judicial functions, may arbitrarily drive out of his house the minister of a God of peace and charity, grown grey in the shadow of the altar." Thus, "everywhere, where disturbances occur on account of religious opinions, and whether these troubles are due to the frantic scourgers of the

70. Duvergier, decree of November 29, 1791.—*Mercure*, November 30, 1791 (article by Mallet-Dupan).

virtuous sisters of charity or to the ruffians armed with cow-hides who, at Nismes and Montpellier, outrage all the laws of decorum and of liberty for six whole months, the nonjuring priests are to be punished with banishment. Torn from their families whose means of living they share, they are sent away to wander on the highways, abandoned to public pity or ferocity the moment any scoundrel chooses to excite a disturbance that he can impute to them."—Thus we see approaching the revolt of the peasantry, the insurrections of Nismes, Franche-Comté, La Vendée, and Brittany, emigration, transportation, imprisonment, the guillotine or drowning for two-thirds of the clergy of France, and likewise for myriads of the loyal, for husbandmen, artisans, day-labourers, sempstresses, and servants, and the humblest among the lower class of the people. This is what the laws of the Constituent Assembly are leading to.—In the institution of the clergy, as in that of the nobles and the King, it demolished a solid wall in order to dig through it an open door, and it is nothing strange if the whole structure tumbles down on the heads of its inmates. The true course was to respect, to reform, to utilise rank and corporations: all that the Assembly thought of was the abolition of these in the name of abstract equality and of national sovereignty. In order to abolish these it executed, tolerated, or initiated all the attacks on persons and on property. Those it is about to commit are the inevitable result of those which it has already committed; for, through its Constitution, bad is changed to worse, and the social edifice, already half in ruins through the clumsy havoc that is effected in it, will fall in completely under the weight of the incongruous or extravagant constructions which it proceeds to extemporise.

CHAPTER III

Construction—The Constitution of 1791— I. *Powers of the Central Government—The Assembly on the partition of power—Rupture of every tie between the Legislature and the King—The Assembly on the subordination of the executive power—How this is nullified—Certainty of a conflict—The deposition of the King inevitable—* II. *Administrative powers—The Assembly on the hierarchy—Grades abolished—Collective powers—Election introduced, and the influence of subordinates in all branches of the service—Certainty of disorganization—Power in the hands of municipal bodies—* III. *The Municipal bodies—Their great task—Their incapacity—Their feeble authority—Insufficiency of their means of action—The rôle of the National Guard—* IV. *The National Guard as electors—Its great power—Its important task—The work imposed on active citizens—They avoid it—* V. *The restless minority—Its elements—The clubs—Their ascendency—How they interpret the Rights of Man—Their usurpations and violence—* VI. *Summary of the work of the Constituent Assembly.*

THAT which is called a Government is a concert of powers, each with a distinct function, and all working towards a final and complete end. The merit of a Government consists in the attainment of this end; the worth of a machine depends upon the work it accomplishes. The important thing is not to produce a good mechanical design on paper, but to see that the machine works well when set up on the ground. In vain might its conductors allege the beauty of their plan and the logical connection of their theorems; they are not required to furnish either plan or theorems, but an implement.—Two conditions are requisite to render this implement serviceable and effective. In the first place, the public powers must harmonize with each other, or one neutralises the other; in the second place they must be obeyed, or they are null. The Constituent Assembly made no provision for securing this harmony or this obedience. In the machine which it constructed the motions all counteract each other; the impulse is not transmitted; the gearing is not complete between the centre and the extremities; the large central and upper wheels turn to no purpose; the innumerable small wheels near the ground break or get out of order: the machine, by virtue of its own mechanism, remains useless, overheated, under clouds of waste steam, creaking and thumping in such a manner as to show clearly that it must explode.

I

Let us first consider the two central powers, the Assembly and the King.—Ordinarily when distinct powers of different origin are established by a Constitution, it makes provision for an umpire, in case of conflict between them, in the institution of an Upper Chamber. Each of these powers, at least, has a hold on the other. The Assembly must have one on the King, which is the right to refuse taxation; the King must have one on the Assembly, which is the right of dissolving it. Otherwise, one of the two being disarmed, the other becomes omnipotent, and, consequently, insane. The peril here is as great for an omnipotent Assembly as it is for an absolute King. If the former is desirous of remaining in its right mind, it needs repression and control as much as the latter, and, if it be wise for the Assembly to restrain the King by refusing him subsidies, it is wise for him to be able to defend himself by appealing to the electors.—But, besides these extreme measures, which are dangerous and rarely resorted to, there is another which is ordinarily employed and is safe, that is, the right of the King to take his ministers from the Chamber. Generally, the leaders of the majority become the ministry, their nomination being the means of restoring harmony between the King and the Assembly; they are at once men belonging to the Assembly and men belonging to the King. Through this expedient not only is the confidence of the Assembly assured, since the Government remains in the hands of its leaders, but also it is under restraint because these become simultaneously both powerful and responsible. Placed at the head of all branches of the service, they are in a position to judge whether a law is useful and practicable; obliged to put it into execution, they can calculate its effects before proposing it or accepting it. Nothing is so healthy for a majority as a ministry composed of its own chiefs; nothing is so effective in repressing rashness or intemperance. A railway conductor is not willing that his locomotive should be deprived of coal, nor to have the rails he is about to run on broken up.—This arrangement, with all its drawbacks and inconveniences, is the best one yet arrived at by human experience for the security of societies against despotism and anarchy. For the absolute power which founds or rescues them, but which oppresses or exhausts them, there is a gradual substitution of differentiated powers, held together through the mediation of a third party (*tiers-arbitre*), by reciprocal dependence and an organ which is common to both.

Experience, however, is of no avail with the members of the Constituent Assembly; under the banner of principles they sunder one after another all the ties which should keep the two powers together harmoniously.—There must not be an Upper Chamber, because this would be an asylum or a nursery for aristocrats. Moreover, "the nation being of one mind," it is averse to "the creation of different organs." So they go on with theoretical definitions and distinctions, in the application of ready-made formulas and metaphors. The King must not have a hold on the legislative body: the executive is an arm, whose business it is to obey; it is absurd for the arm to constrain or direct the head. Scarcely is the monarch allowed a suspensive veto. Sieyès here enters with his protest declaring that this is a "*lettre de cachet* launched against the universal will," and there is excluded from the action of the veto the articles of the Constitution, all money-bills, and some other laws.—Neither the monarch nor the electors of the Assembly are to convoke the Assembly; he has no voice in or oversight of the details of its formation;

the electors are to meet together and vote without his summons or supervision. Once the Assembly is elected he can neither adjourn nor dissolve it. He cannot even propose a law;[1] permission is only granted to him "to invite it to take a subject into consideration." He is limited to his executive duties; and still more, a sort of wall is built up between him and the Assembly, and the opening in it, by which each could take the other's hand, is carefully closed up. The deputies are forbidden to become ministers throughout the term of their service and for two years afterwards: fears are entertained that they might be corrupted through contact with the Court, and, again, whoever the ministers might be, there is no disposition to accept their ascendency.[2] If one of them is admitted into the Assembly it is not for the purpose of giving advice, but to furnish information, reply to interrogatories, and make protestations of his zeal in humble terms and in a dubious position.[3] By virtue of being a royal agent he is under suspicion like the King himself, and he is sequestered in his bureau as the King is sequestered in his palace.—Such is the spirit of the Constitution: by force of the theory, and the better to secure a separation of the powers,[4] a common understanding between them is for ever rendered impossible, and to make up for this impossibility there remains nothing but to make one the master and the other the clerk.

This they did not fail to do, and for greater security, the latter is made an honorary clerk. The executive power is conferred on him

1. The initiative rests with the King on one point: war cannot be decreed by the Assembly except on his formal and preliminary proposition. This exception was secured only after a violent struggle and a supreme effort by Mirabeau.

2. Speech by Lanjuinais, November 7, 1789. "We determined on the separation of the powers. Why, then, should the proposal be made to us to unite the legislative power with the executive power in the persons of the ministers?"

3. See the attendance of the Ministers before the Legislative Assembly.

4. "Any society in which the separation of the powers is not clearly defined has no constitution." (Declaration of Rights, article xvi.)—This principle is borrowed from a text by Montesquieu, also from the American Constitution. In the rest the theory of Rousseau is followed.

nominally and in appearance; he does not possess it in fact, care having been taken to place it in other hands.—In effect, all executive agents and all secondary and local powers are elective. The King has no voice, directly or indirectly, in the choice of judges, public prosecutors, bishops, curés, collectors and assessors of the taxes, commissaries of police, district and departmental administrators, mayors, and municipal officers. At most, should an administrator violate a law, he may annul his acts and suspend him; but the Assembly, the superior power, has the right to cancel this suspension.—As to the armed force, of which he is supposed to be the commander-in-chief, this escapes from him entirely: the National Guard is not to receive orders from him; the gendarmerie and the troops are bound to respond to the requisitions of the municipal authorities, whom the King can neither select nor displace: in short, local action of any kind—that is to say, all effective action—is denied to him.—The executive instrument is purposely destroyed. The connection which existed between the wheels of the extremities and the central shaft is broken, and henceforth, incapable of distributing its energy, this shaft, in the hands of the monarch, stands still or else turns to no purpose. The King, "supreme head of the general administration, of the army, and of the navy, guardian of public peace and order, hereditary representative of the nation," is without the means, in spite of his lofty titles, of directly applying his pretended powers, of causing a schedule of assessments to be drawn up in a refractory commune, of compelling payment by a delinquent tax-payer, of enforcing the free circulation of a convoy of grain, of executing the judgment of a court, of suppressing an outbreak, or of securing protection to persons and property. For he can bring no constraint to bear on the agents who are declared to be subordinate to him; he has no resources but those of warning and persuasion. He sends to each Departmental Assembly the decrees which he has sanctioned, requesting it to transmit them and cause them to be carried out; he receives its correspondence and bestows his censure or approval—and that is all. He is merely a powerless medium of communication, a herald or public advertiser, a sort of central echo, sonorous and empty, to which news is brought, and from which laws depart, to spread abroad like a common rumour.

Such as he is, and thus diminished, he is still considered to be too strong. He is deprived of the right of pardon, "which severs the last artery of monarchical government."[5] All sorts of precautions are taken against him. He cannot declare war without a decree of the Assembly; he is obliged to bring war to an end on the decree of the Assembly; he cannot make a treaty of peace, an alliance, or a commercial treaty, without the ratification of these by the Assembly. It is expressly declared that he is to nominate but two-thirds of the rear-admirals, one-half of the lieutenant-generals, field-marshals, captains of vessels, and colonels of the gendarmerie, one-third of the colonels and lieutenant-colonels of the line, and a sixth of the naval lieutenants. He must not allow troops to stay or pass within 30,000 yards of the Assembly. His guard must not consist of more than 1,800 men, duly verified, and protected against his seductions by the civil oath. The heir-presumptive must not leave the country without the Assembly's assent. It is the Assembly which is to regulate by law the education of his son during minority.—All these precautions are accompanied with threats. There are against him five possible causes of dethronement; against his responsible Ministers, eight causes for condemnation to from twelve to twenty years of constraint, and eight grounds for condemnations to death.[6] Everywhere between the lines of the Constitution, we read the constant disposition to assume an attitude of defence, the secret dread of treachery, the conviction that executive power, of whatever kind, is in its nature inimical to the public welfare.—For withholding the nomination of judges, the reason alleged is that "the Court and the Ministers are the most contemptible portion of the nation."[7] If the nomination of Ministers is conceded, it is on the ground that "Ministers appointed by the people would necessarily be too highly es-

5. *Mercure de France*, an expression by Mallet-Dupan.

6. Constitution of 1791, ch. ii. articles 5, 6, 7.—Decree of September 25–October 6, 1791, section iii. articles 8 to 25.

7. Speeches by Barnave and Roederer in the Constituent Assembly.—Speeches by Barnave and Duport in the Jacobin Club.

teemed." The principle is that "the legislative body alone must possess the confidence of the people," that royal authority corrupts its depository, and that executive power is always tempted to commit abuses and to engage in conspiracies. If it is provided for in the Constitution it is with regret, through the necessity of the case, and on the condition of its being trammelled by impediments; it will prove so much the less baneful in proportion as it is restrained, guarded, threatened, and denounced.—A position of this kind is manifestly intolerable; and only a man as passive as Louis XVI. could have put up with it. Do what he will, however, he cannot make it a tenable one. In vain does he scrupulously adhere to the Constitution, and fulfil it to the letter. Because he is powerless the Assembly regards him as lukewarm, and imputes to him the jarrings of the machine which is not under his control. If he presumes once to exercise his veto it is rebellion, and the rebellion of an official against his superior, which is the Assembly; the rebellion of a subject against his Sovereign, which is the people. In this case dethronement is proper, and the Assembly has only to pass the decree; the people have simply to execute the act, and the Constitution ends in a Revolution.—A piece of machinery of this stamp breaks down through its own movement. In conformity with the philosophic theory the two wheels of government must be separated, and to do this they have to be disconnected and isolated one from the other. In conformity with the popular creed, the driving-wheel must be subordinated and its influence neutralised: to do this it is necessary to reduce its energy to a minimum, break up its connections, and raise it up in the air to turn round like a top, or to remain there as an obstacle to something else. It is certain that, after much ill-usage as a plaything, it will finally be removed as a hindrance.

II

Let us leave the centre for the extremities, and observe the various administrations in working operation.[8]—For any service to work

8. Principal texts. (Duvergier, "Collection des Lois et Décrets.")—Laws on municipal and administrative organization, December 14 and 22, 1789; August

well and with precision, there must first be one head, and, next, this head should have the appointment of his subordinates and be empowered to pay, punish, or dismiss them. For, on the one hand, he stands alone and feels his responsibility; he brings to bear on the management of affairs a degree of attention and consistency, a tact and a power of initiation of which a set of commissioners are incapable; corporate follies or defects do not involve any one in particular, and authority is efficacious only when it is in one hand. On the other hand, being master, he can rely on the subalterns whom he has himself selected, whom he controls through their hopes or fears, and whom he discharges if they do not perform their duties; otherwise he has no hold on them and they are not instruments to be depended on. Only on these conditions can a railway manager be sure that his pointsmen are at their posts. Only on these conditions can the foreman of a foundry engage to execute work by a given day. In every public or private enterprise, direct, immediate authority is the only known, the only human and possible way to ensure the obedience and punctuality of agents.—Administration is thus carried on in all countries, by one or several series of functionaries, each under some central manager who holds the reins in his single grasp.

This is all reversed in the new Constitution. In the eyes of our legislators obedience must be spontaneous and never compulsory, and, in the suppression of despotism, they suppress government. The general rule in the hierarchy which they establish is that the subordinates should be independent of their superior, for he must neither appoint nor displace them: the only right he has is to give them advice and remonstrate with them. At best, in certain cases, he can annul their acts and inflict on them a provisional suspension of their

12–20, 1790; March 15, 1791. On the municipal organization of Paris, May 21st, June 27, 1790.—Laws on the organization of the Judiciary, August 16–24, 1790; September 16–29, 1791; September 29, October 21, 1791.—Laws on military organization, September 23, October 29, 1790; January 16, 1791; July 27, 28, 1791.—Laws on the financial organization, November 14–24, 1790; November 23, 1790; March 17, 1791; September 26, October 2, 1791.

functions, which can be contested and is revocable. We see, thus, that none of the local powers are delegated by the central power; the latter is simply like a man without either hands or arms, seated in a gilt chair. The Minister of the Finances cannot appoint or dismiss either an assessor or a collector; the Minister of the Interior, not one of the departmental, district, or communal administrators; the Minister of Justice, not one judge or public prosecutor. The King, in these three branches of the service, has but one officer of his own, the commissioner whose duty it is to advocate the observance of the laws in the courts, and, on sentence being given, to enforce its execution.—All the muscles of the central power are paralyzed by this stroke, and henceforth each department is a State apart, living by itself.

A like amputation, however, in the department itself, has cut away all the ties by which the superior could control and direct his subordinate.—If the administrators of the department are suffered to act on those of the district, and those of the district on those of the municipality, it is only, again, in the way of council and solicitation. Nowhere is the superior a commander who orders and constrains, but everywhere a censor who gives warning and scolds. To render this already feeble authority still more feeble at each step of the hierarchy, it is divided among several bodies. These consist of superposed councils, which administer the department, the district, and the commune. There is no directing head in any of these councils. Permanency and executive functions throughout are vested in directories of four or eight members, or in bureaux of two, three, four, six, and seven members whose elected chief, a president or mayor,[9] has simply an honorary primacy. Decision and action, everywhere blunted, delayed, or curtailed by talk and the processes of discussion, are brought forth only after the difficult, tumultuous assent of several discordant wills. Elective and collective as these powers are, mea-

9. Decrees of December 14 and December 22, 1789: "In municipalities reduced to three members (communes below five hundred inhabitants), all executive functions shall belong to the mayor alone."

sures are still taken to guard against them. Not only are they subject to the control of an elected council, one-half renewable every two years, but, again, the mayor and public prosecutor of the commune after serving four years, and the *procureur-syndic* of the department or district after eight years' service, and the district collector after six years' service, are not reelected. Should these officials have deserved and won the confidence of the electors, should familiarity with affairs have made them specially competent and valuable, so much the worse for affairs and the public; they are not to be anchored to their post. Should their continuance in office introduce into the service a spirit of order and economy, that is of no consequence; there is danger of their acquiring too much influence, and the law sends them off as soon as they become expert and entitled to rule.—Never has jealousy and suspicion been more on the alert against power, even legal and legitimate. Sapping and mining goes on even in services which are recognised as essential, as the army and the gendarmerie.[10] In the army, on the appointment of a noncommissioned officer, the other noncommissioned officers make up a list of candidates, and the captain selects three, one of whom is chosen by the colonel. In the choice of a sublieutenant, all the officers of the regiment vote, and he who receives a majority is appointed. In the gendarmerie, for the appointment of a gendarme, the directory of the department forms a list; the colonel designates five names on it, and the directory selects one of them. For the choice of a brigadier, quartermaster, or lieutenant, there is, besides the directory and the colonel, another intervention, that of the officers, both commissioned and noncommissioned. It is a system of elective complications and lot-drawings; one which, giving a voice in the choice of officers to the civil authorities and to military subordinates, leaves

10. Laws of September 23–October 29, 1790; January 16, 1791. (Titles ii. and vii.)—Cf. the legal prescriptions in relation to the military tribunals. In every prosecuting or judicial jury one-seventh of the sworn members are taken from the noncommissioned officers, and one-seventh from the soldiers, and again, according to the rank of the accused, the number of those of the same rank is doubled.

the colonel with only a third or one-quarter of his former ascendancy. In relation to the National Guard, the new principle is applied without any reservation. All the officers and underofficers up to the grade of captain are elected by their own men. All the superior officers are elected by the inferior officers. All underofficers and all inferior and superior officers are elected for one year only, and are not eligible for reelection until after an interval of a year, during which they must serve in the ranks.[11]—The result is manifest: command, in every civil and in every military order, becomes enervated; subalterns are no longer precise and trustworthy instruments; the chief no longer has any practical hold on them; his orders, consequently, encounter only tame obedience, doubtful deference, sometimes even open resistance; their execution remains dilatory, uncertain, incomplete, and at length is utterly neglected; a latent and soon flagrant system of disorganization is instituted by the law.

Step by step, in the hierarchy of Government, power has slipped downwards, and henceforth belongs by virtue of the Constitution to the authorities who sit at the bottom of the ladder. It is not the King, or the minister, or the directory of the department or of the district who rules, but its municipal officers; and their sway is as omnipotent as it can be in a small independent republic. They alone have the "strong hand" with which to search the pockets of refractory tax-payers, and ensure the collection of the revenue; to seize the rioter by the throat, and protect life and property; in short, to convert the promises and menaces of the law into acts. Every armed force, the National Guard, the regulars, and the gendarmerie, must march on their requisition. They alone, among the body of administrators, are endowed with this sovereign right; all that the department or the district can do is to invite them to exercise it. It is they who proclaim martial law. Accordingly, the sword is in their hands.[12] Assisted by commissioners who are appointed by the council-general

11. Law of July 28th, August 12, 1791.

12. Laws of November 14, 1789 (article 52), August 10–14, 1789.—Instruction of August 10–20, 1790; § 8.—Law of October 21, November 21, 1789.

of the commune, they prepare the schedule of taxation of real and personal property, fix the quota of each tax-payer, adjust assessments, verify the registers and the collector's receipts, audit his accounts, discharge insolvents, answer for returns, and authorise prosecutions.[13] Private purses are, in this way, at their mercy, and they take from them whatever they determine to belong to the public.—With the purse and the sword in their hands they lack nothing that is necessary to make them masters, and all the more because the application of every law belongs to them; because no orders of the Assembly to the King, of the King to the ministers, of ministers to the departments, of departments to the districts, of the districts to the communes, brings about any real local result except through them; because each measure of general application undergoes their special interpretation, and can always be optionally disfigured, softened, or exaggerated according to their timidity, inertia, violence, or partiality. Moreover, they are not long in discovering their strength. We see them on all sides arguing with their superiors against district, departmental, and ministerial orders, and even against the Assembly itself, alleging circumstances, lack of means, their own danger, and the public safety, failing to obey, acting for themselves, openly disobeying and glorying in the act,[14] and claiming, as a right, the omnipotence which they exercise in point of fact. Those of Troyes, at the festival of the Federation, refuse to submit to the precedence of the department and claim it for themselves, as "immediate representatives of the people." Those of Brest, notwithstanding the reiterated prohibitions of their district, dispatch four

13. Laws of November 14, 23, 1790; January 13th, September 26th, October 9, 1791.

14. Albert Babeau, i. 327 (Fête of the Federation, July 14, 1790).—"Archives Nationales," F[7], 3,215 (May 17, 1791, Deliberation of the council-general of the commune of Brest. May 17 and 19, Letters of the directory of the district).—*Mercure,* March 5, 1791. "Mesdames are stopped until the return of the two deputies, whom the Republic of Arnay-le-Duc has sent to the representatives of the nation to demonstrate to them the necessity of keeping the king's aunts in the kingdom."

hundred men and two cannon to force the submission of a neighbouring commune to a curé who has taken the oath. Those of Arnay-le-Duc arrest *Mesdames* (the King's aunts), in spite of their passport signed by the ministers, hold them in spite of departmental and district orders, persist in barring the way to them in spite of a special decree of the National Assembly, and send two deputies to Paris to obtain the sanction of their decision. What with arsenals pillaged, citadels invaded, convoys arrested, couriers stopped, letters intercepted, constant and increasing insubordination, usurpations without truce or measure, the municipalities arrogate to themselves every species of license on their own territory and frequently outside of it. Henceforth, forty thousand sovereign bodies exist in the kingdom. Force is placed in their hands, and they make good use of it. They make such good use of it that one of them, the commune of Paris, taking advantage of its proximity, lays siege to, mutilates, and rules the National Convention, and through it France.

III

Let us follow these municipal kings into their own domain: the burden on their shoulders is immense, and much beyond what human strength can support. All the details of executive duty are confided to them; they have not to busy themselves with a petty routine, but with a complete social system which is being taken to pieces, while another is reconstructed in its place.—They are in possession of four milliards of ecclesiastical property, real and personal, and soon there will be two and a half milliards of property belonging to the emigrants, which must be sequestered, valued, managed, inventoried, divided, sold, and the proceeds received. They have seven or eight thousand monks and thirty thousand nuns to displace, install, sanction, and provide for. They have forty-six thousand ecclesiastics, bishops, canons, curés, and vicars, to dispossess, replace, often by force, and later on to expel, intern, imprison, and support. They are obliged to discuss, trace out, teach, and make public new territorial boundaries, those of the commune, of the district, and of the department. They have to convoke, lodge, and protect the numerous primary and secondary Assemblies, to supervise their operations, which sometimes last for weeks; to install those elected by them, justices of the peace, officers of the National Guard, judges, public prosecutors, curés, bishops, district and departmental administrators. They are to form new lists of tax-payers, apportion amongst themselves, according to a new system of impost, entirely new real and personal taxes, decide on claims, appoint an assessor, regularly audit his accounts and verify his books, aid him with force, use force in the collection of the excise and salt duties, which being reduced, equalised, and transformed in vain by the National Assembly, afford no returns in spite of its decrees. They are obliged to find the funds for dressing, equipping, and arming the National Guard, to step in between it and the military commanders, and to maintain concord between its diverse battalions. They have to protect forests from pillage, communal land from being invaded, to maintain the *octroi*, to protect former functionaries, ecclesiastics, and nobles, suspected and threatened, and, above all, to provide, no matter how, provisions for the commune which lacks food, and consequently, to raise subscriptions, negotiate purchases at a distance and even abroad, organize escorts, indemnify bakers, supply the market every week notwithstanding the dearth, the insecurity of roads, and the resistance of cultivators.—Even an absolute chief, sent from a distance and from high place, the most energetic and expert possible, supported by the best-disciplined and most obedient troops, would scarcely succeed in such an undertaking; and there is instead only a municipality which has neither the authority, the means, the experience, the capacity, nor the will.

In the country, says an orator in the tribune,[15] "the municipal officers, in twenty thousand out of forty thousand municipalities, do not know how to read or write." The curé, in effect, is excluded from such offices by law, and, save in La Vendée, the noble is excluded by public opinion. Besides, in many of the provinces, nothing

15. *Moniteur,* x. 132. Speech by M. Labergerie, November 8, 1791.

but patois is spoken;[16] the French tongue, especially the philosophic and abstract phraseology of the new laws and proclamations, remains gibberish to their inhabitants. They cannot possibly understand and apply the complicated decrees and fine-spun instructions which reach them from Paris. They hurry off to the towns, get the duties of the office imposed on them explained and commented on in detail, try to comprehend, imagine they do, and then, the following week, come back again without having understood anything, either the mode of keeping state registers, the distinction between feudal rights which are abolished and those retained, the regulations they should enforce in cases of election, the limits which the law imposes as to their powers and subordination. Nothing of all this finds its way into their rude, untrained brains; instead of a peasant who has just left his oxen, there is needed here a legal adept aided by a trained clerk.—Prudential considerations must be added to their ignorance. They do not wish to make enemies for themselves in their commune, and they abstain from any positive action, especially in all tax matters. Nine months after the decree on the patriotic contribution, "twenty-eight thousand municipalities are behindhand, not having (yet) returned either rolls or estimates."[17] At the end of January, 1792, "out of forty thousand nine hundred and eleven municipalities, only five thousand four hundred and forty-eight have deposited their registers; two thousand five hundred and eighty rolls only are definitive and in process of collection. A large number have not even begun their sectional statements."[18]—It is much worse when, thinking that they do understand it, they under-

16. At Montauban, in the intendant's salon, the ladies of the place spoke patois only, the grandmother of the gentleman who gives me this fact not understanding any other language.

17. *Moniteur,* v. 163, sitting of July 18, 1791. Speech by M. Lecoulteux, reporter.

18. *Moniteur,* xi. 283, sitting of February 2, 1792. Speech by Cambon: "They go away thinking that they understand what is explained to them, but return the following day to obtain fresh explanations. The attorneys refuse to give the municipalities any assistance, stating that they know nothing about these matters."

take to do their work. In their minds, incapable of abstraction, the law is transformed and deformed by extraordinary interpretations. We shall see what it becomes when it is brought to bear on feudal dues, on the forests, on communal rights, on the circulation of corn, on the taxes on provisions, on the supervision of the aristocrats, and on the protection of persons and property. According to them, it authorises and invites them to do by force, and at once, whatever they need or desire for the time being.—The municipal officers of the large boroughs and towns, more acute and often able to comprehend the decrees, are scarcely in a better condition to carry them out effectually. They are undoubtedly intelligent, inspired by the best disposition, and zealous for the public welfare. During the first two years of the Revolution it is, on the whole, the best informed and most liberal portion of the bourgeoisie which, in the department as in the district, undertakes the management of affairs. Almost all are men of the law, advocates, notaries, and attorneys, with a small number of the old privileged class imbued with the same spirit, a canon at Besançon, a gentleman at Nismes. Their intentions are of the very best; they love order and liberty, they give their time and their money, they hold permanent sessions and accomplish an incredible amount of work, and they often voluntarily expose themselves to great danger.—But they are bourgeois philosophers, and, in this latter particular, similar to their deputies in the National Assembly, and, with this twofold character, as incapable as their deputies of governing a disintegrated nation. In this twofold character they are ill-disposed towards the ancient régime, hostile to Catholicism and feudal rights, unfavourable to the clergy and the nobility, inclined to extend the bearing and exaggerate the rigour of recent decrees, partisans of the rights of man, and, therefore, humanitarians and optimists, disposed to excuse the misdoings of the people, hesitating, tardy and often timid in the face of an outbreak—in short, admirable writers, exhorters, and reformers, but good for nothing when it comes to breaking heads and risking their own bones. They have not been brought up in such a way as to become men of action in a single day. Up to this time they have always lived as passive administrators, as quiet individuals, as studious men and clerks, domesticated, conversational, and polished, to whom words concealed facts, and who, on their evening promenade, warmly discussed important principles of government, without any consciousness of the practical machinery which, with a police-system for its ultimate wheel, rendered themselves, their promenade, and their conversation perfectly secure. They are not imbued with that sentiment of social danger which produces the veritable chief, the man who subordinates the emotions of pity to the exigences of the public service. They are not aware that it is better to mow down a hundred conscientious citizens rather than let them hang a culprit without a trial. Repression, in their hands, is neither prompt, rigid, nor constant. They continue to be in the Hôtel-de-Ville what they were when they went into it, so many legists and scribes, fruitful in proclamations, reports, and correspondence. Such is wholly their rôle, and, if any amongst them, with more energy, desires to depart from it, he has no hold on the commune which, according to the Constitution, he has to direct, and on that armed force which is intrusted to him with a view to ensure the observance of the laws.

To ensure respect for authority, indeed, it must not spring up on the spot and under the hands of its subordinates. It loses its prestige and independence when those who create it are precisely those who have to submit to it. For, in submitting to it, they remember that they have created it. This or that candidate among them who has but lately solicited their suffrages is now a magistrate who issues orders, and this sudden transformation is their work. It is with difficulty that they pass from the rôle of sovereign electors to that of docile subjects of the administration, and recognise a commander in one of their own creatures. On the contrary, they will submit to his control only in their own fashion, reserving to themselves in practice the powers the right to which they have conferred on him. "We gave him his place, and he must do as we want him to do"—which popular reasoning is the most natural in the world. It is as applicable to the municipal officer wearing his scarf as to the officer in the National Guard wearing his epaulettes; the former as well as the latter being conferred by the arbitrary voice of the electors, and always seeming to them a gift which is revocable at their pleasure. The superior always, and more particularly in times of danger or of great public excitement, seems, if directly appointed by those whom he commands, to be their clerk.—Such is municipal authority at this epoch, intermittent, uncertain, and weak; and all the weaker because the sword, whose hilt the men of the Hôtel-de-Ville seem to hold, does not always leave its scabbard at their bidding. They alone are empowered to summon the National Guard, but it does not depend on them, and it is not at their disposal. To obtain its support it is needful that its independent chiefs should be willing to respond to their requisition; that the men should willingly obey their elected officers; that these improvised soldiers should consent to quit their ploughs, their stores, their workshops and offices, to lose their day, to patrol the streets at night, to be pelted with stones, to fire on a riotous crowd whose enmities and prejudices they often share. Undoubtedly, they will fire on some occasions, but generally they will remain quiet, with their arms at rest; and, at last, they will grow weary of a trying, dangerous, and constant service, which is disagreeable to them, and for which they are not fitted. They will not answer the summons, or, if they do, they will come too late, and in too small a number. In this event, the regulars who are sent for, will do as they do and remain quiet, following their example, while the municipal magistrate, into whose hands the sword has glided, will be able to do no more than make grievous reports, to his superiors of the department or district, concerning the popular violence of which he is a powerless witness.—In other cases, and especially in the country, his condition is worse. The National Guard, preceded by its drums, will come and take him off to the town hall to authorise by his presence, and to legalise by his orders, the outrages that it is about to commit. He marches along seized by the collar, and affixes his signature at the point of the bayonet. In this case not only is his instrument taken away from him, but it is turned against himself. Instead of holding it by the hilt, he feels the point: the armed force which he ought to make use of makes use of him.

IV

Behold, accordingly, the true sovereign, the elector, both National Guard and voter. This is the King desired by the Constitution; there he is, in every hierarchical stage, with his suffrage, with which to delegate authority, and his gun to assure its exercise.—Through his free choice he creates all local powers, intermediary, central, legislative, administrative, ecclesiastical, and judiciary. He appoints directly, and in the primary assemblies, the mayor, the municipal board, the public prosecutor and council of the commune, the justice of the peace and his assessors, and the electors of second degree. Indirectly, and through these elected electors, he appoints the administrators and *procureurs-syndics* of both district and department, the civil and criminal judges, the public prosecutor, bishops, and curés, the members of the National Assembly, and jurors of the higher National Court.[19] All these commissions which he issues are of short date, the principal ones, those of municipal officer, elector, and deputy, having but two years to run; at the end of this brief term their recipients are again subject to his vote, in order that, if he is displeased with them, he may replace them by others. He must not be fettered in his choice; in every well-conducted establishment the legitimate proprietor must be free easily and frequently to renew his staff of clerks. He is the only one in whom confidence can be placed, and, for greater security, all arms are given up to him. When his clerks wish to employ force he is the one to place it at their disposal. Whatever he desired as elector he executes as National Guard. On two occasions he interferes, both times in a decisive manner; and his control over the legal powers is irresistible because these are born out of his vote and are obeyed only through his support.—But these rights are, at the same time, burdens. The Constitution describes him as an "active citizen," and this he eminently is or should be, since public action begins and ends with him, since everything depends on his zeal and capacity, since the machine is

19. Law of May 11–15, 1791.

good and only works well in proportion to his discernment, punctuality, calmness, firmness, discipline at the polls, and in the ranks. The law requires his services incessantly day and night, in body and mind, as gendarme and as elector.—How burdensome this service of gendarme must be, can be judged of by the number of riots. How burdensome that of elector must be, the list of elections will show.

In February, March, April, and May, 1789, there are prolonged parish meetings, for the purpose of choosing electors and writing out grievances, also bailiwick meetings of still longer duration to choose deputies and draw up the memorial. During the months of July and August, 1789, there are spontaneous gatherings to elect or confirm the municipal bodies; other spontaneous meetings by which the militia is formed and officered; and then, following these, constant meetings of this same militia to fuse themselves into a National Guard, to renew officers and appoint deputies to the federative assemblies. In December, 1789, and January, 1790, there are primary meetings, to elect municipal officers and their councils. In May, 1790, there are primary and secondary meetings, to appoint district and departmental administrators. In October, 1790, there are primary meetings, to elect the justice of the peace and his assessors, also secondary meetings, to elect the district courts. In November, 1790, there are primary meetings, to renew one-half of the municipal bodies. In February and March, 1791, there are secondary meetings, to nominate the bishop and curés. In June, July, August, September, 1791, there are primary and secondary meetings, to renew one-half of the district and departmental administrators, to nominate the president, the public prosecutor, and the clerk of the criminal court, and to choose deputies. In November, 1791, there are primary meetings to renew one-half of the municipal council. Observe that many of these elections drag along because the voters lack experience, because the formalities are complicated, and because opinions are divided. In August and September, 1791, at Tours, they are prolonged for thirteen days;[20] at Troyes, in January, 1790, instead of three days

20. *Procès-verbal* of the Electoral Assembly of the Department of Indre-et-Loire (1791, printed).

they last for three weeks; at Paris, in September and October, 1791, only for the purpose of choosing deputies, they last for thirty-seven days; in many places their proceedings are contested, annulled, and begun over again. To these universal gatherings, which put all France in motion, we must add the local gatherings by which a commune approves or gainsays its municipal officers, makes claims on the department, on the King, or on the Assembly, demands the maintenance of its curé, the provisioning of its market, the arrival or dispatch of a military detachment—and think of all that these meetings, petitions, and nominations presuppose in the way of preparatory committees and preliminary meetings and debates! Every public representation begins with rehearsals in secret session. In the choice of a candidate, and, above all, of a list of candidates; in the appointment in each commune of from three to twenty-one municipal officers, and from six to forty-two notables; in the selection of twelve district administrators and thirty-six departmental administrators, especially as the list must be of a double length and contain twice as many officers as there are places to fill, immediate agreement is impossible. In every important election the electors are sure to be in a state of agitation a month beforehand, while four weeks of discussion and caucus is not too much to give to inquiries about candidates, and to canvassing voters. Let us add, accordingly, this long preface to each of the elections, so long and so often repeated, and now sum up the mass of these disarrangements and disturbances, all this loss of time, all the labour which the process demands. Each convocation of the primary assemblies summons to the town-hall or principal town of the canton, for one or for several days, about three million five hundred thousand electors of the first degree. Each convocation of the assemblies of the second class compels the attendance and sojourn at the principal town of the department, and again in the principal town of the district, of about three hundred and fifty thousand elected electors. Each revision or reelection in the National Guard gathers together on the public square, or subjects to roll-call at the town-hall, three or four millions of National Guards. Each federation, after exacting the same gathering or the same roll-call, sends delegates by hundreds of thousands to the principal towns of the districts and departments, and tens of thousands to Paris.—The powers thus instituted at the cost of so great an effort, require an equal effort to make them work; one branch alone of the administration[21] keeps two thousand nine hundred and eighty-eight officials busy in the departments, six thousand nine hundred and fifty in the districts, one million one hundred and seventy-five thousand in the communes—in all, nearly one million two hundred thousand administrators, whose places, as we have seen above, are no sinecures. Never did a political machine require so prodigious an expenditure of force to set it up and keep it in motion. In the United States, where it is now deranged by its own action, it has been estimated that, to meet the intentions of the law and keep each wheel in its proper place, it would be necessary for each citizen to give one whole day in each week, or one-sixth of his time, to public business. In France, under the newly adopted system, where disorder is universal, where the duty of National Guard is added to and complicates that of elector and administrator, I estimate that two days would be necessary. This is what the Constitution comes to, this is its essential and supreme requirement: each active citizen has to give up one-third of his time to public affairs.

Now, these twelve hundred thousand administrators and three or four million electors and National Guards, are just the men in France who have the least leisure. The class of active citizens, indeed, comprises about all the men who labour with their hands or with their heads. The law exempts only domestics devoted to personal service or common labourers who, possessing no property or income, earn less than twenty-one sous a day. Every journeyman-miller, the smallest farmer, every village proprietor of a cottage or of a vegetable-garden, any ordinary workman, votes at the primary meetings, and may become a municipal officer. Again, if he pays ten francs a year direct tax, if he is a farmer or yeoman on any property which brings him in four hundred francs, if his rent is one hundred and fifty francs, he may become an elected elector and an administrator of the district

21. De Ferrières, i. 367.

or department. According to this standard the eligible are innumerable; in Doubs, in 1780,[22] they form two-thirds of the active citizens. Thus, the way to office is open to all, or almost all, and the law has taken no precaution whatever to reserve or provide places for the élite, who could best fill them. On the contrary, the nobles, the ecclesiastical dignitaries, the members of the parliaments, the grand functionaries of the ancient régime, the upper class of the bourgeoisie, almost all the rich who possess leisure, are practically excluded from the elections by violence, and from the various offices by public opinion: they soon retire into private life, and, through discouragement or disgust, through monarchical or religious scruples, abandon entirely a public career.—The burden of the new system falls, accordingly, on the most occupied portion of the community: on merchants, manufacturers, agents of the law, employés, shopkeepers, artisans, and cultivators. They are the people who must give up one-third of their time already appropriated, neglect private for public business, leave their harvests, their bench, their shop, or their briefs to escort convoys and patrol the highways, to run off to the principal town of the canton, district, or department, and stay and sit there in the town-hall,[23] subject to a deluge of phrases and papers, conscious that they are forced to gratuitous drudgery, and that this drudgery is of little advantage to the public.—For the first six months they do it with a good grace; their zeal in penning memorials, in providing themselves with arms against "brigands," and in suppressing taxes, rents, and tithes, is active enough. But now

22. Sauzay, i. 191 (21,711 are eligible out of 32,288 inscribed citizens).

23. Official report of the Electoral Assembly of the Department of Indre-et-Loire, Aug. 27, 1791. "A member of the Assembly made a motion that all the members composing it should be indemnified for the expenses which would be incurred by their absence from home and the long sojourn they had to make in the town where the Assembly was held. He remarked that the inhabitants of the country were those who suffered the most, their labour being their sole riches; that if no attention was paid to this demand, they would be obliged, in spite of their patriotism, to withdraw and abandon their important mission; that the electoral assemblies would then be deserted, or would be composed of those whose resources permitted them to make this sacrifice."

that this much is obtained or extorted, decreed as a right, or accomplished in fact, they must not be further disturbed. They need the whole of their time: they have their crops to get in, their customers to serve, their orders to give, their books to make up, their credits to adjust, all which are urgent matters, and neither ought to be neglected or interrupted. Under the lash of necessity and of the crisis they have done a heavy piece of collar-work, and, if we take their word for it, they hauled the public cart out of the mud; but they had no idea of putting themselves permanently in harness to drag it along themselves. Confined as this class has been for centuries to private life, each has his own wheelbarrow to trundle along, and it is for this, before all and above all, that he holds himself responsible. From the beginning of the year 1790 the returns of the votes taken show that as many are absent as present; at Besançon there are only nine hundred and fifty-nine voters out of thirty-two hundred inscribed; four months after this more than one-half of the electors fail to come to the polls;[24] and throughout France, even at Paris, the indifference to voting keeps on increasing. Puppets of such an administration as that of Louis XV. and Louis XVI. do not become Florentine or Athenian citizens in a single night. The hearts and heads of three or four millions of men are not suddenly endowed with faculties and habits which render them capable of diverting one-third of their energies to work which is new, disproportionate, gratuitous, and supererogatory.—A fallacy of measureless falsehood lies at the basis of the political combinations of the day and those of the next ten years. Arbitrarily, and without examining it, a certain weight and a certain power of resistance are attributed to the human metal employed. It is found on trial to have ten times less resistance and twenty times more weight than was supposed.

V

In default of the majority, who shirk their responsibilities, it is the minority which does the work and assumes the power. The majority

24. Sauzay, i. 147, 192.

having resigned, the minority becomes sovereign, and public business, abandoned by the hesitating, weak, and absent multitude, falls into the hands of the resolute, energetic, ever-present few who find the leisure and the disposition to assume the responsibility. In a system in which all offices are elective, and in which elections are frequent, politics becomes a profession for those who subordinate their private interests to it, and who find it of personal advantage; every village contains five or six men of this class, every borough twenty or thirty, every town its hundreds, and Paris its many thousands.[25] These are the veritable *active citizens*. They alone give all their time and attention to public matters, correspond with the newspapers and with the deputies at Paris, receive and spread abroad the party-cry on every important question, hold caucuses, get up meetings, make motions, draw up addresses, overlook, rebuke, or denounce the local magistrates, form themselves into committees, publish and push candidates, and go into the suburbs and the country to canvass for votes. They hold the power in recompense for their labour, for they manage the elections, and are elected to office or provided with places by the successful candidates. There is a prodigious number of these offices and places, not only those of officers of the National Guard and the administrators of the commune, the district, and the department, whose duties are gratuitous, or little short of it, but a quantity of others which are paid[26]—eighty-three bishops, seven hundred and fifty deputies, four hundred criminal judges, three thousand and seven civil judges, five thousand justices of the peace, twenty thousand assessors, forty thousand communal collectors, forty-six thousand curés, without counting the accessory or insignificant places which exist by tens and hundreds of thousands, from secretaries, clerks, bailiffs, and notaries, to gendarmes, constables, office-clerks, beadles, grave-diggers, and keepers of sequestered goods. The pasture is vast for the ambitious; it is not small for the needy, and they seize upon it.—Such is the rule in pure democracies:

25. For the detail of these figures, see vol. ii. book iv.
26. De Ferrières, i. 367. Cf. the various laws above mentioned.

hence the swarm of politicians in the United States. When the law incessantly calls all citizens to political action, there are only a few who devote themselves to it; these become experts in this particular work, and, consequently, preponderant. But they must be paid for their trouble, and the election secures to them their places because they manage the elections.

Two sorts of men furnish the recruits for this dominant minority: on the one hand the enthusiasts, and on the other those who have no social position. Towards the end of 1789, moderate people, who are minding their own business, retire into privacy, and are daily less disposed to show themselves. The public square is occupied by others who, through zeal and political passion, abandon their pursuits, and by those who, finding themselves hampered in their social sphere, or repelled from ordinary circles, were merely awaiting a new opening to take a fresh start. In these utopian and revolutionary times, there is no lack of either class. Flung out by handfuls, the dogma of popular sovereignty falls around like so much seed scattered broadcast, vegetating in the heated brains, in the narrow and rash minds which, once possessed by an idea, adhere to it and are mastered by it. It falls amongst a class of reasoners who, starting from a principle, dash forward like a horse who has had blinders put on; and this is especially the case with the legal class, whose profession accustoms them to deductions; nor less with the village attorney, the unfrocked monk, the "intruding" and excommunicated curé, and above all, the journalist and the local orator, who, for the first time in his life, finds that he has an audience, applause, influence, and a future before him. These are the only people who can do the complicated and constant work which the new Constitution calls for; for they are the only men whose desires are unlimited, whose dreams are coherent, whose doctrine is explicit, whose enthusiasm is contagious, who cherish no scruples, and whose presumption is unbounded. Thus has the rigid will been wrought and tempered within them, the inward spring of energy which, being daily more tightly wound up, urges them on to propagandism and to action.—During the second half of the year 1790 we see them everywhere following the example of the Paris Jacobins, styling themselves friends of the Constitution, and grouping themselves together in popular associations. Each town and village gives birth to a club of patriots who regularly every evening, or several times a week, meet "for the purpose of cooperating for the safety of the commonwealth."[27] This is a new and spontaneous organ, an excrescence and a parasite, which develops itself in the social body alongside of its legal organizations. Its growth insensibly increases, attracting to itself the substance of the others, employing them for its own ends, substituting itself for them, acting by and for itself alone, a sort of omnivorous outgrowth the encroachment of which is irresistible, not only because circumstances and the working of the Constitution nourish it, but also because its germ, deposited at a great depth, is a living portion of the Constitution itself.

For, placed at the head of the Constitution, as well as of the decrees which are attached to it, stands the Declaration of the Rights of Man.—According to this, and by the avowal of the legislators themselves, there are two parts to be distinguished in the law, the one superior, eternal, inviolable, which is the self-evident principle, and the other inferior, temporary, and open to discussion, which comprehends more or less exact or erroneous applications of this principle. No application of the law is valid if it derogates from the principle. No institution or authority is entitled to obedience if it is opposed to the rights which it aims to guarantee. These sacred rights, anterior to all society, take precedence of every social convention, and whenever we would know if a legal order is legitimate, we have merely to ascertain if it is in conformity with natural right. Let us, accordingly, in every doubtful or difficult case, refer to this philosophic gospel, to this incontestable catechism, this primordial creed proclaimed by the National Assembly.—The National Assembly itself invites us to do so. For it announces that "ignorance,

27. Constant, "Histoire d'un Club Jacobin en Provence" (Fontainebleau), p. 15. (*Procès-verbaux* of the founding of the clubs of Moret, Thomery, Nemours, and Montereau.)

neglect, or contempt of the rights of man are the sole causes of public misfortune, and of the corruption of governments." It declares that "the object of every political association is the preservation of natural and imprescriptible rights." It enunciates them, "in order that the acts of legislative power and the acts of executive power may at once be compared with the purpose of every political institution." It desires "that every member of the social body should have its declaration constantly in mind."—Thus we are told to control all acts of application by the principle, and also we are provided with the rule by which we may and should accord, measure, or even refuse our submission to, deference for, and toleration of established institutions and legal authority.

What are these superior rights, and, in case of dispute, who will decide as arbitrator? There is nothing here like the precise declarations of the American Constitution,[28] those positive prescriptions which serve to sustain a judicial appeal, those express prohibitions which prevent beforehand certain species of laws from being passed, which prescribe limits to public powers, which mark out the province not to be invaded by the State because it is reserved to the individual.

On the contrary, in the declaration of the National Assembly, most of the articles are abstract dogmas, metaphysical definitions, more or less literary axioms, that is to say, more or less false, now vague and now contradictory, open to various interpretations and to opposite constructions, good for platform display but bad in practice, mere stage effect, a sort of pompous standard, useless and heavy, which, hoisted in front of the Constitutional house and shaken every day by violent hands, cannot fail soon to tumble on the heads of

28. Cf. the Declaration of Independence, July 4, 1776 (except the first phrase, which is a catchword thrown out for the European philosophers).—Jefferson proposed a Declaration of Rights for the Constitution of March 4, 1789, but it was refused. They were content to add to it the eleven amendments which set forth the fundamental rights of the citizen.

the passers-by.[29] Nothing is done to ward off this visible danger. There is nothing here like that Supreme Court which, in the United States, guards the Constitution even against its Congress, and which, in the name of the Constitution, actually invalidates a law, even when it has passed through all formalities and been voted on by all the powers; which listens to the complaints of the individual affected by an unconstitutional law; which stays the sheriff's or collector's hand raised against him, and which above their heads gives judgment on his interests and wrongs. Ill-defined and discordant laws are proclaimed without any provision being made for their interpretation, application, or sanction. No means are taken to have them specially expounded. No district tribunal is assigned to consider the claims which grow out of them, to put an end to litigation legally, peacefully, on a last appeal, and through a final decision which becomes a precedent and fixes the loose sense of the text. All this is made the duty of everybody, that is to say of those who are disposed to charge themselves with it—in other words, the active minority in council assembled.—Thus, in each town or village it is the local club which, by the authorisation of the legislator himself, becomes the champion, judge, interpreter, and administrator of the rights of man, and which, in the name of these superior rights, may protest or rebel, as it seems best, not only against the legitimate acts of legal powers, but also against the authentic text of the Constitution and the Laws.

Consider, indeed, these rights as they are proclaimed, along with the commentary of the haranguer who expounds them at the club before an audience of heated and daring spirits, or in the street to

29. Article 1. "Men are born and remain free and equal in rights common to all. Social distinctions are founded solely on public utility."

The first phrase condemns the hereditary royalty which is sanctioned by the Constitution. The second phrase can be used to legitimate hereditary monarchy and an aristocracy.—Articles 10 and 11 bear upon the manifestations of religious conviction; and on freedom of speech and of the press. By virtue of these two articles worship, speech, and the press may be made subject to the most repressive restrictions, &c.

the rude and fanatical multitude. Every article in the Declaration is a dagger pointed at human society, and the handle has only to be pressed to make the blade enter the flesh.[30] Among "these natural and imprescriptible rights" the legislator has placed "resistance to oppression." We are oppressed: let us resist and take up arms. According to this legislator, "society has the right to bring every public agent of the Administration to account." Let us away to the Hôtel-de-Ville, and interrogate our lukewarm or suspected magistrates, and watch their sessions to see if they prosecute priests and disarm the aristocrats; let us stop their intrigues against the people; let us force these slow clerks to hasten their steps.—According to this legislator "all citizens have the right to take part in person, or through their representatives, in the formation of the law." There must thus be no more electors privileged by their payment of a three-franc tax. Down with the new aristocracy of active citizens! Let us restore to the two millions of proletaires the right of suffrage, of which the Constitution has unjustly defrauded them!—According to this legislator, "men are born and remain free, and equal in their rights." Consequently, let no one be excluded from the National Guard; let everybody, even the pauper, have some kind of weapon, a pike or gun, to defend his freedom!—In the very terms of the Declaration "there is no longer hereditary right to any public office." Hereditary royalty is therefore illegitimate; let us go to the Tuileries and overthrow the throne! In the very terms of the Declaration "the law is the expression of the universal will." Listen to these clamours in the open streets, to these petitions flowing in from the towns on all sides; behold the universal will, the living law which abolishes the written law! On the strength of this the leaders of a few clubs in Paris are to depose the King, to violate the Legislative Assembly and decimate the National Convention.—In other terms, the turbulent, factious minority is to supplant the sovereign nation, and

30. Roux and Buchez, xi. 237. (Speech by Malouet in relation to the revision, August 5, 1791.) "You constantly tempt the people with sovereignty without giving them the immediate use of it."

henceforth there is nothing to hinder it from doing what it pleases just when it pleases. The operation of the Constitution has given to it the reality of power, while the preamble of the Constitution clothes it with the semblance of right.

VI

Such is the work of the Constituent Assembly. In several of its laws, especially those which relate to private interests, in the institution of civil regulations, in the penal and rural codes,[31] in the first attempts at, and the promise of, a uniform civil code, in the enunciation of a few simple regulations regarding taxation, procedure, and administration, it planted good seed. But in all that relates to political institutions and social organization its proceedings are those of an academy of Utopians, and not those of practical legislators.—On the sick body intrusted to it, it performed amputations which were as useless as they were excessive, and applied bandages as inadequate as they were injurious. With the exception of two or three restrictions admitted inadvertently, and the maintenance of the show of royalty, also the obligation of a small electoral qualification, it carried out its principle to the end, the principle of Rousseau. It deliberately refused to consider man as he really was under its own eyes, and persisted in seeing nothing in him but the abstract being created in books. Consequently, with the blindness and obstinacy characteristic of a speculative surgeon, it destroyed, in the society submitted to its scalpel and to its theories, not only the tumours, the enlargements, and the inflamed parts of the organs, but also the organs themselves, and even the vital governing centres around which the cells arrange themselves to recompose an injured organ. That is, the Assembly destroyed on the one hand the time-honoured, spontaneous, and lasting societies formed by geographical position, history, common occupations, and interests, and on the other, those natural chiefs whose name, repute, education, independence, and earnestness des-

31. Decrees of September 25–October 6, 1791; September 28–October 6, 1791.

ignated them as the best qualified to occupy high positions. In one direction it despoils and permits the ruin and proscription of the superior class, the nobles, the members of Parliament, and the upper middle class. In another it dispossesses and breaks up all historic or natural corporations, religious congregations, clerical bodies, provinces, parliaments, societies of art and of all other professions and pursuits. This done, every tie or bond which holds men together is found to be severed; all subordination and every graduated scale of rank have disappeared. There is no longer rank and file, or commander-in-chief. Nothing remains but individual particles, twenty-six millions of equal and disconnected atoms. Never was so much disintegrated matter, less capable of resistance, offered to hands undertaking to mould it. Harshness and violence will be sufficient to ensure success. These brutal hands are ready for the work, and the Assembly which has reduced the material to powder has likewise provided the mortar and pestle. As awkward in destruction as it is in construction, it invents for the restoration of order in a society which is turned upside down a machine which would, of itself, create disorder in a tranquil society. The most absolute and most concentrated government would not be strong enough to effect without disturbance a similar equalization of ranks, the same dismemberment of associations, and the same displacement of property. No social transformation can be peacefully accomplished without a well-commanded army, obedient and everywhere present, as was the case in the emancipation of the Russian serfs by the Emperor Alexander. The new Constitution,[32] on the contrary, reduces the

32. Impartial contemporaries, those well qualified to judge, agree as to the absurdity of the Constitution.

"The Constitution was a veritable monster. There was too much of monarchy in it for a republic, and too much of a republic for a monarchy. The King was a side-dish, *un hors d'oeuvre,* everywhere present in appearance but without any actual power." (Dumont, 339.)

"It is a general and almost universal conviction that this Constitution is inexecutable. The makers of it to a man condemn it." (G. Morris, September 30, 1791.)

King to the position of an honorary president, suspected and called in question by a disorganized State. Between him and the legislative body it interposes nothing but sources of conflict, and suppresses all means of concord. The monarch has no hold whatever on the administrative departments which he must direct; and the mutual independence of the powers, from the centre to the extremities of the State, everywhere produces indifference, negligence, and disobedience between the injunctions issued and their execution. France is a federation of forty thousand municipal sovereignties, in which the authority of legal magistrates varies according to the caprice of active citizens; in which active citizens, overtasked, avoid the performance of public duty; in which a minority of fanatics and of the ambitious monopolize all organs of communication, all influence, all rights of suffrage, all power, and all action, and sanction their multiplied usurpations, their unbridled despotism, their increasing encroachments by the Declaration of the Rights of Man. The masterpiece of ideal abstractions and of practical absurdities is perfected; spontaneous anarchy, by means of the Constitution, becomes legalised anarchy. The latter is more perfect; nothing finer of the kind has been seen since the ninth century.

"Every day proves more clearly that their new Constitution is good for nothing." (*Ibid.*, December 27, 1791.)

Cf. the sensible and prophetic speech made by Malouet (August 5, 1791, Roux and Buchez, xi. 237).

BOOK III

The Application of the Constitution

CHAPTER I

I. *The Federations—Popular application of philosophic theory—Idyllic celebration of the Contrat-Social—Two phases of human volition—Permanent disorder—* II. *Independence of the municipalities—The causes of their initiative—Sentiment of danger—Issy-l'Evêque in 1789—Exalted pride—Brittany in 1790—Usurpations of the municipalities—Capture of the citadels—Violence increased against their commanders—Stoppage of convoys—Powerlessness of the Directories and of the ministers—Marseilles in 1790—* III. *Independent Assemblies—Why they took the initiative—The people in council—Powerlessness of the municipalities—The violence to which they are subject—Aix in 1790—Government disobeyed and perverted everywhere.*

IF THERE ever was an Utopia which seemed capable of realisation, or, what is still more to the purpose, was really applied, converted into a fact, fully established, it is that of Rousseau, in 1789 and during the three following years. For, not only are his principles embodied in the laws, and the Constitution throughout animated with his spirit, but it seems as if the nation looked upon his ideological gambols, his abstract fiction, as serious. This fiction it carried out in every particular. A social contract, at once spontaneous and practical, an immense gathering of men associating together freely for the first time for the recognition of their respective rights, forming a specific compact, and binding themselves by a solemn oath: such is the social recipe prescribed by the philosophers, and which is carried out to the letter. Moreover, as this recipe is esteemed infallible, the imagination is worked upon and the sensibilities of the day are brought into play. It is admitted that men, on again becoming equals, have again become brothers.[1] The sudden and surprising concord of all volitions and all intelligences is to revive the golden age on earth. It is proper, accordingly, to regard the social contract as a festival, an affecting, sublime idyl, in which, from one end of France to the other, all, hand in hand, should assemble and swear to the new compact, with song, with dance, with tears of joy, with shouts of gladness, the worthy beginning of public felicity. With unanimous assent, indeed, the idyl is performed as if according to a written programme.

On the 29th of November, 1789, at Etoile, near Valence, the federations began.[2] Twelve thousand National Guards, from the two banks of the Rhône, promise "to remain for ever united, to ensure the circulation of grain, and to maintain the laws passed by the National Assembly." On the 13th of December, at Montélimart, six thousand men, the representatives of twenty-seven thousand other men, take a similar oath and confederate themselves with the foregoing.—Upon this the excitement spreads from month to month and from province to province. Fourteen towns of the bailiwicks of Franche-Comté form a patriotic league. At Pontivy, Brittany enters into federal relations with Anjou. One thousand National Guards of Vivarais and Languedoc send their delegates to Voute. Forty-eight thousand in the Vosges send their deputies to Epinal. During February, March, April, and May, 1790, in Alsace, Champagne, Dauphiny, Orléanais, Touraine, Lyonnais, and Provence, there is the same spectacle. At Draguignan eight thousand National Guards take the oath in the presence of twenty thousand spectators. At Lyons fifty thousand men, delegates of more than five hundred thousand others, take the civic oath.—But local unions are not sufficient to complete the organization of France; a general union of all French-

1. See the address of the commune of Paris, June 5, 1790. "Let the most touching of all utterances be heard on this day (the anniversary of the taking of the Bastille), *Frenchmen, we are brothers!* Yes, brothers, freemen and with a country!" Roux et Buchez, vi. 275.

2. Roux and Buchez, iv. 3, 309; v. 123; vi. 274, 399.—Duvergier, Collection of Laws and Decrees. Decree of June 8 and 9, 1790.

men must take place. Many of the various National Guards have already written to Paris for the purpose of affiliating themselves with the National Guard there; and, on the 5th of June, the Parisian municipal body having proposed it, the Assembly decrees the universal federation. It is to take place on the 14th of July, everywhere on the same day, both at the centre and at the extremities of the kingdom. There is to be one in the principal town of each district and of each department, and one at the capital. To the latter, each body of National Guards is to send deputies in the proportion of one man to every two hundred; and each regiment one officer, one noncommissioned officer, and four privates. Fourteen thousand representatives of the National Guard of the provinces appear on the Champ de Mars, the theatre of the festival; also eleven to twelve thousand representatives of the land and marine forces, besides the National Guard of Paris, and sixty thousand spectators on the surrounding slopes, with a still greater crowd on the heights of Chaillot and of Passy. All rise to their feet and swear fidelity to the nation, to the law, to the King, and to the new Constitution. When the report of the cannon is heard which announces the taking of the oath, those of the Parisians who have remained at home, men, women, and children, raise their hands in the direction of the Champ de Mars and likewise make their affirmation. In every principal town of every district, department, and commune in France there is the same oath on the same day. Never was there a more perfect social compact heard of. Here, for the first time in the world, everybody beholds a veritable legitimate society, for it is founded on free pledges, on solemn stipulations, and on actual consent. They possess the authentic act and the dated official report of it.

There is still something more—the time and the occasion betoken a union of all hearts. The barriers which have hitherto separated men from each other are all removed and without effort. Provincial antagonisms are now to cease: the confederates of Brittany and Anjou write that they no longer desire to be Angevins and Bretons, but simply Frenchmen. All religious discords are to come to an end: at Saint-Jean-du-Gard, near Alais, the Catholic curé and the Protestant pastor embrace each other at the altar; the pastor occupies the best seat in the church, and at the Protestant meeting-house the curé has the place of honour, and listens to the sermon of the pastor.[3] Distinctions of rank and condition will no longer exist; at Saint-Andéol "the honour of taking the oath in the name of the people is conferred on two old men, one ninety-three and the other ninety-four years of age, one a noble and a colonel of the National Guard, and the other a simple peasant." At Paris, two hundred thousand persons of all conditions, ages, and sexes, officers and soldiers, monks and actors, school-boys and masters, dandies and ragamuffins, elegant ladies and fishwomen, workmen of every class, and the peasants from the vicinity, all flocked to the Champ de Mars to dig the earth which was not ready, and in a week, trundling wheelbarrows and handling the pick-axe as equals and comrades, all voluntarily yoked in the same service, converted a flat surface into a valley between two hills.—At Strasbourg, General Luckner, commander-in-chief, worked a whole afternoon in his shirt-sleeves just like the commonest labourer. The confederates are fed, housed, and have their expenses paid everywhere on all the roads. At Paris the publicans and keepers of furnished houses lower their prices of their own accord, and do not think of robbing their new guests. "The districts," moreover, "feast the provincials to their heart's content.[4] There are meals every day for from twelve to fifteen hundred people." Provincials and Parisians, soldiers and bourgeois, seated and mingled together, drink each other's health and embrace. The soldiers, especially, and the inferior officers are surrounded, welcomed, and regaled to such an extent that they lose their heads, their health, and more besides. One "old trooper, who had been over fifty years in the service, died on the way home, used up with cordials and excess of pleasure." In short, the joy is excessive, as it should

3. Michelet, "Histoire de la Révolution Française," ii. 470, 474.

4. De Ferrières, ii. 91.—Albert Babeau, i. 340. (Letter addressed to the Chevalier de Poterat, July 18, 1790.)—De Dammartin, "Evénements qui se sont passés sous mes yeux," &c., i. 155.

be on the great day when the wish of an entire century is accomplished.—Behold ideal felicity, as displayed in the books and illustrations of the time! The natural man buried underneath an artificial civilisation is disinterred, and again appears as in early days, as in Otaheite, as in philosophic and literary pastorals, as in bucolic and mythological operas, confiding, affectionate, and happy. "The sight of all these beings again restored to the sweet sentiments of primitive brotherhood is an exquisite delight almost too great for the soul to support," and the Frenchman, more light-hearted and far more childlike than he is today, gives himself up unrestrainedly to his social, sympathetic, and generous instincts.

Whatever the imagination of the day offers him to increase his emotion, all the classical, rhetorical, and dramatic material at his command, are employed for the embellishment of his festival. Already wildly enthusiastic, he is anxious to increase his enthusiasm.—At Lyons, the fifty thousand confederates from the south range themselves in line of battle around an artificial rock, fifty feet high, covered with shrubs, and surmounted by a Temple of Concord in which stands a huge statue of Liberty; the steps of the rock are decked with flags, and a solemn mass precedes the administration of the oath.—At Paris, an altar dedicated to the country is erected in the middle of the Champ de Mars, which is transformed into a colossal circus. The regular troops and the federations of the departments stand in position around it, the King being in front with the Queen and the dauphin, while near them are the princes and princesses in a gallery, and the members of the National Assembly in an amphitheatre; two hundred priests, draped in their albs and with tricoloured belts, officiate around the Bishop of Autun; three hundred drums and twelve hundred musicians all play at once; forty pieces of cannon are discharged at one volley, and four hundred thousand cheers go up as if from one throat. Never was such an effort made to intoxicate the senses and strain the nerves beyond their powers of endurance!—The moral machine is made to vibrate to the same and even to a greater extent. For more than a year past, harangues, proclamations, addresses, newspapers, and events have daily added one degree more to the pressure. On this occasion, thousands of speeches, multiplied by myriads of newspapers, carry the enthusiasm to the highest pitch. Declamation foams and rolls along in a steady stream of rhetoric everywhere throughout France. In this state of excitement the difference between magniloquence and sincerity, between the false and the true, between show and substance, is no longer distinguishable. The Federation becomes an opera which is seriously played in the open street—children have parts assigned them in it; it occurs to no one that they are puppets, and that the words taken for an expression of the heart are simply memoriter speeches that have been put into their mouths. At Besançon, on the return of the confederates, hundreds of "youthful citizens" from twelve to fourteen years of age,[5] in the national uniform, "with sword in hand," march up to the standard of Liberty. Three little girls from eleven to thirteen years old and two little boys of nine years each pronounce "a discourse full of fire and breathing nothing but patriotism"; after which, a young lady of fourteen, raising her voice and pointing to the flag, harangues in turn the crowd, the deputies, the National Guard, the mayor, and the commander of the troops, the scene ending with a ball. This is the universal finale—men and women, children and adults, common people and men of the world, chiefs and subordinates, all, everywhere, frisk about as in the last act of a pastoral drama. At Paris, writes an eye-witness, "I saw chevaliers of Saint-Louis and chaplains dancing in the street with people belonging to their department."[6] At the Champ de Mars, on the day of the Federation, notwithstanding that rain was falling in torrents, "the first arrivals began to dance, and those who came after them, joining in, formed a circle which soon spread over a portion of the Champ de Mars. . . . Three hundred thousand spectators kept time with their hands." On the following days dancing is kept up on the Champ de Mars and in the streets, and there is drinking and carousing; "there was a ball with

5. Sauzay, i. 202.

6. Albert Babeau, *ibid.* i 330.—De Ferrières, ii. 92.

refreshments at the Corn-Exchange, and on the site of the Bastille."—At Tours, where fifty-two detachments from the neighbouring provinces are collected, about four o'clock in the afternoon,[7] through an irresistible outburst of insane gaiety, "the officers, inferior officers, and soldiers, pell-mell, race through the streets, some with sabre in hand and others dancing and shouting 'Vive le Roi!' 'Vive la Nation!' flinging up their hats and compelling every one they met to join in the dance. One of the canons of the cathedral, who happens to be passing quietly along, has a grenadier's cap put on his head," and is dragged into the circle, and after him two monks; "they are often embraced," and then allowed to depart. The carriages of the mayor and the Marquise de Montausier arrive; people mount up behind, get inside, and seat themselves in front, as many as can find room, and force the coachmen to parade through the principal streets in this fashion. There is no malice in it, nothing but sport and the overflow of spirits. "Nobody was maltreated or insulted, although almost every one was drunk."—Nevertheless, there is one bad symptom: the soldiers of the Anjou regiment leave their barracks the following day and "pass the whole night abroad, no one being able to hinder them." And there is another of still graver aspect; at Orleans, after the companies of the National Militia had danced on the square in the evening, "a large number of volunteers marched in procession through the town with drums, shouting out with all their might that the aristocracy must be destroyed, and that priests and aristocrats should be strung up to the lantern." They enter a suspected coffee-house, drive out the inmates with insults, lay hands on a gentleman who is supposed not to have cried out as correctly and as lustily as themselves, and come near hanging him.[8]—Such is the fruit of the susceptibility and philosophy of the

7. "Archives Nationales," H. 1453. Correspondence of M. de Bercheney, May 23, 1790.

8. "Archives Nationales," *ibid.* May 13, 1790. "M. de la Rifaudière was dragged from his carriage and brought to the guard-house, which was immediately filled with people, shouting, 'To the lantern, the aristocrat!'—The fact is this: after his having repeatedly shouted *Vive le Roi et la Nation!* they wanted

eighteenth century. Men believed that, for the organization of a perfect society and the permanent establishment of freedom, justice, and happiness on earth, an inspiration of sentiment and an act of the will would suffice. The inspiration has come and the act is fulfilled; the transports and the ravishment have been experienced, and minds have been wrought up to the highest pitch of excitement. Now comes the reaction, when they have to fall back upon themselves. The effort has succeeded in accomplishing all that it could accomplish, namely, a deluge of effusions and phrases, a verbal and not a real contract, ostentatious fraternity skin-deep, a well-meaning masquerade, an ebullition of feeling evaporating through its own pageantry—in short, an agreeable carnival of a day's duration.

The reason is that in the human will there are two strata, one superficial, of which men are conscious, the other deep down, of which they are unconscious; the former unstable and vacillating like shifting sand, the latter stable and fixed like a solid rock, to which their caprices and agitations never descend. The latter alone determines the general inclination of the soil, the main current of human activity necessarily following the bent thus prepared for it.—Certainly embraces have been interchanged and oaths have been taken; but after, as before the ceremony, men are just what many centuries of administrative thraldom and one century of political literature have made them. Their ignorance and presumption, their prejudices, hatreds, and distrusts, their inveterate intellectual and emotional habits are still preserved. They are human, and their stomachs need to be filled daily. They have imagination, and, if bread be scarce, they fear that they may not get enough of it. They prefer to keep their money rather than to give it away. For this reason they spurn the claims which the State and individuals have upon them as much as possible. They avoid paying their debts. They willingly lay their

---

him to shout *Vive la Nation!* alone, upon which he gave *Vive la Nation tant qu'ell pourra.*"—At Blois, on the day of the Federation, a mob promenade the streets with a wooden head covered with a wig, and a placard stating that the aristocrats must be decapitated.

hands on public property which is badly protected; finally, they are disposed to regard gendarmes and proprietors as baneful, and all the more so because this has been repeated to them over and over again, day after day, for a whole year.—On the other hand there is no change in the situation of things. They are ever living in a disorganized community, under an impracticable constitution, the passions which sap public order being only the more stimulated by the semblance of fraternity under which they seemed to be allayed. Men cannot be persuaded with impunity that the millennium has come, for they will want to enjoy it immediately, and will tolerate no deception practised on their expectations. In this violent state, due to unbounded hopes, every prompting of their will seems legitimate, and all opinions are stamped with certainty. They are no longer capable of self-distrust and self-restraint. In their brain, overflowing with emotions and enthusiasm, there is no room but for one intense, absorbing, fixed idea. Each is confident and overconfident in his own opinion; all become impassioned, imperious, and intractable. Having assumed that all obstacles are taken out of the way, they grow indignant at each obstacle they actually encounter. Whatever it may be, they shatter it on the instant, and their overexcited imagination clothes with the fine name of patriotism their natural appetite for despotism and usurpation.

France, accordingly, in the three years which follow the taking of the Bastille, presents a strange spectacle. Everywhere there is philanthropy in words and symmetry in the laws; everywhere there is violence in acts and disorder in all things. Afar, is the reign of philosophy; at hand is the chaos of the Carlovingian era. "Foreigners," remarks an observer,[9] "are not aware that, with a great extension of political rights, the liberty of the individual is in law reduced to nothing, while in practice it is subject to the caprice of sixty thousand constitutional assemblies; that no citizen enjoys any protection against the annoyances of these popular assemblies; that,

9. *Mercure de France*, the articles by Mallet-Dupan (June 18th and August 16, 1791; April 14, 1792).

according to the opinions which they entertain of persons and things, they act in one place in one way and in another place in another way. Here, a department, acting for itself and without referring elsewhere, puts an embargo on vessels, while there another orders the expulsion of a military detachment essential for the security of places devastated by ruffians; and the minister, who responds to the demands of those interested, replies: '*Such are the orders of the department.*' Elsewhere are administrative bodies which, the moment the Assembly decrees relief of consciences and the freedom of non-juring priests, order the latter out of their homes within twenty-four hours. Always in advance of or lagging behind the laws; alternately bold and pusillanimous; daring all things when seconded by public license, and daring nothing to repress it; eager to abuse their momentary authority against the weak in order to acquire titles to popularity in the future; incapable of maintaining order except at the expense of public safety and tranquillity; entangled in the reins of their new and complex administration, adding the fury of passion to incapacity and inexperience—such are, for the most part, the men sprung from nothing, void of ideas and drunk with pretension, on whom now rests responsibility for public powers and resources, the interest of security, and the foundations of the might of government. In all sections of the empire, in every branch of the administration, in every report, we detect the confusion of authorities, the uncertainty of obedience, the dissolution of all restraints, the absence of all resources, the deplorable complication of enervated springs, without one of the means of real power, and, for their sole support, laws which, in supposing France to be peopled with men without vices or passions, abandon humanity to its primitive state of independence." A few months after this, in the beginning of 1792, Malouet sums up all in one phrase: "It is the Government of Algiers without the Dey."

II

Things could not work otherwise. For, before the 6th of October, and the King's captivity in Paris, the Government had already been destroyed. Now, through the successive decrees of the Assembly, it is legally done away with, and each local group is left to itself.—The intendants have fled, military commanders are not obeyed, the bailiwicks dare hold no courts, the parliaments are suspended, and seven months elapse before the district and department administrations are elected, a year before the new judgeships are instituted, while afterwards, as well as before, the real power is in the hands of the commune.—The commune must arm itself, appoint its own chiefs, provide its own supplies, protect itself against brigands, and feed its own poor. It has to sell its national property, install the constitutional curé, and accomplish the transformation by which an old society takes the place of a new society, amidst so many eager passions and so many injured interests. It alone has to ward off the perpetual or constantly reviving dangers which assail it or which it imagines. These are great, and it exaggerates them. It is inexperienced and alarmed. It is not surprising that, in the exercise of its extemporised power, it should pass beyond its natural or legal limit, and without being aware of it, overstep the metaphysical line which the Constitution defines between its rights and the rights of the State. Neither hunger, fear, rage, nor any of the popular passions can wait; there is no time to refer to Paris. Action is necessary, immediate action, and, with the means at hand, they must save themselves as well as they can. This or that mayor of a village is soon to find himself a general and a legislator. This or that petty town is to give itself a charter like Laon or Vezelay in the twelfth century. "On the 6th of October, 1789,[10] near Autun, the market-town of Issy-l'Evêque declares itself an independent State. The parish assembly is convoked by the curé, M. Carion, who is appointed member of the administrative committee and of the new military staff. In full session he secures the adoption of a complete code, political, judiciary, penal, and military, consisting of sixty articles. Nothing is overlooked; we find ordinances concerning "the town police, the laying out of streets and public squares, the repair of prisons, the

10. *Moniteur*, iv. 560 (sitting of June 5, 1790), report of M. Freteau. "These facts are attested by fifty witnesses."—Cf. the number of April 19, 1791.

road taxes and price of grain, the administration of justice, fines, confiscations, and the diet of the National Guards." He is a provincial Solon, zealous for the public weal, and a man of executive power. He expounds his ordinances from the pulpit, and threatens the refractory. He passes decrees and renders judgments in the town-hall: outside the town limits, at the head of the National Guard, sabre in hand, he will enforce his own decisions. He causes it to be decided that, on the written order of the committee, every citizen may be imprisoned. He imposes and collects *octrois;* he has boundary walls thrown down; he goes in person to the houses of cultivators and makes requisitions for grain; he seizes the convoys which have not deposited their quota in his own richly stored granaries. One day, preceded by a drummer, he marches outside the walls, makes proclamation of "his agrarian laws," and proceeds at once to the partition of the territory, and, by virtue of the ancient communal or curial right, to assign to himself a portion of it. All this is done in public and conscientiously, the notary and the scrivener being called in to draw up the official record of his acts; he is satisfied that human society has come to an end, and that each local group has the right to begin over again and apply in its own way the Constitution which it has accorded to itself without reference to anybody else.—This man, undoubtedly, talks too loudly, and proceeds too quickly; and first the bailiwick, next the Châtelet, and afterwards the National Assembly temporarily put a stop to his proceedings; but his principle is a popular one, and the forty thousand communes of France are about to act like so many distinct republics, under the sentimental and constantly more powerless reprimands of the central authority.

Excited and invigorated by a new sentiment, men now abandon themselves to the proud consciousness of their own power and independence. Nowhere is greater satisfaction found than among the new local chiefs, the municipal officers and commanders of the National Guard, for never before has such supreme authority and such great dignity fallen upon men previously so submissive and so insignificant. Formerly the subordinates of an intendant or subdelegate, appointed, maintained, and ill used by him, kept aloof from transactions of any importance, unable to defend themselves except by humble protestations against the aggravations of taxation, concerned with precedences and the conflicts of etiquette,[11] plain townspeople or peasants who never dreamt of interfering in military matters, henceforth become sovereigns in all military and civil affairs. This or that mayor or syndic of a little town or parish, a petty bourgeois or villager in a blouse, whom the intendant or military commander could imprison at will, now orders a gentleman, a captain of dragoons, to march or stand still, and the captain stands still or marches at his command. On this same bourgeois or villager depends the safety of the neighbouring chateau, of the large landowner and his family, of the prelate, and of all the prominent personages of the district. In order that they may be out of harm's way he must protect them; they will be pillaged if, in case of insurrection, he does not send troops and the National Guard to their assistance. It is he who, with his communal council, fixes their rate of taxation as he pleases. It is he who, granting or refusing a passport, obliges them to stay at home or allows them to depart. It is he who, lending or refusing public force to the collection of their rents, gives them or deprives them of the means of living. He accordingly rules, and on the sole condition of ruling according to the wishes of his equals, the vociferous multitude, the restless, dominant mob which has elected him.—In the towns, especially, and notably in the large towns, the contrast between what he was and what he is is immense, since to the plenitude of his power is added the extent of his jurisdiction. Judge of the effect on his brain in cities like those of

11. "Archives Nationales," KK. 1105. Correspondence of M. de Thiard, military commandant in Brittany (September, 1789). "There are in every petty village three conflicting powers, the *présidial,* the bourgeois militia, and the permanent committee. Each is anxious to take precedence of the other, and, on this occasion, a scene happened to come under my eyes at Landivisiau which might have had a bloody termination, but which turned out to be simply ridiculous. A lively dispute arose between three haranguers to determine which should make the first address. They appealed to me to decide. Not to offend either of the parties, I decided that all three should speak at the same time; which decision was immediately carried out."

Marseilles, Bordeaux, Nantes, Rouen, and Lyons, where he holds in his hand the lives and property of eighty or a hundred thousand men. And the more as, amid the municipal officers of the towns, three-quarters of them, *procureurs* or advocates, are imbued with the new dogmas, and are persuaded that in themselves alone, the directly elected of the people, is vested all legitimate authority. Bewildered by their recent elevation, distrustful as parvenus, in revolt against all ancient or rival powers, they are additionally alarmed by their imagination and ignorance, their minds being vaguely disturbed by the contrast between their rôle in the past and their present rôle: anxious on account of the State, anxious on their own account, they find no security but in usurpations. The municipalities, on the strength of the reports which emanate from the coffee-houses, decide that the ministry are traitors. With an obstinacy of conviction and a boldness of presumption alike extraordinary, they believe that they have the right to act without and against their orders, and against the orders of the National Assembly itself, as if, in the now disintegrated France, each municipality constituted the nation.

Thus, if the armed force of the country is now obedient to anybody, it is to them and to them alone, and not only the National Guard, but also the regular troops which, placed under the orders of municipalities by a decree of the National Assembly,[12] will comply with no other. Military commanders in the provinces, after September, 1787, declare themselves powerless; when they and the municipality give orders, it is only those of the municipality which the troops recognise. "However pressing may be the necessity for moving the troops where their presence is required, they are stopped by the resistance of the village committee."[13] "Without any reasonable motive," writes the commander of the forces in Brittany, "Vannes and Auray made opposition to the detachment which I thought it

12. Decree of August 10–14, 1789.

13. "Archives Nationales," KK. 1105. Correspondence of M. de Thiard, September 11, 1789. "The troops now obey the municipalities only." Also July 30th, August 11, 1790.

prudent to send to Belle-Ile, to replace another one. . . . The Government cannot move without encountering obstacles. . . . The Minister of War no longer has the direction of the army. . . . No orders are executed. . . . Every one wants to command, and no one to obey. . . . How could the King, the Government, or the Minister of War send troops where they are wanted if the towns believe that they have the right to countermand the orders given to the regiments and change their destination?"—And it is still worse, for, "on the false supposition of brigands and conspiracies which do not exist,[14] the towns and villages make demands on me for arms and even cannon. . . . The whole of Brittany will soon be in a frightful belligerent state on this account, for, having no real enemies, they will turn their arms against each other."—This is of no consequence. The panic is an "epidemic." People are determined to believe in "brigands and enemies." At Nantes, the assertion is constantly repeated that the Spaniards are going to land, that the French regiments are going to make an attack, that an army of brigands is approaching, that the castle is threatened, that it is threatening, and that it contains too many engines of war. The commandant of the province writes in vain to the mayor to reassure him, and to explain to him that "the municipality, being master of the chateau, is likewise master of its magazine. Why then should it entertain fear about that which is in its own possession? Why should any surprise be manifested at an arsenal containing arms and gunpowder?"—Nothing is of any effect. The chateau is invaded; two hundred workmen set to work to demolish the fortifications; they listen only to their fears, and cannot exercise too great precaution. However inoffensive the citadels may be, they are held to be dangerous; however accommodating the commanders may be, they are regarded with suspicion. The people chafe against the bridle, relaxed and slack as it is: it is broken and cast aside, that it may not be used again when occasion requires. Each municipal body, each company of the National

14. "Archives Nationales," KK. 1105. Correspondence of M. de Thiard, September 11 and 25, November 20, December 25 and 30, 1789.

Guard, wants to reign on its own plot of ground out of the way of any foreign control; and this is what is called liberty. Its adversary, therefore, is the central power; this must be disarmed for fear that it may interpose, and, on all sides, with a sure and persistent instinct, through the capture of fortresses, the pillage of arsenals, the seduction of the soldiery, and the expulsion of generals, the municipality ensures its omnipotence by guaranteeing itself beforehand against all repression.

At Brest the municipal authorities insist that a naval officer shall be surrendered to the people, and on the refusal of the King's lieutenant to give him up, the permanent committee orders the National Guard to load its guns.[15] At Nantes the municipal body refuses to recognise M. d'Hervilly, sent to take command of a camp, and the towns of the province write to declare that they will suffer no other than the federated troops on their territory. At Lille the permanent committee insists that the military authorities shall place the keys of the town in its keeping every evening, and, a few months after this, the National Guard, joined by mutinous soldiers, seize the citadel and the person of Livarot, its commander. At Toulon the commander of the arsenal, M. de Rioms, and several naval officers, are put in the dungeon. At Montpellier the citadel is surprised, and the club writes to the National Assembly to demand its demolition. At Valence, the commandant, M. de Voisin, on taking measures of defence, is massacred, and henceforth the municipality issues all orders to the garrison. At Bastia, Colonel de Rully falls under a shower of bullets, and the National Guard takes possession of the citadel and the powder magazine. These are not passing outbursts: at the end of two years the same insubordinate spirit is apparent everywhere.[16]

15. Roux and Buchez, v. 304 (April, 1790).—"Archives Nationales." Papers of the Committee of Investigation, DXXIX. I (note of M. Latour-du-Pin, October 28, 1789).—Roux and Buchez, iv. 3 (December 1, 1789); iv. 390 (February, 1790); vi. 179 (April and May, 1790).

16. *Mercure de France,* Report of M. Emery, sitting of July 21, 1790, Number for July 31.—"Archives Nationales," F[7], 3,200. Letter of the directory of Calvados, September 26 and October 20, 1791.

In vain do the commissioners of the National Assembly seek to transfer the Nassau regiment from Metz. Sedan refuses to receive it; while Thionville declares that, if it comes, she will blow up the bridges, and Sarrelouis threatens, if it approaches, that it will open fire on it. At Caen neither the municipality nor the directory dares enforce the law which assigns the castle to the troops of the line; the National Guard refuses to leave it, and forbids the director of the artillery to inspect the munitions.—In this state of things a Government subsists in name but not in fact, for it no longer possesses the means of enforcing obedience. Each commune arrogates to itself the right of suspending or preventing the execution of the simplest and most urgent orders. Arnay-le-Duc, in spite of passports and legal injunctions, persists in retaining *Mesdames;* Arcis-sur-Aube retains Necker, and Montigny is about to retain M. Caillard, Ambassador of France.[17]—In the month of June, 1791, a convoy of eighty thousand crowns of six livres sets out from Paris for Switzerland; this is a repayment by the French Government to that of Soleure; the date of payment is fixed, the itinerary marked out; all the necessary documents are provided; it is important that it should arrive on the day when the bill falls due. But they have counted without the municipalities and the National Guards. Arrested at Bar-sur-Aube, it is only at the end of a month, and on a decree of the National Assembly, that the convoy can resume its march. At Belfort it is seized again, and it still remains there in the month of November. In vain has the directory of the Bas-Rhin ordered its release; the Belfort municipality paid no attention to the order. In vain the same directory dispatches a commissioner, who is near being cut to pieces. The personal interference of General Luckner, with the strong arm, is necessary, before the convoy can pass the frontier, after five months of delay.[18] In the month of July, 1791, a French vessel on

17. "Archives Nationales," F^7, 3,207. Letter of the minister Dumouriez, June 15, 1792. Report of M. Caillard, May 29, 1792.

18. *Mercure de France,* No. for July, 1791 (sitting of the 6th); Nos. for November 5 and 26, 1791.

the way from Rouen to Caudebec, said to be loaded with kegs of gold and silver, is stopped. On the examination being made, it has a right to leave; its papers are all correct, and the department enjoins the district to respect the law. The district, however, replies that it is impossible, for "all the municipalities on the banks of the Seine have armed and are awaiting the passing of the vessel," and the National Assembly itself is obliged to pass a decree that the vessel shall be discharged.

If the rebellion of the small communes is of this stamp, what must be that of the larger ones?[19] The departments and districts summon the municipality in vain; it disobeys or pays no attention to the summons. "Since the session began," writes the directory of Saône-et-Loire, "the municipality of Maçon has taken no step in relation to us which has not been an encroachment; it has not uttered a word which has not been an insult; it has not entered upon a deliberation which has not been an outrage." "If the regiment of Aunis is not ordered here immediately," writes the directory of Calvados, "if prompt and efficient measures are not taken to provide us with an armed force, we shall abandon a post which we are prevented from holding amidst insubordination, license, contempt for all the authorities, and, consequently, the absolute impossibility of performing the duties which were imposed upon us." The directory of the Bouches-du-Rhône, on being attacked, flies before the bayonets of Marseilles. The members of the directory of Gers, in conflict with the municipality of Auch, are almost beaten to death. As to the ministers, who are distrusted by virtue of their office, they are still

19. Albert Babeau, "Histoire de Troyes," vol. i *passim*.—"Archives Nationales," F^7, 3,257. Address of the Directory of Saône-et-Loire to the National Assembly, November 1, 1790.—F^7, 3,200. Letter of the Directory of Calvados, November 9, 1791.—F^7, 3,105. *Procès-verbal* of the municipality of Aix, March 1, 1792 (on the events of February 26th); letter of M. Villard, President of the Directory, March 10, 1792.—F^7, 3,220. Extracts from the deliberations of the Directory of Gers, and a letter to the King, January 28, 1792. Letter of M. Lafitau, President of the Directory, January 30. (He was dragged along by his hair and obliged to leave the town.)

less respected than the directories; they are constantly denounced to the Assembly, while the municipalities send back their dispatches without deigning to open them,[20] and, towards the end of 1791, their increasing powerlessness ends in complete annihilation. We can judge of this by one example. In the month of December, 1791, Limoges is not allowed to carry away the grain which it had just purchased in Indre, a force of sixty horsemen being necessary to protect its transportation; the directory of Indre at once calls upon the ministers to furnish them with this small troop.[21] After trying for three weeks, the minister replies that it is out of his power; he has knocked at all doors in vain. "I have pointed out one way," he says, "to the deputies of your department in the National Assembly, namely, to withdraw the 20th regiment of cavalry from Orleans, and I have recommended them to broach the matter to the deputies of Loiret." The answer is still delayed: the deputies of the two departments have to come to an agreement, for, otherwise, the minister dares not displace sixty men to protect a convoy of grain. It is plain enough that there is no longer any executive power, that there is no longer a central authority, that there is no longer a France, but merely so many disintegrated and independent communes, like Orleans and Limoges, which, through their representatives, carry on negotiations with each other, one to secure itself from a deficiency of troops, and the other to secure itself from a want of bread.

Let us consider this general dissolution on the spot, and take up a case in detail. On the 18th of January, 1790, the new municipal authorities of Marseilles enter upon their duties. As is generally the case, the majority of the electors have had nothing to do with the balloting, the mayor, Martin, having been elected by only an eighth of the active citizens.[22] If, however, the dominant minority is a small

20. *Mercure de France,* No. for October 30, 1790.

21. "Archives Nationales," F^7, 3226. Letter of the Directory of Indre to M. Cahier, minister, December 6, 1791.—Letter of M. Delessart, minister, to the Directory of Indre, December 31, 1791.

22. Fabre, "Histoire de Marseille," ii. 442. Martin had but 3,555 votes, when shortly after the National Guard numbered 24,000 men.

one, it is resolute and not inclined to stop at trifles. "Scarcely is it organized,"[23] when it sends deputies to the King to have him withdraw his troops from Marseilles. The King, always weak and accommodating, finally consents; and, the orders to march being prepared, the municipality is duly advised of them. But the municipality will tolerate no delay, and immediately "draws up, prints, and issues a denunciation to the National Assembly" against the commandant and the two ministers who, according to it, are guilty of having forged or suppressed the King's orders. In the meantime it equips and fortifies itself as for a combat. At its first establishment the municipality broke up the bourgeois guard, which was too great a lover of order, and organized a National Guard, in which those who have no property are soon to be admitted. "Daily additions are made to its military apparatus;[24] entrenchments and barricades, at the Hôtel-de-Ville, are increasing, also the artillery; the town is filled with the excitement of a military camp in the immediate presence of an enemy."—Thus, in possession of force, it makes use of it, and in the first place against justice.

A popular insurrection had been suppressed in the month of August, 1789, and the three principal leaders, Rebecqui, Pascal, and Granet, had been imprisoned in the Chateau d'If. They are the friends of the municipal authorities, and they must be set free. At the demand of this body the affair is taken out of the hands of the *grand-prévôt,* and put into those of the *sénéchaussée,* the former, meanwhile, together with his councillors, undergoing punishment for having performed their duty: the municipality, on its own authority, interdicts them from further exercise of their functions. They are publicly denounced, "threatened with poniards, the scaffold, and every species of assassination."[25] No printer dares publish their de-

23. "Archives Nationales," F^7, 3,196. Letter of the minister, M. de Saint-Priest, to the President of the National Assembly, May 11, 1790.

24. "Archives Nationales," F^7, 3,196. Letters of the military commandant, M. de Miran, March 6, 14, 30, 1790.

25. "Archives Nationales," F^7, 3,196. Letter of M. de Bournissac, *grand-prévôt,* March 6, 1790.

fence, for fear of "municipal annoyances." It is not long before the royal *procureur* and a councillor are reduced to seeking refuge in Fort Saint-Jean, while the *grand-prévôt,* after having resisted a little longer, leaves Marseilles in order to save his life. As to the three imprisoned men, the municipal authorities visit them in a body and demand their provisional release; one of them having made his escape, they refuse to give the commandant the order for his rearrest, while the other two triumphantly leave the chateau on the 11th of April, escorted by eight hundred National Guards. They go, for form's sake, to the prisons of the *sénéchaussée,* but the next day are set at liberty, and further prosecution ceases. As an offset to this, M. d'Ambert, colonel in the Royal Marine, guilty of expressing himself too warmly against the National Guard, although acquitted by the tribunal before which he was brought, can be set at liberty only in secret and under the protection of two thousand soldiers: the populace want to burn the house of the criminal lieutenant that dared absolve him; the magistrate himself is in danger, and is forced to take refuge in the house of the military commander.[26] Meanwhile, printed and written papers, insulting libels by the municipal body and the club, the seditious or violent discussions of the district assemblies, and a lot of pamphlets, are freely distributed among the people and the soldiers: the latter are purposely stirred up in advance against their chiefs.—In vain are the officers mild, conciliatory, and cautious. In vain does the commander-in-chief depart with a portion of the troops. The object now is to dislodge the regiment occupying the three forts. The club sets the ball in motion, and, forcibly or otherwise, the will of the people must be carried out. On the 29th of April, two actors, supported by fifty volunteers, surprise a sentinel and get possession of Notre-Dame de la Garde. On the same day, six thousand National Guards invest the forts of Saint-Jean and Saint-Nicolas. The municipal authorities, summoned to respect the fortresses, reply by demanding the opening of the gates to the Na-

26. "Archives Nationales," F[7], 3,196. Letters of M. du Miran, April 11th and 16th, and May 1, 1790.

tional Guard, that it may do duty jointly with the soldiers. The commandants hesitate, refer to the law, and demand time to consult their superiors. A second requisition, more urgent, is made; the commandants are held responsible for the disturbances which they provoke by their refusal, and if they resist they are declared promoters of civil war.[27] They accordingly yield and sign a capitulation. One among them, the Chevalier de Beausset, major in Fort Saint-Jean, is opposed to this, and refuses his signature. On the following day he is seized as he is about to enter the Hôtel-de-Ville, and massacred, his head being borne about on the end of a pike, while the band of assassins, the soldiers, and the rabble dance about and shout over his remains.—"It is a sad accident," writes the municipality.[28] How does it happen that, "after having thus far merited and obtained all praise, a Beausset, whom we were unable to protect against the decrees of Providence, should sully our laurels? Having had nothing to do with this tragic affair, it is not for us to prosecute the authors of it." Moreover, he was "culpable . . . rebellious, condemned by public opinion, and Providence itself seems to have abandoned him to the irrevocable decrees of its vengeance."—As to the taking of the forts, nothing is more legitimate. "These places were in the hands of the enemies of the State, while now they are in the hands of the defenders of the Constitution of the empire. Woe to whoever would take them from us again, to convert them into a focus of counterrevolution!"—M. de Miran, commandant of the province, has, it is true, made a demand for them. But, "is it not somewhat pitiable to see the requisition of a *Sieur* de Miran, made in the name of the King he betrays, to surrender to his Majesty's troops places which, henceforth in our hands, guarantee public security to the nation, to the law, and to the King?" In vain does the King, at the request of the National Assembly,[29] order the munici-

27. "Archives Nationales," F^7, 3,196. *Procès-verbal* of events on the 30th of April.

28. "Archives Nationales," F^7, 3,196. Letters of the Municipality of Marseilles to the National Assembly, May 5 and 20, 1790.

29. "Archives Nationales," F^7, 3,196. Order of the king, May 10. Letter of

pality to restore the forts to the commandants, and to make the National Guards leave them. The municipal authorities become indignant, and resist. According to them the wrong is all on the side of the commandant and the ministers. It is the commandants who, "with the threatening equipment of their citadels, their stores of provisions and of artillery, are disturbers of the public peace. What does the minister mean by driving the national troops out of the forts, in order to entrust their guardianship to foreign troops? His object is apparent in this plan . . . he wants to kindle civil war."—"All the misfortunes of Marseilles originate in the secret understanding existing between the ministers and the enemies of the State." The municipal corps is at last obliged to evacuate the forts, but it is determined not to give them up; and, the day following that on which it receives the decree of the National Assembly, it conceives the design of demolishing them. On the 17th of May, two hundred labourers, paid in advance, begin the work of destruction. To save appearances the municipal body betakes itself at eleven o'clock in the morning to the different localities, and orders them to stop. But, on its departure, the labourers keep on; and, at six o'clock in the evening, a resolution is passed that, "to prevent the entire demolition of the citadel, it is deemed advisable to authorise only that of the part overlooking the town." On the 18th of May the Jacobin club, at once agent, accomplice, and councillor of the municipal body, compels private individuals to contribute something towards defraying the expenses of the demolition, and "sends round to every house, and to the *syndics* of all corporations, exacting their quotas, and making all citizens subscribe a document by which they appear

---

M. de Saint-Priest to the National Assembly, May 11. Decree of the National Assembly, May 12. Letter of the Municipality to the King, May 20. Letter of M. de Rubum, May 20. Note sent from Marseilles, May 31. Address of the Municipality to the President of the Friends of the Constitution, at Paris, May 5. In his narration of the taking of the forts we read the following sentence: "We arrived without hindrance in the presence of the commandant, whom we brought to an agreement by means of the influence which force, fear, and reason give to persuasion."

to sanction the action of the municipal body, and to express their thanks to it. People had to sign it, pay, and keep silent. Woe to any one that refused!" On the 20th of May the municipal body presumes to write to the Assembly, that "this threatening citadel, this odious monument of a stupendous despotism, is about to disappear"; and, to justify its disobedience, it takes occasion to remark, "that the love of country is the most powerful and most enduring of an empire's ramparts." On the 28th of May it secures the performance in two theatres of a piece representing the capture of the forts of Marseilles, for the benefit of the men engaged in their demolition. Meanwhile, it has summoned the Paris Jacobins to its support; it has proposed to invite the Lyons federation and all the municipalities of the kingdom to denounce the minister; it has forced M. de Miran, threatened with death and watched by a party in ambush on the road, to quit Aix, and then demands his recall,[30] and only on the 6th of June does it decide, at the express command of the National Assembly, to suspend the almost completed demolition.—Authorities to which obedience is due could not be treated more insolently. The end, however, is attained; there is no longer a citadel, and the troops have departed; the regiment commanded by Ernest alone remains, to be tampered with, insulted, and then sent off. It is ordered to Aix, and the National Guard of Marseilles will go there to disarm and disband

30. "Archives Nationales," F[7], 3,196. Letter of M. de Miran, May 5. The spirit of the ruling party at Marseilles is indicated by several printed documents joined to the *dossier*, and, among others, by a "Requête à Desmoulins, *procureur-général* de la Lanterne." It relates to a "patriotic inkstand," recently made out of the stones of the demolished citadel, representing a hydra with four heads, symbolizing the nobility, the clergy, the ministry, and the judges. "It is from the four patriotic skulls of the hydra that the ink of proscription will be taken for the enemies of the Constitution. This inkstand, cut out of the first stone that fell in the demolition of Fort Saint-Nicolas, is dedicated to the patriotic Assembly of Marseilles. The magic art of the hero of the liberty of Marseilles, that Renaud who, under the mask of devotion, surprised the watchful sentinel of Notre-Dame de la Garde, and whose manly courage and cunning ensured the conquest of that key of the great focus of counterrevolution, has just given birth to a new trait of genius: a new Deucalion, he personifies this stone which Liberty has flung from the summit of our menacing Bastilles, &c."

it. Henceforth the municipal body has full sway, "observes only those laws which suit it, makes others to its own liking, and, in short, governs in the most despotic and arbitrary manner,"[31] not only at Marseilles, but throughout the department where, under no authority but its own, it undertakes armed expeditions and makes raids and sudden attacks.

III

Were it but possible for the dissolution to stop here! But each commune is far from being a tranquil little state under the rule of a body of respected magistrates. The same causes which render municipalities rebellious against the central authority render individuals rebellious against local authority. They also feel that they are in danger and want to provide for their own safety. They also, in virtue of the Constitution and of circumstances, believe themselves appointed to save the country. They also consider themselves qualified to judge for themselves on all points and entitled to carry out their judgments with their own hands. The shopkeeper, workman, or peasant, at once elector and National Guard, furnished with his vote and a musket, suddenly becomes the equal and master of his superiors; instead of obeying, he commands, while all who see him again after some years' absence, find that "in his demeanour and manner all is changed." "There was great agitation everywhere,"[32] says M. de Ségur; "I noticed groups of men talking earnestly in the streets and on the squares. The sound of the drum struck my ear in the villages, while I was astonished at the great number of armed men I encountered in the little towns. On interrogating various persons among the lower classes they would reply with a proud look and in a bold and confident tone. I observed everywhere the effect of those sentiments of equality and liberty which had then become such violent passions."—Thus exalted in their own eyes they believed

31. "Archives Nationales," F^7, 3,198. Letters of the royal commissioners, April 13 and 15, 1791.

32. De Ségur, "Mémoires," iii. 482 (early in 1790).

themselves qualified to take the lead in everything, not only in local affairs, but also in general matters. France is to be governed by them; by virtue of the Constitution they arrogate to themselves the right, and, by dint of ignorance, attribute to themselves the capacity, to govern it. A torrent of new, shapeless, and disproportionate ideas have taken possession of their brains in the space of a few months. Vast interests about which they have never thought, have to be considered—government, royalty, the church, creeds, foreign powers, internal and external dangers, what is occurring at Paris and at Coblentz, the insurrection in the Low Countries, the acts of the cabinets of London, Vienna, Madrid, Berlin; and, of all this, they inform themselves as they best can. An officer,[33] who traverses France at this time, narrates that at the post-stations they made him wait for horses until he had "given them details. The peasants stopped my carriage in the middle of the road and overwhelmed me with questions. At Autun, I was obliged, in spite of the cold, to talk out of a window opening upon the square and tell what I knew about the Assembly."—These *on-dits* are all changed and amplified in passing from mouth to mouth. They finally become circumstantial stories adapted to the calibre of the minds they pass into and to the dominant passion that propagates them. Trace the effect of these fables in the house of a peasant or fishwoman in an outlying village or a populous suburb, on imbruted or almost brutal minds, especially when they are lively, heated, and overexcited—the effect is tremendous. For, in minds of this stamp, belief is at once converted into action, and into rude and destructive action. It is an acquired self-control, reflection, and culture which interposes between belief and action the solicitude for social interests, the observance of forms and respect for the law. These restraints are all wanting in the new sovereign. He does not know how to stop and will not suffer himself to be stopped. Why so many delays when the peril is urgent? What is the use of observing formalities when the safety of the people is at stake? What is there sacred in the law when it protects public

33. De Dammartin, i. 184 (January, 1791).

enemies? What is more pernicious than passive deference and patient waiting under timid or blind magistrates? What can be more just than to do one's self justice at once and on the spot?—Precipitation and passion, in their eyes, are both duties and merits. One day "the militia of Lorient decide upon marching to Versailles and to Paris without considering how they are to get over the ground or what they will do on their arrival."[34] Were the central government within reach they would lay their hands on it. In default of this they substitute themselves for it on their own territory, and exercise its functions with a full conviction of right, principally those of gendarme, judge, and executioner.

During the month of October, 1789, at Paris, after the assassination of the baker François, the leading murderer, who is a porter at the grain depôt, declares "that he wanted to avenge the nation." It is quite probable that this declaration is sincere. In his mind, assassination is one of the forms of patriotism, and it does not take long for his way of thinking to become prevalent. In ordinary times, social and political ideas slumber in uncultured minds in the shape of vague antipathies, restrained aspirations, and fleeting desires. Behold them aroused—energetic, imperious, stubborn, and unbridled. Objection or opposition is not to be tolerated; dissent, with them, is a sure sign of treachery.—Apropos of the nonjuring priests,[35] five hundred and twenty-seven of the National Guards of Arras write, "that no one could doubt their iniquity without being suspected of being their accomplices. . . . Should the whole town combine and express a contrary opinion, it would simply show that it is filled

34. "Archives Nationales," KK. 1105. Correspondence of M. de Thiard (October 12, 1789).

35. "Archives Nationales," F^7, 3,250. *Procès-verbal* of the directory of the department, March 18, 1792. "As the ferment was at the highest point and fears were entertained that greater evils would follow, M. le Président, with painful emotion declared that he yielded and passed the unconstitutional act." Reply of the minister, June 23: "If the constituted authorities are thus forced to yield to the arbitrary will of a wild multitude, government no longer exists and we are in the saddest stage of anarchy. If you think it best I will propose to the King to reverse your last decision."

with enemies of the Constitution"; and forthwith, in spite of the law and the remonstrances of the authorities, they insist on the closing of the churches. At Boulogne-sur-Mer, an English vessel having shipped a quantity of poultry, game, and eggs, "the National Guards, of their own authority," go on board and remove the cargo. On the strength of this, the accommodating municipal body approves of the act, declares the cargo confiscated, orders it to be sold, and awards one-half of the proceeds to the National Guards and the other half to charitable purposes. The concession is a vain one, for the National Guards consider that one-half is too little, "insult and threaten the municipal officers," and immediately proceed to divide the booty in kind, each one going home with a share of stolen hams and chickens.[36] The magistrates must necessarily keep quiet with the guns of those they govern pointed at them.—Sometimes, and it is generally the case, they are timid, and do not try to resist. At Douai,[37] the municipal officers, on being summoned three times to proclaim martial law, refuse, and end by avowing that they dare not unfold the red flag: "Were we to take this course we should all be sacrificed on the spot." Neither the troops nor the National Guards, in fact, are to be relied on. In this universal state of apathy the field is open to savages, and a dealer in wheat is hung.—Sometimes the administrative corps tries to resist, but in the end it has to succumb to violence. "For more than six hours," writes one of the members of the district of Étampes,[38] "we were closed in by bayonets levelled at us and with pistols at our breasts"; and they were obliged to sign a

36. "Archives Nationales," F^7, 3,250. Letter of M. Duport, minister of justice, December 24, 1791.

37. "Archives Nationales," F^7, 3,248, *Procès-verbal* of the members of the department, finished March 18, 1791.—Roux and Buchez, ix. 240 (Report of M. Alquier).

38. "Archives Nationales," F^7, 3,268. Extract from the deliberations of the directory of Seine-et-Oise, with the documents relating to the insurrection at Étampes, September 16, 1791. Letter of M. Venard, administrator of the district, September 20—"I shall not set foot in Étampes until the reestablishment of order and tranquillity, and the first thing I shall do will be to record my resignation in the register. I am tired of making sacrifices for ungrateful wretches."

dismissal of the troops which had arrived to protect the market. At present "we are all away from Étampes; there is no longer a district or a municipality"; almost all have handed in their resignations, or are to return for that purpose.—Sometimes, and this is the rarest case,[39] the magistrates do their duty to the end, and perish. In this same town, six months later, Simoneau, the mayor, having refused to cut down the price of wheat, is beaten with iron-pointed sticks, and his corpse is riddled with balls by the murderers.—Municipal bodies must take heed how they undertake to stem the torrent; the slightest opposition will soon be at the expense of their lives. In Touraine,[40] "as the publication of the tax-rolls takes place, riots break out against the municipal authorities; they are forced to surrender the rolls they have drawn up, and their papers are torn up." And still more, "they kill, they assassinate the municipal authorities." In that large commune men and women "beat and kick them with their fists and *sabots*. . . . The mayor is laid up after it, and the *procureur* of the commune died between nine and ten o'clock in the morning. Véteau, a municipal officer, received the last sacrament this morning"; the rest have fled, being constantly threatened with death and incendiarism. They do not, consequently, return, and "no one now will take the office of either mayor or administrator."—The outrages which the municipalities thus commit against their superiors are committed against themselves, the National Guards, the mob, the controlling faction, arrogating to themselves in the commune the same violent sovereignty which the commune pretends to exercise against the State.

I should never finish if I undertook to enumerate the outbreaks in which the magistrates are constrained to tolerate or to sanction popular usurpations, to shut up churches, to drive off or imprison

39. *Moniteur,* March 16, 1792. Mortimer-Ternaux, "Histoire de la Terreur" (Proceedings against the assassins of Simoneau), i. 381.

40. "Archives Nationales," F^{7}, 3,226. Letter and memorial of Chenantin, cultivator, November 7, 1792. Extract from the deliberations of the directory of Langeais, November 5, 1792 (sedition at Chapelle-Blanche, near Langeais, October 5, 1792).

priests, to suppress *octrois,* tax grain, and allow clerks, bakers, corn-dealers, ecclesiastics, nobles, and officers to be hung, beaten to death, or to have their throats cut. Ninety-four thick files of records in the national archives are filled with these acts of violence, and do not contain two-thirds of them. It is worth while to take in detail one case more, a special one, and one that is authentic, which serves as a specimen, and which presents a foreshortened image of France during one tranquil year. At Aix, in the month of December, 1790,[41] in opposition to the two Jacobin clubs, a club had been organized, had complied with all the formalities, and, like the "Club des Monarchiens" at Paris, claimed the same right of meeting as the others. But here, as at Paris, the Jacobins recognise no rights but for themselves alone, and refuse to admit their adversaries to the privileges of the law. Moreover, alarming rumours are circulated. A person who has arrived from Nice states that he had "heard that there were twenty thousand men between Turin and Nice, under the pay of the emigrants, and that at Nice a *neuvaine*[42] was held in Saint-François-de-Paule to pray God to enlighten the French." A counterrevolution is certainly under way. Some of the aristocrats have stated "with an air of triumph, that the National Guard and municipalities are a mere toy, and that this sort of thing will not last long." One of the leading members of the new club, M. de Guiramand, an old officer

41. "Archives Nationales," F^7, 3,195. Report of the Commissioners sent by the National Assembly and the King, February 23, 1791. (On the events of December 12 and 14, 1790.)—*Mercure de France,* February 29, 1791. (Letters from Aix, and notably a letter from seven officers shut up in the prison at Aix, January 30, 1791.) The oldest Jacobin club, formed in February, 1790, was entitled "Club des vrais amis de la Constitution." The second Jacobin club, formed in October, 1790, was "composed from the beginning of artisans and labourers from the faubourgs and suburbs." Its title was "Société des frères anti-politiques," or "frères vrais, justes et utiles à la patrie." The opposition club, formed in December, 1790, bore the title, according to some, of "Les Amis du Roi, de la paix et de la religion"; according to others, "Les amis de la paix"; and finally, according to another report, "Les Défenseurs de la religion, des personnes et des propriétés."

42. A special series of religious services.

of seventy-eight years, makes speeches in public against the National Assembly, tries to enlist artisans in his party, "affects to wear a white button on his hat fastened by pins with their points jutting out," and, as it is stated, he has given to several mercers a large order for white cockades. In reality, on examination, not one is found in any shop, and all the dealers in ribbons, on being interrogated, reply that they know of no transaction of that description. But this simply proves that the culprit is a clever dissimulator, and the more dangerous because he is eager to save the country.—On the 12th of December, at four o'clock in the afternoon, the two Jacobin clubs fraternise, and pass in long procession before the place of meeting, "where some of the members, a few officers of the Lyons regiment and other individuals, are quietly engaged at play or seeing others play." The crowd hoot, but they remain quiet. The procession passes by again, and they hoot and shout, "Down with the aristocrats! To the lantern with them!" Two or three of the officers standing on the threshold of the door become irritated, and one of them, drawing his sword, threatens to strike a young man if he keeps on. Upon this the crowd cries out, "Guard! help! an assassin!" and rushes at the officer, who withdraws into the house, exclaiming, "To arms!" His comrades, sword in hand, descend in order to defend the door; M. de Guiramand fires two pistol shots and receives a stab in the thigh. A shower of stones smashes in the windows, and the door is on the point of being burst open when several of the members of the club save themselves by taking to the roof. About a dozen others, most of them officers, form in line, penetrate the crowd with uplifted swords, strike and get struck, and escape, five of them being wounded. The municipality orders the doors and windows of the club-house to be walled up, sends the Lyons regiment away, decrees the arrest of seven officers and of M. de Guiramand, and all this in a few hours, with no other testimony than that of the conquerors.

But these prompt, vigorous, and partial measures are not sufficient for the club; other conspirators must be seized, and it is the club which designates them and goes to take them.—Three months before this, M. Pascalis, an advocate, on addressing along with some of his professional brethren the parliament which had been dissolved, deplored the blindness of the people, "exalted by prerogatives of which they knew not the danger." A man who dared talk in this way is evidently a traitor.—There is another, M. Morellet de la Roquette, who refused to join the proscribed club. His former vassals, however, had been obliged to bring an action against him to make him accept the redemption of his feudal dues; also, six years before this, his carriage, passing along the public promenade, had run over a child; he likewise is an enemy of the people. While the municipal officers are deliberating, "a few members of the club" get together and decide that M. Pascalis and M. de la Roquette must be arrested. At eleven o'clock at night eighty trustworthy National Guards, led by the president of the club, travel a league off to seize them in their beds and lodge them in the town prison.—Zeal of this kind excites some uneasiness, and if the municipality tolerates the arrests, it is because it is desirous of preventing murder. Consequently, on the following day, December 13th, it sends to Marseilles for four hundred men of the Swiss Guard commanded by Ernest, and four hundred National Guards, adding to these the National Guard of Aix, and orders this company to protect the prison against any violence. But, along with the Marseilles National Guards, there came a lot of armed people who are volunteers of disorder. On the afternoon of the 13th, the first mob strives to force the prison, and the next day, fresh squads congregate around it demanding the head of M. Pascalis. The members of the club head the riot with "a crowd of unknown men from outside the town, who give orders and carry them out." During the night the populace of Aix are tampered with, and the dykes all give way at the same moment. At the first clamours the National Guard on duty on the public promenade disband and disperse, while, as there is no signal for the assemblage of the others, notwithstanding the regulations, the general alarm is not sounded. "The largest portion of the National Guard draws off so as not to appear to authorise by its presence outrages which it has not been ordered to prevent. Peaceable citizens are in great consternation"; each one takes to flight or shuts himself up in his house, the streets being deserted and silent. Meanwhile the prison gates are shattered with axes. The *procureur-syndic* of the department, who requests the commandant of the Swiss regiment to protect the prisoners, is seized, borne off, and runs the risk of losing his life. Three municipal officers in their scarfs, who arrive on the ground, dare not give the order which the commandant requires, plainly showing that at this decisive moment, when it is necessary to shed blood and kill a number of men, they fear to take the responsibility; their reply is, "We have no orders to give."—An extraordinary spectacle now presents itself in this barrack courtyard surrounding the prison. On the side of the law stand eight hundred armed men, four hundred of the "Swiss" and four hundred of the National Guard of Marseilles, drawn up in battle array, with guns to their shoulders, with special orders repeated the evening before at three different times by the municipal district and departmental authorities, possessing the sympathies of all honest people and of most of the National Guard. But the legal indispensable phrase does not pass the lips of those who by virtue of the Constitution should utter it, and a small group of convicts are found to be sovereign.—The three municipal officers are seized in their turn under the eyes of their own soldiers who remain motionless, and "with bayonets at their breasts they sign, under constraint, the order to give up M. Pascalis to the people." M. de la Roquette is likewise surrendered. "The only portion of the National Guard of Aix which was visible," that is to say, the Jacobin minority, form a circle around the gate of the prison and organize themselves into a council of war. And there they stand, at once "accusers, witnesses, judges, and executioners." A captain conducts the two victims to the public promenade where they are hung. Very soon after this old M. de Guiramand, whom the National Guard of his village have brought a prisoner to Aix, is hung in the same manner.

There is no prosecution of the assassins. The new tribunal, frightened or forestalled, has for some time back ranged itself on the popular side; its writs, consequently, are served on the oppressed, against the members of the assaulted club. Writs of arrest, summonses to attend court, searches, seizures of correspondence, and other proceedings, rain down upon them. Three hundred witnesses are examined. Some of the arrested officers are "loaded with chains and thrust into dungeons." Henceforth the club rules, and "makes everybody tremble."[43] "From the 23rd to the 27th of December, more than ten thousand passports are delivered at Aix." "If the emigrations continue," write the commissioners, "there will be no one left at Aix but workmen without work and with no resources. Whole streets are uninhabited. . . . As long as such crimes can be permitted with impunity fear will drive out of this town every one who has the means of living elsewhere."—Many come back after the arrival of the commissioners, hoping to obtain justice and security through them. But, "if a prosecution is not ordered, we shall scarcely have left Aix when three or four hundred families will abandon it. . . . And what man in his senses would dare guarantee that each village will not soon have some one hung in it? . . . Country valets arrest their masters. . . . The hope of doing evil deeds with impunity leads the inhabitants of villages to commit all sorts of depredations in the forests, which is exceedingly dangerous in a region where woods are very scarce. They set up the most absurd and most unjust pretensions against rich proprietors, and the fatal rope is ever the interpreter and the signal of their will." There is no refuge against these outrages. "The department, the districts, the municipalities, administer only in conformity with the multiplied petitions of the club." In the sight of all, and on one solemn day, a crushing defeat has demonstrated the weakness of the magistrates; and, bowed beneath the yoke of their new masters, they preserve their legal authority only on the condition that it remains at the service of the victorious party.

43. "Archives Nationales," F[7], 3,195. Letters of the commissioners, March 20, February 11, May 10, 1791.

CHAPTER II

The sovereignty of unrestrained passions— I. *Old religious rancours—Montauban and Nismes in 1790*— II. *Passion supreme—Dread of hunger its acutest form—The noncirculation of grain—Intervention and usurpations of the electoral assemblies—The rural code in Nivernais—The four central provinces in 1790—Why high prices are kept up—Anxiety and insecurity—Stagnation of the grain market—The departments near Paris in 1791—The supply and price of grain regulated by force—The mobs in 1792—Village armies of Eure and of the lower Seine and of Aisne—Aggravation of the disorder after August 10th—The dictation of unbridled instinct—Its practical and political expedients*— III. *Egotism of the tax-payer—Issoudun in 1790—Rebellion against taxation—Indirect taxes in 1789 and 1790—Abolition of the salt-tax, excise, and* octrois*—Direct taxation in 1789 and 1790—Delay and insufficiency of the returns—New levies in 1791 and 1792—Delays, partiality, and concealment in preparing the rolls—Insufficiency of, and the delay in, the returns—Payment in assignats—The tax-payer relieves himself of one-half—Devastation of the forests—Division of the communal property*— IV. *Cupidity of tenants—The third and fourth jacquerie—Brittany and other provinces in 1790 and 1791—The burning of chateaux—Title-deeds destroyed.—Refusal of claims—Destruction of reservoirs—Principal characteristics, prime motive, and ruling passion of the Revolution.*

IN THIS state of things the passions have full sway. Any one of them that is powerful enough to group together a few hundred men suffices for the formation of a faction or band, which dashes through the relaxed or feeble meshes of a government that is passive or disregarded. An experiment on a grand scale is about to be made on human society; owing to the slackening of the regular restraints which have maintained it, it is possible to measure the force of the permanent instincts which attack it. They are always there even in ordinary times; we do not notice them because they are kept in check; but they are not the less energetic and effective, and, moreover, indestructible. The moment their repression ceases, their power of mischief is shown; just as that of the water which floats a ship, but which at the first leak enters into it and sinks it.

I

Religious passions, to begin with, are not to be kept down by federations, embraces, and effusions of fraternity. In the south, where the Protestants have been persecuted for more than a century, hatreds exist more than a century old.[1]—In vain have the odious edicts which oppressed them fallen into desuetude for the past twenty years; in vain have civil rights been restored to them since 1787: the past still lives in transmitted recollections; and two groups are confronting each other, one Protestant and the other Catholic, each defiant, hostile, ready to act on the defensive, and interpreting the preparations of its adversary as a plan of attack. Under such circumstances the guns go off of their own accord.—On a sudden alarm at Uzès[2] the Catholics, two thousand in number, take possession of the bishop's palace and the Hôtel-de-Ville; while the Protestants, numbering four hundred, assemble outside the walls on the esplanade, and pass the night under arms, each troop persuaded that the other is going to massacre it, one party summoning the Catholics of Jalès to its aid, and the other the Protestants of Gardonnenque.—There is but one way of avoiding civil war between parties in such an attitude, and that is the ascendancy of an energetic third party, impartial and on the spot. A plan to this effect, which promises well, is proposed by the military commandant of Languedoc.[3] According

1. The expression is that of Jean Bon Saint-André to Mathieu Dumas, sent to reestablish tranquillity in Montauban (1790): "The day of vengeance, which we have been awaiting for a hundred years, has come!"

2. De Dammartin, i. 187 (an eye-witness).

3. "Archives Nationales," F[7], 3,223 and 3,216. Letters of M. de Bouzols, major-general, residing at Montpellier, May 21, 25, 28, 1790.

to him the two firebrands are, on the one hand, the bishops of Lower Languedoc, and on the other, MM. Rabaut-Saint-Etienne, father and two sons, all three being pastors. Let them be responsible "with their heads" for any mob, insurrection, or attempt to debauch the army; let a tribunal of twelve judges be selected from the municipal bodies of twelve towns, and all delinquents be brought before it; let this be the court of final appeal, and its sentence immediately executed. The system in vogue, however, is just the reverse. Both parties being organized into a body of militia, each takes care of itself, and is sure to fire on the other; and the more readily, inasmuch as the new ecclesiastical regulations, which are issued from month to month, strike like so many hammers on Catholic sensibility, and scatter showers of sparks on the primings of the already loaded guns.

At Montauban, on the 10th of May, 1790, the day of the inventory and expropriation of the religious communities,[4] the commissioners are not allowed to enter. Women in a state of frenzy lie across the thresholds of the doors, and it would be necessary to pass over their bodies; a large mob gathers around the "Cordeliers," and a petition is signed to have the convents maintained.—The Protestants who witness this commotion become alarmed, and eighty of their National Guards march to the Hôtel-de-Ville, and take forcible possession of the guard-house which protects it. The municipal authorities order them to withdraw, which they refuse to do. Thereupon the Catholics assembled at the "Cordeliers" begin a riot, throw stones, and drive in the doors with pieces of timber, while a cry is heard that the Protestants, who have taken refuge in the guard-house, are firing from the windows. The enraged multitude immediately invade the arsenal, seize all the guns they can lay their hands on, and fire volleys on the guard-house, the effect of which is to kill five of the Protestants and wound twenty-four others. The rest are saved by a municipal officer and the police; but they are obliged to appear, two and two, before the cathedral in their shirts, and do

4. Mary Lafon, "Histoire d'une Ville Protestante" (with original documents derived from the archives of Montauban).

public penance, after which they are put in prison. During the tumult political shouts have been heard: "Hurrah for the nobles! Hurrah for the aristocracy! Down with the nation! Down with the tricolour flag!" Bordeaux, regarding Montauban as in rebellion against France, dispatches fifteen hundred of its National Guard to set the prisoners free. Toulouse gives its aid to Bordeaux. The fermentation is frightful. Four thousand of the Protestants of Montauban take flight; armed cities are about to contend with each other, as formerly in Italy. It is necessary that a commissioner of the National Assembly and of the King, Mathieu Dumas, should be dispatched to harangue the people of Montauban, obtain the release of the prisoners, and reestablish order.

One month after this a more bloody affray takes place at Nismes[5] against the Catholics. The Protestants, in fact, are but twelve thousand out of fifty-four thousand inhabitants, but the principal trade of the place is in their hands; they hold the manufactories and support thirty thousand workmen; in the elections of 1789 they furnished five out of the eight deputies. The sympathies of that time were in their favour; nobody then imagined that the dominant Church was exposed to any risk. It is to be attacked in its turn, and the two parties are seen confronting each other.—The Catholics sign a petition,[6] hunt up recruits among the market-gardeners of the suburbs, retain the white cockade, and, when this is prohibited, re-

5. "Archives Nationales," F^7, 2,216. *Procès-verbal* of the Municipality of Nismes and report of the Abbé de Belmont.—Report of the Administrative Commissioners, June 28, 1790.—Petition of the Catholics, April 20.—Letters of the Municipality, the Commissioners, and M. de Nausel, on the events of May 2 and 3.—Letter of M. Rabaut-Saint-Etienne, May 12.—Petition of the widow Gas, July 30.—Report (printed) of M. Alquier, February 19, 1791.—Memoir (printed) of the massacre of the Catholics at Nismes, by Froment (1790).—New address of the Municipality of Nismes, presented by M. de Marguerite, mayor and deputy (1790), printed.—*Mercure de France,* February 23, 1791.

6. The petition is signed by 3,127 persons, besides 1,560 who put a cross declaring that they could not write. The counterpetition of the club is signed by 162 persons.

place it with a red rosette, another sign of recognition. At their head is an energetic man named Froment, who has vast projects in view; but as the soil on which he treads is undermined, he cannot prevent the explosion. It takes place naturally, by chance, through the simple collision of two equally distrustful bodies; and before the final day it has commenced and recommenced twenty times, through mutual provocations and denunciations, through insults, libels, scuffles, stone-throwing, and gun-shots.—On the 13th of June, 1790, the question is which party shall furnish administrators for the district and department, and the conflict begins in relation to the elections. The Electoral Assembly is held at the guard-house of the bishop's palace, where the Protestant and patriotic dragoons arrive "three times as many as usual, with loaded muskets and pistols, and with full cartridge-boxes," and they patrol the surrounding neighbourhood. The red rosettes, on their side, royalists and Catholics, complain of being threatened and "treated contemptuously" (*nargués*). They give notice to the gate-keeper "not to let any dragoon enter the town either on foot or mounted, at the peril of his life," and declare that "the bishop's quarters were not made for a guard-house."—A mob forms, and shouting takes place under the windows; stones are thrown; the bugle of a dragoon, who sounds the roll-call, is broken and two shots are fired.[7] The dragoons immediately fire a volley, which wounds a good many people and kills seven. From this moment, firing goes on during the evening and all night, in every quarter of the town, each party believing that the other wants to exterminate it, the Protestants satisfied that it is another St. Bartholomew, and the Catholics that it is "a Michelade."[8] There is no one to act between them. The municipality authorities, far from issuing orders, receive them: they are roughly handled, hustled and jostled about, and made to march about like servants.

7. This last item, stated in M. Alquier's report, is denied by the municipality. According to it, the red rosettes gathered around the bishop's quarters had no guns.

8. An insurrection in the sixteenth century, when the Protestants fired on the Catholics on St. Michael's Day.—[Tr.]

The patriots seize the Abbé de Belmont, a municipal officer, at the Hôtel-de-Ville, order him, on pain of death, to proclaim martial law, and place the red flag in his hand. "March, rascal, you ——! Hold up your flag—higher up still—you are big enough to do that!" Blows follow with the but-ends of their muskets. The poor man spits blood, but this is of no consequence; he must be in full sight at the head of the crowd, like a target, whilst his conductors prudently remain behind. Thus does he advance, exposed to bullets, holding the flag, and finally becomes the prisoner of the red rosettes, who release him, but keep his flag. There is a second march with a red flag held by a town valet, and fresh gunshots; the red rosettes capture this flag also, as well as another municipal officer. The rest of the municipal body, with a royal commissioner, take refuge in the barracks and order out the troops. Meanwhile Froment, with his three companies, posted in their towers and in the houses on the ramparts, resist to the last extremity. Daylight comes, the tocsin is sounded, the drums beat to arms, and the patriot militia of the neighbourhood, the Protestants from the mountains, the rude Cévenols, arrive in crowds. The red rosettes are besieged; a Capuchin convent, from which it is pretended that they have fired, is sacked, and five of the monks are killed. Froment's tower is demolished with cannon and taken by assault. His brother is massacred and thrown from the walls, while a Jacobin convent next to the ramparts is sacked. Towards night, all the red rosettes who have fought are slain or have fled, and there is no longer any resistance.—But the fury still lasts; the fifteen thousand rustics who have flooded the town think that they have not yet done enough. In vain are they told that the other fifteen companies of red rosettes have not moved; that the pretended aggressors "did not even put themselves in a state of defence"; that during the battle they remained at home, and that afterwards, through extra precaution, the municipal authorities had made them give up their arms. In vain does the Electoral Assembly, preceded by a white flag, march to the public square and exhort the people to keep the peace. "Under the pretext of searching suspicious houses, they pillage or destroy, and whatever cannot be carried away is broken." One hundred and twenty houses are sacked in Nismes alone, while the same ravages are committed in the environs, the damage, at the end of three days, amounting to seven or eight hundred thousand livres. A number of poor creatures, workmen, merchants, old and infirm men, are massacred in their houses; some, "who have been bed-ridden for many years, are dragged to the sills of their doors to be shot." Others are hung on the esplanade and at the Cours Neuf, while others have their noses, ears, feet, and hands cut off, and are hacked to pieces with sabres and scythes. Horrible stories, as is commonly the case, provoke the most atrocious acts. A publican, who refuses to distribute anti-Catholic lists, is supposed to have a mine in his cellar filled with kegs of gunpowder and with sulphur matches all ready; he is hacked to pieces with a sabre, and twenty guns are discharged into his corpse: they expose the body before his house with a long loaf of bread on his breast, and they again stab him with bayonets, saying to him, "Eat, you ——, eat!" More than five hundred Catholics were assassinated, and many others, covered with blood, "are crowded together in the prisons, while the search for the proscribed is continued; whenever they are seen, they are fired upon like so many wolves." Thousands of the inhabitants, accordingly, demand their passports and leave the town. The rural Catholics, meanwhile, on their side, massacre six Protestants in the environs—an old man of eighty-two years, a youth of fifteen, and a husband and his wife in their farmhouse. In order to put a stop to the murderous acts, the National Guard of Montpellier have to be summoned. But the restoration of order is for the benefit of the victorious party. Three-fifths of the electors have fled; one-third of the district and departmental administrators have been appointed in their absence, and the majority of the new directories is taken from the club of patriots. It is for this reason that those who are held in durance are prejudged as guilty. "No officer of the court dare give them the benefit of his services; they are not allowed to bring forward justificatory facts in evidence, while everybody knows that the judges are not free."[9]

9. "Archives Nationales," F[7], 3,216. Letter of M. de Lespin, Major at Nismes, to the Commandant of Provence, M. de Perigord, July 27, 1790: "The

Thus do the violent measures of political and religious discord come to an end. The victor stops the mouth of the law when it is about to speak in his adversary's behalf; and, under the legal iniquity of an administration which he has himself established, he crushes those whom the illegal force of his own strong hand has stricken down.

II

Passions of this stamp are the product of human cultivation, and break loose only within narrow bounds. Another passion exists which is neither historic nor local, but natural and universal, the most indomitable, most imperious, and most formidable of all, namely, the fear of hunger. There is no such thing with this passion as delay, or reflection, or looking beyond itself. Each commune or canton wants its bread, and a sure and unlimited supply of it. Our neighbour may provide for himself as best he can, but let us look out for ourselves first and then for other people. Each group of people, accordingly, through its own decrees, or by main force, keeps for itself whatever subsistences it possesses, or takes from others the subsistences which it does not possess.

At the end of 1789,[10] "Roussillon refuses aid to Languedoc; Upper Languedoc to the rest of the province, and Burgundy to Lyonnais; Dauphiny shuts herself up, and Normandy retains the wheat purchased for the relief of Paris." At Paris, sentinels are posted at the doors of all the bakers; on the 21st of October one of the latter is lanterned, and his head is borne about on a pike. On the 27th of October, at Vernon, a corn-merchant named Planter, who the preceding winter had supported the poor for six leagues around, has to

---

plots and conspiracies which were attributed to the vanquished party, and which, it was believed, would be discovered in the depositions of the four hundred men in prison, vanish as the proceedings advance. The veritable culprits are to be found among the informers."

10. Roux and Buchez, iii. 240 (Memorial of the Ministers, October 28, 1789).—"Archives Nationales," D. xxix. 3.—Deliberation of the Municipal Council of Vernon (November 4, 1789).

take his turn. At the present moment the people do not forgive him for having sent flour to Paris, and he is hung twice, but is saved through the breaking of the rope each time.—It is only by force and under an escort that it is possible to ensure the arrival of grain in a town; the excited people or the National Guards constantly seize it on its passage. In Normandy the militia of Caen stops wheat on the highways which is destined for Harcourt and elsewhere.[11] In Brittany, Auray and Vannes retain the convoys for Nantes, and Lannion those for Brest. Brest having attempted to negotiate, its commissioners are seized, and, with knives at their throats, are forced to sign a renunciation, pure and simple, of the grain which they have paid for, and they are led out of Lannion and stoned on the way. Eighteen hundred men, consequently, leave Brest with four cannon, and go to recover their property with their guns loaded. These are the customs prevalent during the great famines of feudal times; and, from one end of France to the other, to say nothing of the outbreaks of the famished in the large towns, similar outrages or attempts at recovery are constantly occurring.—"The armed population of Nantua, Saint-Claude, and Septmoncel," says a dispatch,[12] "have again cut off provisions from the Gex region; there is no wheat coming there from any direction, all the roads being guarded. Without the aid of the government of Geneva, which is willing to lend to this region eight hundred cuttings of wheat, we should either die of starvation or be compelled to take grain by force from the municipalities which keep it to themselves." "Narbonne starves Toulon; the navigation of the Languedoc canal is intercepted; the people on its banks repulse two companies of soldiers, burn a large building, and want to destroy the canal itself." Boats are stopped, waggons are pillaged, bread is forcibly lowered in price, stones are thrown and guns discharged; the populace contend with

11. "Archives Nationales," KK. 1105. Correspondence of M. de Thiard, November 4, 1789.—See similar occurrences, September 4, October 23, November 4 and 19, 1789, January 27 and March 27, 1790.

12. "Archives Nationales," F^7, 3,257. Letter from Gex, May 29, 1790.—Roux and Buchez, vii. 198, 369 (September, October, 1790).

the National Guard, peasants with townsmen, purchasers with dealers, artisans and labourers with farmers and landowners, at Castelnaudary, Niort, Saint-Etienne, in Aisne, in Pas-de-Calais, and especially along the line stretching from Montbrison to Angers—that is to say, for almost the whole of the extent of the vast basin of the Loire—such is the spectacle presented by the year 1790.—And yet the crop has not been a bad one. But there is no circulation of grain. Each petty centre has formed a league for the monopoly of food; and hence the fasting of others and the convulsions of the entire body are the first effects of the unbridled freedom which the Constitution and circumstances have conferred on each local group.

"We are told to assemble, vote, and elect men that will attend to our business; let us attend to it ourselves. We have had enough of talk and hypocrisy. Bread at two sous, and let us go after wheat where it can be found!" Such is the reasoning of the peasantry, and, in Nivernais, Bourbonnais, Berri, and Touraine, electoral gatherings are the firebrands of the insurrections.[13] At Saint-Sauge, "the first work of the primary meeting is to oblige the municipal officers to fix the price of wheat under the penalty of being decapitated." At Saint-Géran the same course is taken with regard to bread, wheat, and meat; at Châtillon-en-Bayait it is done with all supplies, and always a third or a half under the market price, without mentioning other exactions.—They come by degrees to the drafting of a tariff for all the valuables they know, proclaiming the maximum price which an article may reach, and so establishing a complete code of rural and social economy. We see in the turbulent and spasmodic wording of this instrument their dispositions and sentiments, as in a mirror.[14] It is the programme of villagers. Its diverse articles, save

13. "Archives Nationales," H. 1453. Correspondence of M. de Bercheny, Commandant of the four central provinces. Letters of May 25, June 11, 19, and 27, 1790.—"Archives Nationales," D. xxix. 4. Deliberations of the district administrators of Bourbon-Lancy, May 26.

14. "Archives Nationales," H. 1453. *Procès-verbal* of a dozen parishes in Nivernais, June 4. "White bread is to be 2 sous, and brown bread 1½ sous. Husbandmen are to have 30 sous, reapers 10 sous, wheelwrights 10 sous, bailiffs

local variations, must be executed, now one and now the other, according to the occasion, the need, and the time, and, above all, whatever concerns provisions. The wish, as usual, is the father of the thought; the peasantry thinks that it is acting by authority: here, through a decree of the King and the National Assembly, there, by a commission directly entrusted to the Comte d'Estrées. Even before this, in the market-place of Saint-Amand, "a man jumped on a heap of wheat and cried out, 'In the name of the King and the nation, wheat at one-half the market-price!'" An old officer of the Royal Grenadiers, a chevalier of the order of Saint-Louis, is reported to be marching at the head of several parishes, and promulgating ordinances in his own name and that of the King, imposing a fine of eight livres on whoever may refuse to join him.—On all sides

---

6 sous per league. Butter is to be at 8 sous, meat at 5 sous, pork at 8 sous, oil at 8 sous the pint, a square foot of masonry-work 40 sous, a pair of large sabots 3 sous. All rights of pasturage and of forests are to be surrendered. The roads are to be free everywhere, as formerly. All seignorial rents are to be suppressed. Millers are to take only one thirty-second of a bushel. The seignieurs of our department are to give up all servile holidays and ill-acquired property. The curé of Bièze is simply to say mass at nine o'clock in the morning and vespers at two o'clock in the afternoon, in summer and winter; he must marry and bury gratis, it being reserved to us to pay him a salary. He is to be paid 6 sous for masses, and not to leave his *cure* except to repeat his breviary and make proper calls on the men and women of his parish. Hats must be had from 3 livres to 30 sous. Nails 3 livres the gross. Curés are to have none but circumspect females of fifty for domestics. Curés are not to go to either fairs or markets. All curés are to be on the same footing as the one at Bièze. There must be no more wholesale dealers in wheat. Law officers who make unjust seizures must return the money. Farm leases must expire on St. Martin's Day. M. le Comte, although not there, M. de Tontenelle, and M. de Commandant must sign this document without difficulty. M. de Mingot is formally to resign his place in writing: he went away with his servant-woman—he even missed his mass on the first Friday of the Fête-Dieu, and it is supposed that he slept in the woods. Joiners' wages shall be fixed at the same rate as wheelwrights'. Ox-straps are not to cost over 40 sous, yokes 10 sous. Masters must pay one-half of the *tailles.* Notaries are to take only the half of what they had formerly, as well as comptrollers. The Commune claims the right of protest against whatever it may have forgotten in the present article, in fact or in law." It is signed by about twenty persons, several of them being mayors and municipal clerks.

there is a swarm of blouses, and resistance is fruitless. There are too many of them, the constabulary being drowned in the flood. For, these rustic legislators are the National Guard itself, and when they vote reductions upon, or requisitions for, subsistences, they enforce their demands with their guns.

The municipal officials, willingly or unwillingly, must needs serve the insurgents. At Donjon the Electoral Assembly has seized the mayor of the place and threatened to kill him, or to burn his house, if he did not put the cutting of wheat at forty sous; whereupon he signs, and all the mayors with him, "under the penalty of death." As soon as this is done the peasants, "to the sound of fifes and drums," spread through the neighbouring parishes and force the delivery of wheat at forty sous, and show such a determined spirit that the four brigades of gendarmes sent out against them think it best to retire.—Not content with taking what they want, they provide for reserve supplies; wheat is a prisoner. In Nivernais and Bourbonnais, the peasants trace a boundary line over which no sack of grain of that region must pass; in case of any infraction of this law the rope and the torch are close at hand for the delinquent.—It remains to see that this rule is enforced. In Berri bands of peasants visit the markets to see that their tariff is everywhere maintained. In vain are they told that they are emptying the markets; "they reply that they know how to make grain come, that they will take it from private hands, and money besides, if necessary." In fact, the granaries and cellars belonging to a large number of persons are pillaged. Farmers are constrained to put their crops into a common granary, and the rich are put to ransom; "the nobles are compelled to contribute, and obliged to give entire domains as donations; cattle are carried off, and they want to take the lives of the proprietors," while the towns, which defend their storehouses and markets, are openly attacked.[15] Bourbon-Lancy, Bourbon-l'Archambault, Saint-

15. "Archives Nationales," H. 1453. The same correspondence, May 29, June 11 and 17, September 15, 1790.—*Ibid.*, F^{7}, 3,257. Letter of the municipal authorities of Marsigny, May 3; of the municipal officers of Bourbon-Lancy, June 5. Extract from letters written to M. Amelot, June 1.

Pierre-le-Moutier, Montluçon, Saint-Amand, Chateau-Gontier, Decises, each petty community is an islet assailed by the mounting tide of rustic insurrection. The militia pass the night under arms; detachments of the National Guards of the large towns with regular troops come and garrison them. The red flag is continuously raised for eight days at Bourbon-Lancy, and cannon stand loaded and pointed in the public square. On the 24th of May an attack is made on Saint-Pierre-le-Moutier, and fusillades take place all night on both sides. On the 2nd of June, Saint-Amand, menaced by twenty-seven parishes, is saved only by the preparations it makes and by the garrison. About the same time Bourbon-Lancy is attacked by twelve parishes combined, and Chateau-Gontier by the *sabotiers* of the forests in the vicinity. A band of from four to five hundred villagers arrests the convoys of Saint-Amand, and forces their escorts to capitulate; another band intrenches itself in the Chateau de la Fin, and fires throughout the day on the regulars and the National Guard.—The large towns themselves are not safe. Three or four hundred rustics, led by their municipal officers, forcibly enter Tours, to compel the municipality to lower the price of corn and diminish the rate of leases. Two thousand slate-quarry-men, armed with guns, spits, and forks, force their way into Angers to obtain a reduction on bread, fire upon the guard, and are charged by the troops and the National Guard; a number remain dead in the streets, two are hung that very evening, and the red flag is displayed for eight days. "The town," say the dispatches, "would have been pillaged and burnt had it not been for the Picardy regiment." Fortunately, as the crop promises to be a good one, prices fall. As the Electoral Assemblies are closed, the fermentation subsides; and towards the end of the year, like a clear spell in a steady storm, the gleam of a truce appears in the civil war excited by hunger.

But the truce does not last long, as it is broken in twenty places by isolated explosions; and towards the month of July, 1791, the disturbances arising from the uncertainty of subsistences begin again, to cease no more. We will consider but one group in this universal state of disorder—that of the eight or ten departments which surround Paris and furnish it with supplies. These districts,

Brie and Beause, are rich wheat regions, and not only was the crop of 1790 good, but that of 1791 is ample. Information is sent to the minister from Laon[16] that, in the department of Aisne, "there is a supply of wheat for two years . . . that the barns, generally empty by the month of April, will not be so this season before July," and, consequently, "subsistences are assured." But this does not suffice, for the source of the evil is not in a scarcity of wheat. In order that everybody, in a vast and populous country, where the soil, cultivation, and occupations differ, may eat, it is essential that food should be attainable by the nonproducers; and for it to reach them freely, without delay, solely by the natural operation of supply and demand, it is essential that there should be a police able to protect property, transactions, and transport. Just in proportion as the authority of a State becomes weakened, and in proportion as security diminishes, the distribution of subsistences becomes more and more difficult: a gendarmerie, therefore, is an indispensable wheel in the machine by which we are able to secure our daily bread. Hence it is that, in 1791, daily bread is wanting to a large number of men. Simply through the working of the Constitution, all restraints, already slackened both at the extremities and at the centre, are becoming looser and more loose each day. The municipalities, which are really sovereign, repress the people more feebly, some because the latter are the bolder and themselves more timid, and others because they are more radical and always consider them in the right. The National Guard is wearied, never comes forward, or refuses to use its arms. The active citizens are disgusted, and remain at home. At Étampes,[17] where they are convoked by the commissioners of the department to take steps to reestablish some kind of order, only twenty assemble; the others excuse themselves by saying that, if the populace knew that they opposed its will, "their houses would be burnt," and they

16. "Archives Nationales," F[7], 3,185, 3,186. Letter of the President of the Tribunal of the district of Laon, February 8, 1792.

17. "Archives Nationales," F[7], 3,268. *Procès-verbal* and observations of the two commissioners sent to Étampes, September 22–25, 1791.

accordingly stay away. "Thus," write the commissioners, "the common-weal is given up to artisans and labourers whose views are limited to their own existence."—It is, accordingly, the lower class which rules, and the information upon which it bases its decrees consists of rumours which it accepts or manufactures, to hide by an appearance of right the outrages which are due to its cupidity or to the brutalities of its hunger. At Étampes, "they have been made to believe that the grain which had been sold for supplying the departments below the Loire, is shipped at Paimboeuf and taken out of the kingdom from there to be sold abroad." In the suburbs of Rouen they imagine that grain is purposely "ingulfed in the swamps, ponds, and clay-pits." At Laon, imbecile and Jacobin committees attribute the dearness of provisions to the avidity of the rich and the malevolence of the aristocrats: according to them, "jealous millionaires grow rich at the expense of the people. They know the popular strength," and, not daring to measure their forces with it, "in an honourable fight," have recourse "to treachery." To conquer the people easily they have determined to reduce them in advance by extreme suffering and by the length of their fast, and hence they monopolize "wheat, rye, and meal, soap, sugar, and brandy."[18]—Similar reports suffice to excite a suffering crowd to acts of violence, and it must inevitably accept for its leaders and advisers those who urge it forward on the side to which it is inclined. The people always

18. "Archives Nationales," F^7, 3,265. The following document, among many others, shows the expedients and conceptions of the popular imagination. Petition of several inhabitants of the commune of Forges (Seine Inférieure) "to the good and incorruptible Minister of the Interior" (October 16, 1792). "After three good crops in succession, the famine still continues. Under the ancient régime wheat was superabundant; hogs were fed with it, and calves were fattened with bread. It is certain, therefore, that wheat is diverted by monopolizers and the enemies of the new regime. The farms are too large; let them be divided. There is too much pasture-ground: sow it with wheat. Compel each farmer and landowner to give a statement of his crop: let the quantity be published at the church service, and in case of falsehood let the man be put to death or imprisoned, and his grain be confiscated. Oblige all the cultivators of the neighbourhood to sell their wheat at Forges only, &c."

require leaders, and they are chosen wherever they can be found, at one time amongst the élite, and at another amongst the dregs. Now that the nobles are driven out, the *bourgeoisie* in retirement, the large cultivators under suspicion, while animal necessities exercise their blind and intermittent despotism, the appropriate popular ministers consist of adventurers and of bandits. They need not be very numerous, for in a place full of combustible matter a few firebrands suffice to start the conflagration. "About twenty, at most, can be counted in the towns of Étampes and Dourdan, men with nothing to lose and everything to gain by disturbances; they are those who always produce excitement and disorder, while other citizens afford them the means through their indifference." Those whose names are known among the new guides of the crowd are almost all escaped convicts whose previous habits have accustomed them to blows, violence, frequently to murder, and always to contempt for the law. At Brunoy,[19] the leaders of the outbreak are "two deserters of the 18th regiment, sentenced and unpunished, who, in company with the vilest and most desperate of the parish, always go about armed and threatening." At Étampes, "the two principal assassins of the mayor are a poacher repeatedly condemned for poaching, and an old carbineer dismissed from his regiment with a bad record against him."[20] Around these are artisans "without a known residence," wandering workmen, journeymen and apprentices, vagrants and highway rovers, who flock into the towns on market-days and are always ready for mischief when an opportunity occurs. Vagabonds, indeed, now roam about the country everywhere, all restrictions against them having ceased.

19. "Archives Nationales," F[7], 3,268. Report of the commissioners sent by the department, March 11, 1792 (apropos of the insurrection of March 4).—Mortimer-Pernaux, i. 381.

20. "Archives Nationales," F[7], 3,268. Letters of several mayors, district administrators, cultivators of Velizy, Villadoublay, La Celle-Saint-Cloud, Montigny, &c. November 12, 1791.—Letter of M. de Narbonne, January 13, 1792; of M. Sureau, justice of the peace in the canton of Étampes, September 17, 1791.—Letter of Bruyères-le-Chatel, January 28, 1792.

"For a year past," write several parishes in the neighbourhood of Versailles, "we have seen no gendarmes except those who come with decrees," and hence the multiplication of "murders and brigandage" between Étampes and Versailles, on the highways and in the country. Bands of thirteen, fifteen, twenty, and twenty-two beggars rob the vineyards, enter farmhouses at night, and compel their inmates to lodge and feed them, returning in the same way every fortnight, all farms or isolated dwellings being their prey. An ecclesiastic is killed in his own house in the suburbs of Versailles, on the 26th of September, 1791, and, on the same day, a bourgeois and his wife are garotted and robbed. On the 22nd of September, near Saint-Rémi-Honoré, eight bandits ransack the dwelling of a farmer. On the 25th of September, at Villérs-le-Sec, thirteen others strip another farmer, and then add with much politeness, "It is lucky for your masters that they are not here, for we would have roasted them at yonder fire." Six similar outrages are committed by armed ruffians in dwelling-places, within a radius of from three to four leagues, accompanied with the threats of the *chauffeurs*.[21] "After enterprises of such force and boldness," write the people of this region, "there is not a well-to-do man in the country who can rely upon an hour's security in his house. Already many of our best cultivators are giving up their business, while others threaten to do the same in case these disorders continue."—What is worse still is the fact that in these outrages most of the bandits were "in the national uniform." The most ignorant, the poorest, and most fanatical of the National Guard thus enlist for the sake of plunder. It is so natural for men to believe in their right to that of which they feel the need, that the possessors of wheat thus become its monopolizers, and the superfluity of the rich the property of the poor! This is what the peasants say who devastate the forest of Bruyères-le-Chatel: "We have neither wood, bread, nor work—necessity knows no law."

21. A term applied to brigands at this epoch who demand money and objects of value, and force their delivery by exposing the soles of the feet of their victims to a fire.—[Tr.]

The necessaries of life are not to be had cheap under such a system. There is too much anxiety, and property is too precarious; there are too many obstacles to commerce; purchases, sales, shipments, arrivals, and payments are too uncertain. How are goods to be stored and transported in a country where neither the central government, the local authorities, the National Guard, nor the regular troops perform their duties, and where every transaction in produce, even the most legal and the most serviceable, is subject to the caprice of a dozen villains whom the populace obey? Wheat remains in the barn, or is secreted, or is kept waiting, and only reaches by stealth the hands of those who are rich enough to pay, not only its price, but the extra cost of the risk. Thus forced into a narrow channel, it rises to a rate which the depreciation of the *assignats* augments, its dearness being not only maintained, but ever on the increase.—Thereupon popular instinct invents for the cure of the evil a remedy which serves to aggravate it: henceforth, wheat must not travel; it is impounded in the canton in which it is gathered. At Laon, "the people have sworn to die rather than let their food be carried off." At Étampes, to which the municipality of Angers dispatches an administrator of its hospital to buy two hundred and fifty sacks of flour, the commission cannot be executed, the delegate not even daring to avow for several days the object of his coming; all he can do is "to visit incognito, and at night, the different flour-dealers in the valley, who would offer to furnish the supply, but fear for their lives and *dare not even leave their houses.*"—The same violence is shown in the more distant circle of departments which surround the first circle. At Aubigny, in Cher,[22] grain-waggons are

22. "Archives Nationales," F[7], 3,203. Letter of the Directory of Cher, August 25, 1791.—F[7], 3,240. Letter of the Directory of Haute Marne, November 6, 1791.—F[7], 3,248. *Procès-verbal* of the members of the department of the North, March 18, 1791.—F[7], 3,250. *Procès-verbal* of the municipal officers of Montreuil-sur-Mer, October 16, 1791.—F[7], 3,265. Letter of the Directory of Seine Inférieure, July 22, 1791.—D. xxix. 4. Remonstrances of the municipalities assembled at Tortes, July 21, 1791. Petitions of the municipal officers of the districts of Dieppe, Cany, and Caudebec, July 22, 1791.

stopped, the district administrators are menaced; two have a price set on their heads; a portion of the National Guard sides with the mutineers. At Chaumont, in Haute-Marne, the whole of the National Guard is in a state of mutiny; a convoy of over three hundred sacks is stopped, the Hôtel-de-Ville forced, and the insurrection lasts four days; the directory of the department takes flight; and the people seize on the powder and cannons. At Douai, in the Nord, to save a grain-dealer, he is put in prison; the mob forces the gates, the soldiers refuse to fire, and the man is hung, while the directory of the department takes refuge in Lille. At Montreuil-sur-Mer, in Pas-de-Calais, the two leaders of the insurrection, a brazier and a horse-shoer, "Bèquelin, called Petit-Gueux," the latter with his sabre in hand, reply to the summons of the municipal authorities, that "not a grain shall go now that they are masters," and that if they dare to make such proclamations "they will cut off their heads." There are no means of resistance. The National Guard, when it is convoked, does not respond; the volunteers when called upon turn their muskets down, and the crowd, assembled beneath the windows, shouts out its huzzahs. So much the worse for the law when it opposes popular passion: "We will not obey it," they say; "*people make laws to please themselves.*"—By way of practical illustration, at Tortes, in Seine-Inférieure, six thousand armed men belonging to the surrounding parishes form a deliberative armed body; the better to establish their rights, they bring two cannon with them fastened by ropes on a couple of carts; twenty-two companies of the National Guard, each under its own banner, march beside them, while all peaceable inhabitants are compelled to fall in "under penalty of death," the municipal officers being at their head. This improvised parliament promulgates a complete law in relation to grain, which, as a matter of form, is sent for acceptance to the department, and to the National Assembly; and one of its articles declares that all husbandmen shall be forbidden "to sell their wheat elsewhere than on the market-places." With no other outlet for it, wheat must be brought to the corn-markets (*halles*), and when these are full the price must necessarily fall.

What a profound deception! Even in the granary of France wheat remains dear, and costs about one-third more than would be necessary to secure the sale of bread at two sous the pound, in conformity with the will of the people. For instance,[23] at Gonesse, Dourdan, Corbeil, Mennecy, Brunoy, Limours, Brie-Comte-Robert, and especially at Étampes and Montlhéry, the holders of grain are compelled almost weekly, through the clamours and violence of the people, to reduce prices one-third and more. It is impossible for the authorities to maintain, on their corn-exchange, the freedom of buying and selling. The regular troops have been sent off by the people beforehand. Whatever the tolerance or connivance of the soldiers may be, the people have a vague sentiment that they are not there to permit the ripping open of sacks of flour, or the seizing of farmers by the throat. To get rid of all obstacles and of being watched, they make use of the municipality itself, and force it to effect its own disarmament. The municipal officers, besieged in the town-hall, at times threatened with pistols and bayonets,[24] dispatch to the detachments they are expecting an order to turn back, and entreat the Directory not to send any more troops, for, if any come, they have been told that "they will be sorry for it." Nowhere are there regular troops. At Étampes, the people repeat that "they are sent for and paid by the flour-dealers"; at Montlhéry, that "they merely serve to arm citizens against each other"; at Limours, that "they make grain dearer." All pretexts seem good in this direction; the popular will is absolute, and the authorities complacently meet its decrees half-way. At Montlhéry, the municipal body orders the gendarmerie to remain

23. "Archives Nationales," F[7], 3,268 and 3,269, *passim.*

24. "Archives Nationales," F[7], 3,268 and 3,269, *passim.* Deliberation of the Directory of Seine-et-Oise, September 20, 1791 (apropos of the insurrection, September 16, at Étampes).—Letter of Charpentier, president of the district, September 19.—Report of the Department Commissioners, March 11, 1792 (on the insurrection at Brunoy, March 4).—Report of the Department Commissioners, March 4, 1792 (on the insurrection at Montlhéry, February 13 to 20).—Deliberation of the Directory of Seine-et-Oise, September 16, 1791 (on the insurrection at Corbeil).—Letters of the mayors of Limours, Lonjumeau, &c.

at the gates of the town, which gives full play to the insurrection.—The administrators, however, are not relieved by leaving the people free to act; they are obliged to sanction their exactions by ordinances. They are taken out of the Hôtel-de-Ville, led to the market-place, and there forthwith, under the dictation of the uproar which establishes prices, they, like simple clerks, proclaim the reduction. When, moreover, the armed rabble of a village marches forth to tyrannize over a neighbouring market, it carries its mayor along with it in spite of himself, as an official instrument which belongs to it.[25] "There is no resistance against force," writes the mayor of Vert-le-Petit; "we had to set forth immediately."—"They assured me," says the mayor of Fontenay, "that, if I did not obey them, they would hang me."—On any municipal officer hazarding a remonstrance, they tell him that "he is getting to be an aristocrat." "Aristocrat" and "the gallows" argument is irresistible, and all the more so because it is practically applied. At Corbeil, the *procureur-syndic* who tries to enforce the law is almost beaten to death, and three houses in which they try to find him are demolished. At Montlhéry, a seedsman, accused of mixing the flour of beans (twice as dear) with wheaten flour, is massacred in his own house. At Étampes, the mayor who promulgates the law is cudgelled to death. Mobs talk of nothing but "burning and destroying," while the farmers, abused, hooted at, forced to sell, threatened with death, and robbed, run away, declaring they will never return to the market again.

Such is the first effect of popular dictatorship. Like all unintelligent forces, it operates in a direction the reverse of its intention: to dearness it adds dearth, and empties, instead of replenishing, the markets. That of Étampes often contained fifteen or sixteen hundred sacks of flour; the week following this insurrection there were, at

25. "Archives Nationales," F^7, 3,268 and 3,269, *passim.*—*Procès-verbal* of the Municipality of Montlhéry, February 28, 1792: "We cannot enter into fuller details without exposing ourselves to extremities which would be only disastrous to us."—Letter of the justice of the peace of the canton, February 25: "Public outcry teaches me that if I issue writs of arrest against those who massacred Thibault, the people would rise."

most, sixty brought to it. At Montlhéry, where six thousand men had collected together, each one obtains for his share only a small measure, while the bakers of the town have none at all. This being the case, the enraged National Guards tell the farmers that they are coming to see them on their farms. And they really go.[26] Drums roll constantly on the roads around Montlhéry, Limours, and other large market-towns. Columns of two, three, and four hundred men are seen passing under the lead of their commandant and of the mayor whom they take along with them. They enter each farm, mount into the granaries, estimate the quantity of grain thrashed out, and force the proprietor to sign an agreement to bring it to market the following week. Sometimes, as they are hungry, they compel people to give them something to eat and drink on the spot, and it will not do to enrage them—a farmer and his wife come near being hung in their own barn.

Useless pains. Wheat is impounded and hunted up in vain; it takes to the earth or slips off like a frightened animal. In vain do insurrections continue. In vain do armed mobs, in all the market-towns of the department,[27] subject grain to a forced reduction of price. Wheat becomes scarcer and dearer from month to month, rising in price from twenty-six francs to thirty-three. And because the outraged farmer "brings now a very little," just "what is necessary to sacrifice in order to avoid threats, he sells at home, or in the inns, to the flour-dealers from Paris."—The people, in running after abundance, have thus fallen deeper down into want: their brutality has aggravated their misery, and it is to themselves that their starvation is owing. But they are far from attributing all this to their own insubordination; the magistrates are accused; these, in the eyes of the populace, are "in league with the monopolizers." On this

26. "Archives Nationales," F^7, 3,268 and 3,269, *passim*. Reports of the gendarmerie, February 24, 1792, and the following days.—Letter of the Brigadier of Limours, March 2; of the manager of the farm of Plessis-le-Comte, February 23.

27. "Archives Nationales," F^7, 3,268 and 3,269, *passim*.—Memorial to the National Assembly by the citizens of Rambouillet, September 17, 1792.

incline no stoppage is possible. Distress increases rage, and rage increases distress; and on this fatal declivity men are precipitated from one outrage to another.

After the month of February, 1792, such outrages are innumerable; the mobs which go in quest of grain or which cut down its price consist of armies. One of six thousand men comes to control the market of Montlhéry.[28] There are seven to eight thousand men who invade the market-place of Verneuil, and there is an army of ten and another of twenty-five thousand men, who remain organized for ten days near Laon. One hundred and fifty parishes have sounded the tocsin, and the insurrection spreads for ten leagues around. Five boats loaded with grain are stopped, and, in spite of the orders of district, department, minister, King, and National Assembly, they refuse to surrender them. Their contents, in the meantime, are made the most of. "The municipal officers of the different parishes, assembled together, pay themselves their fees, to wit: one hundred sous per diem for the mayor, three livres for the municipal officers, two livres ten sous for the guards, two livres for the porters. They have ordered that these sums should be paid in grain, and they reduce grain, it is said, fifteen livres the sack. It is certain that they have divided it amongst themselves, and that fourteen hundred sacks have been distributed." In vain do the commissioners of the National Assembly make speeches to them three hours in length. The discourse being finished, they deliberate, in presence of the commissioners, whether the latter shall be hung, drowned, or cut up, and their heads put on the five points of the middle of the abbey railing. On being threatened with military force, they make their dispositions accordingly. Nine hundred men who relieve each other watch day and night on the ground, in a well-chosen and permanent encampment, while signalmen stationed in the belfries of the surround-

28. "Archives Nationales," F^7, 3,268 and 3,269, *passim*. *Procès-verbal* of the Municipality of Montlhéry, February 27, 1792.—Roux and Buchez, xiii. 421, March, 1792, and xiii. 317.—*Mercure de France*, February 25, 1792. (Letters of M. Dauchy, President of the Directory of the Department; of M. de Gouy, messenger sent by the minister, &c.)—*Moniteur*, sitting of February 15, 1792.

ing villages have only to sound the alarm to bring together twenty-five thousand men in a few hours.—So long as the Government remains on its feet it carries on the combat as well as it can; but it grows weaker from month to month, and, after the 10th of August, when it lies on the ground, the mob takes its place and becomes the universal sovereign. From this time forth not only is the law which protects subsistences powerless against the disturbers of sale and circulation, but the Assembly actually sanctions their acts, since it decrees[29] the stoppage of all proceedings commenced against them, remits sentences already passed, and sets free all who are imprisoned or in irons. Behold every administration, with merchants, proprietors, and farmers abandoned to the famished, the furious, and to robbers; henceforth subsistences are for those who are disposed and able to take them. "You will be told," says a petition,[30] "that we violate the law. We reply to these perfidious insinuations that the salvation of the people is the supreme law. We come in order to keep the markets supplied, and to ensure an uniform price for wheat throughout the Republic. For, there is no doubt about it, the purest patriotism dies out (*sic*) when there is no bread to be had. . . . Resistance to oppression—yes, resistance to oppression is the most sacred of duties; is there any oppression more terrible than that of wanting bread? Undoubtedly, no. . . . Join us and 'Ça ira, ça ira!' We cannot end our petition better than with this patriotic air." This supplication was written on a drum, amidst a circle of firearms; and with such accompaniments it is equivalent to a command.—They are well aware of it, and of their own authority they often confer upon themselves not only the right but also the title. In Loire-et-Cher,[31] a band of from four to five thousand men assume the name

29. Decree of September 3, 1792.

30. "Archives Nationales," F[7], 3,268 and 3,269. Petition of the citizens of Montfort-l'Amaury, Saint-Leger, Gros-Rouvre, Gelin, Laqueue, and Méré, to the citizens of Rambouillet.

31. "Archives Nationales," F[7], 3,230. Letter of an administrator of the district of Vendôme, with the deliberation of the commune of Vendôme, November 24, 1792.

of "Sovereign Power." They go from one market-town to another, to Saint-Calais, Montdoubleau, Blois, Vendôme, reducing the cost of provisions, their troop rolling up like a snowball—for they threaten "to burn the effects and set fire to the houses of all who are not as courageous as themselves."

In this state of social disintegration, insurrection is a gangrene in which the healthy are infected by the morbid parts. Mobs are everywhere produced and reproduced, incessantly, large and small, like abscesses which break out side by side, and painfully irritate each other and finally combine. There are the towns against the rural districts and rural districts against the towns. On the one hand "every farmer who contributes anything to the market passes (at home) for an aristocrat,[32] and becomes the horror of his fellow-citizens in the village." On the other hand the National Guards of the towns spread themselves through the rural districts and make raids to save themselves from death by hunger.[33] It is admitted in the rural districts that each municipality has the right to isolate itself from the rest. It is admitted in the towns that each town has the right to derive its provisions from the country. It is admitted by the indigent of each commune that the commune must provide bread gratis or at a cheap rate. On the strength of this there is a shower of stones and a fusillade; department against department, district against district, canton against canton, all fight for food, and the strongest get it and keep it for themselves.—I have simply described the north, where, for the past three years, the crops are good. I have

32. "Archives Nationales," F^7, 3,255. Letter of the Administrators of the Department of Seine-Inférieure, October 23, 1792.—Letters of the Special Committee of Rouen, October 22 and 23, 1792: "The more the zeal and patriotism of the cultivators is stimulated, the more do they seem determined to avoid the market-places, which are always in a state of absolute destitution."

33. "Archives Nationales," F^7, 3,265. Letter of David, a cultivator, October 10, 1792.—Letter of the Department Administrators, October 13, 1792, &c.—Letter (printed) of the minister to the Convention, November 4.—Proclamation of the Provisional Executive Council, October 31, 1792. (The *setier* of grain of two hundred and forty pounds is sold at 60 francs in the south, and at half that sum in the north.)

omitted the south, where trade is interrupted on the canal of the Deux Mers, where the *procureur-syndic* of Aude has lately been massacred for trying to secure the passage of a convoy; where the harvest has been poor; where, in many places, bread costs eight sous the pound; where, in almost every department, a bushel of wheat is sold twice as dear as in the north!

Strange phenomenon! and the most instructive of all, for in it we see down into the depths of humanity; for, as on a raft of shipwrecked beings without food, there is a reversion to a state of nature. The light tissue of habit and of rational ideas in which civilisation has enveloped man, is torn asunder and is floating in rags around him; the bare arms of the savage show themselves, and they are striking out. The only guide he has for his conduct is that of primitive days, the startled instinct of a craving stomach. Henceforth that which rules in him and through him is animal necessity with its train of violent and narrow suggestions, sometimes sanguinary and sometimes grotesque. Incompetent or savage, in all respects like a negro monarch, his sole political expedients are either the methods of a slaughter-house or the dreams of a carnival. Two commissioners whom Roland, Minister of the Interior, sends to Lyons, are able to see within a few days the carnival and the slaughter-house.[34]—On the one hand the peasants, all along the road, arrest everybody; the people regard every traveller as an aristocrat who is running away—which is so much the worse for those who fall into their hands. Near Autun, four priests who, to obey the law, are betaking themselves to the frontier, are put in prison "for their own protection"; they are taken out a quarter of an hour later, and, in spite of thirty-two of the mounted police, are massacred. "Their carriage was still burning as I passed, and the corpses were stretched out not far off. Their driver was still in durance, and it was in vain that I solicited his release."—On the other hand, at Lyons, the power has fallen into the hands of the degraded women of the streets. "They seized the

34. "Archives Nationales," F[7], 3,255. Letters of Bonnemant, September 11, 1792; of Laussel, September 22, 1792.

central club, constituted themselves commissaries of police, signed notices as such, and paid visits of inspection to store-houses"; they drew up a tariff of provisions, "from bread and meat up to common peaches, and peaches of fine quality." They announced that "whoever dared to dispute it would be considered a traitor to the country, an adherent of the civil list, and prosecuted as such." All this is published, proclaimed, and applied by "female commissaries of police," themselves the dregs of the lowest sinks of corruption. Respectable housewives and workwomen had nothing to do with it, nor "working-people of any class." The sole actors of this administrative parody are "scamps, a few bullies of houses of ill-fame, and a portion of the dregs of the female sex."—To this end comes the dictatorship of instinct, yonder let loose on the highway in a massacre of priests, and here, in the second city of France, in the government of strumpets.

III

The fear of starvation is only the sharper form of a more general passion, which is the desire of possession, and the determination not to give up the possessions attained. No popular instinct had been longer, more rudely, more universally tried under the ancient régime; and there is none which gushes out more readily under constraint, none which requires a higher or broader public barrier, or one more entirely constructed of solid blocks, to keep it in check. Hence it is that this passion from the commencement breaks down or engulfs the slight and low boundaries, the tottering embankments of crumbling earth between which the Constitution pretends to confine it.—The first flood sweeps away the pecuniary claims of the State, of the clergy, and of the noblesse. The people regard them as abolished, or, at least, they consider their debts discharged. Their idea, in relation to this, is formed and fixed; for them it is that which constitutes the Revolution. The people have no longer a creditor; they are determined to have none, they will pay nobody, and first of all, they will make no further payment to the State.

On the 14th of July, 1790, the day of the Federation, the population of Issoudun, in Touraine, solemnly convoked for the purpose, had just taken the solemn oath which was to ensure public peace, social harmony, and respect for the law for evermore.[35] Here, probably, as elsewhere, arrangements had been made for an affecting ceremonial; there were young girls dressed in white, and learned and impressionable magistrates were to pronounce philosophical harangues. All at once they discover that the people gathered on the public square are provided with clubs, scythes, and axes, and that the National Guard will not prevent their use; on the contrary, the Guard itself is composed almost wholly of vine-dressers and others interested in the suppression of the duties on wine, of coopers, innkeepers, workmen, carters of casks, and others of the same stamp, all rough fellows who have their own way of interpreting the Social Contract. The whole mass of decrees, acts, and rhetorical flourishes which are dispatched to them from Paris, or which emanate from the new authorities, are not worth a halfpenny tax maintained on each bottle of wine. There are to be no more excise duties; they will only take the civic oath on this express condition, and that very evening they hang, in effigy, their two deputies, who "had not supported their interests" in the National Assembly. A few months later, of all the National Guard called upon to protect the clerks, only the commandant and two officers respond to the summons. If a docile tax-payer happens to be found, he is not allowed to pay the dues; this seems a defection and almost treachery. An entry of three puncheons of wine having been made, they are stove in with stones, a

35. "Archives Nationales," H. 1453. Correspondence of M. de Bercheny, July 28, October 24 and 26, 1790.—The same disposition lasted. An insurrection occurred in Issoudun after the three days of July, 1830, against the combined imposts. Seven or eight thousand vine-dressers burnt the archives and tax-offices and dragged an employé through the streets, shouting out at each street-lamp, "Let him be hung!" The general sent to repress the outbreak entered the town only through a capitulation; the moment he reached the Hôtel-de-Ville a man of the Faubourg de Rome put his pruning-hook around his neck, exclaiming, "No more clerks where there is nothing to do!"

portion is drunk, and the rest taken to the barracks to debauch the soldiers; M. de Sauzay, commandant of the "Royal Roussillon," who was bold enough to save the clerks, is menaced, and for this misdeed he barely escapes being hung himself. When the municipal body is called upon to interpose and employ force, it replies that "for so small a matter, it is not worth while to compromise the lives of the citizens," and the regular troops sent to the Hôtel-de-Ville are ordered by the people not to go except with the but-ends of their muskets in the air. Five days after this the windows of the excise office are smashed, and the public notices are torn down; the fermentation does not subside, and M. de Sauzay writes that a regiment would be necessary to restrain the town. At Saint-Amand the insurrection breaks out violently, and is only put down by violence. At Saint-Etienne-en-Forez, Berthéas, a clerk in the excise office, falsely accused of monopolizing grain,[36] is fruitlessly defended by the National Guard; he is put in prison, according to the usual custom, to save his life, and, for greater security, the crowd insist on his being fastened by an iron collar. But, suddenly changing its mind, it breaks upon the door and drags him to death. Stretched on the ground, his head still moves and he raises his hand to it, when a woman, picking up a large stone, smashes his skull.—These are not isolated occurrences. During the months of July and August, 1789, the tax offices are burnt in almost every town in the kingdom. In vain does the National Assembly order their reconstruction, insist on the maintenance of duties and *octrois,* and explain to the people the public needs, pathetically reminding them, moreover, that the Assembly has already given them relief—the people prefer to relieve themselves instantly and entirely. Whatever is consumed must no longer be taxed, either for the benefit of the State or for that of the towns. "Entrance dues on wine and cattle," writes the municipality

36. "Archives Nationales," F^7, 3,203. Letter of the Directory of Cher, April 9, 1790.—*Ibid.,* F^7, 3,255. Letter of August 4, 1790. Verdict of the *présidial,* November 4, 1790.—Letter of the Municipality of Saint-Etienne, August 5, 1790.

of Saint-Etienne, "scarcely amount to anything, and our powers are inadequate for their enforcement." At Cambrai, two successive outbreaks compel the excise office and the magistracy of the town[37] to reduce the duties on beer one-half. But "the evil, at first confined to one corner of the province, soon spreads"; the *grands baillis* of Lille, Douai, and Orchies write that "we have hardly a bureau which has not been molested, and in which the taxes are not wholly subject to popular discretion." Those only pay who are disposed to do so, and, consequently, "greater fraud could not exist." The tax-payers, indeed, cunningly defend themselves, and find plenty of arguments or quibbles to avoid paying their dues. At Cambrai they allege that, as the privileged now pay as well as the rest, the Treasury must be rich enough.[38] At Noyon, Ham, and Chauny, and in the surrounding parishes, the butchers, innkeepers, and publicans combined, who have refused to pay excise duties, pick flaws in the special decree by which the Assembly subjects them to the law, and a second special decree is necessary to circumvent these new legists. The process at Lyons is simpler. Here the thirty-two sections appoint commissioners; these decide against the *octroi,* and request the municipal authorities to abolish it. They must necessarily comply, for the people are at hand and are furious. Without waiting, however, for any legal measures, they take the authority on themselves, rush to the toll-houses, and drive out the clerks, while large quantities of provisions, which "through a singular predestination" were waiting at the gates, come in free of duty.

The Treasury defends itself as it best can against this universally bad disposition of the tax-payer, against these irruptions and infiltrations of fraud; it repairs the dyke where it has been carried away, stops up the fissures, and again resumes collections. But how can these be regular and complete in a State where the courts dare not

37. "Archives Nationales," F^7, 3,248. Letter of M. Sénac de Meilhan, April 10, 1790.—Letter of the *grands baillis,* June 30, 1790.

38. Roux and Buchez, vi. 403. Report of Chabrond on the insurrection at Lyons, July 9 and 10, 1790.—Duvergier, "Collection des Décrets."—Decrees of August 4 and 15, 1790.

condemn delinquents, where public force dares not support the courts,[39] where popular favour protects the most notorious bandits and the worst vagabonds against the tribunals and against the public powers? At Paris, where, after eight months of impunity, proceedings are begun against the pillagers who on the 13th of August, 1789, set fire to the tax-offices, the officers of the election, "considering that their audiences have become too tumultuous, that the thronging of the people excites uneasiness, that threats have been uttered of a kind calculated to create reasonable alarm," are constrained to suspend their sittings and refer matters to the National Assembly, while the latter, considering that "if prosecutions are authorised in Paris it will be necessary to authorise them throughout the kingdom," decides that it is best "to veil the statue of the Law."[40] Not only does the Assembly veil the statue of the Law, but it takes to pieces, remakes, and mutilates it, according to the requirements of the popular will; and, in the matter of indirect imposts, all its decrees are forced upon it. The outbreak against the salt impost was terrible from the beginning; sixty thousand men in Anjou alone combined to destroy it, and the price of salt had to be reduced from sixteen to six sous.[41] The people, however, are not satisfied with this. This monopoly has been the cause of so much suffering that they are not disposed to put up with any remains of it, and are always on the side of the smugglers against the excise officers. In the month of

39. "Archives Nationales," F[7], 3,255. Letter of the Minister, July 2, 1790, to the Directory of Rhone-et-Loire. "The King is informed that, throughout your department, and especially in the districts of Saint-Etienne and Montbrison, license is carried to the extreme; that the judges dare not prosecute; that in many places the municipal officers are at the head of the disturbances; and that, in others, the National Guard do not obey requisitions."—Letter of September 5, 1790. "In the bourg of Thisy, brigands have invaded divers cotton-spinning establishments and partially destroyed them, and, after having plundered them, they have sold the goods by public auction."

40. Roux and Buchez, vi. 545. Report of M. Muguet, July 1, 1790.

41. *Procès-verbaux* of the National Assembly. (Sitting of October 24, 1789.)—Decree of September 27, 1789, applicable the 1st of October. There are other modifications applicable on the 1st of January, 1790.

January, 1790, at Béziers, thirty-two employés, who had seized a quantity of contraband salt on the persons of armed smugglers,[42] are pursued by the crowd to the Hôtel-de-Ville; the consuls decline to defend them and run away; the troops defend them, but in vain. Five are tortured, horribly mutilated, and then hung. In the month of March, 1790, Necker states that, according to the returns of the past three months, the deficit in the salt-tax amounts to more than four millions a month, which is four-fifths of the ordinary revenue, while the tobacco monopoly is no more respected than that of salt. At Tours,[43] the bourgeois militia refuse to give assistance to the employés, and "openly protect smuggling," "and contraband tobacco is publicly sold at the fair, under the eyes of the municipal authorities, who dare make no opposition to it." All receipts, consequently, diminish at the same time.[44] From the 1st of May, 1789, to the 1st of May, 1790, the general collections amount to one hundred and twenty-seven millions instead of one hundred and fifty millions; the dues and excise combined return only thirty-one, instead of fifty millions. The streams which filled the public exchequer are more and more obstructed by popular resistance, and under the popular pressure, the Assembly ends by closing them entirely. In the

42. *Mercure de France,* February 27, 1790. (Memorial of the *garde des sceaux,* January 16.)—Observations of M. Necker on the report made by the Financial Committee, at the sitting of March 12, 1790.

43. "Archives Nationales," H. 1453. Correspondence of M. de Bercheny, April 24, May 4 and 6, 1790: "It is much to be feared that the tobacco-tax will share the fate of the salt-tax."

44. *Mercure de France,* July 31, 1790 (sitting of July 10). M. Lambert, Comptroller-General of the Finances, informs the Assembly of "the obstacles which continual outbreaks, brigandage, and the maxims of anarchical freedom impose, from one end of France to the other, on the collection of the taxes. On one side, the people are led to believe that, if they stubbornly refuse a tax contrary to their rights, its abolition will be secured. Elsewhere, smuggling is openly carried on by force; the people favour it, while the National Guards refuse to act against the nation. In other places hatred is excited, and divisions between the troops and the overseers at the toll-houses: the latter are massacred, the bureaus are pillaged, and the prisons are forced open."—Memorial to the National Assembly by M. Necker, July 21, 1790.

month of March, 1790,[45] it abolishes salt duties, internal customs-duties, taxes on leather, on oil, on starch, and the stamp of iron. In February and March, 1791, it abolishes *octrois* and entrance-dues in all the cities and boroughs of the kingdom, all the excise duties and those connected with the excise, especially all taxes which affect the manufacture, sale, or circulation of beverages. The people have at last carried everything, and on the 1st of May, 1791, the day of the application of the decree, the National Guard of Paris parades around the walls playing patriotic airs. The cannon of the Invalides and those on the Pont-Neuf thunder out as if for an important victory. There is an illumination in the evening, there is drinking all night, a universal revel. Beer, indeed, is to be had at three sous the pot, and wine at six sous a pint, which is a reduction of one-half; no conquest could be more popular, since it brings intoxication within easy reach of all topers.[46]

The object, now, is to provide for the expenses which have been defrayed by the suppressed *octrois*. In 1790, the *octroi* of Paris had produced 35,910,859 francs, of which 25,059,446 went to the State, and 10,851,413 went to the city. How is the city going to pay for its watch, the lighting and cleaning of its streets, and the support of its hospitals? What are the twelve hundred other cities and boroughs going to do which are brought by the same stroke to the same situation? What will the State do, which, in abolishing the general revenue from all entrance-dues and excise, is suddenly deprived of two-fifths of its revenue?—In the month of March, 1790, when the Assembly suppressed the salt and other duties, it established in the place of these a tax of fifty millions, to be divided between the direct imposts and dues on entrance to the towns. Now, consequently, that the entrance-dues are abolished, the new charge falls entirely *upon the direct imposts*. Do returns come in, and will they come in?—In

45. Decrees of March 21 and 22, 1790, applicable April 21 following.—Decrees of February 19 and March 2, 1791, applicable May 1 following.

46. De Goncourt, "La Société Française pendant la Révolution," 204.—Maxime du Camp, "Paris, sa Vie et ses Organes," vi. 11.

the face of so many outbreaks, any indirect taxation is, certainly, difficult to collect. Nevertheless it is not so repulsive as the other because the levies of the State disappear in the price of the article, the hand of the Exchequer being hidden by the hand of the dealer. The Government clerk formerly presented himself with his stamped paper and the seller handed him the money without much grumbling, knowing that he would soon be more than reimbursed by his customer: the indirect tax is thus collected. Should any difficulty arise, it is between the dealer and the tax-payer who comes to his shop to lay in his little store; the latter grumbles, but it is at the high price which he feels, and possibly at the seller who pockets his silver; he does not find fault with the clerk of the Exchequer, whom he does not see and who is not then present. In the collection of the direct tax, on the contrary, it is the clerk himself whom he sees before him, who abstracts the precious piece of silver. This authorised robber, moreover, gives him nothing in exchange; it is an entire loss. On leaving the dealer's shop he goes away with a jug of wine, a pot of salt, or similar commodities; on leaving the tax-office he has nothing in hand but an acquittance, a miserable bit of scribbled paper.—But now he is master in his own commune, an elector, a National Guard, mayor, the sole authority in the use of armed force, and charged with his own taxation. Come and ask him to unearth the buried mite on which he has set all his heart and all his soul, the earthen pot wherein he has deposited his cherished pieces of silver one by one, and which he has laid by for so many years at the cost of so much misery and fasting, in the very face of the bailiff, in spite of the prosecutions of the subdelegate, commissioner, collector, and clerk!

From the 1st of May, 1789, to the 1st of May, 1790,[47] the general returns, the *taille* and its accessories, the poll-tax, and "twentieths,"

47. "Compte des Revenus et Dépenses au 1er Mai, 1789."—Memorial of M. Necker, July 21, 1790.—Memorials presented by M. de Montesquiou, September 9, 1791.—*Comptes-rendus* by the minister, Clavières, October 5, 1792, February 1, 1792.—Report of Cambon, February, 1793.

instead of yielding 161,000,000 francs, yield but 28,000,000 francs in the provinces which impose their own taxes (*pays d'États*); instead of 28,000,000 francs, the Treasury obtains but 6,000,000. On the patriotic contribution which was to deduct one-quarter of all incomes over four hundred livres, and to levy two and a half per cent. on plate, jewels, and whatever gold and silver each person has in reserve, the State received 9,700,000 francs. As to patriotic gifts, their total, comprising the silver buckles of the deputies, reaches only 361,587 francs; and the closer our examination into the particulars of these figures, the more do we see the contributions of the villager, artisan, and former subjects of the *taille* diminish.—Since the month of October, 1789, the privileged classes, in fact, appear in the tax-rolls, and they certainly form the class which is best off, the most alive to general ideas and the most truly patriotic. It is therefore probable that, of the forty-three millions of returns from the direct imposts and from the patriotic contribution, they have furnished the larger portion, perhaps two-thirds of it, or even three-quarters. If this be the case, the peasant, the former tax-payer, gave nothing or almost nothing from his pocket during the first year of the Revolution. For instance, in regard to the patriotic contribution, the Assembly left it to the conscience of each person to fix his own quota; at the end of six months, consciences are found too elastic, and the Assembly is obliged to confer this right on the municipalities. The result is[48] that this or that individual who taxed himself at forty-eight livres, is taxed at a hundred and fifty; another, a cultivator, who had offered six livres, is judged to be able to pay over one hundred. Every regiment contains a small number of select brave men, and it is always these who are ready to advance under fire. Every State contains a select few of honest men who advance to meet the tax-collector. Some effective constraint is essential in the regiment to supply those with courage who have but little, and in the State to supply those with probity who do not possess it. Hence, during the eight months which follow, from May 1st, 1790, to Jan-

48. Boivin-Champeaux, 231.

uary 1st, 1791, the patriotic contribution furnishes but 11,000,000 livres. Two years later, on the 1st of February, 1793, out of the forty thousand communal tax-rolls which should provide for it, there are seven thousand which are not yet drawn up; out of 180,000,000 livres which it ought to produce, there are 70,000,000 livres which are still due.—The resistance of the tax-payer produces a similar deficit, and similar delays in all branches of the national income.[49] In the month of June, 1790, a deputy declares in the tribune that "out of thirty-six millions of imposts which ought to be returned each month only nine have been received."[50] In the month of November, 1791, a reporter on the budget states that the receipts, which should amount to forty or forty-eight millions a month, do not reach eleven millions and a half. On February 1, 1793, there remains still due on the direct taxes of 1789 and 1790 one hundred and seventy-six millions.—It is evident that the people struggle with all their might against the old taxes, even authorised and prolonged by the Constituent Assembly, and all that is obtained from them is wrested from them.

Will the people be more docile under the new taxation? The Assembly exhorts them to be so and shows them how, with the relief they have gained and with the patriotism they ought to possess, they can and should discharge their dues. The people are able to do it because, having got rid of tithes, feudal dues, the salt-tax, *octrois*, and excise duties, they are in a comfortable position. They should do so, because the taxation adopted is indispensable to the State, equitable, assessed on all in proportion to their fortune, collected and expended under rigid scrutiny, without perversion or waste, according to precise, clear, periodical, and audited accounts. No doubt exists that, after the 1st of January, 1791, the date when the new financial scheme comes into operation, each tax-payer will gladly pay as a good citizen, and the two hundred and forty millions

49. *Mercure de France*, May 28, 1791. (Sitting of May 22.) Speech of M. d'Allarde: "Burgundy has paid nothing belonging to 1790."

50. *Moniteur*, sitting of June 1, 1790. Speech by M. Freteau.—*Mercure de France*, November 26, 1791. Report by Lafont-Ladebat.

of the new tax on real property, and the sixty millions of that on personal property, leaving out the rest—registries, license, and customs duties—will flow in regularly and easily of their own accord.

Unfortunately, before the tax-gatherer can collect the first two levies these have to be assessed, and as there are complicated writings and formalities, claims to settle amidst great resistance and local ignorance, the operation is indefinitely prolonged. The personal and land-tax schedule of 1791 is not transmitted to the departments by the Assembly until June, 1791. The departments do not distribute it among the districts until the months of July, August, and September, 1791. It is not distributed by the districts among the communes before October, November, and December, 1791. Thus in the last month of 1791 it is not yet distributed to the tax-payers by the communes; from which it follows that on the budget of 1791 and throughout that year, the tax-payer has paid nothing.—At last, in 1792, everybody begins to receive this assessment. It would require a volume to set forth the partiality and dissimulation of these assessments. In the first place the office of assessor is one of danger; the municipal authorities, whose duty it is to assign the quotas, are not comfortable in their town quarters. Already, in 1790,[51] the municipal officers of Monbazon have been threatened with death if they dared to tax industrial pursuits on the tax-roll, and they escaped to Tours in the middle of the night. Even at Tours, three or four hundred insurgents of the vicinity, dragging along with them the municipal officers of three market-towns, come and declare to the town authorities "that for all taxes they will not pay more than forty-

51. "Archives Nationales," H. 1453. Correspondence of M. de Bercheny, June 5, 1790, &c.—F[7], 3,226. Letters of Chenantin, cultivator, November 7, 1792, also of the *procureur-syndic*, November 6.—F[7], 3,202. Letter of the Minister of Justice, Duport, January 3, 1792. "The utter absence of public force in the district of Montargis renders every operation of the Government and all execution of the laws impossible. The arrears of taxes to be collected is here very considerable, while all proceedings of constraint are dangerous and impossible to execute, owing to the fears of the bailiffs, who dare not perform their duties, and the violence of the tax-payers, on whom there is no check."

five sous per household." I have already narrated how, in 1792, in the same department, "they kill, they assassinate the municipal officers" who presume to publish the tax-rolls of personal property. In Creuse, at Clugnac, the moment the clerk begins to read the document, the women spring upon him, seize the tax-roll, and "tear it up with countless imprecations"; the municipal council is assailed, and two hundred persons stone its members, one of whom is thrown down, has his head shaved, and is promenaded through the village in derision.—When the small tax-payer defends himself in this manner, it is a warning that he must be humoured. The assessment, accordingly, in the village councils is made amongst a knot of cronies. Each relieves himself of the burden by shoving it off on somebody else. "They tax the large proprietors, whom they want to make pay the whole tax." The noble, the old seigneur, is the most taxed, and to such an extent that in many places his income does not suffice to pay his quota.—In the next place they make themselves out poor, and falsify or elude the prescriptions of the law. "In most of the municipalities, houses, tenements, and factories[52] are estimated according to the value of the area they cover, and considered as land of the first class, which reduces the quota to almost nothing." And this fraud is not practised in the villages alone. "Communes of eight or ten thousand souls might be cited which have arranged matters so well amongst themselves in this respect that not a house is to be found worth more than fifty sous."—Last expedient of all, the commune defers as long as it can the preparation of its tax-rolls. On the 30th of January, 1792, out of 40,211, there are only 2,560 which are complete; on the 5th of October, 1792, the schedules are not made out in 4,800 municipalities, and it must be noted that all this relates to a term of administration which has been finished for more than nine months. At the same date, there are more than six thousand communes which have not yet begun to collect the land-tax of 1791, and more than fifteen thousand communes which have not yet begun

52. Report of the Committee on Finances, by Ramel, 19th Floréal, year II. (The Constituent Assembly had fixed the real tax of a house at one-sixth of its letting value.)

to collect the personal tax; the Treasury and the departments have not yet received 152,000,000 francs, there being still 222,000,000 to collect. On the 1st February, 1793, there still remains due on the same period 161,000,000 francs, while of the 50,000,000 assessed in 1790, to replace the salt-tax and other suppressed duties, only 2,000,000 have been collected. Finally, at the same date, out of the two direct taxes of 1792, which should produce 300,000,000, less than 4,000,000 have been received.—It is a maxim of the debtor that he must put off payment as long as possible. Whoever the creditor may be, the State or a private individual, a leg or a wing may be saved by dint of procrastination. The maxim is true, and, on this occasion, success once more demonstrates its soundness. During the year 1792, the peasant begins to discharge a portion of his arrears, *but it is with assignats.* In January, February, and March, 1792, the *assignats* diminish thirty-four, forty-four, and forty-five per cent. in value; in January, February, and March, 1793, forty-seven and fifty per cent.; in May, June, and July, 1793, fifty-four, sixty, and sixty-seven per cent. Thus has the old credit of the State melted away in its hands; those who have held on to their crowns gain fifty per cent. and more. Again, the greater their delay the more their debts diminish, and already, on the strength of this, the way to release themselves at half-price is found.

Meanwhile, hands are laid on the badly defended landed property of this feeble creditor.—It is always difficult for rude brains to form any conception of the vague, invisible, abstract entity called the State, to regard it as a veritable personage and a legitimate proprietor, especially when they are persistently told that the State is everybody. The property of all is the property of each, and as the forests belong to the public, the first-comer has a right to profit by them. In the month of December, 1789,[53] bands of sixty men or more chop down the trees in the Bois de Boulogne and at Vincennes. In

53. *Mercure de France,* December 12, 1789.—"Archives Nationales," F^7, 3,268. Memorial of the officers in command of the detachment of the Paris National Guard stationed at Conflans-Sainte-Honorine (April, 1790). Certificate of the Municipal Officers of Poissy, March 31.

April, 1790, in the forest of Saint-Germain, "the patrols arrest all kinds of delinquents day and night": handed over to the National Guards and municipalities in the vicinity, these are "almost immediately released, even with the wood which they have cut down against the law." There is no means of repressing "the reiterated threats and insults of the low class of people." A mob of women, urged on by an old French guardsman, come and pillage under the nose of the escort a load of faggots confiscated for the benefit of a hospital; and, in the forest itself, bands of marauders fire upon the patrols.—At Chantilly, three game-keepers are mortally wounded;[54] both parks are devastated for eighteen consecutive days; the game is all killed, transported to Paris, and sold.—At Chambord the lieutenant of the constabulary writes to announce his powerlessness; the woods are ravaged and even burnt; the poachers are now masters of the situation; breaches in the wall are made by them, and the water from the pond is drawn off to enable them to catch the fish.—At Claix, in Dauphiny, an officer of the jurisdiction of woods and forests, who has secured an injunction against the inhabitants for cutting down trees on leased ground, is seized, tortured during five hours, and then stoned to death.—In vain does the National Assembly issue three decrees and regulations, placing the forests under the supervision and protection of administrative bodies—the latter are too much afraid of their charge. Between the central power, which is weak and remote, and the people, present and strong, they always decide in favour of the latter. Not one of the five municipalities surrounding Chantilly is disposed to assist in the execution of the laws, while the directories of the district and department respectively,

54. *Mercure de France,* March 12 and 26, 1791.—"Archives Nationales," H. 1453. Letter of the police-lieutenant of Blois, April 22, 1790.—*Mercure de France,* July 24, 1790. Two of the murderers exclaimed to those who tried to save one of the keepers, "Hanging is well done at Paris! Bah, you are aristocrats! We shall be talked about in the gazettes of Paris." (Deposition of witnesses.)—Decrees and proclamations regarding the protection of the forests, November 3 and December 11, 1789.—Another in October, 1790.—Another June 20, 1791.

sanction their inertia. Similarly, near Toulouse,[55] where the magnificent forest of Larramet is devastated in open day and by an armed force, where the wanton destruction by the populace leaves nothing of the underwood and shrubbery but "a few scattered trees and the remains of trunks cut at different heights," the municipalities of Toulouse and of Tournefeuille refuse all aid. And worse still, in other provinces, as for instance in Alsace, "whole municipalities, with their mayors at the head, cut down woods which are confided to them, and carry them off."[56] If some tribunal is disposed to enforce the law, it is to no purpose; it takes the risk, either of not being allowed to give judgment, or of being constrained to reverse its decision. At Paris the judgment prepared against the incendiaries of the tax-offices could not be given. At Montargis, the sentence pronounced against the marauders who had stolen cartloads of wood in the national forests had to be revised, and by the judges themselves. The moment the tribunal announced the confiscation of the carts and horses which had been seized, there arose a furious outcry against it; the court was insulted by those present; the condemned parties openly declared that they would have their carts and horses back by force. Upon this "the judges withdrew into the council-chamber, and when soon after they resumed their seats, that part of their decision which related to the confiscation was cancelled."

And yet this administration of justice, ludicrous and flouted as it may be, is still a sort of barrier. When it falls, along with the Government, everything is exposed to plunder, and there is no such thing as public property.—After August 10, 1792, each commune or individual appropriates whatever comes in its way, either products or the soil itself. Some of the depredators go so far as to say that, since the Government no longer represses them, they act under its

55. "Archives Nationales," F[7], 3,219. Letter of the *bailli* of Virieu, January 26, 1792.

56. *Mercure de France,* December 3, 1791. (Letter from Sarrelouis, November 15, 1791.)—"Archives Nationales," F[7], 3,223. Letter of the Municipal Officers of Montargis, January 8, 1792.

authority.[57] "They have destroyed even the recent plantation of young trees." "One of the villages near Fontainebleau cleared off and divided an entire grove. At Rambouillet, from August 10th to the end of October," the loss is more than 100,000 crowns; the rural agitators demand with threats the partition of the forest among the inhabitants. "The destruction is enormous" everywhere, prolonged for entire months, and of such a kind, says the minister, as to dry up this source of public revenue for a long time to come.—Communal property is no more respected than national property. In each commune, these bold and needy folk, the rural populace, are privileged to enjoy and make the most of it. Not content with enjoying it, they desire to acquire ownership of it, and, for days after the King's fall, the Legislative Assembly, losing its footing in the universal breaking up, empowers the indigent to put in force the agrarian law. Henceforth it suffices in any commune for one-third of its inhabitants of both sexes, servants, common labourers, shepherds, farm-hands, or cowherds, and even paupers, to demand a partition of the communal possessions. All that the commune owns, save public edifices and woods, is to be cut up into as many equal lots as there are heads, the lots to be drawn for, and each individual to take possession of his or her portion.[58] The operation is carried out, for "those who are least well off are infinitely flattered by it." In the district of Arcis-sur-Aube, there are not a dozen communes out of ninety in which more than two-thirds of the voters had the good sense to pronounce against it. From this time forth the commune ceases to be an independent proprietor; it has nothing to fall back

57. "Archives Nationales," F[7], 3,268. Letter of the overseer of the national domains at Rambouillet, October 31, 1792.—*Compte-rendu* of the minister Clavières, February 1, 1793.

58. Decrees of August 14, 1792, June 10, 1793.—"Archives Nationales," Missions des Représentants, D. § 7. (Deliberation of the district of Troyes, 2 Ventose, an. III.)—At Thunelières, the drawing took place on the 10th Fructidor, year II., and was done over again in behalf of a servant of Billy, an influential municipal officer who "was the soul of his colleagues."—*Ibid.* Abstract of operations in the district of Arcis-sur-Aube, 30 Pluviose, year III. "Two-thirds of the communes hold this kind of property. Most of them have voted on and effected the partition, or are actually engaged on it."

upon. In case of distress it is obliged to lay on extra taxes and obtain, if it can, a few additional sous. Its future revenue is at present in the tightly buttoned pockets of the new proprietors.—The prevalence of short-sighted views is once more due to the covetousness of individuals. Whether national or communal, it is always public interest which succumbs, and it succumbs always under the usurpations of indigent minorities, at one time through the feebleness of public authority, which dares not oppose their violence, and at another through the complicity of public authority, which has conferred upon them the rights of the majority.

IV

When there is a lack of public force for the protection of public property, there is also a lack of it for the protection of private property, for the same greed and the same needs attack both. Let a man owe anything either to the State or to an individual, and the temptation not to pay is equally the same. In both cases it suffices to find a pretext for denying the debt; in finding this pretext the cupidity of the tenant is as good as the selfishness of the tax-payer. Now that the feudal system is abolished let nothing remain of it: let there be no more seignorial claims. "If the Assembly has maintained some of them, yonder in Paris, it did so inadvertently or through corruption: we shall soon hear of all being suppressed. In the meantime we will relieve ourselves, and burn the agreements in the places where they are kept."

Such being the argument, the jacquerie breaks out afresh: in truth, it is permanent and universal. Just as in a body in which some of the elements of its vital substance are affected by an organic disease, the evil is apparent in the parts which seem to be sound: even where as yet no outbreak has occurred, one is imminent; constant anxiety, a profound restlessness, a low fever, denote its presence. Here, the debtor does not pay, and the creditor is afraid to prosecute him. In other places isolated eruptions occur. At Auxon,[59] on an estate spared

59. *Mercure de France,* January 7, 1790. (Chateau of Auxon, in Haute-Saone.)—"Archives Nationales," F^7, 3,255. (Letter of the minister to the Di-

by the great jacquerie of July, 1789, the woods are ravaged, and the peasants, enraged at being denounced by the keepers, march to the chateau, which is occupied by an old man and a child; everybody belonging to the village is there, men and women; they hew down the barricaded door with their axes, and fire on the neighbours who come to the assistance of its inmates.—In other places, in the districts of Saint-Etienne and Montbrison, "the trees belonging to the proprietors are carried away with impunity, and the walls of their grounds and terraces are demolished, the complainants being threatened with death or with the sight of the destruction of their dwellings." Near Paris, around Montargis, Nemours, and Fontainebleau, a number of parishes refuse to pay the tithes and ground-rent (*champart*) which the Assembly has a second time sanctioned; gibbets are erected and the collectors are threatened with hanging, while, in the neighbourhood of Tonnerre, a mob of debtors fire upon the body of police which comes to enforce the claims.—Near Amiens, the Comtesse de la Mire,[60] on her estate of Davencourt, is visited by the municipal authorities of the village, who request her to renounce her right to ground-rent (*champart*) and thirds (*tiers*). She refuses and they insist, and she refuses again, when they inform her that "some misfortune will happen to her." In effect, two of the municipal officers cause the tocsin to be rung, and the whole village rushes to arms. One of the domestics has an arm broken by a ball, and for three hours the countess and her two children are subject to the grossest insults and to blows: she is forced to sign a paper which she is not allowed to read, and, in warding off the stroke of a sabre, her arm is cleft from the elbow to the wrist; the chateau is pillaged, and she owes her escape to the zeal of some of her servants.—Large eruptions take place at the same time over entire provinces; one

---

rectory of Rhone-et-Loire, July 2, 1790.)—*Mercure de France,* July 17, 1790. (Report of M. de Broglie, July 13, and decree of July 13–18.)—"Archives Nationales," H. 1453. (Correspondence of M. de Bercheny, July 21, 1790.)

60. *Mercure de France,* March 19, 1790. Letter from Amiens, February 28. (Mallet-Dupan publishes in the *Mercure* only letters which are signed and authentic.)

succeeds the other almost without interruption, the fever encroaching on parts which were supposed to be cured, and to such an extent that the virulent ulcers finally combine and form one over the whole surface of the social body.

By the end of December, 1789, the chronic fermentation comes to a head in Brittany. Imagination, as usual, has forged a plot, and, as the people say, if they make an attack it is in their own defence.—A report spreads[61] that M. de Goyon, near Lamballe, has assembled in his chateau a number of gentlemen and six hundred soldiers. The mayor and National Guard of Lamballe immediately depart in force; they find everything tranquil there, and no company but two or three friends, and no other arms than a few fowling-pieces.—The impulse, however, is given, and, on the 15th of January, the great federation of Pontivy has excited the wildest enthusiasm. The people drink, sing, and shout in honour of the new decrees before armed peasants who do not comprehend the French tongue, still less legal terms, and who, on their return home, arguing with each other in *bas-breton,* interpret the law in a peculiar way. "A decree of the Assembly, in their eyes, is a *decree of arrest,*" and as the principal decrees of the Assembly are issued against the nobles, they are so many decrees of arrest against them.—Some days after this, about the end of January, during the whole of February, and down to the month of April, the execution of this theory is tumultuously carried out by mobs of villagers and vagabonds around Nantes, Auray, Redon, Dinan, Ploërmel, Rennes, Guingamp, and other villages. Everywhere, writes the Mayor of Nantes,[62] "the country-people believe that in burning deeds and contracts they get rid of their debts; the very best of them concur in this belief," or let things take their

61. "Archives Nationales," KK. 1105. (Correspondence of M. de Thiard; letters of Chevalier de Bévy, December 26, 1789, and others up to April 5, 1790.)—*Moniteur,* sitting of February 9, 1790.—*Mercure de France,* February 6 and March 6, 1790 (list of chateaux).

62. "Archives Nationales," KK. 1105. (Correspondence of M. de Thiard.) Letters of the Mayor of Nantes, February 16, 1790, of the Municipality of Redon, February 19, &c.

course; the excesses are enormous, because many gratify "special animosities, and all are heated with wine."—At Beuvres, "the peasants and vassals of the manor, after burning title-deeds, establish themselves in the chateau, and threaten to fire it if other papers, which they allege are concealed there, are not surrendered." Near Redon the Abbey of Saint-Sauveur is reduced to ashes. Redon is menaced, and Ploërmel almost besieged. At the end of a month thirty-seven chateaux are enumerated as attacked: twenty-five in which the title-deeds are burnt, and twelve in which the proprietors are obliged to sign an abandonment of their rights. Two chateaux which began to burn are saved by the National Guard. That of Bois-au-Voyer is entirely consumed, and several have been sacked. By way of addition, "more than fifteen *procureurs-fiscaux,* clerks, notaries, and officers of seignorial courts have been plundered or burnt," while proprietors take refuge in the towns because the country is now uninhabitable for them.

A second tumour makes its appearance at the same time at another point.[63] It showed itself in Lower Limousin in the beginning of January. From thence the purulent inflammation spreads to Quercy, Upper Languedoc, Perigord, and Rouergue, and in February from Tulle to Montauban, and from Agen to Périgueux and Cahors, extending over three departments.—Then, also, expectancy is the creator, according to rule, of its own object. By dint of longing for a law for the suppression of all claims, it is imagined that it is passed, and the statement is current that "the King and the National Assembly have ordered deputations to set up the maypole[64] and to '*light up*' the chateaux."—Farther, and quite according to custom, bandits,

63. *Mercure de France,* February 6 and 27, 1790. (Speech of M. de Foucault, sittings of February 2 and 6). —*Moniteur* (same dates). (Report of Grégoire, February 9; speeches by MM. Sallé de Chaux and de Noailles, February 9.)—Memorial of the deputies of the town of Tulle, drawn up by the Abbé Morellet (from the deliberations and addresses of eighty-three boroughs and cities in the province).

64. In allusion to the feudal custom of paying seignorial dues on the first of May around a maypole. See further on.—[Tr.]

people without occupation, take the lead of the furious crowd and manage things their own way. As soon as a band is formed it arrests all the peaceable people it can find on the roads, in the fields, and in isolated farmhouses, and takes good care to put them in front in case of blows.—These miscreants add terror to compulsion. They erect gibbets for any one that pays casual duties or annual dues, while the parishes of Quercy threaten their neighbours of Perigord with fire and sword in a week's time if they do not do in Perigord as they have done in Quercy.—The tocsin rings, the drums beat, and "the ceremony" is performed from commune to commune. The keys of the church are forcibly taken from the curé, the seats are burned, and, frequently, the woodwork marked with the seigneur's arms. They march to the seigneur's mansion, tear down his weathercocks, and compel him to furnish his finest tree, together with feathers and ribbons with which to deck it, without omitting the three measures which he uses in the collection of his dues in grain or flour. The maypole is planted in the village square, and the weathercocks, ribbons, and feathers are attached to its top, together with the three measures and this inscription, "By order of the King and National Assembly, the final quittance for all rentals." When this is done it is evident that the seigneur, who no longer possesses weathercocks, or a seat in the church, or measures to rate his dues by, is no longer a seigneur, and can no longer put forth claims of any kind. Huzzahs and acclamations accordingly burst forth, and there is a revel and an orgy on the public square. All who can pay—the seigneur, the curé, and the rich—are put under contribution for the festival, while the people eat and drink "without any interval of sobriety."—In this condition, being armed, they strike, and when resistance is offered they burn. In Agénois: a chateau belonging to M. de Lameth, and another of M. d'Aiguillon; in Upper Languedoc, that of M. de Bournazel, and in Perigord that of M. de Bar, are burnt down: M. de Bar is almost beaten to death, while six others are killed in Quercy. A number of chateaux in the environs of Montauban and in Limousin are assaulted with firearms, and several are pillaged.—Bands of twelve hundred men swarm the country; "they have a spite against every estate"; they redress wrongs; "they try over again cases disposed of thirty years ago, and give judgments which they put into execution."—If anybody fails to conform to the new code he is punished, and to the advantage of the new sovereigns. In Agénois, a gentleman having paid the rent which was associated with his fief, the people take his receipt from him, mulct him in a sum equal to that which he paid, and come under his windows to spend the money on good cheer, in triumph and with derision.

Many of the National Guards who still possess some degree of energy, several of the municipalities which still preserve some love of order, and a number of the resident gentry, employ their arms against these excited swarms of brutal usurpers. Some of the ruffians, taken in the act, are judged somewhat after the fashion of a drumhead court-martial, and immediately executed as examples. Everybody in the country sees that the peril to society is great and urgent, and that if such acts go unpunished, there will be no such thing as law and property in France. The Bordeaux parliament, moreover, insists upon prosecutions. Eighty-three boroughs and cities sign addresses, and send a special deputation to the National Assembly to urge on prosecutions already commenced, the punishment of criminals under arrest, and, above all, the maintenance of the *prévôtés*.[65] In reply to this, the Assembly inflicts upon the parliament of Bordeaux its disapprobation in the rudest manner, and enters upon the demolition of every judicial corporation.[66] After this, the execution of all *prévotal* decisions is adjourned. A few months later the Assembly will oblige the King to declare that the proceedings begun against the jacquerie of Brittany shall be regarded as null and void, and that the arrested insurgents shall be set free. For repressive purposes, it dispatches a sentimental exhortation to the French people, consisting of twelve pages of literary insipidity, which Florian might have composed for his Estilles and his Nemorins.[67]—New

65. Criminal courts without appeal.—[TR.]

66. *Moniteur,* sitting of March 4, 1790.—Duvergier, decrees of March 6, 1790, and August 6–10, 1790.

67. The address is dated February 11, 1793. This singularly comic document

conflagrations, as an inevitable consequence, kindle around live coals which have been imperfectly extinguished. In the district of Saintes,[68] M. Dupaty, counsellor of the parliament of Bordeaux, after having exhausted mild resources, and having concluded by issuing writs against those of his tenantry who would not pay their rents, the parish of Saint-Thomas de Cosnac, combined with five or six others, puts itself in motion and assails his two chateaux of Bois-Roche and Saint-George-des-Agouts; these are plundered and then set on fire, his son escaping through a volley of musket-balls. They visit Martin, the notary and steward, in the same fashion; his furniture is pillaged and his money is taken, and "his daughter undergoes the most frightful outrages." Another detachment pushes on to the house of the Marquis de Cumont, and forces him, under the penalty of having his house burnt down, to give a discharge for all the claims he has upon them. At the head of these incendiaries are the municipal officers of Saint-Thomas, except the mayor, who has taken to flight.

The electoral system organized by the Constituent Assembly is beginning to take effect. "Almost everywhere," writes the royal commissioner, "the large proprietors have been eliminated, and the offices have been filled by men who strictly fulfil the conditions of eligibility. The result is a sort of rage of the petty rich to annoy those who enjoy large heritages."—Six months later, the National Guards and village authorities in this same department at Aujean, Migron, and Varaise, decide that no more tithes, *agriers*, or *champarts*, nor any of the dues which are retained, shall be paid. In vain does the department annul the decision, and send its commissioners, gendarmes, and law-officers. The commissioners are driven away, and the officers and gendarmes are fired upon; the vice-president of the district, who was on his way to make his report to the department, is seized on the road and forced to give in his resignation.

---

would alone suffice to make the history of the Revolution perfectly comprehensible.

68. "Archives Nationales," F[7], 3,203. (Letters of the royal commissioner, April 30 and May 9, 1790.)—Letter of the Duc de Maillé, May 6.—*Procès-verbaux* of the department of administrators, November 12, 1790.—*Moniteur,* vi. 515.

Seven parishes have coalesced with Aujean and ten with Migron; Varaise has sounded the tocsin, and the villages for four leagues round have risen; fifteen hundred men, armed with guns, scythes, hatchets, and pitchforks, lend their aid. The object is to set free the principal leader at Varaise, one Planche, who was arrested, and to punish the mayor of Varaise, Latierce, who is suspected of having denounced Planche. Latierce is unmercifully beaten, and "forced to undergo a thousand torments during thirty hours"; then they set out with him to Saint-Jean-d'Angely, and demand the release of Planche. The municipality at first refuses, but finally consents on the condition that Latierce be given up in exchange for him. Planche, consequently, is set at liberty and welcomed with shouts of triumph. Latierce, however, is not given up; on the contrary, he is tormented for an hour and then massacred, while the directory of the district, which is less submissive than the municipal body, is forced to fly.—Symptoms of this kind are not to be mistaken, and similar ones exist in Brittany. It is evident that the minds of the people are permanently in revolt. Instead of the social abscess being relieved by the discharge, it is always filling up and getting more inflamed. It will burst a second time in the same places; in 1791 as in 1790, the jacquerie overspreads Brittany as it has spread over Limousin.

This is owing to the will of the peasant being of another nature than our will, possessing a great deal more fixity and tenacity. When an idea obtains a hold on him it takes root in an obscure and profound conviction upon which neither discussion nor argument have any effect; once planted, it vegetates according to his notions, not according to ours, and no legislative text, no judicial verdict, no administrative remonstrance can change in any respect the fruit it produces. This fruit, developed during centuries, is the feeling of an excessive spoliation, and, consequently, the need of an absolute release. Too much having been paid to everybody, the peasant now is not disposed to pay anything to anybody, and this idea, vainly repressed, always rises up in the manner of an instinct.—In the month of January, 1791,[69] bands again form in Brittany, owing to

69. "Archives Nationales," F^7, 3,225. Letter of the Directory from Ile-et-

the proprietors of the ancient fiefs having insisted on the payment of their rents. At first the coalesced parishes refuse to pay the stewards, and after this the rustic National Guards enter the chateaux to constrain the proprietors. Generally, it is the commander of the National Guard, and sometimes the communal attorney, who dictates to the lord of the manor the renunciation of his claims; they oblige him, moreover, to sign notes for the benefit of the parish, or for that of various private individuals. This is considered by them to be compensation for damages; all feudal dues being abolished, he must return what he received from them during the past year, and as they have been put to inconvenience he must indemnify them by "paying them for their time and journey." Such are the operations of two of the principal bands, one of them numbering fifteen hundred men, around Dinan and St. Malo; for greater security they burn title-deeds in the chateaux of Saint-Tual, Besso, Beaumanoir, La Rivière, La Bellière, Chateauneuf, Chenay, Chausavoir, Tourdelon, and Chalonge; and as a climax they set fire to Chateauneuf, just before the arrival of the regular troops.—In the beginning, a dim conception of legal and social order seems to be floating in their brains; at Saint-Tual, before taking 2,000 livres from the steward, they oblige the mayor to give them his consent in writing; at Yvignac, their chief, called upon to show the authority under which he acted, declares that "he is authorised by the general will of the populace of the nation."[70]—But when, at the end of a month, they are beaten by the regular troops, made furious by the blows given and taken, and excited by the weakness of the municipal authorities who release their prisoners, they then become bandits of the worst species. During the night of the 22nd of February, the chateau of Villefranche, three leagues from Malestroit, is attacked. Thirty-two rascals with their faces masked, and led by a chief in the national uniform, break open the door. The domestics are garrotted. The

---

Vilaine, January 30, 1791, and letter from Dinan, January 29.—*Mercure de France*, April 2 and 16, 1791. Letters from Rennes, March 20th; from Redon, March 12.

70. So expressed in the *procès-verbal*.

proprietor, M. de la Bourdonnaie, an old man, with his wife aged sixty, are half killed by blows and tied fast to their bed, and after this a fire is applied to their feet and they are *warmed* (*chauffé*). In the meantime the plate, linen, stuffs, jewellery, two thousand francs in silver, and even watches, buckles, and rings—everything is pillaged, piled on the backs of the eleven horses in the stables, and carried off.—When property is concerned, one sort of outrage provokes another, the narrow cupidity of the lease-holder being completed by the unlimited rapacity of the brigand.

Meanwhile, in the south-western provinces, the same causes have produced the same results; and towards the end of autumn, when the crops are gathered in and the proprietors demand their dues in money or in produce, the peasant, immovably fixed in his idea, again refuses.[71] In his eyes, any law that may be against him is not that of the National Assembly, but of the so-called *seigneurs*, who have extorted or manufactured it; and therefore it is null. The department and district administrators may promulgate it as much as they please: it does not concern him, and if the opportunity occurs, he knows how to make them smart for it. The village National Guards, who are lease-holders like himself, side with him, and instead of repressing him give him their support. As a commencement, he replants the maypoles, as a sign of emancipation, and erects the gibbet by way of a threat.—In the district of Gourdon, the regulars and the police having been sent to put them down, the tocsin is at once sounded: a crowd of peasants, amounting to four or five thousand, arrives from every surrounding parish, armed with scythes and guns; the soldiers, forming a body of one hundred, retire into a church, where they capitulate after a siege of twenty-four hours, being obliged to give the names of the proprietors who demanded their intervention of the district, and who are Messrs. Hébray, de Fon-

71. *Moniteur,* sitting of December 15, 1790. (Address of the department of Lot, December 7.)—Sitting of December 20 (Speech by M. de Foucault.)—*Mercure de France,* December 18, 1790. (Letter from Belves, in Perigord, December 7.)—*Ibid.,* January 22, 29, 1791. (Letter from M. de Clarac, January 18.)

tange, and many others. All their houses are destroyed from top to bottom, and they effect their escape in order not to be hung. The chateaux of Repaire and Salviat are burned. At the expiration of eight days Quercy is in flames and thirty chateaux are destroyed.—The leader of a band of rustic National Guards, Joseph Linard, at the head of a village army, penetrates into Gourdon, instals himself in the Hôtel-de-Ville, declares himself the people's protector against the directory of the district, writes to the department in the name of his "companions in arms," and vaunts his patriotism. Meanwhile he commands as a conqueror, throws open the prisons, and promises that, if the regular troops and police be sent off, he and his companions will withdraw in good order.—This species of tumultuary authority, however, instituted by acclamation for attack, is powerless for resistance. Scarcely has Linard retired when savagery is let loose. "A price is set upon the heads of the administrators; their houses are the first devastated; all the houses of wealthy citizens are pillaged; and the same is the case with all chateaux and country habitations which display any signs of luxury."—Fifteen gentlemen, assembled together at the house of M. d'Escayrac, in Castel, appeal to all good citizens to march to the assistance of the proprietors who may be attacked in this jacquerie, which is spreading everywhere;[72] but there are too few proprietors in the country, and none of the towns have too many of them for their own protection. M. d'Escayrac, after a few skirmishes, abandoned by the municipal officers of his village, and wounded, withdraws to the house of the Comte de Clarac, a major-general, in Languedoc. Here, too, the chateau is surrounded,[73] blockaded, and besieged by the local National Guard. M. de Clarac descends and tries to hold a parley with the attacking party, and is fired upon. He goes back inside and throws money out of the window; the money is gathered up, and he is again fired upon. The chateau is set on fire, and M. d'Escayrac receives five shots, and is killed. M. de Clarac, with another person, having taken refuge in a

72. December 17, 1790.

73. January 7, 1791.

subterranean vault, are taken out almost stifled the next morning but one by the National Guard of the vicinity, who conduct them to Toulouse, where they are kept in prison and where the public prosecutor takes proceedings against them. The chateau of Bagat, near Montcuq, is demolished at the same time. The abbey of Espagnac, near Figeac, is assaulted with fire-arms; the abbess is forced to refund all rents she has collected, and to restore four thousand livres for the expenses of a trial which the convent had gained twenty years before.

After such successes, the extension of the revolt is inevitable; and at the end of some weeks and months it becomes permanent in the three neighbouring departments.—In Creuse,[74] the judges are threatened with death if they order the payment of seignorial dues, and the same fate awaits all proprietors who claim their rents. In many places, and especially in the mountains, the peasants, "considering that they form the nation, and that clerical possessions are national," want to have these divided amongst themselves, instead of their being sold. Fifty parishes around La Souterraine receive incendiary letters inviting them to come in arms to the town, in order to secure by force, and by staking their lives, the production of all titles to rentals. The peasants, in a circle of eight leagues, are all stirred up by the sound of the tocsin, and preceded by the municipal officers in their scarves; there are four thousand of them, and they drag with them a waggon full of arms: this is for the revision and reconstitution of the ownership of the soil.—In Dordogne, self-appointed arbitrators interpose imperiously between the proprietor and the small farmer, at the time of harvest, to prevent the proprietor from claiming, and the farmer from paying, the tithes or the *rève;*[75] any agreement to this end is forbidden; whoever shall transgress the new order of things, proprietor or farmer, shall be hung. Accord-

74. Revolutionary archives of the department of Creuse, by Duval. (Letter of the administrators of the department, March 31, 1791.)—"Archives Nationales," F^7, 3,200. (Deliberation of the Directory of the Department, May 12, 1791.—*Procès-verbal* of the municipality of La Souterraine, August 23, 1791.)

75. A sort of export duty.—[Tr.]

ingly, the rural militia in the districts of Bergerac, Excideuil, Ribérac, Mucidan, Montignac, and Perigueux, led by the municipal officers, go from commune to commune in order to force the proprietors to sign an act of desistance; and these visits "are always accompanied with robberies, outrages, and ill-treatment from which there is no escape but in absolute submission." Moreover, "they demand the abolition of every species of tax and the partition of the soil."—It is impossible for "proprietors moderately rich" to remain in the country; on all sides they take refuge in Perigueux, and there, organizing in companies, along with the gendarmerie and the National Guard of the town, overrun the cantons to restore order. But there is no way of persuading the peasantry that it is order which they wish to restore. With that stubbornness of the imagination which no obstacle arrests, and which, like a vigorous spring, always finds some outlet, the people declare that "the gendarmes and National Guard" who come to restrain them "are priests and gentlemen in disguise."—The new theories, moreover, have struck down to the lowest depths; and nothing is easier than to draw from them the abolition of debts, and even the agrarian law. At Ribérac, which is invaded by the people of the neighbouring parishes, a village tailor, taking the catechism of the Constitution from his pocket, argues with the *procureur-syndic*, and proves to him that the insurgents are only exercising the rights of man. The book states, in the first place, "that Frenchmen are equals and brethren, and that they should give each other aid"; and that "the masters should share with their fellows, especially this year, which is one of scarcity." In the next place, it is written that "all property belongs to the nation," and that is the reason why "it has taken the possessions of the Church." Now, the nation is composed of all Frenchmen, and the conclusion is clearly apparent. Since, in the eyes of the tailor, the property of individual Frenchmen belongs to all the French, he, the tailor, has a right to at least the quota which belongs to him.—One travels fast and far on this road, for every mob considers that this means immediate enjoyment, and enjoyment according to its own ideas. There is no care for neighbours or for consequences, even when imminent and physical, and in twenty places the property which is usurped perishes in the hands of the usurpers.

This voluntary destruction of property can be best observed in the third department, that of Corrèze.[76] Not only have the peasants here refused to pay rents from the beginning of the Revolution; not only have they "planted maypoles, supplied with iron hooks, to hang" the first one that dared to claim or to pay them; not only are violent acts of every description committed "by entire communes," "the National Guards of the small communes participating in them"; not only do the culprits, whose arrest is ordered, remain at liberty, while "nothing is spoken of but the hanging of the constables who serve writs," but farther, together with the ownership of the water-sources, the power of collecting, directing, and distributing the water is overthrown, and, in a country of steep declivities, the consequences of such an operation may be imagined. Three leagues from Tulle, in a valley forming a semicircle, a pond twenty feet in depth, and covering an area of three hundred acres, was enclosed by a broad embankment on the side of a very deep gorge, which was completely covered with houses, mills, and cultivation. On the 17th of April, 1791, a troop of five hundred armed men assembled by the beat of a drum, and collected from three villages in the vicinity, set themselves to demolish the dyke. The proprietor, M. de Sedières, a substitute-deputy in the National Assembly, is not advised of it until eleven o'clock in the evening. Mounting his horse, along with his guests and domestics, he makes a charge on the insane wretches, and, with the aid of pistol and gun-shots, disperses them. It was time, for the trench they had dug was already eight feet deep, and the water was nearly on a level with it: a half-hour later and the terrible rolling mass of waters would have poured out on the inhabitants of the gorge.—But such vigorous strokes, which are rare

76. "Archives Nationales," F[7], 3,204.—Letters from the Directory of the Department, June 2, 1791; September 8 and 22.—Letter from the Minister of Justice, May 15, 1791.—Letter from M. de Lentilhac, September 2.—Letter from M. Melon-Padon, Royal Commissioner, September 8.—*Mercure de France,* May 14, 1791. (Letter of an eye-witness, M. de Loyac, April 25, 1791.)

and hardly ever successful, are no defence against universal and continuous attacks. The regular troops and the gendarmerie, both of which are in the way of reorganization or of dissolution, are not trustworthy, or are too weak. There are no more than thirty of the cavalry in Creuse, and as many in Corrèze. The National Guards of the towns are knocked up by expeditions into the country, and there is no money with which to provide for their change of quarters. And finally, as the elections are in the hands of the people, this brings into power men disposed to tolerate popular excesses. At Tulle, the electors of the second class, almost all chosen from among the cultivators, and, moreover, catechized by the club, nominate for deputies and public prosecutor only the candidates who are pledged against rentals and against water privileges.—Accordingly, the general demolition of the dykes begins as the month of May approaches. This operation continues unopposed on a vast pond, a league and a half from the town, and lasts for a whole week; elsewhere, on the arrival of the guards or of the gendarmerie, they are fired upon. Towards the end of September, all the embankments in the department are broken down: nothing is left in the place of the ponds but fetid marshes; the mill-wheels no longer turn, and the fields are no longer watered. But those who demolish them carry away baskets full of fish, and the soil of the ponds again becomes communal.—Hatred is not the motive which impels them, but the instinct of acquisition: all these violent outstretched hands, which rigidly resist the law, are directed against property, but not against the proprietor; they are more greedy than hostile. One of the noblemen of Corrèze,[77] M. de Saint-Victour, has been absent for five years. From the beginning of the Revolution, although his feudal dues constitute one-half of the income of his estate, he has given orders that no rigorous measures shall be employed in their collection, and the result is that, since 1789, none of them were collected. Moreover,

77. "Archives Nationales," F[7], 3,204. Letters from M. de Saint-Victour, September 25, October 2 and 10, 1791.—Letter from the steward of his estate, September 18.

having a reserve stock of wheat on hand, he lent grain, to the amount of four thousand francs, to those of his tenants who had none. In short, he is liberal, and, in the neighbouring town, at Ussel, he even passes for a Jacobin. In spite of all this, he is treated just like the rest. It is because the parishes in his domain are "clubbist," governed by associations of moral and practical levellers; in one of them "the brigands have organized themselves into a municipal body," and have chosen their leader as *procureur-syndic.* Consequently, on the 22nd of August, eighty armed peasants opened the dam of his large pond, at the risk of submerging a village in the neighbourhood, the inhabitants of which came and closed it up. Five other ponds belonging to him are demolished in the course of the two following weeks; fish to the value of from four to five thousand francs are stolen, and the rest perish in the weeds. In order to make this expropriation sure, an effort is made to burn his title-deeds; his chateau, twice attacked in the night, is saved only by the National Guard of Ussel. His farmers and domestics hesitate, for the time being, whether or not to cultivate the ground, and come and ask the steward if they could sow the seeds. There is no recourse to the proper authorities: the administrators and judges, even when their own property is concerned, "dare not openly show themselves," because "they do not find themselves protected by the buckler of the law."—Popular will, traversing both the old and the new law, obstinately persists in its work, and forcibly attains its ends.

Thus, whatever the grand terms of liberty, equality, and fraternity may be, with which the Revolution graces itself, it is, in its essence, a *transfer of property;* in this alone consists its chief support, its enduring energy, its primary impulse, and its historical significance.—Formerly, in antiquity, similar movements were accomplished, debts were abolished or lessened, the possessions of the rich were confiscated, and the public lands were divided; but this operation was confined to a city and limited to a small territory. For the first time it takes place on a large scale and in a modern State.—Thus far, in these vast States, when the deeper foundations have been disturbed, it has ever been on account of foreign domination or on account of an oppression of conscience. In France in the fifteenth century, in Holland in the sixteenth, and in England in the seventeenth century, the peasant, the mechanic, and the labourer had taken up arms against an enemy or in behalf of their faith. On religious or patriotic zeal has followed the craving for prosperity and comfort, and the new motive is as powerful as the others; for in our industrial, democratic, and utilitarian societies it is this which governs almost all lives, and excites almost all efforts. Kept down for centuries, the passion recovers itself by throwing off government and privilege, the two great weights which have borne it down. At the present time this passion launches itself impetuously with its whole force, with brutal insensibility, athwart every kind of proprietorship that is legal and legitimate, whether it be public or private. The obstacles it encounters only render it the more destructive; beyond property it attacks proprietors, and completes spoliation with proscriptions.

CHAPTER III

Development of the ruling passion— I. *Attitude of the nobles—Their moderate resistance*— II. *Workings of the popular imagination with respect to them—The monomania of suspicion—The nobles distrusted and treated as enemies—Situation of a gentleman on his domain—M. de Bussy*— III. *Domiciliary visits—The fifth jacquerie—Burgundy and Lyonnais in 1791—M. de Chaponay and M. Guillin-Dumoutet*— IV. *The nobles obliged to leave the rural districts—They take refuge in the towns—The dangers they incur—The eighty-two gentlemen of Caen*— V. *Persecutions in private life*— VI. *Conduct of officers—Their self-sacrifice—Disposition of the soldiery—Military outbreaks—Spread and increase of insubordination—Resignation of the officers*— VII. *Emigration and its causes—The first laws against the emigrants*— VIII. *Attitude of the nonjuring priests—How they become distrusted—Illegal arrests by local administrations—Violence or complicity of the National Guards—Outrages by the populace—Executive power in the south—The sixth jacquerie—Its two causes—Isolated outbreaks in the north, east, and west—General eruption in the south and in the centre*— IX. *General state of opinion—The three convoys of nonjuring priests on the Seine—Psychological aspect of the Revolution.*

I

IF popular passion ended in murder it was not because resistance was great or violent. On the contrary, never did an aristocracy undergo dispossession with so much patience, or employ less force in the defence of its prerogatives, or even of its property. To speak with exactness, the class in question receives blows without returning them, and when it does take up arms, it is always with the bourgeois and the National Guard, at the request of the magistrates, in conformity with the law, and for the protection of persons and property. The nobles try to avoid being either killed or robbed, nothing more: for nearly three years they raise no political banner. In the towns where they exert the most influence and which are denounced as rebellious, for example in Mende and Arles, their opposition is limited to the suppression of riots, the restraining of the common people, and ensuring respect for the law. It is not the new order of things against which they conspire, but against brutal disorder.—"At Mende," says the municipal body,[1] "we had the honour of being the first to furnish the contributions of 1790. We supplied the place of our bishop and installed his successor without disturbance, and without the assistance of any foreign force. . . . We dispersed the members of a cathedral body to which we were attached by the ties of blood and friendship; we dismissed all, from the bishop down to the children of the choir. We had but three communities of mendicant monks, and all three have been suppressed. We have sold all national possessions without exception."—The commander of their gendarmerie is, in fact, an old member of the body-guard, while the superior officers of the National Guard are gentlemen, or belong to the order of Saint-Louis. It is very evident that, if they defend themselves against Jacobins, they are not insurgent against the National Assembly.—In Arles,[2] which has put down its populace, which has armed itself, which has shut its gates, and which passes for a focus of royalist conspiracy, the commissioners sent by the King and by the National Assembly, men of discretion and of consideration,

1. *Moniteur,* xi. 763. (Sitting of March 28, 1792.)—"Archives Nationales," F[7], 3,235. (Deliberation of the Directory of the Department, November 29, 1791, and January 27, 1792.—Petition of the Municipality of Mende and of forty-three others, November 30, 1791.)

2. "Archives Nationales," F[5], 3,198. *Procès-verbal* of the municipal officers of Arles, September 2, 1791.—Letters of the Royal Commissioners and of the National Assembly, October 24, November 6, 14, 17, 21, and December 21, 1791.—The commissioners, to be impartial, attend in turn a mass by a nonjuring priest and one by a priest of the opposite side. "The church is full" with the former, and "always empty" with the latter.

find nothing, after a month's investigation, but submission to the decrees and zeal for the public welfare. "Such," they say, "are the men who have been calumniated because, cherishing the Constitution, they hold fanaticism, demagogues, and anarchy, in horror. If the citizens had not roused themselves when the moment of danger arrived, they would have been slaughtered like their neighbours (of Avignon). It is this insurrection against crime which the brigands have slandered." If their gates were shut it was because "the National Guard of Marseilles, the same which behaved so badly in the Comtat, flocked there under the pretext of maintaining liberty and of forestalling the counterrevolution, but, in reality, to pillage the town." *Vive la Nation! Vive la Loi! Vive le Roi!* were the only cries heard at the very quiet and orderly elections that had just taken place. "The attachment of the citizens to the Constitution has been spoken of. . . . Obedience to the laws, the readiest disposition to discharge public contributions, were remarked by us among these pretended counterrevolutionists. Those who are subject to the license-tax came in crowds to the Hôtel-de-Ville." Scarcely "was the bureau of receipts opened when it was filled with respectable people; those on the contrary who style themselves *good patriots*, republicans or anarchists, were not conspicuous on this occasion; but a very small number among them have made their submission. The rest are surprised at being called upon for money; they had been flattered by such different hopes."

In short, during more than thirty months, and under a steady fire of threats, outrages, and spoliations, the nobles who remain in France neither commit nor undertake any hostile act against the Government that persecutes them. None of them, not even M. de Bouillé, attempts to carry out any real plan of civil war; I find but one resolute man in their ranks at this date, ready for action, and who labours to form one militant party against another militant party: he is really a politician and conspirator; he has an understanding with the Comte d'Artois; he gets petitions signed for the freedom of the King and of the Church; he organizes armed companies; he recruits the peasants; he prepares a Vendée for Languedoc and Provence;

and *this person is a bourgeois,* Froment of Nismes.[3] But, at the moment of action, he finds only three out of eighteen companies, supposed by him to be enlisted in his cause, that are willing to march with him. Others remain in their quarters until, Froment being overcome, they are found there and slaughtered; the survivors, who escape to Jalès, find, not a stronghold, but a temporary asylum, where they never succeed in transforming their inclinations into determinations.[4]—The nobles too, like other Frenchmen, have been subject to the lasting pressure of monarchical centralization. They no longer form one body; they have lost the instinct of association. They no longer know how to act for themselves; they are the puppets of administration awaiting an impulse from the centre, while at the centre the King, their hereditary general, a captive in the hands of the people, commands them to be resigned and to do nothing. Moreover, like other Frenchmen, they have been brought up in the philosophy of the eighteenth century. "Liberty is so precious," wrote the Duc de Brissac,[5] "that it may well be purchased with some suffering; a destroyed feudalism will not prevent the good and the true from being respected and loved."—They persist in this illusion for a long time and remain optimists. As they feel kindly towards the people, they cannot comprehend that the people should entertain other sentiments toward them; they firmly believe that the troubles are transient. Immediately on the proclamation of the Constitution they return in crowds from Spain, Belgium, and Germany; at Troyes

3. "Mémoire" of M. Mérilhon, for Froment, *passim.*—Report of M. Alquier, p. 54.—De Dammartin, i. 208.

4. De Dammartin, i. 208. They would exclaim to the Catholic peasants: "Allons, mes enfans, Vive le Roi!" (shouts of enthusiasm): "those wretches of democrats, let us make an example of them, and restore the sacred rights of the throne and the altar!"—"As you please," replied the rustics in their patois, "but we must hold fast to the Revolution, for there are some good things about it."—They remain calm, refuse to march to the assistance of Uzès, and withdraw into their mountains on the first sign of the approach of the National Guard.

5. Dauban, "La Demagogie à Paris," p. 598: Letter of M. de Brissac, August 25, 1789.

there are not enough post-horses for many days to supply the emigrants who are coming back.[6] Thus they accept not only the abolition of feudalism with civil equality, but also political equality and numerical sovereignty.

Some consideration for them, some outward signs of respect, a few bows, would, in all probability, have rallied them sincerely to democratic institutions. They would soon consent to be confounded with the crowd, to submit to the common level, and to live as private individuals. Had they been treated like the bourgeois or the peasant, their neighbours, had their property and persons been respected, they might have accepted the new régime without any bitterness of feeling. That the leading emigrant nobles and those forming a part of the old court carry on intrigues at Coblentz or at Turin is natural, since they have lost everything: authority, places, pensions, sinecures, pleasures, and the rest. But, to the gentry and inferior nobles of the provinces, chevaliers of Saint-Louis, subaltern officers, and resident proprietors, the loss is insignificant. The law has suppressed one-half of their seignorial dues; but by virtue of the same law their lands are no longer burdened with tithes. Popular elections will not provide them with places, but they did not enjoy them under ministerial favour. Little does it matter to them that power, whether ministerial or popular, has changed hands: they are not accustomed to its favours, and will pursue their ordinary avocations—the chase, promenading, reading, visiting, and conversing—provided they, like the first-comer, the grocer at the corner, or their farm-servant, find protection, safety, and security on the public road and in their dwellings.[7]

6. *Moniteur,* x. 339. (*Journal de Troyes,* and a letter from Perpignan, November, 1791.)

7. *Mercure de France,* No. for September 3, 1791. "Let Liberty be presented to us, and all France will kneel before her; but noble and proud hearts will eternally resist the oppression which assumes her sacred mask. They will invoke liberty, but liberty without crime, the liberty which is maintained without dungeons, without inquisitors, without incendiaries, without brigands, without forced oaths, without illegal coalitions, without mob outrages; that liberty, fi-

II

Popular passion, unfortunately, is a blind power, and, for lack of enlightenment, suffers itself to be guided by spectral illusions. Imaginary conceptions work, and work in conformity with the structure of the excited brain which has given birth to them. What if the ancient régime should return! What if we were obliged to restore the property of the clergy! What if we should be again forced to pay the salt-tax, the excise, the *taille,* and other dues which, thanks to the law, we no longer pay, besides other taxes and dues that we do not pay in spite of the law! What if all the nobles whose chateaux are burnt, and who have given rent acquittances at the point of the sword, should find some way to avenge themselves and recover their former privileges! Undoubtedly they brood over these things, make agreements amongst each other, and plot with the foreigners; at the first opportunity they will fall upon us: we must watch them, repress them, and, if needs be, destroy them.—This instinctive process of reasoning prevailed from the outset, and, in proportion as excesses increase, prevails to a much greater extent. The noble is ever the past, present, and future *creditor,* or, at the very least, a possible one, which means that he is the worst and most odious of enemies. All his ways are suspicious, even when he is doing nothing; whatever he may do it is with a view of arming himself.—M. de Gilliers, who lives with his wife and sister one league out of Romans in Dauphiny,[8] amuses himself by planting trees and flowers; a few steps from his house, on another domain, M. de Montchorel, an old soldier, and M. Osmond, an old lawyer from Paris, with their wives and children, occupy their leisure hours in somewhat the same manner. M. de Gilliers having ordered and received wooden water-pipes, the report spreads that they are cannon. His guest, M. Servan, receives an

---

nally, which allows no oppressor to go unpunished, and which does not crush peaceable citizens beneath the weight of the chains it has broken."

8. Rivarol, "Mémoires," p. 367. (Letter of M. Servan, published in the "Actes des Apôtres.")

English travelling-trunk, which is said to be full of pistols. When M. Osmond and M. Servan stroll about the country with pencils and drawing-paper, it is averred that they are preparing topographical plans for the Spaniards and Savoyards. The four carriages belonging to the two families go to Romans to fetch some guests: instead of four there are nineteen, and they are sent for aristocrats who are coming to hide away in underground passages. M. de Senneville, decorated with a *cordon rouge* (red ribbon), pays a visit on his return from Algiers: the decoration becomes a blue one, and the wearer is the Comte d'Artois in person. There is certainly a plot brewing, and at five o'clock in the morning eighteen communes (two thousand armed men) arrive before the doors of the two houses; shouts and threats of death last for eight hours; a gun fired a few paces off at the inmates happens to flash in the pan; a peasant who is aiming at them says to his neighbour, "Give me a twenty-four-sous piece, and I will plant both my balls in their bodies!" Finally, M. de Gilliers, who was absent, attending a baptism, returns with the Royal Chasseurs of Dauphiny and the National Guard of Romans, and with their assistance delivers his family.—It is only in the towns, that is, in a few towns, and for a very short time, that an inoffensive noble who is attacked obtains any aid; the phantoms which people create for themselves there are less gross; a certain degree of enlightenment, and a remnant of common sense, prevent the hatching of too absurd stories.—But in the dark recesses of rustic brains nothing can arrest the monomania of suspicion. Fancies multiply there like weeds in a dark hole: they take root and vegetate until they become belief, conviction, and certainty; they produce the fruit of hostility and hatred, homicidal and incendiary ideas. With eyes constantly fixed on the chateau, the village regards it as a Bastille which must be captured, and, instead of saluting the lord of the manor, it thinks only of firing at him.

Let us take up one of these local histories in detail.[9] In the month

9. "Archives Nationales," F[7], 3,257. Official reports, investigations, and correspondence in relation to the affair of M. de Bussy (October, 1790).

of July, 1789, during the jacquerie in Mâconnais, the parish of Villiers appealed for assistance to its lord, M. de Bussy, a former colonel of dragoons. He had returned home, treated the people of his village to a dinner, and attempted to form them into a body of guards to protect themselves against incendiaries and brigands; along with the well-disposed men of the place "he patrolled every evening to restore tranquillity to the parish." On a rumour spreading that "the wells were poisoned," he placed sentinels alongside of all the wells except his own, "to prove that he was acting for the parish and not for himself." In short, he did all he could to conciliate the villagers, and to interest them in the common safety.—But, by virtue of being a noble and an officer he is distrusted, and it is Perron, the syndic of the commune, to whom the commune now listens. Perron announces that the King "having abjured his sworn word," no more confidence is to be placed in him, and, consequently, neither in his officers nor in the gentry. On M. de Bussy proposing to the National Guards that they should go to the assistance of the chateau of Thil, which is in flames, Perron prevents them, declaring that "these fires are kindled by the nobles and the clergy." M. de Bussy insists, and entreats them to go, offering to abandon "his *terrier,*" that is to say all his seignorial dues, if they will only accompany him and arrest this destruction. They refuse to do so. He perseveres, and, on being informed that the chateau of Juillenas is in peril, he collects, after great efforts, a body of one hundred and fifty men of his parish, and, marching with them, arrives in time to save the chateau, which a mob was about to set on fire. But the popular excitement, which he had just succeeded in calming at Juillenas, has gained the upper hand amongst his own troop: the brigands have seduced his men, "which obliges him to lead them back, while, along the road, they seem inclined to fire at him."—Having returned, he is followed with threats even to his own house: a band comes to attack his chateau; finding it on the defensive, they insist on being led to that of Courcelles.—In the midst of all this violence M. de Bussy, with about fifteen friends and tenants, succeeds in protecting himself, and, by dint of patience, energy, and cool blood, without killing or wounding a single man, ends in bringing back security throughout the whole canton. The jacquerie subsides, and it seems as if the newly restored order would be maintained. He sends for Madame de Bussy to return, and some months pass away.—The popular imagination, however, is poisoned, and whatever a gentleman may do, he is no longer tolerated on his estate. A few leagues from there, on April 29, 1790, M. de Bois-d'Aisy, deputy to the National Assembly, had returned to his parish to vote at the new elections.[10] "Scarcely has he arrived," when the commune of Bois-d'Aisy gives him notice through its mayor "that it will not regard him as eligible." He attends the electoral meeting which is held in the church: there, a municipal officer in the pulpit inveighs against nobles and priests, and declares that they must not take part in the elections. All eyes turn upon M. de Bois-d'Aisy, who is the only noble present. Nevertheless, he takes the civic oath, which nearly costs him dear, for murmurs arise around him, and the peasants say that he ought to have been hanged like the lord of Sainte-Colombe, to prevent his taking the oath. In fact, the evening before, the latter, M. de Vitteaux, an old man of seventy-four years of age, was expelled from the primary assembly, then torn out of the house in which he had sought refuge, half killed with blows, and dragged through the streets to the open square; his mouth was stuffed with manure, a stick was thrust into his ears, and "he expired after a martyrdom of three hours." The same day, in the church of the Capuchins, at Sémur, the rural parishes which met together excluded their priests and gentry in the same fashion. M. de Damas and M. de Sainte-Maure were beaten with clubs and stones; the curé of Massigny died after six stabs with a knife, and M. de Virieu saved himself as he best could.—With such examples before them it is probable that many of the nobles will no longer exercise their right of suffrage. M. de Bussy does not pretend to do it. He merely tries to prove that he is loyal to the nation, and that

10. *Mercure de France,* May 15, 1790. (Letter of Baron de Bois-d'Aisy, April 29, read in the National Assembly.)—*Moniteur,* iv. 302. Sitting of May 6. (Official statement of the Justice of the Peace of Vitteaux, April 28.)

he meditates no wrong to the National Guard or to the people. He proposed, at the outset, to the volunteers of Mâcon to join them, along with his little troop; they refused to have him and thus the fault is not on his side. On the 14th of July, 1790, the day of the Federation on his domain, he sends all his people off to Villiers, furnished with the tricolour cockade. He himself, with three of his friends, attends the ceremony to take the oath, all four in uniform, with the cockade on their hats, without any weapons but their swords and a light cane in their hands. They salute the assembled National Guards of the three neighbouring parishes, and keep outside the enclosure so as not to give offence. But they have not taken into account the prejudices and animosities of the new municipal bodies. Perron, the former syndic, is now mayor. A man named Bailly, who is the village shoemaker, is another of the municipal officers; their councillor is an old dragoon, one of those soldiers probably who have deserted or been discharged, and who are the firebrands of almost every riot that takes place. A squad of a dozen or fifteen men leave the ranks and march up to the four gentlemen, who advance, hat in hand, to meet them. Suddenly the men aim at them, and Bailly, with a furious air, demands: "What the devil do you come here for?" M. de Bussy replies that, having been informed of the Federation, he had come to take the oath like the rest of the people. Bailly asks why he had come armed. M. de Bussy remarks that "having been in the service, the sword was inseparable from the uniform," and had they come there without that badge they would have been at fault; besides, they must have observed that they had no other arms. Bailly, still in a rage, and, moreover, exasperated by such good reasons, turns round with his gun in his hand towards the leader of the squad and asks him three times in succession, "Commander, must I fire?" The commander not daring to take the responsibility of so gratuitous a murder, remains silent, and finally orders M. de Bussy to "clear out"; "which I did," says M. de Bussy. —Nevertheless, on reaching home, he writes to the municipal authorities clearly setting forth the motive of his coming, and demands an explanation of the treatment he had received. Mayor Perron throws aside his letter without reading it, and, on the following day, on leaving the mass, the National Guards come, by way of menace, to load their guns in sight of M. de Bussy, round his garden.—A few days after this, at the instigation of Bailly, two other proprietors in the neighbourhood are assassinated in their houses. Finally, on a journey to Lyons, M. de Bussy learns "that the chateaux in Poitou are again in flames, and that the work is to begin again everywhere."—Alarmed at all these indications, "he resolves to form a company of volunteers, which, taking up their quarters in his chateau, can serve the whole canton on a legal requisition." He thinks that about fifteen brave men will be sufficient. He has already six men with him in the month of October, 1790; green coats are ordered for them, and buttons are bought for the uniform. Seven or eight domestics may be added to the number. In the way of arms and munitions the chateau contains two kegs of gunpowder which were on hand before 1789, seven blunderbusses, and five cavalry sabres, left there in passing by M. de Bussy's old dragoons: to these must be added two double-barrelled fowling-pieces, three soldiers' muskets, five brace of pistols, two poor common guns, two old swords, and a hunting-knife. Such is the garrison, such the arsenal, and these are the preparations, so well justified and so slight, which prejudice conjointly with gossip is about to transform into a great conspiracy.

The chateau, in effect, was an object of suspicion in the village from the very first day. All its visitors, whenever they went out or came in, with all the details of their actions, were watched, denounced, exaggerated, and misinterpreted. If, through the awkwardness or carelessness of so many inexperienced National Guards, a stray ball reaches a farmhouse one day in broad daylight, it comes from the chateau; it is the aristocrats who have fired upon the peasants.—There is the same state of suspicion in the neighbouring towns. The municipal body of Valence, hearing that two youths had ordered coats made "of a colour which seemed suspicious," send for the tailor; he confesses the fact, and adds that "they intended to put the buttons on themselves." Such a detail is alarming. An inquiry is set on foot and the alarm increases; people in a strange uniform have been seen passing on their way to the chateau of Villiers; from thence, on reaching the number of two hundred, they will go and join the garrison of Besançon; they will travel four at a time in order to avoid detection. At Besançon they are to meet a corps of forty thousand men, commanded by M. Autichamp, which corps is to march on to Paris to carry off the King, and break up the National Assembly. The National Guards along the whole route are to be forced into the lines. At a certain distance each man is to receive 1,200 francs, and, at the end of the expedition, is to be enrolled in the Artois Guard, or sent home with a recompense of 12,000 francs.—Meanwhile, the Prince de Condé, with forty thousand men, will come by the way of Pont Saint-Esprit in Languedoc, rally the disaffected of Carpentras and of the Jalès camp to his standard, and occupy Cette and the other seaports; and finally, the Comte d'Artois, on his side, will enter by Pont-Beauvoisin with thirty thousand men.—A horrible discovery! The municipal authorities of Valence immediately inform those of Lyons, Besançon, Chalons, Mâcon, and others beside. On the strength of this the municipal body of Mâcon, "considering that the enemies of the Revolution are ever making the most strenuous efforts to annihilate the Constitution which secures the happiness of this empire," and "that it is highly important to frustrate their designs," sends two hundred men of its National Guard to the chateau of Villiers, "empowered to employ armed force in case of resistance." For greater security, this troop is joined by the National Guards of the three neighbouring parishes. M. de Bussy, on being told that they were springing over into his garden, seizes a gun and takes aim, but does not fire, and then, the requisition being legal, throws all open to them. There are found in the house six green coats, seven dozens of large buttons, and fifteen dozens of small ones. The proof is manifest. He explains what his project was and states his motive—it is a mere pretext. He makes a sign, as an order, to his valet—there is a positive complicity. M. de Bussy, his six guests, and the valet, are arrested and transported to Mâcon. A trial takes place, with depositions and interrogatories, in which the truth is elicited in spite of the most adverse testimony; it is clear that M. de Bussy never intended to do more than defend himself.—But prejudice is a blinder to hostile eyes. It cannot be admitted that, under a constitution which is perfect, an innocent man could incur danger; the objection is made to him that "it is not natural for an armed company to be formed to resist a massacre by which it is not menaced"; they are convinced beforehand that he is guilty. On a decree of the National Assembly the minister had ordered all accused persons to be brought to Paris by the constabulary and hussars; the National Guard of Mâcon, "in the greatest state of agitation," declares that, "as it had arrested M. de Bussy, it would not consent to his transport by any other body. . . . Undoubtedly, the object is to allow him to escape on the way," but it will know how to keep its captive secure. The guard, in fine, of its own authority, escorts M. de Bussy to Paris, into the Abbaye prison, where he is kept confined for several months—so long, indeed, that, after a new trial and investigation, the absurdity of the accusation being too palpable, they are obliged to set him at liberty.—Such is the situation of most of the gentry on their own estates, and M. de Bussy, even acquitted and vindicated, will act wisely in not returning home.

III

He would be nothing but a hostage there. Alone against thousands, sole survivor and representative of an abolished régime which all detest, it is the noble against whom everybody turns whenever a political shock seems to shake the new régime. He is at least disarmed, as he might be dangerous, and, in these popular executions, brutal instincts and appetites break loose like a bull that dashes through a door and rages through a dwelling-house. In the same department, some months later, on the news arriving of the arrest of the King at Varennes, "all nonjuring[11] priests and *ci-devant* nobles

11. "Archives Nationales," DXXIX. 4. Letter of M. Belin-Chatellenot (near Arnay-le-Duc) to the President of the National Assembly, July 1, 1791. "In the realm of liberty we live under the most cruel tyranny, and in a state of the

are exposed to the horrors of persecution." Bands forcibly enter houses to seize arms: Commarin, Grosbois, Montculot, Chaudenay, Créancé, Toisy, Chatellenot, and other houses are thus visited, and several are sacked. During the night of June 26–27, 1791, at the chateau of Créancé, "there is pillaging throughout; the mirrors are broken, the pictures are torn up, and the doors are broken down." The master of the house, "M. de Comeau-Créancé, Knight of St. Louis, horribly maltreated, is dragged to the foot of the stairs, where he lies as if dead": previous to this, "he was forced to give a considerable contribution, and to refund all penalties collected by him before the Revolution as the local lord of the manor."—Two other proprietors in the neighbourhood, Knights of St. Louis, are treated in the same way. "That is the way in which three old and brave soldiers are rewarded for their services!" A fourth, a peaceable man, escapes beforehand, leaving his keys in the locks and his gardener in the house. Notwithstanding this, the doors and the clothes-presses were broken open, the pillaging lasting five hours and a half, with threats of setting the house on fire if the seigneur did not make his appearance. Questions were asked "as to whether he attended the mass of the new curé, whether he had formerly exacted fines, and finally, whether any of the inhabitants had any complaint to make

---

completest anarchy, while the administrative bodies and the police, still in their infancy, seem to act only in fear and trembling. . . . So far, in all crimes, they are more concerned with extenuating the facts than in punishing the offence. The result is that the guilty have had no other restraint on them than a few gentle phrases like this: 'Dear brothers and friends, you are in the wrong, be careful,'" &c.—*Ibid.*, F^7, 3,229. Letter of the Directory of the Department of Marne, July 13, 1791. (Searches by the National Guard in chateaux and the disarmament of formerly privileged persons.) "None of our injunctions were obeyed." For example, there is breakage and violence in the residence of M. Guinaumont at Merry; the gun, shot, and powder of the game-keeper even are carried off. "M. de Guinaumont is without the means of defending himself against a mad dog or any other savage brute that might come into his woods or into his courtyard." The Mayor of Merry, with the National Guard, under compulsion, tells them in vain that they are breaking the law.—Petition of Madame d'Ambly, wife of the deputy, June 28, 1791. Not having the guns which she had already given up, she is made to pay 150 francs.

against him." No complaint is made; on the contrary, he is rather beloved.—But, in tumults of this sort, a hundred madmen and fifty rogues prescribe the law to the timid and the indifferent. These outlaws declared that "they were acting under orders; they compelled the mayor and prosecuting attorney to take part in their robberies; they likewise took the precaution to force a few honest citizens, by using the severest threats, to march along with them." These people come the next day to apologize to the pillaged proprietor, while the municipal officers draw up a statement of the violence practised against them. The violence, nevertheless, is accomplished, and, as it will go unpunished, it is soon to be repeated.

A beginning and an end are already made in the two neighbouring departments. There, especially in the south, nothing is more instructive than to see how an outbreak stimulated by enthusiasm for the public good immediately degenerates under the impulse of private interest, and ends in crime.—Around Lyons,[12] under the same pretext and at the same date, similar mobs perform similar visitations, and, on all these occasions, "the rent-rolls are burnt, and houses are pillaged and set on fire. Municipal authority, organized for the security of property, is in many hands but one facility more for its violation. The National Guard seems to be armed merely for the protection of robbery and disorder."—For more than thirty years, M. de Chaponay, the father of six children of whom three are in the service, expended his vast income on his estate of Beaulieu, giving occupation to a number of persons, men, women, and children. After the hailstorm of 1761, which nearly destroyed the village of Moranée, he rebuilt thirty-three houses, furnished others with timber for the framework, supplied the commune with wheat, and, for several years, obtained for the inhabitants a diminution of their taxation. In 1790, he celebrated the Federation Festival on a magnificent scale, giving two banquets, one of a hundred and thirty seats, for the

12. "Archives Nationales," DXXIX. 4. Letters of the Administrators of the Department of Rhône-et-Loire, July 6, 1791. (M. Vilet is one of the signers.)—*Mercure de France,* October 8, 1791.

municipal bodies and officers of the National Guards in the vicinity, and the other of a thousand seats for the privates. If any of the gentry had reason to believe himself popular and safe it was certainly this man.—On the 24th of June, 1791, the municipal authorities of Moranée, Lucenay, and Chazelai, with their mayors and National Guards, in all nearly two thousand men, arrive at the chateau with drums beating and flags flying. M. de Chaponay goes out to meet them, and begs to know to what he owes "the pleasure" of their visit. They reply that they do not come to offend him, but to carry out the orders of the district, which oblige them to take possession of the chateau and to place in it a guard of sixty men: on the following day the "district" and the National Guard of Villefranche are to come and inspect it.—Be it noted that these orders are imaginary, for M. de Chaponay asks in vain to see them; they cannot be produced. The cause of their setting out, probably, is the false rumour that the National Guard of Villefranche is coming to deprive them of a booty on which they had calculated.—Nevertheless M. de Chaponay submits; he merely requests the municipal officers to make the search themselves and in an orderly manner. Upon this the commandant of the National Guard of Lucenay exclaims, with some irritation, that "all are equal and all must go in," and at the same moment all rush forward. "M. de Chaponay orders the apartments to be opened; they immediately shut them up, purposely to let the sappers break through the doors with their axes."—Everything is pillaged, "plate, *assignats,* stocks of linen, laces, and other articles; the trees of the avenues are hacked and mutilated; the cellars are emptied, the casks are rolled out on the terrace, the wine is suffered to run out, and the chateau keep is demolished. . . . The officers urge on those that are laggard." Towards nine o'clock in the evening M. de Chaponay is informed by his servants that the municipal authorities have determined upon forcing him to sign an abandonment of his feudal dues and afterwards beheading him. He escapes with his wife through the only door which is left unguarded, wanders about all night, exposed to the gun-shots of the squads which are on his track, and reaches Lyons only on the following day.—Meanwhile the pillagers send him notice that if he does not abandon his rentals, they will cut down his forests and burn up everything on his estate. The chateau, indeed, is fired three distinct times, while, in the interval, the band sack another chateau at Bayère, and, on again passing by that of M. de Chaponay, demolish a dam which had cost 10,000 livres.—The public prosecutor, for his part, remains quiet, notwithstanding the appeals to him: he doubtless says to himself that a gentleman whose house has been searched is lucky to have saved his life, and that others, like M. Guillin-Dumoutet, for example, have not been as fortunate.

The latter gentleman, formerly captain of a vessel belonging to the India Company, afterwards Commandant at Senegal, now retired from active life, occupied his chateau of Poleymieux with his young wife and two infant children, his sisters, nieces, and sister-in-law—in all, ten women belonging to his family and domestic service—one negro servant, and himself, an old man of sixty years of age; here is a haunt of militant conspirators which must be disarmed as soon as possible.[13] Unfortunately, a brother of M. Guillin, accused of treason to the nation, had been arrested ten months previously, which was quite sufficient for the clubs in the neighbourhood. In the month of December, 1790, the chateau had already been ransacked by the people of the parishes in the vicinity: nothing was found, and the Department first censured and afterwards interdicted these arbitrary searches. On this occasion they will manage things better.—On the 26th of June, 1791, at ten o'clock in the morning, the municipal body of Poleymieux, along with two other bodies in their scarfs, and three hundred National Guards, are seen approaching, under the usual pretext of searching for arms. Madame Guillin presents herself, reminds them of the interdict of the Department,

13. *Mercure de France*, August 20, 1791, the article by Mallet-Dupan. "The details of the picture I have just sketched were all furnished me by Madame Dumoutet herself." I am "authorised by her signature to guarantee the accuracy of this narrative."

and demands the legal order under which they act. They refuse to give it. M. Guillin descends in his turn and offers to open his doors to them if they will produce the order. They have no order to show him. During the colloquy a certain man named Rosier, a former soldier who had deserted twice, and who is now in command of the National Guard, seizes M. Guillin by the throat; the old captain defends himself, presents a pistol at the man, which misses fire, and then, throwing the fellow off, withdraws into the house, closing the door behind him.—Soon after this, the tocsin sounds in the neighbourhood, thirty parishes start up, and two thousand men arrive. Madame Guillin, by entreaties, succeeds in having delegates appointed, chosen by the crowd, to inspect the chateau. These delegates examine the apartments, and declare that they can find nothing but the arms ordinarily kept on hand. This declaration is of no effect: the multitude, whose excitement is increased by waiting, feel their strength, and have no idea of returning empty-handed. A volley is fired, and the chateau windows are riddled with balls. As a last effort Madame Guillin, with her two children in her arms, comes out, and going to the municipal officers, calls upon them to do their duty. Far from doing this they retain her as a hostage, and place her in such a position that, if there is firing from the chateau, she may receive the bullets. Meanwhile, the doors are forced, the house is pillaged from top to bottom, and then set on fire; M. Guillin, who seeks refuge in the keep, is almost reached by the flames. At this moment, some of the assailants, less ferocious than the rest, prevail upon him to descend, and they answer for his life. Scarcely has he shown himself when others fall on him; they cry that he must be killed, that he has a life-rent of 36,000 francs from the State, and "this will be so much saved for the nation." "He is hacked to pieces alive"; his head is cut off and borne upon a pike; his body is cut up, and sent piece by piece to each parish; several wash their hands in his blood, and besmear their faces with it. It seems as if tumult, clamour, incendiarism, robbery, and murder had aroused in them not only the cruel instincts of the savage, but the carnivorous appetites of the brute; some of them, seized by the gendarmerie at Chasselay, had roasted the dead man's arm and dined upon it.[14]—Madame Guillin, who is saved through the compassion of two of the inhabitants of the place, succeeds, after encountering many dangers, in reaching Lyons; she and her children lost everything, "the chateau, its dependencies, the crop of the preceding year, wine, grain, furniture, plate, ready money, *assignats,* notes, and contracts." Ten days later, the department gives notice to the National Assembly that "similar projects are still being plotted and arranged, and that there are (always) threats of burning chateaux and rent-rolls"; that no doubt of this can possibly exist: "the inhabitants of the country only await the opportunity, to renew these scenes of horror."[15]

IV

Amidst these multiplied and reviving jacqueries there is nothing left but flight, and the nobles, driven out of the rural districts, seek refuge in the towns. But here also a jacquerie awaits them.—As the effects of the Constitution are developed, successive administrations become feebler and more partial; the unbridled populace has become more excitable and more violent; the enthroned club has become more suspicious and more despotic. Henceforth the club, through or in opposition to the administrative bodies, leads the populace, and the nobles will find it as hostile as the peasants. All their reunions, even when liberal, are closed like that in Paris, through the illegal interference of mobs, or through the iniquitous action of the popular magistrates. All their associations, even when legal and salutary, are broken up by brute force or by municipal intolerance. They are punished for having thought of defending themselves, and slaughtered because they try to avoid assassination.—Three or four

14. *Mercure de France,* August 20, 1791, the article by Mallet-Dupan. "The proceedings instituted at Lyons confirmed this cannibal banquet."

15. The letter of the Department ends with this either naïve or ironical expression: "You have one triumph to complete, that of the obedience and submission of the people to the law."

hundred gentlemen, who were threatened on their estates, sought refuge with their families in Caen;[16] and they trusted to find one there, for, by three different resolutions, the municipal body promised them aid and protection. Unfortunately, the club thinks otherwise, and, on August 23, 1791, prints and posts up a list of their names and residences, declaring that since "their suspected opinions have compelled them to abandon the rural districts," they are emigrants in the interior; from which it follows that "their conduct must be scrupulously watched," because "it may be the effect of some dangerous plot against the country." Fifteen are especially designated; among others "the former curé of Saint-Loup, the great bloodhound of the aristocrats, and all of them very suspicious persons, harbouring the worst intentions."—Thus denounced and singled out, it is evident that they can no longer sleep tranquilly: moreover, now that their addresses are published, they are openly threatened with domiciliary visits and violence. As to the administrative authorities, their interference cannot be depended on; the department itself gives notice to the minister that, as the law stands, it cannot put the chateau in the hands of the regulars,[17] as this would, it is said, excite the National Guard. "Besides, how without an army is this post to be wrested from the hands which hold it? It is impossible with only the resources which the Constitution affords us." Thus, in the defence of the oppressed, the Constitution is a dead letter.—Hence it is that the refugees, finding protection only in

16. "Archives Nationales," F[7], 3,200. See documents relating to the affair of November 5, 1791, and the events which preceded it or followed it, and among others "Lettres du Directoire et du Procureur-syndic du Department"; Pétition et Mémoire pour les Déténus"; Lettres d'un Témoin," M. de Morant.—*Moniteur,* x. 356. "*Procès-verbal* de la Municipalité de Caen" and of the "Directoire du Département," xi. 164, 206. "Rapport de Guadet," and documents of the trial.—"Archives Nationales," *ibid.*—"Lettres de M. Cahier," Minister of the Interior, January 26, 1792; of M. G—d de Pontécoulant, President of the Department Directory, February 3, 1792.—Proclamation by the Directory.

17. "Archives Nationales," F[7], 3,200. Letter of September 26, 1791.—Letter found on one of the arrested gentlemen. "A cowardly bourgeoisie, directors in cellars, a clubbist municipality, waging the most illegal war against us."

themselves, undertake to help each other. No association can be more justifiable, more pacific, more innocent. Its object is "to demand the execution of the laws constantly violated, and to protect persons and property." In each quarter they will try to bring together "all good citizens"; they will form a committee of eight members, and, in each committee, there will always be "an officer of justice or a member of the administrative body with an officer or subaltern of the National Guard." Should any citizen be attacked in person or property the association will draw up a petition in his favour. Should any particular act of violence require the employment of public force, the members of the district will assemble under the orders of the officer of justice and of the National Guard to enforce obedience. "In all possible cases" they "will avoid with the greatest care any insult of individuals; they will consider that the object of the meeting is solely to ensure public peace, and that protection from the law to which every citizen is entitled."—In short, they are *volunteer constables.* Turn the inquiry which way they will, a hostile municipality and a prejudiced tribunal can put no other construction upon it; they find nothing else. The only evidence against one of the leaders is a letter in which he tries to prevent a gentleman from going to Coblentz, striving to prove to him that he will be more useful at Caen. The principal evidence against the association is that of a townsman whom they wished to enrol, and of whom they demanded his opinions. He had stated that he was in favour of the execution of the laws; upon which they told him: "In this case you belong to us, and are more of an aristocrat than you think you are." Their aristocracy, in effect, consists wholly in the suppression of brigandage. No claim is more unpalatable, because it interposes an obstacle to the arbitrary acts of a party which thinks it has a right to do as it pleases.—On the 4th of October the regiment of Aunis left the town, and all good citizens were handed over to the militia, "in uniform or not," they alone being armed. That day, for the first time in a long period, M. Bunel, the former curé of Saint-Jean, with the consent and assistance of his sworn successor, officiates at the mass. There is a large gathering of the orthodox, which causes uneasiness among the patriots. The following day M. Bunel is to say mass again; whereupon, through the municipal authorities, the patriots forbid him to officiate, to which he submits. Nevertheless, for lack of due notice, a crowd of the faithful have arrived and the church is filled. A dangerous mob! The patriots and National Guards arrive "to preserve order," which has not been disturbed, and which they alone disturb. Threatening words are exchanged between the servants of the nobles and the National Guard. The latter draw their swords, and a young man is hewn down and trampled on; M. de Saffrey, who comes to his assistance unarmed, is himself cut down and pierced with bayonets, and two others are wounded.—Meanwhile, in a neighbouring street, M. Achard de Vagogne, seeing a man maltreated by armed men, approaches, in order to make peace. The man is shot down and M. Achard is covered with sabre and bayonet gashes: "there is not a thread on him which is not dyed with the blood that ran down even into his shoes." In this condition he is led to the chateau along with M. de Saffrey. Others break down the door of the house of M. du Rosel, an old officer of seventy-five years, of which fifty-nine have been passed in the service, and pursue him even over the wall of his garden. A fourth squad seizes M. d'Héricy, another venerable officer, who, like M. du Rosel, was ignorant of all that was going on, and was quietly leaving for his country seat.—The town is full of tumult, and, through the orders of the municipal authorities, the general alarm is sounded.

The time for the special constables to act has come; about sixty gentlemen, with a number of merchants and artisans, set out. According to the rules of their association, and with significant scruple, they beg an officer of the National Guard, who happens to be passing, to put himself at their head; they reach the Place Saint-Sauveur, encounter the superior officer sent after them by the municipal authorities, and, at his first command, follow him to the Hôtel-de-Ville. On reaching this, without any resistance on their part, they are arrested, disarmed, and searched. The rules and regulations of their league are found on their persons; they are evidently hatching a counterrevolution. The uproar against them is terrible. "To keep them safe," they are conducted to the chateau, while many of them are cruelly treated on the way by the crowd. Others, seized in their houses—M. Levaillant and a servant of M. d'Héricy—are carried off bleeding and pierced with bayonets. Eighty-two prisoners are thus collected, while fears are constantly entertained that they may escape. "Their bread and meat are cut up into little pieces, to see that nothing is concealed therein; the surgeons, who are likewise treated as aristocrats, are denied access to them." Nocturnal visits are, at the same time, paid to their houses; every stranger is ordered to present himself at the Hôtel-de-Ville, to state why he comes to the town to reside, and to give up his arms; every nonjuring priest is forbidden to say mass. The Department, which is disposed to resist, has its hands tied and confesses its powerlessness. "The people," it writes, "know their strength: they know that we have no power; excited by disreputable citizens, they permit whatever serves their passions or their interests; they influence our deliberations, and force us to those which, under other circumstances, we should carefully avoid."—Three days after this the victors celebrate their triumph "with drums, music, and lighted torches; the people are using hammers to destroy on the mansions the coats-of-arms which had previously been covered over with plaster"; the defeat of the aristocrats is accomplished.—And yet their innocence is so clearly manifest that the Legislative Assembly itself cannot help recognising it. After eleven weeks of durance the order is given to set them free, with the exception of two, a youth of less than eighteen years and an old man, almost an octogenarian, on whom two letters, misunderstood, still leave a shadow of suspicion.—But it is not certain that the people are disposed to give them up. The National Guard refuses to discharge them in open daylight and serve as their escort. Even the evening before "numerous groups of women, a few men mingled with them, talk of murdering all those fellows the moment they set foot outside the chateau." They have to be let out at two o'clock in the morning, secretly, under a strong guard, and to leave the town at once as six months before they left the rural districts.—

Neither in the country nor in the town[18] are they under the protection of civil or religious law; a gentleman, who is not compromised in the affair, remarks that their situation is worse than that of Protestants and vagabonds during the worst years of the ancient régime. "Does not the law allow (nonjuring) priests the liberty of saying mass? Why then can we not listen to their mass except at the risk of our lives? Does not the law command all citizens to preserve the public peace? Why then are those whom the cry *to arms* has summoned forth to maintain public order, assailed as aristocrats? Why is the refuge of citizens which the laws have declared sacred, violated without orders, without accusation, without any appearance of wrong-doing? Why are all prominent citizens and those who are well off disarmed in preference to others? Are weapons exclusively made for those but lately deprived of them and who abuse the use of them? Why should one be on an equality for purposes of payment, and distinguished only for purposes of annoyance and insult?"—He has spoken right, and that which rules henceforth is an aristocracy in an inverse sense, contrary to the law, and yet more contrary to nature. For, by a violent inversion, the lower grades in the graduated scale of civilisation and culture now are found uppermost, while the superior grades are found undermost. The Constitution having suppressed inequality, this has again arisen in an inverse sense. The populace, both of town and country, taxes, imprisons, pillages, and slays more arbitrarily, more brutally, more unjustly than feudal barons, and for its serfs or villains it has its ancient chieftains.

18. "Archives Nationales," F[7], 3,200. Letter of the Attorney-General of Bayeux, May 14, 1702, and of the Directory of Bayeux, May 21, 1792.—At Bayeux, likewise, the refugees are denounced and in peril. According to their verified statements they scarcely amounted to one hundred. "Several nonjuring priests, indeed, are found among them; (but) the rest, for the most part, consist of the heads of families who are known to reside habitually in neighbouring districts, and who have been forced to leave their firesides after having been, or fearing to become, victims of religious intolerance or of the threats of factions and of brigands."

V

Let us suppose that, in order not to excite suspicion, they are content to be without arms, to form no more associations, not to attend elections, to shut themselves up at home, to strictly confine themselves within the harmless precincts of domestic life. The same distrust, the same animosity, still pursues them there.—At Cahors,[19] where the municipal authorities, in spite of the law, had just expelled the Carthusians who, under legal sanction, chose to remain and live in common, two of the monks, before their departure, give to M. de Beaumont, their friend and neighbour, four dwarf pear-trees and some onions in blossom in their garden. On the strength of this, the municipal body decree that "the *sieur* Louis de Beaumont, formerly count, is guilty of having audaciously and maliciously damaged national property," condemns him to pay a fine of three hundred livres, and orders "that the four pear-trees, pulled up in the so-called Carthusian garden, be brought on the following day, Wednesday, to the door of the said *sieur* de Beaumont, and there remain for four consecutive days, guarded, day and night, by two fusiliers, at the expense of the said *sieur* de Beaumont; and upon the said trees shall be placed the following inscription, to wit: Louis de Beaumont, destroyer of the national property. And the judgment herewith rendered shall be printed to the number of one thousand copies, read, published, and posted at the expense of the said *sieur* de Beaumont, and duly addressed throughout the department of Lot to the districts and municipalities thereof, as well as to all societies of the Friends of the Constitution and of Liberty." Every line of this legal invective discloses the malignant envy of the local recorder, who revenges himself for having formerly bowed too low.—The following year, M. de Beaumont, having formally bought in, under notarial sanction, a church which was sold by the district, along with the ornaments and objects of worship it contained, the mayor and municipal offi-

19. *Mercure de France,* June 4, 1790 (letter from Cahors, May 17, and an Act of the Municipality, May 10, 1790).

cers, followed by a lot of workmen, come and carry away and destroy everything—confessionals, altars, and even the saint's canonised body, which had been interred for one hundred and fifty years: so that, after their departure, "the edifice resembled a vast barn filled with ruins and rubbish."[20] It must be noted that, at this very time, M. de Beaumont is military commandant at Perigord. The treatment he undergoes shows what is in reserve for ordinary nobles. I do not recommend them to attend official sales of property.[21]—Will they even be free in their domestic enjoyments, and on entering a drawing-room are they sure of quietly passing an evening there?—At Paris, even, a number of persons of rank, among them the ambassadors of Denmark and Venice, are listening to a concert in a mansion in the Faubourg Saint-Honoré, given by a foreign virtuoso, when a cart enters the court loaded with fifty bundles of hay, the monthly supply for the horses. A patriot, who sees the cart driven in, imagines that the King is concealed underneath the hay, and that he has come there for the purpose of plotting with the aristocrats about his flight. A mob gathers, and the National Guard arrives, along with a commissioner, while four grenadiers stand guard around the cart. The commissioner, in the meantime, inspects the hotel; he sees music-stands, and the arrangements for a supper; comes back, has the cart unloaded, and states to the people

20. "Archives Nationales," F^7, 3,223. Letter of Comte Louis de Beaumont, November 9, 1791. His letter, in a very moderate tone, thus ends: "You must admit, sir, that it is very disagreeable and even incredible, that the Municipal Officers should be the originators of the disorders which occur in this town."

21. *Mercure de France,* January 7, 1702. M. Granchier de Riom petitions the Directory of his Department in relation to the purchase of the cemetery, where his father had been interred four years before; his object is to prevent it from being dug up, which was decreed, and to preserve the family vault. He at the same time wishes to buy the church of Saint-Paul, in order to ensure the continuance of the masses in behalf of his father's soul. The Directory replies (December 5, 1791): "Considering that the motives which have determined the petitioner in his declaration are a pretence of good feeling under which there is hidden an illusion powerless to pervert a sound mind, the Directory decides that the application of the *sieur* Granchier cannot be granted."

that he has found nothing suspicious. The people do not believe him, and demand a second inspection. This is made by twenty-four delegates; the bundles of hay, moreover, are counted, and several of them are unbound, but all in vain. Disappointed and irritated, having anticipated a spectacle, the crowd insists that all the invited guests, men and women, should leave the house on foot, and only get into their carriages at the end of the street. "First comes a file of empty carriages"; next, "all the guests in their evening attire, and the ladies in full dress, trembling with fear, with downcast eyes, between two rows of men, women, and children, who stare them in the face, and overwhelm them with insults."[22]

Suspected of holding secret meetings, and called to account in his own house, has the noble at least the right to frequent a public saloon, to eat in a restaurant, and to take the fresh air in a balcony?—The Vicomte de Mirabeau, who has just dined in the Palais-Royal, stands at the window to take the air, and is recognised; there is a gathering, and the cry is soon heard, "Down with Mirabeau-Tonneau (barrel-Mirabeau)!"[23] "Gravel is flung at him from all sides, and occasionally stones. One of the window-panes is broken by a stone. Immediately picking up the stone, he shows it to the crowd, and, at the same time, quietly places it on the sill of the window, in token of moderation." There is a loud outcry; his friends force him to withdraw inside, and Bailly, the mayor, comes in person to quiet the aggressors. In this case there are good reasons for their hatred. The gentleman whom they stone is a bon-vivant, large and fat, fond of rich epicurean suppers; and on this account the populace imagine him to be a monster, and even worse, an ogre. With regard to these nobles, whose greatest misfortune is to be overpolished and too worldly, the overexcited imagination revives its old nursery tales.—M. de Montlosier, living in the Rue Richelieu, finds that he is watched on his way to the National Assembly. One woman especially, from thirty to thirty-two years of age, who sold meat at a

22. De Ferrières, ii. 268 (April 19, 1791).
23. De Montlosier, ii. 307, 309, 312.

stall in the Passage Saint-Guillaume, "regarded him with special attention. As soon as she saw him coming she took up a long, broad knife which she sharpened before him, casting furious looks at him." He asks his housekeeper what this means. Two children of that quarter have disappeared, carried off by gipsies, and the report is current that M. de Montlosier, the Marquis de Mirabeau, and other deputies of the "right," meet together "to hold orgies in which they eat little children."

In this state of public opinion there is no crime which is not imputed to them, no insult which is not freely bestowed on them. "Traitors, tyrants, conspirators, assassins," such is the current vocabulary of the clubs and newspapers in relation to them. "Aristocrat" signifies all this, and whoever dares to refute the calumny is himself an aristocrat.—At the Palais-Royal, it is constantly repeated that M. de Castries, in his last duel, made use of a poisoned sword, and an officer of the navy who protests against this false report is himself accused, tried on the spot, and condemned "to be shut up in the guard-house or thrown into the fountain."[24]—The nobles must beware of defending their honour in the usual way and of meeting an insult with a challenge! At Castelnau, near Cahors,[25] one of those who, the preceding year, marched against the incendiaries, M. de Bellud, Knight of Saint-Louis, on coming down the public square with his brother, a guardsman, is greeted with cries of "The aristocrat! to the lantern!" His brother is in a morning coat and slippers, and not wishing to get into trouble they do not reply. A squad of the National Guard, passing by, repeats the cry, but they still remain silent. The shout continues, and M. de Bellud, after some time has elapsed, begs the captain to order his men to be quiet. He refuses, and M. de Bellud demands satisfaction outside the town. At these words the National Guards rush at M. de Bellud with fixed

24. *Moniteur,* vi. 556. Letter of M. d'Aymar, commodore, November 18, 1790.

25. *Mercure de France,* May 28, and June 16, 1791 (letters from Cahors and Castelnau, May 18).

bayonets. His brother receives a sabre-cut on the neck, while he, defending himself with his sword, slightly wounds the captain and one of the men. The two brothers, alone against the whole body, fight on, retreating to their house, in which they are blockaded. Towards seven o'clock in the evening, two or three hundred National Guards from Cahors arrive to reinforce the besiegers. The house is taken, and the guardsman, escaping across the fields, sprains his ancle and is captured. M. de Bellud, who has found his way into another house, continues to defend himself there: the house is set on fire and burnt, together with two others alongside of it. Taking refuge in a cellar he still keeps on firing. Bundles of lighted straw are thrown in at the air-holes. Almost suffocated, he springs out, kills his first assailant with a shot from one pistol, and himself with another. His head is cut off with that of his servant. The guardsman is made to kiss the two heads, and, on his demanding a glass of water, they fill his mouth with the blood which drops from the severed head of his brother. The victorious gang then set out for Cahors, with the two heads stuck on bayonets, and the guardsman in a cart. It comes to a halt before a house in which a literary circle meets, suspected by the Jacobin club. The wounded man is made to descend from the cart and is hung: his body is riddled with balls, and everything the house contains is broken up, "the furniture is thrown out of the windows, and the house pulled down."—Every popular execution is of this character, at once prompt and complete, similar to those of an Oriental monarch who, on the instant, without inquiry or trial, avenges his offended majesty, and, for every offence, knows no other punishment than death. At Tulle, M. de Massy,[26] lieutenant of the "Royal Navarre," having struck a man that insulted him, is seized in the house in which he took refuge, and, in spite of

26. *Mercure de France,* Number of May 28, 1791. At the festival of the Federation, M. de Massy would not order his cavalry to put their chapeaux on the points of their swords, which was a difficult manoeuvre. He was accused of treason to the nation on account of this, and obliged to leave Tulle for several months.—"Archives Nationales," F^7, 3,204. Extract from the minutes of the tribunal of Tulle, May 10, 1791.

the three administrative bodies, is at once massacred.—At Brest, two antirevolutionary caricatures having been drawn with charcoal on the walls of the military coffee-house, the excited crowd lay the blame of it on the officers; one of these, M. Patry, takes it upon himself, and, on the point of being torn to pieces, attempts to kill himself. He is disarmed, but, when the municipal authorities come to his assistance, they find him "already dead through an infinite number of wounds," and his head is borne about on the end of a pike.[27]

VI

Much better would it be to live under an Eastern king, for he is not found everywhere, nor always furious and mad, like the populace. Nowhere are the nobles safe, neither in public nor in private life, neither in the country nor in the towns, neither associated together nor separate. Popular hostility hangs over them like a dark and threatening cloud from one end of the territory to the other, and the tempest bursts upon them in a continuous storm of vexations, outrages, calumnies, robberies, and acts of violence; here, there, and almost daily, bloody thunderbolts fall haphazard on the most inoffensive heads, on an old man asleep, on a Knight of Saint-Louis taking a walk, on a family at prayers in a church. But, in this aristocracy, crushed down in some places and attacked everywhere, the thunderbolt finds one predestined group which attracts it and on which it constantly falls, and that is the corps of officers.

With the exception of a few fops, frequenters of drawing-rooms, and the court favourites who have reached a high rank through the intrigues of the antechamber, it was in this group, especially in the medium ranks, that true moral nobility was then found. Nowhere in France was there so much tried, substantial merit. A man of genius, who associated with them in his youth, rendered them this homage: many among them are men possessing "the most amiable

27. "Archives Nationales," F^7, 3,215. "*Procès-verbal* des Officiers Municipaux de Brest," June 23, 1791.

characters and minds of the highest order."[28] Indeed, for most of them, military service was not a career of ambition, but an obligation of birth. It was the rule in each noble family for the eldest son to enter the army, and advancement was of but little consequence. He discharged the debt of his rank; this sufficed for him, and, after twenty or thirty years of service, the order of Saint-Louis, and sometimes a meagre pension, were all he had a right to expect. Amongst nine or ten thousand officers, the great majority coming from the lower and poorer class of provincial nobles, body-guards, lieutenants, captains, majors, lieutenant-colonels, and even colonels, have no other pretension. Satisfied with favours[29] restricted to their subordinate rank, they leave the highest grades of the service to the heirs of the great families, to the courtiers or to the parvenus at Versailles, and content themselves with remaining the guardians of public order, and the brave defenders of the State. Under this system, when the heart is not depraved it becomes exalted; it is made a point of honour to serve without compensation; there is nothing but the public welfare in view, and all the more because, at this moment, it is the absorbing topic of all minds and of all literature. Nowhere has practical philosophy, that which consists in a spirit of abnegation, more deeply penetrated than among this unrecognised nobility. Under a polished, brilliant, and sometimes frivolous exterior, they have

28. "Mémoires de Cuvier" ("Eloges Historiques," by Flourens), i. 177. Cuvier, who was then in Havre (1788), had pursued the higher studies in a German administrative school. "M. de Sarville," he says, "an officer in the Artois regiment, has one of the most refined minds and most amiable characters I ever encountered. There were a good many of this sort among his comrades, and I am always astonished how such men could vegetate in the obscure ranks of an infantry regiment."

29. De Dammartin, i. 133. At the beginning of the year 1790, "inferior officers said: 'We ought to demand something, for we have at least as many grievances as our men.' "—M. de la Rochejacquelein, after his great success in La Vendée, said: "I hope that the King, when once he is restored, will give me a regiment." He aspired to nothing more ("Mémoires de Madame de la Rochejacquelein").—Cf. "Un Officier royaliste au Service de la République," by M. de Bezancenet, in the letters and biography of General de Dommartin, killed in the expedition to Egypt.

a serious soul; the old sentiment of honour is converted into one of patriotism. Set to execute the laws, with force in hand to maintain peace through fear, they feel the importance of their mission, and, for two years, fulfil its duties with extraordinary moderation, gentleness, and patience, not only at the risk of their lives, but amidst great and multiplied humiliations, through the sacrifice of their authority and self-esteem, through the subjection of their intelligent will to the dictation and incapacity of the masters imposed upon them. For a noble officer to respond to the requisitions of an extemporised bourgeois municipal body,[30] to subordinate his competence, courage, and prudence to the blunders and alarms of five or six inexperienced, frightened, and timid attorneys, to place his energy and daring at the service of their presumption, feebleness, and lack of decision, even when their orders or refusal of orders are manifestly absurd or injurious, even when they are opposed to the previous instructions of his general or of his minister, even when they end in the plundering of a market, the burning of a chateau, the assassination of an innocent person, even when they impose upon him the obligation of witnessing crime with his sword sheathed and arms folded[31]—this is a hard task. It is hard for the noble officer to see independent, popular, and bourgeois troops organized in the face of his own troops, rivals and even hostile, in any case ten times as numerous and no less exacting than sensitive—hard to be expected to show them deference and extend civilities to them, to surrender to them posts, arsenals, and citadels, to treat their chiefs as equals, however ignorant or unworthy, and whatever they may be—here a

30. Correspondence of MM. de Thiard, de Caraman, de Miran, de Bercheny, &c., above cited, *passim*.—Correspondence of M. de Thiard, May 5, 1790: "The town of Vannes has an authoritative style which begins to displease me. It wants the King to furnish drum-sticks. The first log of wood would provide these, with greater ease and promptness."

31. "Archives Nationales," F^7, 3,248, March 16, 1791. At Douai, Nicolon, a grain-dealer, is hung because the municipal authorities did not care to proclaim martial law. The commandant, M. de la Noue, had not the right of ordering his men to move, and the murder took place before his eyes.

lawyer, there a Capuchin, elsewhere a brewer or a shoemaker, most generally some demagogue, and, in many a town or village, some deserter or soldier drummed out of his regiment for bad conduct, perhaps one of the noble's own men, a scamp whom he has formerly discharged with the yellow cartouch, telling him to go and be hung elsewhere. It is hard for the noble officer to be publicly and daily calumniated on account of his rank and title, to be characterized as a traitor at the club and in the newspapers, to be designated by name as an object of popular suspicion and fury, to be hooted at in the streets and in the theatre, to submit to the disobedience of his men, to be denounced, insulted, arrested, fleeced, hunted down, and slaughtered by them and by the populace, to see before him a cruel, ignoble, and unavenged death—that of M. de Launay, murdered at Paris—that of M. de Belzunce, murdered at Caen—that of M. de Beausset, murdered at Marseilles—that of M. de Voisins, murdered at Valence—that of M. de Rully, murdered at Bastia, or that of M. de Rochetailler, murdered at Port-au-Prince.[32] All this is endured by the officers among the nobles. Not one of the municipalities, even Jacobin, can find any pretext which will warrant the charge of disobeying orders. Through tact and deference they avoid all conflict with the National Guards. Never do they give provocation, and, even when insulted, rarely defend themselves. Their gravest faults consist of imprudent conversations, vivacious expressions, and witticisms. Like good watch-dogs amongst a frightened herd which trample them under foot, or pierce them with their horns, they allow themselves to be pierced and trampled on without biting, and would remain at their post to the end were they not driven away from it.

All to no purpose: doubly suspicious as members of a proscribed class, and as heads of the army, it is against them that public distrust excites the most frequent explosions, and so much the more as the instrument they handle is singularly explosive. Recruited by vol-

32. The last named, especially, died with heroic meekness (*Mercure de France*, June 18, 1791).—Sitting of June 9, speeches by two officers of the regiment of Port-au-Prince, one of them an eye-witness.

unteer enlistments "amongst a passionate, turbulent, and somewhat debauched people," the army is composed of "all that are most fiery, most turbulent, and most debauched in the nation."[33] Add to these the sweepings of the alms-houses, and you find a good many blackguards in uniform! When we consider that the pay is small, the food bad, discipline severe, no promotion, and desertion endemic, we are no longer surprised at the general disorder: license, to such men, is too powerful a temptation. With wine, women, and money they have from the first been made turncoats, and from Paris the contagion has spread to the provinces. In Brittany,[34] the grenadiers and chasseurs of Ile-de-France "sell their coats, their guns, and their shoes, exacting advances in order to consume it in the tavern"; fifty-six soldiers of Penthièvre "wanted to murder their officers," and it is foreseen that, left to themselves, they will soon, for lack of pay, "betake themselves to the highways, to rob and assassinate." In Eure-et-Loir, the dragoons,[35] with sabre and pistols in hand, visit the farmers' houses and take bread and money, while the foot soldiers of the "Royal-Comtois" and the dragoons of the "Colonel-Général" desert in bands in order to go to Paris, where amusement is to be had. The main thing with them is "to have a jolly time." In fact, the extensive military insurrections of the earliest date, those of Paris, Versailles, Besançon, and Strasbourg, began or ended with

33. "De Dammartin," ii. 214. Desertion is very great, even in ordinary times, supplying foreign armies with "a fourth of their effective men." Towards the end of 1789, Dubois de Crancé, an old musketeer and one of the future "mountain," stated to the National Assembly that the old system of recruiting supplied the army with "men without home or occupation, who often became soldiers to avoid civil penalties" (*Moniteur,* ii. 376, 381, sitting of December 12, 1789).

34. "Archives Nationales," KK. 1105. Correspondence of M. de Thiard, September 4 and 7, 1789, November 20, 1789, April 28, and May 29, 1790. "The spirit of insubordination which begins to show itself in the Bassigny regiment is an epidemic disease which is insensibly spreading among all the troops. . . . The troops are all in a state of gangrene, while all the municipalities oppose the orders they receive concerning the movements of troops."

35. "Archives Nationales," H. 1453. Correspondence of M. de Bercheny, July 12, 1790.

a revel.—Out of these depths of gross desires there has sprung up natural or legitimate ambitions. A number of soldiers, for twenty years past, have learned how to read, and think themselves qualified to be officers. One-quarter of those enlisted, moreover, are young men born in good circumstances, and whom a caprice has thrown into the army. They choke in this narrow, low, dark, confined passage where the privileged by birth close up the issue, and they will march over their chiefs to secure advancement. These are the discontented, the disputants, the orators of the mess-room, and between these barrack politicians and the politicians of the street an alliance is at once formed.—Starting from the same point they march on to the same end, and the imagination which has laboured to blacken the Government in the minds of the people, blackens the officers in the minds of the soldiers.

The Treasury is empty and there are arrears of pay. The towns, burdened with debt, no longer furnish their quotas of supplies; and at Orleans, with the distress of the municipality before them, the Swiss of Chateauvieux were obliged to impose on themselves a stoppage of one sou per day and per man to have wood in winter.[36] Grain is scarce, the flour is spoilt, and the army bread, which was bad, has become worse. The administration, worm-eaten by old abuses, is deranged through the new disorder, the soldiers suffering as well through its dissolution as through their extravagance.—They think themselves robbed and they complain, at first with moderation; and justice is done to their well-founded claims. Soon they exact accounts, and these are made out for them. At Strasbourg, on these being verified before Kellermann and a commissioner of the National Assembly, it is proved that they have not been wronged out of a sou; nevertheless a gratification of six francs a head is given to them, and they cry out that they are content and have nothing more to

36. "Mémoire justificatif" (by Grégoire), on behalf of two soldiers, Emery and Delisle.—De Bouillé, "Mémoires."—De Dammartin. i. 128, 144.—"Archives Nationales," KK. 1105. Correspondence of M. de Thiard, July 2 and 9, 1790.—*Moniteur,* sittings of September 3 and June 4, 1790.

ask for. A few months after this fresh complaints arise, and there is a new verification: an ensign, accused of malversation and whom they wished to hang, is tried in their presence; he is clearly irresponsible; none of them can cite against him a proven charge, and, once more, they remain silent. On other occasions, after hearing the reading of registers for several hours, they yawn, cease to listen, and go outside to get something to drink.—But the figures of their demands, as these have been summed up by their mess-room calculators, remain implanted in their brains; they have taken root there, and are constantly springing up without any account or refutation being able to extirpate them. No more writings nor speeches—what they want is money: 11,000 livres for the Beaune regiment, 39,500 livres for that of Forez, 44,000 livres for that of Salm, 200,000 livres for that of Chateauvieux, and similarly for the rest. So much the worse for the officers if the money-chest does not suffice for them; let them assess each other, or borrow on their note of hand from the municipality, or from the rich men of the town.—For greater security, in divers places, the soldiers take possession of the military chest and mount guard around it: it belongs to them, since they form the regiment, and, in any case, it is better that it should be in their hands than in suspected hands.—Already, on the 4th of June, 1790, the Minister of War announces to the Assembly that "the military body threatens to fall into the completest state of anarchy." His report shows "the most incredible pretensions put forth in the most plain-spoken way—orders without force, chiefs without authority, the military chest and flags carried away, the orders of the King himself openly defied, the officers condemned, insulted, threatened, driven off, some of them even captive amidst their own troops, leading a precarious life in the midst of mortifications and humiliations, and, as the climax of horror, commanders slaughtered under the eyes and almost in the arms of their own soldiers."

It is much worse after the July Federation. Regaled, caressed, and indoctrinated at the clubs, their delegates, inferior officers and privates, return to the regiment Jacobins; and henceforth correspond with the Jacobins of Paris, "receiving their instructions and reporting to them."[37]—Three weeks later, the Minister of War gives notice to the National Assembly that there is no limit to the license in the army. "Couriers, the bearers of fresh complaints, are arriving constantly." In one place "a statement of the fund is demanded, and it is proposed to divide it." Elsewhere, a garrison, with drums beating, leaves the town, deposes its officers, and comes back sword in hand. Each regiment is governed by a committee of soldiers. "It is in this committee that the detention of the lieutenant-colonel of Poitou has been twice arranged; here it is that 'Royal-Champagne' conceived the insurrection" by which it refused to recognise a sublieutenant sent to it. "Every day the minister's cabinet is filled with soldiers who are deputed to him, and who proudly come and intimate to him the will of their constituents." Finally, at Strasbourg, seven regiments, each represented by three delegates, formed a military congress. The same month, the terrible insurrection of Nancy breaks out—three regiments in revolt, the populace with them, the arsenal pillaged, three hours of furious fighting in the streets, the insurgents firing from the windows of the houses and from the cellar openings, five hundred dead among the victors, and three thousand among the vanquished.—The following month, and for six weeks,[38] there is

37. De Bouillé, p. 127.—*Moniteur*, sitting of August 6, 1790, and that of May 27, 1790.—Full details in authentic documents of the affair at Nancy, *passim*.—Report of M. Emmery, August 16, 1790, and other documents in Roux and Buchez, vii. 59–162.—De Bezancenet, p. 35. Letters of M. de Dommartin (Metz, August 4, 1790). "The Federation there passed off quietly, only, a short time after, some soldiers of a regiment took it into their heads to divide the (military) fund, and at once placed sentinels at the door of the officer having charge of the chest, compelling him to open it (*désacquer*). Another regiment has since put all its officers under arrest. A third has mutinied, and wanted to take all its horses to the market-place and sell them. . . . Everywhere the soldiers are heard to say that if they want money they know where to find it."

38. "Archives Nationales," F[7], 3,215. Letters of the Royal Commissioners, September 27, October 1, 4, 8, 11, 1790. "What means can four commissioners employ to convince 20,000 men, most of whom are seduced by the real enemies of the public welfare? In consequence of the replacing of the men the crews are, for the most part, composed of those who are almost ignorant of the sea,

another insurrection, less bloody, but more extensive, better arranged, and more obstinate, that of the whole squadron at Brest, a mutiny of twenty thousand men, at first against their admiral and their officers, then against the new penal code and against the National Assembly itself. The latter, after remonstrating in vain, is obliged not only not to take rigorous measures, but again to revise its laws.[39]

From this time forth, I cannot enumerate the constant outbreaks in the fleet and in the army.—Authorised by the minister, the soldier goes to the club, where he is repeatedly told that his officers, being aristocrats, are traitors. At Dunkirk, he is additionally taught how to get rid of them. Clamours, denunciations, insults, musket-shots—these are the natural means, and they are put in practice: but there is another, recently discovered, by which an energetic officer of whom they are afraid may be driven away. Some patriotic bully is found who comes and insults him. If the officer fights and is not killed, the municipal authorities have him arraigned, and his chiefs send him off along with his seconds "in order not to disturb the harmony between the soldier and the citizen." If he declines the proposed duel, the contempt of his men obliges him to quit the regiment. In either case he is got out of the way.[40]—They have no scruples in relation to him. Present or absent, a noble officer must

---

who know nothing of the rules of subordination, *and who, at the commencement of the Revolution, had most to do with the insurrections in the interior.*"

39. *Mercure de France,* October 2, 1790. Letter of the Admiral, M. d'Albert de Rioms, September 16. The soldiers of the *Majestueux* have refused to drill, and the sailors of the *Patriote* to obey.—"I wished to ascertain beforehand if they had any complaint to make against their captain?—No.—If they complained of myself?—No.—If they had any complaints to make against their officers?—No.—It is the revolt of one class against another class; their sole cry is 'Vive la Nation et les Aristocrates à la lanterne!' The mob have set up a gibbet before the house of M. de Marigny, major-general of marines; he has given in his resignation. M. d'Albert tenders his resignation."—*Ibid.,* June 18, 1791 (letter from Dunkirk, June 3).

40. De Dammartin, i. 222, 219. *Mercure de France,* September 3, 1791. (Sitting of August 23.)—Cf. *Moniteur* (same date). "The Ancient Régime," p. 377.

certainly be plotting with his emigrant companions; and on this a story is concocted. Formerly, to prove that sacks of flour were being thrown into the river, the soldiers alleged that these sacks were tied with *blue cords* (*cordons bleus*). Now, to confirm the belief that an officer is conspiring with Coblentz, it suffices to state that he rides a *white horse;* a certain captain, at Strasbourg, barely escapes being cut to pieces for this crime; "the devil could not get it out of their heads that he was acting as a spy, and that the little grey-hound" which accompanies him on his rides "is used to make signals."—One year after, at the time when the National Assembly completes its work, M. de Lameth, M. Fréteau, and M. Alquier state before it that Luckner, Rochambeau, and the most popular generals, "no longer are responsible for anything." The Auvergne regiment has driven away its officers and forms a separate society, which obeys no one. The second battalion of Beaune is on the point of setting fire to Arras. It is almost necessary to lay siege to Phalsbourg, whose garrison has mutinied. Here, "disobedience to the general's orders is formal." There "are soldiers who have to be urged to stand sentinel; whom they dare not put in confinement for discipline; who threaten to fire on their officers; who stray off the road, pillage everything, and take aim at the corporal who tries to bring them back." At Blois, a part of the regiment "has just arrived without either clothes or arms, the soldiers having sold all on the road to provide for their debauchery." One among them, delegated by his companions, proposes to the Jacobins at Paris to "de-aristocratise" the army by cashiering all the nobles. Another declares, with the applause of the club, that "seeing how the palisades of Givet are constructed, he is going to denounce the Minister of War at the tribunal of the sixth *arrondissement* of Paris."

It is manifest that, for noble officers, the situation is no longer tenable. After waiting patiently for twenty-three months, many of them left through conscientiousness, when the National Assembly, forcing a third oath upon them, struck out of the formula the name of the King, their born general.[41]—Others depart at the end of the

41. Marshal Marmont, "Mémoires," i. 24. "The sentiment I entertained for

Constituent Assembly, "because they are afraid of being hung." A large number resign at the end of 1791 and during the first months of 1792, in proportion as the new code and the new recruiting system for the army develop their results.[42] In fact, on the one hand, through the soldiers and inferior officers having a voice in the election of their chiefs and a seat in the military courts, "there is no longer the shadow of discipline; verdicts are given from pure caprice; the soldier contracts the habit of despising his superiors, of whose punishments he has no fear, and from whom he expects no reward; the officers are paralyzed to such a degree as to become entirely superfluous personages." On the other hand, the majority of the National Volunteers are composed of "men bought by the communes" and administrative bodies, worthless characters of the street-corners, rustic vagabonds forced to march by lot or bribery,"[43] and along with them, enthusiasts and fanatics to such an extent that, from March, 1792, from the spot of their enlistment to the frontier, their track is everywhere marked by pillage, robbery, devastation, and assassinations. Naturally, on the road and at the frontier, they denounce,

---

the person of the King is difficult to define. . . . (It was) a sentiment of devotion of an almost religious character, a profound respect as if due to a being of a superior order. At this time the word *king* possessed a magic power in all pure and upright hearts which nothing had changed. This delicate sentiment . . . still existed in the mass of the nation, especially among the well-born, who, sufficiently remote from power, were rather impressed by its brilliancy than by its imperfections." De Bezancenet, 27. Letter of M. de Dommartin, August 24, 1790. "We have just renewed our oath. I hardly know what it all means. I, a soldier, know only my King; in reality I obey two masters, who, we are told, will secure my happiness and that of my brethren, if they agree together."

42. De Dammartin, i. 179. See the details of these resignations (iii. 185) after June 20, 1792. *Mercure de France,* April 14, 1792. Letter from the officers of the battalion of the Royal Chasseurs of Provence (March 9). They are confined to their barracks by their soldiers, who refuse to obey their orders, and they declare that, on this account, they abandon the service and leave France.

43. Rousset, "Les Volontaires de 1791 à 1794," p. 106. Letter of M. de Biron to the minister (August, 1792); p. 225, letter of Vezu, commander of the 3rd battalion of Paris, to the army of the north (July 24, 1793). "A Residence in France from 1792 to 1795" (September, 1792. Arras). See notes at the end of vol. ii. for the details of these violent proceedings.

drive away, imprison, or murder their officers, and especially the nobles.—And yet, in this extremity, numbers of noble officers, especially in the artillery and engineer corps, persist in remaining at their posts, some through liberal ideas, and others out of respect for their instructions; even after the 10th of August, even after the 2nd of September, even after the 21st of January, like their generals Biron, Custine, de Flers, de Broglie, and de Montesquiou, with the constant perspective of the guillotine that awaits them on leaving the battle-field and even in the ministerial offices of Carnot.

VII

It is, accordingly, necessary that the officers and nobles should go away, should go abroad; and not only they, but their families. "Gentlemen who have scarcely six hundred livres income set out on foot,"[44] and there is no doubt as to the motive of their departure. "Whoever will impartially consider the sole and veritable causes of the emigration," says an honest man, "will find them in anarchy. If the liberty of the individual had not been daily threatened, if," in the civil as in the military order of things, "the senseless dogma, preached by the factions, had not been put in practice, that crimes committed by the mob are the judgments of heaven, France would have preserved three-fourths of her fugitives. Exposed for two years to ignominious dangers, to every species of outrage, to innumerable persecutions, to the steel of the assassin, to the firebrands of incendiaries, to the most infamous informations," to the denunciations of "their corrupted domestics, to domiciliary visits" prompted by the commonest street rumour, "to arbitrary imprisonments by the Com-

44. *Mercure de France,* March 5, June 4, September 3, October 22, 1791. (Articles by Mallet-Dupan.)—*Ibid.,* April 14, 1792. More than six hundred naval officers resigned after the mutiny of the squadron at Brest. "Twenty-two grave insurrectionary acts in the ports remained unpunished, and several of them through the decisions of the naval jury." "There is no instance of any insurrection, in the ports or on shipboard, or any outrage upon a naval officer, having been punished. . . . It is not necessary to seek elsewhere for the causes of the abandonment of the service by naval officers. According to their letters all offer their lives to France, but refuse to command those who will not obey."

mittee of Inquiry," deprived of their civil rights, driven out of primary meetings, "they are held accountable for their murmurs, and punished for a sensibility which would touch the heart in a suffering criminal."—"Resistance is nowhere seen; from the prince's throne to the parsonage of the priest, the tempest has prostrated all malcontents in resignation." Abandoned "to the restless fury of the clubs, to informers, to intimidated officials, they find executioners on all sides where prudence and the safety of the State have enjoined them not even to see enemies. . . . Whoever has detested the enormities of fanaticism and of public ferocity, whoever has awarded pity to the victims heaped together under the ruins of so many legitimate rights and odious abuses, whoever, finally, has dared to raise a doubt or a complaint, has been proclaimed an *enemy of the nation*. After this representation of malcontents as so many conspirators, every crime committed against them has been legitimated in public opinion. The public conscience, formed by the factions and by that band of political corsairs who would be the disgrace of a barbarous nation, have considered attacks against property and towns simply as *national justice,* while, more than once, the news of the murder of an innocent person, or of a sentence which threatened him with death, has been welcomed with shouts of joy. Two systems of natural right, two orders of justice, two standards of morality were accordingly established; by one of these it was allowable to do against one's fellow-creature, a reputed aristocrat, that which would be criminal if he were a patriot. . . . Was it foreseen that, at the end of two years, France, teeming with laws, with magistrates, with courts, with citizen-guards, bound by solemn oaths in the defence of order and the public safety, would still and continually be an arena in which *wild beasts would devour unarmed men*?"—With all, even with old men, widows, and children, it is a crime to escape from their clutches. Without distinguishing between those who fly to avoid becoming a prey, and those who arm to attack the frontier, the Constituent and Legislative Assemblies alike condemn all absentees. The Constituent Assembly[45] trebled their real and personal

45. Duvergier, "Decrees of August 1–6, 1791; February 9–11, 1792; March

taxes, and prescribed that there should be a triple lien on their rents and dues. The Legislative Assembly sequestrates, confiscates, and puts into the market their possessions, real and personal, amounting to nearly fifteen hundred millions of cash value. Let them return and place themselves under the knives of the populace; otherwise they and their posterity shall all be beggars.—At this stroke indignation overflows, and a bourgeois who is liberal and a foreigner, Mallet-Dupan, exclaims,[46] "What! twenty thousand families absolutely ignorant of the Coblentz plans and of its assemblies, twenty thousand families dispersed over the soil of Europe by the fury of clubs, by the crimes of brigands, by constant lack of security, by the stupid and cowardly inertia of petrified authorities, by the pillage of estates, by the insolence of a cohort of tyrants without bread or clothes, by assassinations and incendiarism, by the base servility of silent ministers, by the whole series of revolutionary scourges—what! these twenty thousand desolate families, women and old men, must see their inheritances become the prey of national spoliation! What! Madame Guillin, who was obliged to fly with horror from the land where monsters have burnt her dwelling, slaughtered and eaten her husband, and who live with impunity by the side of her home—shall Madame Guillin see her fortune confiscated for the benefit of the communities to which she owes her dreadful misfortunes! Shall M. de Clarac, under penalty of the same punishment, go and restore the ruins of his chateau, where an army of scoundrels failed to smother him!"—So much the worse for them if they dare not come back! They are to undergo civil death, perpetual banishment, and, in case the ban be violated, they will be given up to the guillotine. In the same case with them are others who, with still greater innocence, have left the territory, magistrates, ordinary rich

---

30 and April 8, 1792; July 24–28, 1792; March 28 and April 5, 1793." Report by Roland, January 6, 1793. He estimates this property at 4,800 millions, of which 1,800 millions must be deducted for the creditors of the emigrants; 3,000 millions remain. Now, at this date, the *assignats* are at a discount of 55 per cent. from their nominal figure.

46. *Mercure de France,* February 18, 1792.

people, burgesses, or peasants, Catholics, and particularly one entire class, the nonjuring clergy, from the cardinal archbishop down to the simple village vicar, all prosecuted, then despoiled, then crushed by the same popular oppression and by the same legislative oppression, each of these two persecutions exciting and aggravating the other to such an extent that, at last, the populace and the law, one the accomplice of the other, no longer leave a roof, nor a piece of bread, nor an hour's safety to a gentleman or to a priest.

VIII

The ruling passion flings itself on all obstacles, even those placed by itself across its own track. Through a vast usurpation the incredulous minority, indifferent or lukewarm, has striven to impose its ecclesiastical forms on the Catholic majority, and the situation thereby created for the Catholic priest is such that unless he becomes schismatic, he cannot fail to appear as an enemy. In vain has he obeyed! He has allowed his property to be taken, he has left his parsonage, he has given the keys of the church to his successor, he has kept aloof, he does not transgress, either by omission or commission, any article of any decree. In vain does he avail himself of his legal right to abstain from taking an oath repugnant to his conscience. This alone makes him appear to refuse the civic oath in which the ecclesiastical oath is included, to reject the constitution which he accepts in full *minus* a parasite chapter, to conspire against the new social and political order of things which he often approves of, and to which he almost always submits.[47] In vain does he confine

47. Cf. on this general attitude of the clergy, Sauzay, v. i. and the whole of v. ii.—*Mercure de France,* September 10, 1791: "No impartial man will fail to see that, in the midst of this oppression, amidst so many fanatical charges of which the reproach of fanaticism and revolt is the pretext, not one act of resistance has yet been manifest. Informers and municipal bodies, governed by clubs, have caused a large number of nonjurors to be cast into dungeons. All have come out of them, or groan there untried, and no tribunal has found any of them guilty."—Report of M. Cahier, Minister of the Interior, February 18, 1792. He declares that "he had no knowledge of any priest being convicted by the

himself to his special and recognised domain, the spiritual direction of things. Through this alone he resists the new legislators who pretend to furnish a spiritual guidance, for, by virtue of being orthodox, he must believe that the priest whom they elect is excommunicated, that his sacraments are vain; and, in his office as pastor, he must prevent his sheep from going to drink at an impure source. In vain might he preach to them moderation and respect. Through the mere fact that the schism is effected, its consequences unfold themselves, and the peasants will not always remain as patient as their pastor. They have known him for twenty years; he has baptized them and married them; they believe that his is the only true mass; they are not satisfied to be obliged to attend another two or three leagues away, and to leave the church, their church which their ancestors built, and where from father to son they have prayed for centuries, in the hands of a stranger, an intruder and heretic, who officiates before almost empty benches, and whom gendarmes, with guns in their hands, have installed. Assuredly, as he passes through the street, they will look upon him askance: it is not surprising that the women and children soon hoot at him, that stones are thrown at night through his windows, that in the strongly Catholic departments, Upper and Lower Rhine, Doubs and Jura, Lozère, Deux Sêvres and Vendée, Finistère, Morbihan, and Côtes-du-Nord, he is greeted with universal desertion, and then expelled through public ill-will. It is not surprising that his mass is interrupted and that his person is threatened;[48] that disaffection, which thus far had only

---

courts as a disturber of the public peace, although several had been accused."—*Moniteur,* May 6, 1792 (Report of Français de Nantes): "Not one has been punished for thirty months."

48. On these spontaneous brutal acts of the Catholic peasants, cf. "Archives Nationales," F^7, 3,236 (Lozère, July–November, 1791). Deliberation of the district of Florac, July 6, 1791, and the official statement of the commissioner of the department on the disturbances in Espagnac. On the 5th of July, Richard, a constitutional curé, calls upon the municipality to proceed to his installation. "The ceremony could not take place, owing to the hootings of the women and children, and the threats of various persons who exclaimed: 'Kill him! strangle him! he is a Protestant, is married, and has children'; and owing to the impos-

reached the upper class, descends to the popular strata; that, from one end of France to the other, a sullen hostility prevails against the new institutions; for now the political and social constitution is joined to the ecclesiastical constitution like an edifice to its spire, and, through this sharp pinnacle, seeks the storm even within the darkening clouds of heaven. The evil all springs out of this unskilful, gratuitous, compulsory fusion, and, consequently, from those who effected it.

But never will a victorious party admit that it has made a mistake. In its eyes the nonjuring priests are alone culpable; it is irritated against their factious conscience; and, to crush the rebellion even in the inaccessible sanctuary of personal conviction, there is no legal or brutal act of violence which it will not allow itself to commit.

Behold, accordingly, a new sport thrown open; and the game is immensely plentiful. For it comprises not only the black or grey robes, more than forty thousand priests, over thirty thousand nuns,

---

sibility of entering the church, the doors of which were obstructed by the large number of women standing in front of them."—On the 6th of July, he is installed, but with difficulty. "Inside the church a crowd of women uttered loud cries and bemoaned the removal of their old curé. On returning, in the streets, a large number of women, unsettled by the sight of the constitutional curé, turned their faces aside . . . and contented themselves with uttering disjointed words . . . without doing anything more than cover their faces with their bonnets, casting themselves on the ground."—July 15. The clerk will no longer serve at the mass nor ring the bells; the curé, Richard, attempting to ring them himself, the people threaten him with ill-treatment if he runs the risk.—September 8, 1791. Letter from the curé of Fau, district of Saint-Chély. "That night I was on the brink of death through a troop of bandits who took my parsonage away from me, after having broken in the doors and windows."—December 30, 1791. Another curé who goes to take possession of his parsonage is assailed with stones by sixty women, and thus pursued beyond the limits of the parish.—August 5, 1791. Petition of the constitutional bishop of Mende and his four vicars. "Not a day passes that we are not insulted in the performance of our duties. We cannot take a step without encountering hootings. If we go out we are threatened with cowardly assassination, and with being beaten with clubs."—F^7, 3,235 (Bas-Rhin, letter from the Directory of the Department, April 9, 1792): "Ten out of eleven, at least, of the Catholics refuse to recognise sworn priests."

and several thousand monks, but also the orthodox that are anywise fervent, that is to say the women of the low or middle class, and, without counting provincial nobles, a majority of the serious, steady bourgeoisie, a majority of the peasantry—almost the whole population of several provinces, east, west, and in the south. A name is bestowed on them, as lately on the nobles; it is that of *fanatic,* which is equivalent to *aristocrat,* for it also designates public enemies likewise placed by it beyond the pale of the law.—Little does it matter whether the law favours them, for it is interpreted against them, arbitrarily construed and openly violated by the partial or intimidated administrative bodies which the Constitution has withdrawn from the control of the central authority and subjected to the authority of popular gatherings. From the first months of 1791, the battue begins; the municipalities, districts, and departments themselves often take the lead in beating up the game. Six months later, the Legislative Assembly, by its decree of November 29,[49] sounds the tally-ho, and, in spite of the King's veto, the hounds on all sides dash forward. During the month of April, 1792, forty-two departments pass against nonjuring priests "acts which are neither prescribed nor authorised by the Constitution," and, before the end of the Legislative Assembly, forty-three others will have followed in their train.—Through this series of illegal acts, without offence, without trial, nonjurors are everywhere in France expelled from their parishes, relegated to the principal town of the department or district, in some places imprisoned, put on the same footing with the emigrants, and despoiled of their property, real and personal.[50]

49. Duvergier, decrees (not sanctioned) of November 29 and May 27, 1792.—Decree of August 26, 1792, after the fall of the throne.—*Moniteur,* xii. 200 (sitting of April 23, 1793). Report of the Minister of the Interior.

50. Lallier, "Le District de Machecoul," p. 261, 263.—"Archives Nationales," F^7, 3,234. Demand of the prosecuting attorney of the commune of Tonneins (December 21, 1791) for the arrest or expulsion of eight priests "at the slightest act of internal or external hostility."—*Ibid.,* F^7, 3,264. Act of the Council-General of Corrèze (July 16, 17, 18, 1792) to place in arrest all nonjuring priests.—Between these two dates, acts of various kinds and of increasing severity are found in nearly all the departments against the nonjurors.

Nothing more is wanting against them but the general decree of deportation which is to come as soon as the Assembly can get rid of the King.

In the meantime, the National Guards, who have extorted the laws, endeavour to aggravate them in their application; and there is nothing strange in their animosity. Commerce is at a stand-still, industry languishes, the artisan and shopkeeper suffer, and, in order to account for the universal discontent, it is attributed to the insubordination of the priest. Were it not for his stubbornness all would go well, since the Constitution is perfect, and he is the only one who does not accept it. But, in not accepting it, he attacks it. He, therefore, is the last obstacle in the way of public happiness; he is the scapegoat, let us drive the obnoxious creature away! And the urban militia, sometimes on its own authority, sometimes instigated by the municipal body its accomplice, is seen disturbing public worship, dispersing congregations, seizing priests by the collar, pushing them by the shoulders out of the town, and threatening them with hanging if they dare to return. At Douay,[51] with guns in hand, they force the directory of the department to order the closing of all the oratories and chapels in hospitals and convents. At Caen, with loaded guns and with a cannon, they march forth against the neighbouring parish of Verson, break into houses, gather up fifteen persons suspected of orthodoxy—canons, merchants, artisans, workmen, women, girls, old men, and the infirm—cut off their hair, strike them with the but-ends of their muskets, and lead them back to Caen fastened to the breach of the cannon; and all this because a nonjuring priest still officiated at Verson, and many pious persons from Caen attended his mass: Verson, consequently, is a focal centre of counterrevolutionary gatherings. Moreover, in the houses which were broken into, the furniture was smashed, casks stove in, and the

51. "Archives Nationales," F[7], 3,250. Official statement by the directory of the department, March 18, 1791, with all the documents in relation thereto.—F[7], 3,200. Letter of the Directory of Calvados, June 13, 1792, with the interrogations. The damages are estimated at 15,000 livres.

linen, money, and plate stolen, the rabble of Caen having joined the expedition.—Here, and everywhere, there is nothing to do but to let this rabble have its own way; and as it operates against the possessions, the liberty, the life, and the sense of propriety of dangerous persons, the National Militia is careful not to interfere with it. Consequently, the orthodox, both priests and believers, men and women, are now at its mercy, and, thanks to the connivance of the armed force, which refuses to interpose, the rabble satiates on the proscribed class its customary instincts of cruelty, pillage, wantonness, and destructiveness.

Whether public or private, the order of the day is always to hinder worship, while the means employed are worthy of those who carry them out.—Here, a nonjuring priest having had the boldness to minister to a sick person, the house which he has just entered is taken by assault, and the door and windows of a house occupied by another priest are shivered to pieces.[52] There, the lodgings of two workmen, who are accused of having had their infants baptized by a refractory priest, are sacked and nearly demolished. Elsewhere, a mob refuses to allow the body of an old curé, who had died without taking the oath, to enter the cemetery. Farther on, a church is assaulted during vespers, and everything is broken to pieces: on the following day it is the turn of a neighbouring church, and, in addition, a convent of Ursuline nuns is devastated.—At Lyons, on Easter-day, 1791, as the people are leaving the six o'clock mass, a troop, armed with whips, falls upon the women.[53] Stripped, bruised,

52. "Archives Nationales," F^7, 3,234. An Act of the Directory of Lot, February 24, 1792, on the disturbances at Marmande.—F^7, 3,239, official statement of the municipal body of Rheims, November 5, 6, 7, 1791. The two workmen are a harness-maker and a wool-carder. The priest who administered the baptism is put in prison as a disturber of the public peace.—F^7, 3,219. Letter of the royal commissioner at the tribunal of Castelsarrasin, March 5, 1792.—F^7, 3,203. Letter of the directory of the district of La Rochelle, June 1, 1792. "The armed force, a witness of these crimes and summoned to arrest these persons in the act, refused to obey."

53. Memorial by Camille Jourdan (Sainte-Beuve, "Causeries du Lundi," xii.

prostrated, with their heads in the dirt, they are not left until they are bleeding and half-dead; one young girl is actually at the point of death; and this sort of outrage occurs so frequently that even ladies attending the orthodox mass in Paris dare not go out without sewing up their garments around them in the shape of drawers.—Naturally, to make the most of the prey offered to them, hunting associations are formed. These exist in Montpellier, Arles, Uzès, Alais, Nismes, Carpentras, and in most of the towns or burgs of Gard, Vaucluse, and l'Hérault, in greater or less number according to the population of the city: some counting from ten to twelve, and others from two to three hundred determined men, of every description: among them are found "strike-hards" (*tape-dur*), former brigands, and escaped convicts with the brand still on their backs. Some of them oblige their members to wear a medal as a visible mark of recognition; all assume the title of *executive power,* and declare that they act of their own authority, and that it is necessary to "quicken the law."[54] Their pretext is the protection of sworn priests; and for twenty months, beginning with April, 1791, they operate to this effect "with heavy knotted clubs garnished with iron points," without counting sabres and bayonets. Generally, their expeditions are nocturnal. Suddenly, the houses of "citizens suspected of a want of patriotism," of nonjuring ecclesiastics, of the monks of the Christian school, are invaded; everything is broken or stolen, and the owner is ordered to leave the place in twenty-four hours: sometimes, doubtless through an excess of precaution, he is beaten

250). The guard refuses to give any assistance, coming too late and merely "to witness the disorder, never to repress it."

54. "Archives Nationales," F^7, 3,217. Letters of the curé of Uzès, January 29, 1792; of the curé of Alais, April 5, 1792; of the administrators of Gard, July 28, 1792; of the *procureur-syndic,* M. Griolet, July 2, 1792; of Castanet, former gendarme, August 25, 1792; of M. Griolet, September 28, 1792.—*Ibid.,* F^7, 3,223. Petition by MM. Thueri and Devès in the name of the oppressed of Montpellier, November 17, 1791; letter of the same to the minister, October 28, 1791; letter of M. Dupin, *procureur-syndic,* August 23, 1791; Act of the Department, August 9, 1791; Petition of the inhabitants of Courmonterral, August 25, 1791.

to death on the spot. Besides this, the band also works by day in the streets, lashes the women, enters the churches sabre in hand, and drives the nonjuring priest from the altar. All of this is done with the connivance and in the sight of the paralyzed or complaisant authorities, by a sort of occult and complementary government, which not only supplies what is missing in the ecclesiastical law, but also searches the pockets of private individuals.—At Nismes, under the leadership of a patriotic dancing-master, not content with "decreeing proscriptions, killing, scourging, and often murdering," these new champions of the Gallician Church undertake to reanimate the zeal of those liable to contribution. A subscription having been proposed for the support of the families of the volunteers about to depart, the *executive power* takes upon itself to revise the list of offerings: it arbitrarily taxes those who have not given, or who, in its opinion, have given too little—some "poor workmen fifty livres, others two hundred, three hundred, nine hundred, and a thousand, under penalty of wrecked houses and severe treatment." Elsewhere, the volunteers of Baux and other communes near Tarascon help themselves freely, and, "under the pretext that they are to march for the defence of the country, levy enormous contributions on proprietors," on one four thousand, and on another five thousand livres. In default of payment, they carry away all the grain on one farm, even to the reserve seed, threatening to make havoc with everything, and even to burn, in case of complaint, so that the owners dare not say a word, while the attorney-general of the neighbouring department, afraid on his own account, begs that his denunciation may be kept secret.—From the slums of the towns the jacquerie has spread into the rural districts. This is the sixth and the most extensive seen for three years.[55]

55. *Moniteur*, xii. 16, sitting of April 1, 1792. Speech by M. Laureau. "Behold the provinces in flames, insurrection in nineteen departments, and revolt everywhere declaring itself. . . . The only liberty is that of brigandage; we have no taxation, no order, no government." *Mercure de France*, April 7, 1792. "More than twenty departments are now participating in the horrors of anarchy and in a more or less destructive insurrection."

Two spurs impel the peasant on.—On the one hand he is frightened by the clash of arms, and the repeated announcements of an approaching invasion. The clubs and the newspapers since the declaration of Pilnitz, and the orators in the Legislative Assembly for four months past, have kept him alarmed with their trumpet-blasts, and he urges on his oxen in the furrow with cries of "Woa, Prussia!" to one, and to the other, "Gee up, Austria!" Austria and Prussia, foreign kings and nobles in league with the emigrant nobles, are going to return in force to reestablish the salt-tax, the excise, feudal dues, tithes, and to retake national property already sold and resold, with the aid of the gentry who have not left, or who have returned, and the connivance of nonjuring priests who declare the sale sacrilegious and refuse to absolve the purchasers.—On the other hand, Holy Week is drawing near, and for the past year qualms of conscience have disturbed the purchasers. Up to March 24, 1791, the sales of national property had amounted to only 180 millions; but, the Assembly having prolonged the date of payment and facilitated further sales in detail, the temptation proves too strong for the peasant; stockings and buried pots are all emptied of their savings. In seven months the peasant has bought to the amount of 1,346 millions,[56] and finally possesses in full and complete ownership the morsel of land which he has coveted for so many years, and sometimes an unexpected plot, a wood, a mill, or a meadow. At the present time he has to settle accounts with the church, and, if the pecuniary settlement is postponed, the Catholic settlement comes on the appointed day. According to immemorial tradition, he is obliged to take the communion at Easter,[57] his wife also, and likewise his mother; and if he, exceptionally, does not think this of consequence,

56. *Moniteur,* xii. 30. Speech by M. Caillasson. The total amount of property sold up to November 1, 1791, is 1,526 millions; the remainder for sale amounts to 669 millions.

57. "Archives Nationales," F^7, 3,225. Letter of the Directory of Ile-et-Vilaine, March 24, 1792. "The National Guards of the district purposely expel all nonjuring priests, who have not been replaced, *under the pretext of the trouble they would not fail to cause at Easter.*"

they do. Moreover, he requires the sacraments for his old sick father, his new-born child, and for his other child of an age to be confirmed. Now, communion, baptism, confession, all the sacraments, to be of good quality, must proceed from a safe source, just as is the case with flour and coin; there is only too much counterfeit money now in the world, and the sworn priests are daily losing credit, like the *assignats.* There is no other course to pursue, consequently, but to resort to the nonjuror, who is the only one able to give valid absolutions. And it so happens that he not only refuses this, but he is said to be inimical to the whole new order of things.—In this dilemma the peasant falls back upon his usual resource, the strength of his arms; he seizes the priest by the throat, as formerly his lord, and extorts an acquittance for his sins as formerly for his feudal dues. At the very least he strives to constrain the nonjurors to swear, to close their separatist churches, and bring the entire canton to the same uniform faith.—Occasionally also he avenges himself against the partisans of the nonjurors, against chateaux and houses of the opulent, against the nobles and the rich, against proprietors of every class. Occasionally, likewise, as, since the amnesty of September, 1791, the prisons have been emptied, as one-half of the courts are not yet installed,[58] as there has been no police for thirty months, the common robbers, bandits, and vagrants, who swarm about without repression or surveillance, join the mob and fill their pockets.

Here, in Pas-de-Calais,[59] three hundred villagers, headed by a drummer, burst open the doors of a Carthusian convent, steal everything, eatables, beverages, linen, furniture, and effects, whilst, in the

58. *Moniteur,* xi. 420. (Sitting of February 18, 1792.) Report by M. Cahier, Minister of the Interior.

59. "Archives Nationales," F^7, 3,250. Deposition of the municipal officers of Gosnay and Hesdiguel (district of Bethune), May 18, 1792. Six parishes took part in this expedition; the mayor's wife had a rope around her neck, and came near being hung.—*Moniteur,* xii. 154, April 15, 1792.—"Archives Nationales," F^7, 3,225. Letter of the Directory of Ile-et-Vilaine, March 24, 1792, and official statement of the commissioners for the district of Vitré; letter of the same directory, April 21, 1792, and report of the commissioners sent to Acigné, April 6.

neighbouring parish, another band operates in the same fashion in the houses of the mayor and of the old curé, threatening "to kill and burn all," and promising to return on the following Sunday.—There, in Bas-Rhin, near Fort Louis, twenty houses of the aristocrats are pillaged.—Elsewhere, in Ile-et-Vilaine, bodies of rural militia, combined, go from parish to parish, and, increasing in consequence of their very violence until they form bands of two thousand men, close churches, drive away nonjuring priests, remove clappers from the bells, eat and drink what they please at the expense of the inhabitants, and often, in the houses of the mayor or tax-registrar, indulge in the pleasure of breaking everything to pieces. Should any public officer remonstrate with them they shout, "At the aristocrat!" One of these unlucky counsellors is struck on the back with the butend of a musket, and two others have guns aimed at them; the chiefs of the expedition are in no better predicament, and, according to their own admission, if they are at the head of the mob it is that they themselves may not be pillaged or hung. The same spectacle presents itself in Mayenne, in Orne, in Moselle, and in the Landes.[60]

These, however, are but isolated irruptions, and very mild; in the south and in the centre, the plague is apparent in an immense leprous spot, which extending from Avignon to Perigueux, and from Aurillac to Toulouse, suddenly overspreads, scarcely with any break, ten departments—Vaucluse, Ardèche, Gard, Cantal, Corrèze, Lot, Dordogne, Gers, Haute-Garonne, and Hérault. Vast rural masses are set in motion at the same time, on all sides and owing to the same causes, the approach of war and the coming of Easter.—In Cantal, at the assembly of the canton held at Aurillac for the recruitment of the army,[61] the commander of a village National Guard demands

60. *Moniteur*, xii. 200. Report of M. Cahier, April 23, 1792. The directories of these four departments refuse to cancel their illegal acts, alleging that "their armed National Guards pursue refractory priests."

61. *Mercure de France*, April 7, 1792. Letters written from Aurillac.—"Archives Nationales," F[7], 3,202. Letter of the Directory of the District of Aurillac, March 27, 1792 (with seven official statements); of the Directory of the District of Saint-Flour, March 19 (with the report of its commissioners); of M. Du-

vengeance "against those who are not patriots," and the report is spread that an order has come from Paris to destroy the chateaux. Moreover, the insurgents allege that the priests, through their refusal to take the oath, are bringing the nation into civil war: "we are tired of not having peace on their account; let them become good citizens, so that everybody may go to mass." On the strength of this, the insurgents enter houses, put the inhabitants to ransom, not only priests and former nobles, "but also those who are suspected of being their partisans, those who do not attend the mass of the constitutional priest," and even poor people, artisans and tillers of the ground, whom they tax five, ten, twenty, and forty francs, and whose cellars and bread-bins they empty. Eighteen chateaux are pillaged, burnt, or demolished, and among others, those of several gentlemen and ladies who have not left the country. One of these, M. d'Humières, is an old officer of eighty years; Madame de Peyronenc saves her son only by disguising him as a peasant; Madame de Beauclerc, who flies across the mountain, sees her sick child die in her arms. At Aurillac, gibbets are set up before the principal houses; M. de Niossel, a former lieutenant of a criminal court, put in prison for his safety, is dragged out, and his severed head is thrown on a dungheap; M. Collinet, just arrived from Malta, and suspected of being an aristocrat, is ripped open, cut to pieces, and his head is carried about on the end of a pike. Finally, when the municipal officers, judges, and royal commissioner commence proceedings against the assassins, they find themselves in such great danger that they are obliged to resign or to run away. In like manner, in Haute-Garonne,[62] it is

---

ranthon, minister of justice, April 22; petition of M. Lorus, municipal officer of Aurillac.—Letter of M. Duranthon, June 9, 1792. "I am just informed by the royal commissioner of the district of Saint-Flour that, since the departure of the troops, the magistrates dare no longer exercise their functions in the midst of the brigands who surround them."

62. "Archives Nationales," F^7, 3,219. Letters of M. Niel, administrator of the Department of Haute-Garonne, February 27, 1792; of M. Sainfal, March 4; of the directory of the department, March 1; of the royal commissioner, tribunal of Castelsarrasin, March 13.

also "against nonjurors and their followers" that the insurrection has begun. This is promoted by the fact that in various parishes the constitutional curé belongs to the club, and demands the riddance of his adversaries. One of them at Saint-Jean-Lorne, "mounted on a cart, preaches pillage to a mob of eight hundred persons." Each band, consequently, begins by expelling refractory priests, and by forcing their supporters to attend the mass of the sworn priest.—But such success, wholly abstract and barren, is of little advantage, and peasants in a state of revolt are not satisfied so easily. When parishes march forth by the dozen and devote their day to the service of the public, they must have some compensation in wood, wheat, wine, or money,[63] and the expense of the expedition may be defrayed by the aristocrats. Not merely the upholders of nonjurors are aristocrats, as, for example, an old lady here and there, "very fanatical, and who for forty years has devoted all her income to acts of philanthropy," "but well-to-do persons, peasants or gentlemen"; for, "by keeping their wine and grain unsold in their cellars and barns, and by not undertaking more work than they need, so as to deprive workmen in the country of their means of subsistence," they design "to starve out" the poor folk. Thus, the greater the pillage, the greater the service to the public. According to the insurgents, it is important "to diminish revenues enjoyed by the enemies of the na-

63. The following are some examples of this rustic creed:—

At Lunel, four thousand peasants and village National Guards strive to enter, to hang the aristocrats; their wives are along with them, leading their donkeys with "baskets which they hope to carry away full." ("Archives Nationales," F^7, 3,223. Letter of the municipal body of Lunel, November 4, 1791.)

At Uzès it is with great difficulty that they can rid themselves of the peasants who came in to drive out the Catholic royalists. In vain "were they given plenty to eat and to drink"; they go away "in bad humour, especially the women who led the mules and asses to carry away the booty, and who had not anticipated returning home with empty hands." (De Dammartin, i. 195.)

In relation to the siege of Nantes by the Vendéans: "An old woman said to me, 'Oh, yes, I was there, at the siege. My sister and myself had brought along our sacks. We were quite sure of their entering at least as far as the Rue de la Casserie'" (the street of jewellers' shops). (Michelet, v. 211.)

tion, in order that they may not send their revenues to Coblentz and other places out of the kingdom." Consequently, bands of six or eight hundred or a thousand men overrun the districts of Toulouse and Castelsarrasin. All proprietors, aristocrats, and patriots are put under contribution. Here, in the house of "the philanthropic but fanatical old maid, they break open everything, destroy the furniture, taking away eighty-two bushels of wheat and sixteen hogsheads of wine." Elsewhere, at Roqueferrière, feudal title-deeds are burnt, and a chateau is pillaged. Farther on, at Lasserre, thirty thousand francs are exacted and the ready money is all carried off. Almost everywhere the municipal officers, willingly or unwillingly, authorise pillaging. Moreover, "they cut down provisions to a price in *assignats* very much less than their current rate in silver," and they double the price of a day's work. In the meantime, other bands devastate the national forests, and the gendarmes, in order not to be called aristocrats, have no idea but of paying court to the pillagers.

After all this, it is manifest that property no longer exists for anybody except for paupers and robbers.—In effect, in Dordogne,[64] "under the pretext of driving away nonjuring priests, frequent mobs pillage and rob whatever comes in their way. . . . All the grain that is found in houses with weathercocks is sequestrated." Rustics turn the forests to account as communal property, the possessions of the emigrants; and this operation is radical; for example, a band, on finding a new barn of which the materials strike them as good, demolish it so as to share with each other the tiles and timber.—In Corrèze, fifteen thousand armed peasants, who have come to Tulle to disarm and drive off the supporters of the nonjurors, break ev-

64. "Archives Nationales," F[7], 3,209. Letters of the royal commissioner at the tribunal of Mucidan, March 7, 1792; of the public prosecutor of the District of Sarlat, January, 1792.—*Ibid.*, F[7], 3,204. Letters of the administrators of the District of Tulle, April 15, 1792; of the directory of the department, April 18; petition of Jacques Labruc and his wife, with official statement of the justice of the peace, April 24. "All these acts of violence were committed under the eyes of the municipal authorities. They took no steps to prevent them, although they had notice given them in time."

erything in suspected houses, and a good deal of difficulty is found in sending them off empty-handed. As soon as they get back home, they sack the chateaux of Saint-Gal, Seilhac, Gourdon, Saint-Basile, and La Rochette, besides a number of country-houses, even of absent plebeians. They have found a quarry, and never was the removal of property more complete. They carefully carry off, says an official statement, all that can be carried—furniture, curtains, mirrors, clothes-presses, pictures, wines, provisions, even floors and wainscotings, "down to the smallest fragments of iron and wood-work," smashing the rest, so that nothing "remains of the house but its four walls, the roof, and the staircase." In Lot, where for two years the insurrection is permanent, the damage is much greater. During the night between the 30th and 31st of January, "all the best houses in Souillac" are broken open, "sacked and pillaged from top to bottom,"[65] their masters being obliged to fly, and so many outbreaks occur in the department, that the directory has no time to render an account of them to the minister. Entire districts are in revolt; as, "in each commune all the inhabitants are accomplices, witnesses cannot be had to support a criminal prosecution, and crime remains unpunished." In the canton of Cabrerets, the restitution of rents formerly collected is exacted, and the reimbursement of charges paid during twenty years past. The small town of Lauzerte is invaded by surrounding bodies of militia, and its disarmed inhabitants are at the mercy of the Jacobin faubourg. For three months, in the district of Figeac, "all the mansions of former nobles are sacked and burnt"; next the pigeon-cots are attacked, "and all country-houses which have a good appearance." Barefooted gangs "enter the houses of well-to-do people, physicians, lawyers, merchants, burst open the

65. "Archives Nationales," F^7, 3,223. Letters of M. Brisson, commissioner of the naval classes of Souillac, February 2, 1792; of the directory of the department, March 14, 1792.—Petition of the brothers Barrié (with supporting documents), October 11, 1791. Letter of the prosecuting attorney of the department, April 4, 1792. Report of the commissioners sent to the District of Figeac, January 5, 1792. Letter of the administrators of the department, May 27, 1792.

doors of cellars, drink the wine," and riot like drunken victors. In several communes these expeditions have become a custom; "a large number of individuals are found in them who live on rapine alone," and the club sets them the example. For six months, in the principal town, a coterie of the National Guard, called the *Black Band,* expel all persons who are displeasing to them, "pillaging houses at will, beating to death, wounding or mutilating by sabre-strokes, all who have been proscribed in their assemblies," without any officer or advocate daring to lodge a complaint. Brigandage, borrowing the mask of patriotism, and patriotism borrowing the methods of brigandage, have combined against property at the same time as against the ancient régime, and, to free themselves from all that inspires them with fear, they seize all which can provide them with booty.

And yet this is merely the outskirts of the storm; the centre is elsewhere, around Nismes, Avignon, Arles, and Marseilles, in a country where, for a long time, the conflict between cities and the conflict between religions have kindled and accumulated malignant passions.[66] Looking at the three departments of Gard, Bouches-de-Rhône, and Vaucluse, one would imagine one's self in the midst of a war with savages. In fact, it is a Jacobin and plebeian invasion, and, consequently, conquest, dispossession, and extermination—in Gard, a swarm of National Guards reproduce the jacquerie: the dregs of the Comtat come to the surface and cover Vaucluse with its scum; an army of six thousand from Marseilles sweeps down on Arles.—In the districts of Nismes, Sommières, Uzès, Alais, Jalais, and Saint-Hippolyte, title-deeds are burnt, proprietors put to ran-

66. "Archives Nationales," F[7], 3,217. Official reports of the commissioners of the Department of Gard, April 1, 2, 3, and 6, 1792, and letter of April 6. One landowner is taxed 100,000 francs.—*Ibid.*, F[7], 3,223. Letter of M. Dupin, prosecuting attorney of l'Hérault, February 17 and 26, 1792. "At the chateau of Pignan, Madame de Lostanges has not one complete piece of furniture left. The cause of these disturbances is religious passion. Five or six nonjuring priests had retreated to the chateau."—*Moniteur,* sitting of April 16, 1792. Letter from the directory of the Department of Gard.—De Dammartin, ii. 85. At Uzès, fifty or sixty men in masks invade the ducal chateau at ten o'clock in the evening, set fire to the archives, and the chateau is burnt.

som, and municipal officers threatened with death if they try to interpose; twenty chateaux and forty country-houses are sacked, burnt, and demolished.—The same month, Arles and Avignon,[67] given up to the bands of Marseilles and of the Comtat, see confiscations and massacres approaching.—Around the commandant, who has received the order to evacuate Arles,[68] "the inhabitants of all parties" gather as suppliants, "clasping his hands, entreating him with tears in their eyes not to abandon them; women and children cling to his boots," so that he does not know how to free himself without hurting them; on his departure twelve hundred families emigrate. After the entrance of the Marseilles band we see eighteen hundred electors proscribed, their country-houses on the two banks of the Rhône pillaged, "as in the times of Saracen pirates," a tax of 1,400,000 livres levied on all people in good circumstances, absent or present, women and girls promenaded about half-naked on donkeys and publicly whipped." "A sabre committee" disposes of lives, proscribes, and executes: it is the reign of sailors, porters, and the dregs of the populace.—At Avignon,[69] it is that of simple brigands, incendiaries, and assassins, who, six months previously, converted the Glacière into a charnel-house. They return in triumph and state that "this time the Glacière will be full." Five hundred families had already sought asylum in France before the first massacre; now, the entire remainder of the honest bourgeoisie, twelve hundred persons, take to flight, and the terror is so great that the small neighbouring

67. "Archives Nationales," F[7], 3,196. Official statements of Augier and Fabre, administrators of the Bouches-du-Rhône, sent to Avignon, May 11, 1792. (The reappearance of Jourdain, Mainvielle, and the assassins of La Glacière took place April 29.).

68. De Dammartin, ii. 63. Portalis, "ll est temps de parler" (pamphlet), *passim*. "Archives Nationales," F[7], 7,090. Memorial of the commissioners of the municipal administration of Arles, year iv., Nivose 22.

69. *Mercure de France,* May 19, 1792. (Sitting of May 4.) Petition of forty inhabitants of Avignon at the bar of the Legislative Assembly.—"Archives Nationales," F[7], 3,195. Letter of the royal commissioners at the tribunal of Apt, March 15, 1792; official report of the municipality, March 21; Letters of the Directory of Apt, March 23 and 28, 1792.

towns dare not entertain emigrants. In fact, from this time forth, both departments throughout Vaucluse and Bouches-de-Rhône are a prey. Bands of two thousand armed men, with women, children, and other volunteer followers, travel from commune to commune to live as they please at the expense of "fanatics"; and well-bred people are not the only ones they despoil. Plain cultivators, taxed at 10,000 livres, have sixty men billeted on them; their cattle are slain and eaten before their eyes, and everything in their houses is broken up; they are driven out of their lodgings and wander as fugitives in the reed-swamps of the Rhône, awaiting a moment of respite to cross the river and take refuge in the neighbouring department.[70] Thus, from the spring of 1792, if any citizen is suspected of unfriendliness or even of indifference towards the ruling faction, if, through but one opinion conscientiously held, he risks the vague possibility of mistrust or of suspicion, he undergoes popular hostility, spoliation, exile, and worse besides; no matter how loyal his conduct may be, nor how loyal he may be at heart, no matter that he is disarmed and inoffensive; it is all the same whether it be a noble, bourgeois, peasant, aged priest, or old woman; and this while public peril is yet neither great, present, nor visible, since France is at peace with Europe, and the government still subsists in its entirety.

IX

What will it be, then, now when the peril, already become palpable and serious, is daily increasing, now when war has begun, when Lafayette's army is falling back in confusion, when the Assembly declares the country in danger, when the King is overthrown, when Lafayette is passing the frontier, when the soil of France is invaded, when the frontier fortresses surrender without resistance, when the Prussians are entering Champagne, when the insurrection in La Ven-

70. "Archives Nationales," *ibid.* Letter of Amiel, president of the bureau of conciliation at Avignon, October 28, 1792, and other letters to the minister Roland.—F^7, 3,217. Letter of the Justice of the Peace at Roque-Maure, October 31, 1792.

dée adds the lacerations of civil war to the threats of a foreign war, and when the cry of treachery arises on all sides?—Already, on the 14th of May, at Metz,[71] M. de Fiquelmont, a former canon, seen chatting with a hussar on the Place Saint-Jacques, was charged with tampering with people on behalf of the princes, carried off in spite of a triple line of guards, and beaten, pierced, and slashed with sticks, bayonets, and sabres, while the mad crowd around the murderers uttered cries of rage: and from month to month, in proportion as popular fears increase, popular imagination becomes more heated and its delirium grows. We can judge of this by one example. On the 31st of August, 1792,[72] eight thousand nonjuring priests, driven out of their parishes, are at Rouen, a town less intolerant than the others, and, in conformity with the decree which banishes them, are preparing to leave France. Two vessels have just carried away about a hundred of them; one hundred and twenty others are embarking for Ostend in a larger vessel. They take nothing with them except a little money, some clothes, and one or at most two portions of their breviary, because they intend to return soon. Each has a regular passport, and, just at the moment of leaving, the National Guard have made a thorough inspection so as not to let a suspected person escape. It makes no difference. On reaching Quilleboeuf the first two convoys are stopped. A report has spread, indeed, that the priests are going to join the enemy and enlist, and the people living round about jump into their boats and surround the vessels. The priests are obliged to disembark amidst a tempest of "yells, blasphemies, insults, and abuse": one of them, a white-headed old man, having fallen into the mud, the cries and shouts redouble; if he is drowned so much the better, there will be one less! On landing all are put in prison, on bare stones, without straw or bread, and word is sent to Paris to know what must be done with so many cassocks.

71. "Archives Nationales," F^7, 3,246. Official report of the municipality of Metz (with supporting documents), May 15, 1792.

72. "Mémoires de l'Abbé Baton," one of the priests of the third convoy (a bishop appointed from Séez), p. 233.

In the meantime the third vessel, short of provisions, has sent two priests to Quilleboeuf and to Pont-Audemer to have twelve hundred pounds of bread baked: pointed out by the village militia, they are chased out like wild beasts, pass the night in a wood, and find their way back with difficulty empty-handed. The vessel itself being signaled, is besieged. "In all the municipalities on the banks of the river drums beat incessantly to warn the population to be on their guard. The appearance of an Algerian or Tripolitan corsair on the shores of the Adriatic would cause less excitement. One of the seamen of the vessel published a statement that the trunks of the priests transported were full of every kind of arms," and the country people constantly imagine that they are going to fall upon them sword and pistol in hand. For several long days the famished convoy remains moored in the stream, and carefully watched. Boats filled with volunteers and peasants row around it uttering insults and threats: in the neighbouring meadows the National Guards form themselves in line of battle. Finally, a decision is arrived at. The bravest, well armed, get into skiffs, approach the vessel cautiously, choose the most favourable time and spot, rush on board, and take possession; and are perfectly astonished to find neither enemies nor arms.—Nevertheless, the priests are confined on board, and their deputies must make their appearance before the mayor. The latter, a former usher and good Jacobin, being the most frightened, is the most violent. He refuses to visé the passports, and, seeing two priests approach, one provided with a sword-cane and the other with an iron-pointed stick, thinks that there is to be a sudden attack. "Here are two more of them," he exclaims with terror; "they are all going to land. My friends, the town is in danger!"—On hearing this the crowd becomes alarmed, and threatens the deputies; the cry of "To the lantern!" is heard, and, to save them, National Guards are obliged to conduct them to prison in the centre of a circle of bayonets.—It must be noted that these madmen are "at bottom the kindest people in the world." After the boarding of the ship, one of the most ferocious, by profession a barber, seeing the long beards of these poor priests, instantly cools down, draws forth his tools, and good-naturedly sets to work, spending several hours in shaving them. In ordinary times ecclesiastics received nothing but salutations; three years previously they were "respected as fathers and guides." But at the present moment the rustic, the man of the lower class, is out of his bearings. Forcibly and against nature, he has been made a theologian, a politician, a police captain, a local independent sovereign; and in such a position his head is turned. Among these people who seem to have lost their senses, only one, an officer of the National Guard, remains cool; he is, besides, very polite, well-behaved, and an agreeable talker; he comes in the evening to comfort the prisoners and to take tea with them in prison; in fact, he is accustomed to tragedies and, thanks to his profession, his nerves are in repose—*this person is the executioner.* The others, "whom one would take for tigers," are bewildered sheep; but they are not the less dangerous; for, carried away by their delirium, they bear down with their mass on whatever gives them umbrage.—On the road from Paris to Lyons[73] Roland's commissioners witness this terrible fright. "The people are constantly asking what our generals and armies are doing; they have vengeful expressions frequently on their lips. Yes, they say, we will set out, but we must (first) purge the interior."

Something appalling is in preparation. The seventh jacquerie is drawing near, this one universal and final—at first brutal, and then legal and systematic, undertaken and carried out on the strength of abstract principles by leaders worthy of the means they employ. Nothing like it ever occurred in history; for the first time we see brutes gone mad, operating on a grand scale and for a long time, under the leadership of blockheads who have become insane.

There is a certain strange malady commonly encountered in the quarters of the poor. A workman, overtaxed with work, in misery and badly fed, takes to drink; he drinks more and more every day, and liquors of the strongest kind. After a few years his nervous system, already weakened by spare diet, becomes overexcited and

73. "Archives Nationales," F^7, 3,225. Letter of citizen Bonnemant, commissioner to minister Roland, September 11, 1792.

out of balance. An hour comes when the brain, under a sudden stroke, ceases to direct the machine; in vain does it command, for it is no longer obeyed; each limb, each joint, each muscle, acting separately and for itself, starts convulsively through discordant impulses. Meanwhile the man is gay; he thinks himself a millionaire, a king, loved and admired by everybody; he is not aware of the mischief he is doing to himself, he does not comprehend the advice given him, he refuses the remedies offered to him, he sings and shouts for entire days, and, above all, drinks more than ever.—At last his face grows dark and his eyes become blood-shot. Radiant visions give way to black and monstrous phantoms; he sees nothing around him but menacing figures, traitors in ambush, ready to fall upon him unawares, murderers with upraised arms ready to cut his throat, executioners preparing torments for him; and he seems to be wading in a pool of blood. Then, he makes a spring, and, in order that he himself may not be killed, he kills. No one is more to be dreaded, for his delirium sustains him; his strength is prodigious, his movements unforeseen, and he endures, without heeding them, suffering and wounds under which a healthy man would succumb.—So France, exhausted by fasting under the monarchy, made drunk by the bad drug of the *Social-Contract,* and countless other adulterated or fiery beverages, is suddenly struck with paralysis of the brain; at once she is convulsed in every limb through the incoherent play and contradictory twitchings of her discordant organs. At this time she has traversed the period of joyous madness, and is about to enter upon the period of sombre delirium: behold her capable of daring, suffering, and doing all, capable of incredible exploits and abominable barbarities, the moment her guides, as erratic as herself, indicate an enemy or an obstacle to her fury.